ARCO
GRE®/GMAT®
Math Review

Sixth Edition

David Frieder, M.A.
Director, Mathworks™

THOMSON
PETERSON'S

Australia • Canada • Mexico • Singapore • Spain • United Kingdom • United States

An ARCO Book

ARCO is a registered trademark of Thomson Learning, Inc., and is used herein under license by Thomson Peterson's.

About Thomson Peterson's

Thomson Peterson's (www.petersons.com) is a leading provider of education information and advice, with books and online resources focusing on education search, test preparation, and financial aid. Its Web site offers searchable databases and interactive tools for contacting educational institutions, online practice tests and instruction, and planning tools for securing financial aid. Thomson Peterson's serves 110 million education consumers annually.

For more information, contact Thomson Peterson's, 2000 Lenox Drive, Lawrenceville, NJ 08648; 800-338-3282; or find us on the World Wide Web at www.petersons.com/about.

Editor: Joe Krasowski; Production Editor: Alysha Bullock; Manufacturing Manager: Ray Golaszewski; Composition Manager: Linda M. Williams.

ISBN 0-7689-1831-6

Printed in the United States of America

10   9   8   7   6   5   4   3   2   07   06   05

Sixth Edition

Petersons.com/publishing

Check out our Web site at www.petersons.com/publishing to see if there is any new information regarding the test and any revisions or corrections to the content of this book. We've made sure the information in this book is accurate and up-to-date; however, the test format or content may have changed since the time of publication.

Other Recommended Titles

Peterson's Ultimate GRE® Tool Kit
Peterson's Ultimate GMAT® Tool Kit
ARCO Master the GRE®
ARCO Master the GMAT®

CONTENTS

CONTENTS

Part II: Mathematics Preparation

CONTENTS

Part III: Practice Tests and Special Format Questions

CONTENTS

PREFACE

This book was written to help people prepare for the mathematics sections of the Graduate Management Admission Test (GMAT) and the Graduate Record Examination (GRE). These tests contain sections that test basic mathematical skills, understanding of elementary mathematical concepts, and ability to solve quantitative problems. Although the formats of these sections vary from test to test, the general content covered is the same—arithmetic, algebra, and geometry.

The book is divided into four parts. **Part I** provides an overview of the tests, including specific information about registering, computer-based tests, test center regulations, test scores, and additional test-prep materials.

Part II provides a thorough review of elementary mathematics. In addition to the chapters on arithmetic, algebra, and geometry, a section on solving word problems is included.

Each section in Part II contains examples demonstrating the principles and procedures discussed in the text. The answers to these problems are accompanied by step-by-step solutions that show how the correct answer was generated. Following the sample problems are more practice problems. In addition to the practice problems, a 25-question practice test is included at the end of each section. The answers to these questions, along with detailed solutions, follow each practice test.

Part III provides tips and strategies for answering the standard multiple-choice questions and the special format questions—Data Sufficiency on the GMAT and Quantitative Comparison on the GRE. Following the tips are several practice tests. These tests have been developed from actual tests and match as closely as possible the format, content, and level of difficulty you will find on the actual GMAT and GRE. All answers are fully explained at the end of each test.

Part IV is an Appendix containing a thorough summary of all the definitions, procedures, and formulas used in the book.

ACKNOWLEDGMENTS

I would like to thank my family and friends for all the encouragement and support they gave me during the writing of this book. I would also like to thank Billy Karp and Jill Israel for providing me with a quiet and comfortable place to write the algebra chapter; Mark Weinfeld, my business partner since 1980, for his help in preparing the practice tests; and Steve Brauch and Nancy Duggan for just being there. The book is dedicated to my two best friends, Tilay and Millie.

Part I

GENERAL EXAM INFORMATION

Chapter 1

ESSENTIALS OF THE GRE & GMAT

In order to evaluate, compare, and select candidates for admission, graduate and professional schools use a variety of information, including undergraduate grades, faculty recommendations, evidence of motivation in a chosen field, and work experience. In addition, most schools use the results of a standardized test as a common measure of verbal, quantitative, and analytical writing abilities. Two of the most common standardized tests are the GMAT® (Graduate Management Admission Test), required by most graduate schools of business and management, and the GRE® (Graduate Record Exam), required by most other types of graduate school programs. Both of these tests are developed and administered by the Educational Testing Service (ETS).

There are several ways to contact ETS to obtain information about the GMAT and GRE.

GMAT
Educational Testing Service
P.O. Box 6103
Princeton, NJ, 08541
Phone: 800-462-8669
gmat@ets.org
Web site: www.mba.com

GRE
Educational Testing Service
P.O. Box 6000
Princeton, NJ, 08541
Phone: 866-473-4373
E-mail: gre-info@ets.org
Web site: www.gre.org

REGISTERING FOR THE EXAMS

One way you can register for the GMAT or GRE is by obtaining a Test Bulletin, which includes registration forms. You can obtain a copy of the Test Bulletin by contacting:

GMAT
Educational Testing Service
P.O. Box 6103
Princeton, NJ 08541
Phone: 800-462-8669

GRE
Educational Testing Service
P.O. Box 6020
Princeton, NJ 08541
Phone: 609-771-7670

You can also register on line. To register for the GMAT, log on to www.mba.com or www.prometric.com. To register for the GRE, log on to www.gre.org or www.prometric.com.

COMPUTER-BASED TESTS

The GMAT and GRE are now given as computer-based tests throughout the world. In both exams, you use the computer as a word processor to type your Analytical Writing Assessment essays. In addition, the Quantitative and Verbal sections are presented as multiple-choice questions.

A computer-based test is also referred to as a computer-adaptive test (CAT) because the sequence of questions depends on how you answered the previous questions. At the start of the test, you are given a question of moderate difficulty. If you answer the question correctly, the computer will follow up with a more difficult question. If you answer the first question incorrectly, your next question will be easier. This process will continue until you complete the section.

As you answer each question, the computer scores that question and uses information about how well you answered all the previous questions to determine which question you should be given next. As long as you respond correctly to each question, you will be presented with questions of increased difficulty. When you enter incorrect responses, the computer will present you with questions of lesser difficulty. Your next question will be the one that best reflects both your previous performance and the requirements of the test design. This means that different test-takers will be given different questions. The selection of questions you will see is based on your responses to all previous questions. Because the CAT adjusts to your individual ability level, you will get very few questions that are either too easy or too difficult for you. In other words, the test adapts itself to your ability level.

MANAGING YOUR TIME

In a computer-based test, you are presented with only one question at a time. Because the computer scores each question before selecting the next one, you may not skip, return to, or change your responses to previous questions.

Since you cannot skip around from question to question, you must answer the question that currently appears on the screen before you can move on to the next one. Once you have selected your answer to a question, you will be asked to confirm it. You should confirm your answer only when you are certain that you want to move on to the next question. You cannot omit questions or go back and change answers. You can, of course, change your answer to the current question at any time before you confirm it by just clicking on a different answer.

Below are some specific test-taking tips for managing your time wisely on a computer-based test:

- **Once you start the test, an on-screen clock will continuously count down your time.** You can hide this display if you want, but it is probably a good idea to check the clock periodically to monitor your progress. The clock will automatically alert you when you have 5 minutes left to complete a section.

- **Pace yourself so that you have enough time to carefully consider and answer every question in the section in which you are working.** For example, on the GMAT Quantitative section you have 75 minutes to answer 37 questions, or about 2 minutes per question. On the GRE Quantitative section you have 45 minutes to answer 28 questions, or a little less than 2 minutes per question.

- **Don't waste time trying to answer a difficult question.** Keep moving through the test and try to finish each section. If you do not finish in the allotted time, you will still receive a score for that section. Since your score reflects the number of questions you answered, you will receive a higher score when you finish all the questions in a section. Therefore, if you are unable to answer a question within a reasonable timeframe, eliminate what you consider to be wrong answers and select the best answer from the remaining choices.

- **If you are running out of time at the end of a section, make every effort to complete all the questions in the section.** Based on analyses of test-takers, a majority will score higher if they finish the section than if they do not attempt to answer all of the questions. The best strategy is to pace yourself so that you have time to consider each question and don't have to guess randomly near the end of the time allotted.

- **Understand the implications of exiting a section or quitting the test.** Once you exit a section, you cannot return to it. Click on the "Test Quit" box at the bottom of your screen only if you decide to end your entire testing session. If you quit the test, you will not receive a score for any section, even for those sections you have already completed. If you click on "Section Exit" or "Test Quit" by mistake, you will be given the opportunity to reverse or confirm your decision.

STRUCTURE OF THE EXAMS

The GMAT contains three parts: an Analytical Writing Assessment section, a Quantitative Ability section, and a Verbal Ability section.

GMAT		
Test Section	*Number of Questions*	*Time Allotted*
Analytical Writing		
Analysis of an Issue	1 writing task	30 minutes
Analysis of an Argument	1 writing task	30 minutes
Quantitative Ability		
Problem Solving and Data Sufficiency	37 multiple-choice questions	75 minutes
Verbal Ability		
Critical Reasoning, Sentence Correction, and Reading Comprehension	41 multiple-choice questions	75 minutes

The GRE contains four parts: Analytical Writing, Quantitative Ability, Verbal Ability, and a second Quantitative or Verbal section. The second Quantitative or Verbal Section does not count toward your score but is used by ETS to experiment with questions for future tests. Since the second section is not identified as experimental, you must treat each Quantitative or Verbal section equally. Note: There are still some places, mostly outside the United States, that offer paper-based versions of the GRE.

GRE		
Test Section	*Number of Questions*	*Time Allotted*
Analytical Writing		
Analysis of an Issue	1 writing task	45 minutes
Analysis of an Argument	1 writing task	30 minutes
Verbal Ability		
Reading Comprehension, Antonyms, Analogies, and Sentence Completions	30 multiple-choice questions	30 minutes
Quantitative Ability		
Problem Solving and Quantitative Comparisons	28 multiple-choice questions	45 minutes
Second Quantitative or Verbal Section	Varies	Varies

TEST CENTER PROCEDURES AND REGULATIONS

The following test center procedures and regulations apply during the entire test administration:

- **The administrator will check your photo identification. ID verification at the test center may include thumb-printing, photographing, videotaping, or other forms of electronic ID confirmation.** If you refuse to comply, you will not be permitted to take the test and will forfeit your registration fee. Note that this is in addition to the requirement that you present acceptable and valid identification.

- **You will be asked to write and sign a confidentiality statement at the test center.** Your signature is required. If you do not write and sign the statement, you will not be permitted to take the test and you will forfeit your registration fee.

- **You must sign your name whenever you enter or leave the testing room.**

- **No testing aids are permitted during the test session or during breaks.** Aids include, but are not limited to, beepers, pagers, pens, calculators, watch calculators, books, pamphlets, notes, rulers, stereos or radios, telephones or cell phones, stop watches, watch alarms (including those with flashing lights or alarm sounds), dictionaries, translators, thesauruses, personal data assistants (PDAs), or any other electronic or photographic devices.

- **You are not be permitted to leave the test center premises during the test session or during breaks.**

- **Access to telephones or cell phones is not be permitted during the test session or during breaks.**

- **You are not allowed to eat, drink, or use tobacco products while in the testing room.** If you want to go outside during a scheduled break, you must inform the test administrator where you are going and you must remain in the immediate vicinity of the test center.

- **The administrator will provide you with six pieces of scratch paper that may be replaced after you have used them all.** If you need more scratch paper during the exam, raise your hand and ask for it. You may not remove this paper from the testing room at any time. All scratch paper MUST be returned at the end of the test session.
- **Under no circumstances may test content or any part of the test content be removed from the test center, reproduced, and/or disclosed by any means (e.g., hard copy, verbally, electronically) to any person or entity.**
- **You may not leave your workstation while timed sections of the test are being administered.** If, due to an emergency, you must leave your seat during the test session, raise your hand and notify the test administrator. Remember, however, that the timing for the test section you are working on will not stop during your absence.
- **If you have placed personal items, such as a cell phone, briefcase, or other study materials in a locker at the test center, you will not have access to these items during the test session or breaks.**
- **If you believe you have a problem with your computer, need more scratch paper, or need assistance for any reason, raise your hand and notify the test administrator.**

TEST SCORES AND SCORE REPORTS

DETERMINING YOUR SCORE

Your score is based on three factors:

1. Number of questions answered
2. Number of questions answered correctly
3. Level of difficulty and other statistical characteristics of each question (NOTE: In a computer-adaptive test, the questions are weighted according to their difficulty and other statistical properties, not to their position on the test.)

YOUR SCORE REPORT

You'll receive four scores for the GMAT, including:

1. A Quantitative score on a 0−60 scale
2. A Verbal score on a 0−60 scale
3. A total score, on a 200−800 scale, based on both your Quantitative and Verbal scores
4. An Analytical Writing score on a 0−6 scale, which averages (to the nearest one-half point) the final scores for each of your two GMAT essays

You'll receive three scores for the GRE, including:

1. A Quantitative score on a 200−800 scale
2. A Verbal score on a 200−800 scale
3. An Analytical Writing score on a 0−6 scale, which averages (to the nearest half-point) the final scores for each of your two GRE essays

You'll also receive a percentile rank (0–99%) for each section of the GMAT and GRE. A percentile rank of 70, for example, indicates that you scored higher than 70 percent of all other test-takers.

When you complete your test, a message will appear on the computer screen asking you if you want to report your scores or cancel them. If you choose to report your scores, you will be able to view and print an unofficial score report that shows you all your scores except for the Analytical Writing score. Official score reports, which include the Analytical Writing score, will be mailed both to you and to your designated score recipients approximately two weeks after the test. Keep in mind that once you choose to report your scores, you cannot cancel them later.

CANCELING YOUR SCORES

The only opportunity you will have to cancel your scores is during the day of the test itself. Immediately after you complete the test, but before you can view your scores, a message will appear asking if you want to cancel your scores. If you choose to cancel your scores, you will not be able to view them. Keep in mind that canceled scores cannot be reinstated later.

EXITING A SECTION OR QUITTING THE TEST EARLY

While taking the test you may decide to exit a section or quit the test early. If you're considering this option, keep the following in mind:

- If you exit a section and confirm you want to exit that section, you won't be able to return to it.
- If you click "Test Quit," you won't receive a score for any section, even if you answered questions for some or all of the sections.
- If you click "Section Exit" or "Test Quit," you will be required to confirm your decision. So, if you inadvertently click on either of these buttons or if you change your mind, you may select the option to "Return to Where I Was."

RESCHEDULING OR CANCELING YOUR TEST

If you decide to reschedule your test appointment, you can do so on line or by phone. You must reschedule your appointment **at least seven calendar days before** your scheduled appointment or you will forfeit your registration fee. Appointments cannot be rescheduled beyond one year of the original appointment date, or six months beyond when you are rescheduling your appointment. You will be charged a rescheduling service fee for each appointment you choose to reschedule.

If you decide to cancel your test appointment, you can also do so on line or by phone. You must cancel your appointment **at least seven calendar days before** your scheduled appointment or you will forfeit your entire registration fee. You will receive a partial refund of your registration fee if your cancellation request is received at least seven days prior to your scheduled appointment.

RETAKING THE TEST

There may be a reason why you decide to retake your test. For example, you may not have felt well on the day of the test, or a graduate school may request more recent scores than you have on record. In this case, the retest policy is as follows: you may take the test only once per calendar month and no more than five times in any 12-month period. This applies even if you canceled your scores on a test taken previously.

If you repeat the GMAT, your scores from the latest test date and the two most recent test dates within the last five years will be reported to your designated score recipients.

If you repeat the GRE, all your scores earned during the past five years will be reported to your designated score recipients. You may not choose to have only certain scores reported.

ADDITIONAL TEST-PREP MATERIALS

As part of your test preparation, it is very important that you familiarize yourself with the mechanics of taking a computer-adaptive test and practice answering questions that are similar to those you will see on the actual test.

Peterson's GMAT® CAT Center: To get the practice you need, a full-length GMAT CAT is your only option. Peterson's offers the only complete practice GMAT CAT available on the Internet. Log on to www.petersons.com/testprepchannel/gmat_index.asp for access to 3 full-length, timed practice tests, detailed answers and explanations for every question, expert strategies, plus 3 hours of live, online tutoring with expert e-tutors.

Peterson's Ultimate GMAT® Tool Kit 2005: This innovative multimedia tool provides the complete package you need to score your personal best on the GMAT and get into your top-choice MBA program. The book is structured so that you gain proven test-taking strategies to do your best on the exam, a thorough review of all content on the GMAT, and three full-length paper tests that include a mix of easy, moderate, and difficult questions. Unlike any other book previously published, this tool kit contains many features that used to be available only to those who purchased expensive test-prep courses.

In addition to the book itself, the tool kit provides a for-fee e-tutor feature that offers one-to-one math help from a live expert when you need it, three additional computer-adaptive tests on a CD that carefully reproduce the experience you can expect on test day, and instant online essay scoring and feedback for your practice essays.

Peterson's GRE® CAT Center: You can get familiar with the GRE and discover where you need more preparation well before test day by logging on to www.petersons.com/testprepchannel/gre_index.asp for access to 3 full-length, timed, computer-adaptive practice tests, detailed answers and explanations for every question, as well as expert strategies, shortcuts, and common mistakes.

Peterson's Ultimate GRE® Tool Kit 2005: The GRE version of Peterson's Ultimate GMAT Tool Kit, this product is the ultimate solution for test preparation for the GRE. It includes both intermediate and advanced learning and practice and affords you the opportunity to chart your own course and choose your own tools for success.
Part III of this book contains more specific suggestions on how to answer the various types of math questions asked on the GMAT and GRE. The GMAT contains standard multiple-choice and data sufficiency questions, and the GRE contains standard multiple-choice and quantitative comparison questions.

Part II

MATHEMATICS PREPARATION

Chapter 2
ARITHMETIC REVIEW

In this chapter, we will review the procedures for:

- Performing operations with whole numbers
- Fractions, decimals, and percents

The emphasis will be on computational skills, not problem-solving skills. Since most of the arithmetic word problems we will look at require algebraic solutions, these problems will be discussed in Chapter 4.

SUMMARY OF SYMBOLS

SYMBOL	MEANING
$=$	is equal to
$\neq$	is not equal to
$\approx$	is approximately equal to
$>$	is greater than
$\geq$	is greater than or equal to
$<$	is less than
$\leq$	is less than or equal to
$\sqrt{}$	square root
$.\overline{6}$	the repeating decimal .666···
$\pm$	plus or minus
r°s't"	r degrees s minutes t seconds
$\angle$	angle
∟	right angle
$\perp$	is perpendicular to
$\parallel$	is parallel to
$\triangle$	triangle
$\sim$	is similar to
$\cong$	is congruent to
Δx	delta x
$\overset{\frown}{ST}$	arc ST
π	pi (3.1415···)

WHOLE NUMBERS

The set of **whole numbers** is an infinite set consisting of all the counting numbers, 1, 2, 3, etc, and 0.

The value of each digit in a whole number is determined by the particular **place** it occupies in the number. For example, in the number 357, the 3 is in the hundreds place and thus represents the value 300; the 5 is in the tens place and thus represents the value 50; and the 7 is in the ones place and thus represents the value 7. A summary of whole number **place-values** is given below.

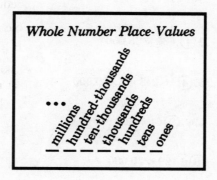

ROUNDING OFF WHOLE NUMBERS

When only an approximate value of a whole number is needed, we use the following procedure to **round off** the number to a particular place. Note in the accompanying example that the symbol ≈ means "is approximately equal to."

> **To Round Off a Whole Number:**
>
> 1. Circle the digit in the place being rounded off.
> 2. If the digit to its right is less than 5, leave the circled digit as it is.
>   If the digit to its right is 5 or more, increase the circled digit by 1.
> 3. Replace all the digits to the right of the circled digit by zeros.

Round off 9371 to the nearest *hundred*.

$$9\,③\,71$$
$$\downarrow$$
$$9\,③\,71$$
$$9\,④\,71$$
$$9400$$
$$9371 \approx 9400$$

Rounding off whole numbers is particularly useful in estimating the results of arithmetic problems. To do this, we usually round off the left most digit of each number in the problem, and replace all the other digits by zeros. For example, to estimate the value of 47 × 624, round off 47 to 50 and 624 to 600 and then multiply. As shown below, this gives us an estimated value of 30,000.

$$47 \times 624 \approx 50 \times 600$$
$$\approx 30,000$$

PRACTICE PROBLEMS

Round off the following whole numbers to the place indicated:

1. 34,682 to the nearest thousand
2. 5,416,248 to the nearest hundred-thousand
3. 299,961 to the nearest hundred
4. 68,199 to the nearest ten-thousand

ANSWERS AND EXPLANATIONS

1. 3④,682 ≈ 35,000

2. 5,④16,248 ≈ 5,400,000

3. 299,⑨61 ≈ 300,000

4. ⑥8,199 ≈ 70,000

FUNDAMENTAL OPERATIONS

Each of the fundamental operations of arithmetic—addition, subtraction, multiplication, and division—has associated with it a special set of terms that identify the numbers used in the operation as well as the result of the operation.

Terms Associated with Operations

Addition: Addend + Addend = Sum
Subtraction: Minuend − Subtrahend = Difference
Multiplication: Factor × Factor = Product
Division: Dividend ÷ Divisor = Quotient

$$\left(\text{Divisor} \overline{)\text{Dividend}}^{\text{Quotient}} \right)$$

Remember that only in addition and multiplication can we reverse the order of the numbers. This property, called the **commutative property** of addition and multiplication, is not true of subtraction or division. In the examples shown below, the symbol ≠ means "is not equal to."

$$3 + 5 = 5 + 3 \qquad\qquad 6 - 2 \neq 2 - 6$$
$$7 \times 9 = 9 \times 7 \qquad\qquad 8 \div 4 \neq 4 \div 8$$

PRIME AND COMPOSITE NUMBERS

A whole number, M, is said to be **divisible** by a whole number, N, if N divides into M without a remainder ("evenly"). For example, since 4 divides into 20 without a remainder, we say that 20 is divisible by 4.

When a whole number, *M*, is divisible by a whole number, *N*, then *N* is said to be a **divisor** or **factor** of *M*, and *M* is said to be a **multiple** of *N*. In the previous example, 4 is a divisor of 20, and 20 is a multiple of 4.

Each whole number greater than 0 has an infinite number of multiples, but only a limited number of divisors. For example, the multiples of 6 are 6, 12, 18, 24, 30, etc., while the divisors of 6 are only 1, 2, 3, and 6.

A whole number that has only two divisors—the number itself and 1—is called a **prime number**. A whole number that has more than two divisors is called a **composite number**. Examples of both types of numbers are shown below. Note that 0 and 1 are not considered either prime numbers or composite numbers. Also note that the only even prime number is 2. All even numbers greater than 2 have 2 as a divisor and are therefore composite numbers.

> **Prime Numbers**
> 2, 3, 5, 7, 11, 13, 17,...
> **Composite Numbers**
> 4, 6, 8, 9, 10, 12, 14,...

Every composite number can be written as a product of prime number factors. One method of doing this is described below.

To Obtain the Prime Factorization of a Number:
1. Find *any* pair of numbers whose product is the given number, and write the pair at the end of two branches leading from the number.
2. Continue this branching process until every number at the end of a branch is a prime number.
3. Form a product of all the prime numbers at the ends of the branches.

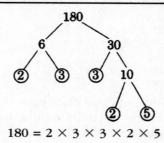

$$180 = 2 \times 3 \times 3 \times 2 \times 5$$

PRACTICE PROBLEMS

Write each of the following composite numbers as a product of prime number factors:

1. 60

2. 315

3. 176

4. 825

ANSWERS AND EXPLANATIONS

1.

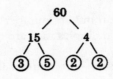

$$60 = 3 \times 5 \times 2 \times 2$$

2.

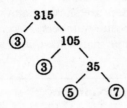

$$315 = 3 \times 3 \times 5 \times 7$$

3.

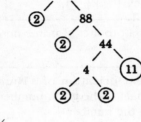

$$176 = 2 \times 2 \times 2 \times 2 \times 11$$

4.

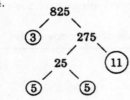

$$825 = 3 \times 5 \times 5 \times 11$$

FRACTIONS

Fractions consist of two numbers separated by a line called a fraction bar. The number above the line is called the **numerator** of the fraction, and the number below the line is called the **denominator**. Depending upon the way a fraction is used, these numbers have several different meanings.

The most common way of using a fraction is to represent a **part of a whole**. For example, the fraction $\frac{3}{4}$ is used to represent 3 of the 4 equal parts into which a whole has been divided.

Another way of using a fraction is to indicate **division** of one number by another. For example, the fraction $\frac{7}{3}$ can be used to indicate the quotient 7 divided by 3 (or equivalently, 3 divided into 7).

A third way of using a fraction is to express a **ratio**, or comparison, between two quantities. For example, the fraction $\frac{25}{10}$ can be used to express the ratio of the number of cents in a quarter to the number of cents in a dime.

These different interpretations of a fraction are summarized on the following page.

> **Interpretations of a Fraction**
>
> 1. A part of a whole: $\dfrac{\text{part}}{\text{whole}}$
>
> 2. Division of one number by another: $\dfrac{\text{dividend}}{\text{divisor}}$
>
> 3. A ratio of two quantities: $\dfrac{\text{quantity A}}{\text{quantity B}}$

TYPES OF FRACTIONS

Fractions are classified into two categories according to the relative size of their numerators and denominators: 1. **proper fractions**—fractions whose numerators are less than their denominators. 2. **improper fractions**—fractions whose numerators are either equal to or greater than their denominators. The value of a proper fraction is always less than 1 (one whole), and the value of an improper fraction is either equal to or greater than 1. Any whole number can be put into the form of an improper fraction by placing it over a denominator of 1. For example $8 = \dfrac{8}{1}$, and $12 = \dfrac{12}{1}$.

> **Proper Fractions**
>
> $\dfrac{3}{4}, \dfrac{5}{9}, \dfrac{1}{2}$
>
> **Improper Fractions**
>
> $\dfrac{5}{2}, \dfrac{7}{7}, \dfrac{9}{4}$

The sum of a whole number and a proper fraction is called a **mixed number**. Mixed numbers are denoted by placing the whole number and fraction side by side without using the addition symbol. For example, $4 + \dfrac{8}{9}$ is written $4\dfrac{8}{9}$.

> **Mixed Numbers**
>
> $5\dfrac{2}{3}, 8\dfrac{2}{7}, 1\dfrac{3}{4}$

A mixed number can be changed into the form of an improper fraction by the following procedure.

> **To Change a Mixed Number into an Improper Fraction:**
> 1. Multiply the denominator of the fraction by the whole number.
> 2. Add the resulting product to the numerator of the fraction and place the sum over the original denominator.

$$\overset{7\times2}{2\dfrac{5}{7}} = \dfrac{7\times2+5}{7}$$

$$2\dfrac{5}{7} = \dfrac{19}{7}$$

By interpreting a fraction as a quotient, we can reverse this procedure and change the improper fraction back into the form of a mixed number.

To Change an Improper Fraction into a Mixed Number:
1. Divide the denominator into the numerator.
2. Express any remainder as a fraction by placing it over the original denominator.

$$\frac{19}{7} = 7\overline{)19} \;\; \genfrac{}{}{0pt}{}{2}{}$$

$$\frac{19}{7} = 2\frac{5}{7}$$

PRACTICE PROBLEMS

Change the following mixed numbers to improper fractions:

1. $5\frac{3}{4}$

2. $7\frac{3}{8}$

3. $6\frac{2}{3}$

4. $12\frac{1}{2}$

Change the following improper fractions to mixed numbers:

5. $\frac{14}{3}$

6. $\frac{27}{2}$

7. $\frac{48}{4}$

8. $\frac{6}{5}$

ANSWERS AND EXPLANATIONS

1. $5\frac{3}{4} = \frac{4 \times 5 + 3}{4} = \frac{23}{4}$

2. $7\frac{3}{8} = \frac{8 \times 7 + 3}{8} = \frac{59}{8}$

3. $6\frac{2}{3} = \frac{3 \times 6 + 2}{3} = \frac{20}{3}$

4. $12\frac{1}{2} = \frac{2 \times 12 + 1}{2} = \frac{25}{2}$

5. $3\overline{)14}^{4} = 4\frac{2}{3}$
   $\frac{12}{2}$

6. $2\overline{)27}^{13} = 13\frac{1}{2}$
   $\frac{26}{1}$

7. $4\overline{)48}^{12}$

8. $5\overline{)6}^{1} = 1\frac{1}{5}$
   $\frac{5}{1}$

RAISING FRACTIONS TO HIGHER TERMS

Fractions that have the same value are said to be **equivalent**. For example, $\frac{2}{4}$, $\frac{3}{6}$, and $\frac{4}{8}$ are equivalent fractions, all having the value $\frac{1}{2}$. Fractions can be changed into equivalent fractions by multiplying or dividing both their numerators and denominators by the same non-zero number.

When both the numerator and denominator of a fraction are *multiplied* by the same number greater than 1, the fraction is said to be **raised to higher terms**. Remember that although the numerator and denominator of the new fraction are larger than those of the original fraction, the fractions are equivalent in *value*.

$$\frac{a}{b} = \frac{a \times c}{b \times c}, c \neq 0$$

If the denominator of the fraction in higher terms is specified in advance, we can find the corresponding numerator by the following procedure:

To Raise a Fraction to Higher Terms:
1. Divide the original denominator into the new, specified denominator.
2. Multiply the result by the original numerator.

$$\frac{3}{5} = \frac{?}{20}$$

$$\frac{3}{5} \underset{4}{\overset{4}{\lessgtr}} \frac{12}{20}$$

PRACTICE PROBLEMS

Change each of the following fractions to an equivalent fraction having the denominator indicated:

1. $\dfrac{3}{4} = \dfrac{?}{20}$

2. $\dfrac{5}{9} = \dfrac{?}{72}$

3. $\dfrac{4}{11} = \dfrac{?}{66}$

4. $\dfrac{8}{3} = \dfrac{?}{12}$

ANSWERS AND EXPLANATIONS

1. $\dfrac{3}{4} \overset{\times 5}{\underset{\times 5}{=}} \dfrac{15}{20}$

2. $\dfrac{5}{9} \overset{\times 8}{\underset{\times 8}{=}} \dfrac{40}{72}$

3. $\dfrac{4}{11} \overset{\times 6}{\underset{\times 6}{=}} \dfrac{24}{66}$

4. $\dfrac{8}{3} \overset{\times 4}{\underset{\times 4}{=}} \dfrac{32}{12}$

REDUCING FRACTIONS TO LOWEST TERMS

When both the numerator and denominator of a fraction are *divided* by the same number greater than 1, the fraction is said to be **reduced to lower terms**. Again, remember that the original fraction and new fraction are equivalent in value. Fractions such as $\dfrac{3}{4}$ and $\dfrac{12}{17}$, which cannot be reduced further, are said to be **reduced to lowest terms**.

$$\frac{a}{b} = \frac{a \div c}{b \div c}, c \neq 0$$

To reduce a fraction to lower terms, we must find a number that can divide evenly into both the numerator and denominator. With the divisibility tests that follow, we can quickly check if the numerator and denominator are both divisible by certain common numbers.

Divisibility Tests for 2, 3, 5, and 10
A number is divisible by:
2, if its last digit is even—0, 2, 4, 6, or 8;
3, if the sum of its digits is a number divisible by 3;
5, if its last digit is 0 or 5; and
10, if its last digit is 0.

These tests are illustrated in the examples below:

Reduce by 2 | **Reduce by 3** | **Reduce by 5** | **Reduce by 10**

$$\frac{14 \div 2}{38 \div 2} = \frac{7}{19}$$

$$\overset{(5+1=6)}{\underset{(7+2=9)}{\frac{51 \div 3}{72 \div 3}}} = \frac{17}{24}$$

$$\frac{15 \div 5}{40 \div 5} = \frac{3}{8}$$

$$\frac{20 \div 10}{30 \div 10} = \frac{2}{3}$$

Although there are no quick divisibility tests for numbers like 7, 11, and 13, we must remember to try them as well. For example, $\frac{21}{28}$ can be reduced to $\frac{3}{4}$ by dividing the numerator and denominator by 7.

Example

Reduce $\frac{1740}{3960}$ to lowest terms.

Procedure

1. Since the numerator and denominator both end in 0, divide them by 10.

$$\frac{1740}{3960} = \frac{1740 \div 10}{3960 \div 10}$$
$$= \frac{174}{396}$$

2. Since the numerator and denominator both end in an even digit, divide them by 2.

$$= \frac{174 \div 2}{396 \div 2}$$
$$= \frac{87}{198}$$

3. The sum of the digits in the numerator is 15, which is divisible by 3, and the sum of the digits in the denominator is 18, which is also divisible by 3. Therefore, divide the numerator and denominator by 3. Since the result cannot be reduced further, it is reduced to lowest terms.

$$= \frac{\overset{(8+7=15)}{87 \div 3}}{\underset{(1+9+8=18)}{198 \div 3}}$$
$$= \frac{29}{66}$$

PRACTICE PROBLEMS

Reduce the following fractions to lowest terms:

1. $\dfrac{24}{72}$

2. $\dfrac{135}{243}$

3. $\dfrac{750}{1250}$

4. $\dfrac{420}{560}$

ANSWERS AND EXPLANATIONS

1. $\dfrac{24}{72} = \dfrac{24 \div 3}{72 \div 2} = \dfrac{12 \div 2}{36 \div 2} = \dfrac{6 \div 2}{18 \div 2} = \dfrac{3 \div 3}{9 \div 3} = \dfrac{1}{3}$

2. $\dfrac{135}{243} = \dfrac{135 \div 3}{243 \div 3} = \dfrac{45 \div 3}{81 \div 3} = \dfrac{15 \div 3}{27 \div 3} = \dfrac{5}{9}$

3. $\dfrac{750}{1250} = \dfrac{750 \div 10}{1250 \div 10} = \dfrac{75 \div 5}{125 \div 5} = \dfrac{15 \div 5}{25 \div 5} = \dfrac{3}{5}$

4. $\dfrac{420}{560} = \dfrac{420 \div 10}{560 \div 10} = \dfrac{42 \div 2}{56 \div 2} = \dfrac{21 \div 7}{28 \div 7} = \dfrac{3}{4}$

ADDING AND SUBTRACTING LIKE FRACTIONS

To add or subtract fractions having the same denominators (**like fractions**), we add or subtract their numerators, and place the result over the common denominator. In each case, we **simplify** the resulting fraction by changing any improper fraction to a mixed number, and by reducing any proper fraction to lowest terms.

$$\frac{a}{c} + \frac{b}{c} = \frac{a+b}{c}$$
$$\frac{a}{c} - \frac{b}{c} = \frac{a-b}{c}$$

$$\frac{7}{8} + \frac{6}{8} - \frac{1}{8} = \frac{7+6-1}{8}$$
$$= \frac{12}{8}$$
$$= 1\frac{4}{8}$$
$$= 1\frac{1}{2}$$

To add or subtract mixed numbers, the whole numbers and fractions are treated separately. This is facilitated by arranging the problem vertically, with the whole numbers and fractions lined up. Remember that the final result should be simplified as much as possible. Consider the examples below. In the one on the left, note that the result, $14\frac{16}{12}$, is simplified by changing $\frac{16}{12}$ to $1\frac{4}{12}$, and then combining it with 14 to give $15\frac{4}{12}$ or $15\frac{1}{3}$.

$$
\begin{array}{r}
8\frac{5}{12} \\
+6\frac{11}{12} \\
\hline
14\frac{16}{12} = 15\frac{4}{12} \\
= 15\frac{1}{3}
\end{array}
\qquad
\begin{array}{r}
9\frac{3}{4} \\
-2\frac{1}{4} \\
\hline
7\frac{2}{4} = 7\frac{1}{2}
\end{array}
$$

Sometimes, when subtracting mixed numbers, it will be necessary to borrow from one of the whole numbers. This is illustrated in the examples that follow:

Example 1

Subtract $6 - 2\frac{3}{7}$.

Procedure

1. Arrange the problem vertically with the whole numbers lined up.

$$
\begin{array}{r}
6 \\
-2\frac{3}{7} \\
\hline
\end{array}
$$

2. Since there is no fraction in the top number, borrow 1 from the whole number 6 and change it into the equivalent fraction, $\frac{7}{7}$, having the same denominator as the bottom fraction. Subtract.

$$
\begin{array}{r}
5\cancel{6}\frac{7}{7} \\
-2\frac{3}{7} \\
\hline
3\frac{4}{7}
\end{array}
$$

Example 2

Subtract $8\frac{2}{9} - 3\frac{5}{9}$.

Procedure

1. Arrange the problem vertically.

$$8\frac{2}{9}$$

$$-3\frac{5}{9}$$

2. Since $\frac{5}{9}$ cannot be subtracted from $\frac{2}{9}$, borrow 1 from the whole number 8 and place it next to $\frac{2}{9}$. Change the mixed number, $1\frac{2}{9}$, to the improper fraction $\frac{11}{9}$, and subtract. Reduce the result to lowest terms.

$$7\overset{\frown}{\cancel{8}}1\frac{2}{9}=7\frac{11}{9}$$

$$-3\frac{5}{9}=3\frac{5}{9}$$

$$4\frac{6}{9}=4\frac{2}{3}$$

PRACTICE PROBLEMS

Perform the following additions and subtractions. Reduce all answers to lowest terms.

1. $5\frac{3}{4}+2\frac{3}{4}$

2. $12\frac{5}{9}-7\frac{2}{9}$

3. $8-5\frac{5}{6}$

4. $16\frac{4}{7}-9\frac{6}{7}$

ANSWERS AND EXPLANATIONS

1.

$$5\frac{3}{4}$$
$$+2\frac{3}{4}$$

$$7\frac{6}{4} = 8\frac{2}{4} = 8\frac{1}{2}$$

2.

$$12\frac{5}{9}$$
$$-7\frac{2}{9}$$

$$5\frac{3}{9} = 5\frac{1}{3}$$

3.

$$7\cancel{8}\frac{6}{6}$$
$$-5\frac{5}{6}$$

$$2\frac{1}{6}$$

4.

$$15\cancel{16}\,1\frac{4}{7} = \frac{11}{7}$$
$$-\ 9\ \ \frac{6}{7} = \frac{6}{7}$$

$$6\ \ \ \ \ \frac{5}{7} = 6\frac{5}{7}$$

ADDING AND SUBTRACTING UNLIKE FRACTIONS

To add or subtract fractions having different denominators (**unlike fractions**), we first change them to equivalent fractions having a common denominator, and then proceed as in the last section.

Consider the sum $\frac{3}{4} + \frac{5}{6}$. Since the fractions have different denominators, we first change them to equivalent fractions having a common denominator. In general, a **common denominator** for a given set of fractions is any number that is divisible by all the denominators, that is, a *common multiple of the denominators*. One such number will always be the *product of the denominators*. Thus, in this case, we can use 24, the product of 4 and 6, or any other common denominator circled below. Note that 12, the smallest possible common denominator, is usually referred to as the **least common denominator**.

$$\text{\emph{Common Denominators of}}\ \frac{3}{4}\ \text{\emph{and}}\ \frac{5}{6}$$

$$\text{\emph{Multiples of 4: 4, 8, }}\textcircled{12}\text{\emph{, 16, 20, }}\textcircled{24}\text{\emph{, 28, 32, }}\textcircled{36}\text{\emph{, ...}}$$

$$\text{\emph{Multiples of 6: 6, }}\textcircled{12}\text{\emph{, 18, }}\textcircled{24}\text{\emph{, 30, }}\textcircled{36}\text{\emph{, ...}}$$

After choosing one of these denominators (the choice is purely arbitrary), we change each of the fractions to an equivalent fraction having this denominator (by using the procedure for changing fractions to higher terms), and then add the resulting numerators. Thus, if we choose the common denominator 12, we get

$$\frac{3}{4} = \frac{9}{12}$$
$$+\frac{5}{6} = \frac{10}{12}$$
$$\overline{\qquad\qquad}$$
$$\frac{19}{12} = 1\frac{7}{12}$$

To Add or Subtract Unlike Fractions:

1. Find a common denominator for the fractions (a common multiple of the denominators). Remember that one can always be obtained by multiplying the denominators.
2. By using the procedure for changing fractions to higher terms, change each of the fractions to the common denominator.
3. Add or subtract the numerators, and place the result over the common denominator.
4. Simplify the resulting fraction.

$$\frac{5}{6} = \frac{40}{48}$$
$$-\frac{3}{8} = \frac{18}{48}$$
$$\overline{\qquad\qquad}$$
$$\frac{22}{48} = \frac{11}{24}$$

Example 1

Add $4\frac{3}{5} + 5\frac{2}{7} + 3\frac{1}{2}$.

Procedure

1. Arrange the problem vertically. Change each of the fractions to the common denominator 70, the product of the denominators. Add the whole numbers and fractions separately, and simplify the result.

$$4\frac{3}{5} = 4\frac{42}{70}$$

$$5\frac{2}{7} = 5\frac{20}{70}$$

$$+3\frac{1}{2} = 3\frac{35}{70}$$

$$12\frac{97}{70} = 13\frac{27}{70}$$

Example 2

Subtract $9\frac{3}{7} - 3\frac{1}{2}$.

Procedure

1. Arrange the problem vertically. Change each of the fractions to the common denominator, 14.

$$9\frac{3}{7} = 9\frac{6}{14}$$

$$-3\frac{1}{2} = 3\frac{7}{14}$$

2. Since we cannot subtract $\frac{7}{14}$ from $\frac{6}{14}$, borrow 1 from 9 and place it next to $\frac{6}{14}$. Change the mixed number $1\frac{6}{14}$ to the improper fraction $\frac{20}{14}$ and subtract.

$$9\frac{3}{7} = 8\,\cancel{9}1\frac{6}{14} = 8\frac{20}{14}$$

$$-3\frac{1}{2} = \quad 3\frac{7}{14} = 3\frac{7}{14}$$

$$5\frac{13}{14}$$

PRACTICE PROBLEMS

Perform the following additions and subtractions. Reduce all answers to lowest terms.

1. $6\frac{3}{5} + 2\frac{5}{7}$

2. $2\frac{2}{3} + 4\frac{1}{4} + 1\frac{3}{5}$

3. $8\frac{2}{3} - 3\frac{1}{2}$

4. $19\frac{2}{5} - 12\frac{3}{4}$

ANSWERS AND EXPLANATIONS

1.
$$6\frac{3}{5} = \frac{21}{35}$$
$$+2\frac{5}{7} = \frac{25}{35}$$
$$8 \quad \frac{46}{35} = 9\frac{11}{35}$$

2.
$$2\frac{2}{3} = \frac{40}{60}$$
$$4\frac{1}{4} = \frac{15}{60}$$
$$+1\frac{3}{5} = \frac{36}{60}$$
$$7 \quad \frac{91}{60} = 8\frac{31}{60}$$

3.
$$8\frac{2}{3} = \frac{4}{6}$$
$$-3\frac{1}{2} = \frac{3}{6}$$
$$5 \quad \frac{1}{6} = 5\frac{1}{6}$$

4.
$$\overset{18}{\cancel{19}}\frac{2}{5} = 1\frac{8}{20} = \frac{28}{20}$$
$$-12\frac{3}{4} = \quad \frac{15}{20} = \frac{15}{20}$$
$$6 \qquad \frac{13}{20} = 6\frac{13}{20}$$

MULTIPLYING FRACTIONS

Multiplication of fractions is usually indicated by the word "of." For example, $\frac{3}{4}$ of $\frac{5}{7}$ means $\frac{3}{4} \times \frac{5}{7}$.

Unlike addition and subtraction of fractions, it is not necessary to change the fractions to a common denominator. Instead, just multiply the numerators by the numerators, and the denominators by the denominators:

$$\boxed{\frac{a}{b} \times \frac{c}{d} = \frac{a \times c}{b \times d}}$$

$$\frac{3}{4} \times \frac{5}{7} = \frac{3 \times 5}{4 \times 7} = \frac{15}{28}$$

If any of the numbers in the product are whole numbers or mixed numbers, they should first be changed to improper fractions before multiplying. Remember that a whole number is changed to an improper fraction by placing it over a denominator of 1. This is illustrated in the example below.

$$\frac{2}{9} \times 5 \times 4\frac{2}{3} = \frac{2}{9} \times \frac{5}{1} \times \frac{14}{3}$$

$$= \frac{2 \times 5 \times 14}{9 \times 1 \times 3}$$

$$= \frac{140}{27}$$

$$= 5\frac{5}{27}$$

Sometimes we can simplify a product of fractions before multiplying by "cancelling" common factors in the numerators and denominators.

For example, in the product $\frac{5}{6} \times \frac{9}{20}$ divide out ("cancel") a common factor of 5 in 5 and 20, and a common factor of 3 in 6 and 9. (Notice that the numerator and denominator do not have to be part of the same fraction.) Then, multiply the remaining factors and get the result $\frac{3}{8}$. This result is the same as the one we would get by multiplying first and reducing after:

Cancel First	**Multiply First**
$\frac{5}{6} \times \frac{9}{20} = \frac{\overset{1}{\cancel{5}}}{\underset{2}{\cancel{6}}} \times \frac{\overset{3}{\cancel{9}}}{\underset{4}{\cancel{20}}}$	$\frac{5}{6} \times \frac{9}{20} = \frac{45}{120}$
$= \frac{1}{2} \times \frac{3}{4}$	$= \frac{45 \div 5}{120 \div 5}$
$= \frac{3}{8}$	$= \frac{9 \div 3}{24 \div 3}$
	$= \frac{3}{8}$

It is usually much easier to find common factors to cancel before multiplying than it is to find common factors to reduce after multiplying.

Example

Multiply $\dfrac{4}{5} \times 15 \times 1\dfrac{3}{8}$.

Procedure

1. Change the whole number and mixed number into improper fractions.

$$\dfrac{4}{5} \times 15 \times 1\dfrac{3}{8}$$

$$= \dfrac{4}{5} \times \dfrac{15}{1} \times \dfrac{11}{8}$$

2. Cancel the common factors in the numerators and denominators, and multiply the remaining factors.

$$= \dfrac{\overset{1}{\cancel{4}}}{\underset{1}{\cancel{5}}} \times \dfrac{\overset{3}{\cancel{15}}}{1} \times \dfrac{11}{\underset{2}{\cancel{8}}}$$

$$= \dfrac{33}{2}$$

3. Simplify the final result.

$$= 16\dfrac{1}{2}$$

PRACTICE PROBLEMS

Perform the following multiplications. Reduce all answers to lowest terms.

1. $\dfrac{2}{3} \times \dfrac{6}{7} \times \dfrac{3}{4}$

2. $2\dfrac{2}{3} \times 1\dfrac{4}{5}$

3. $5 \times \dfrac{2}{3} \times 1\dfrac{1}{5}$

4. $1\dfrac{4}{5} \times 2\dfrac{2}{3} \times 2\dfrac{1}{2}$

ANSWERS AND EXPLANATIONS

1. $\dfrac{\overset{1}{\cancel{2}}}{\underset{1}{\cancel{3}}} \times \dfrac{\overset{3}{\cancel{6}}}{7} \times \dfrac{\overset{1}{\cancel{3}}}{\underset{12}{\cancel{4}}} = \dfrac{3}{7}$

2. $2\dfrac{2}{3} \times 1\dfrac{4}{5} = \dfrac{8}{\underset{1}{\cancel{3}}} \times \dfrac{\overset{3}{\cancel{9}}}{5} = \dfrac{24}{5} = 4\dfrac{4}{5}$

3. $5 \times \dfrac{2}{3} \times 1\dfrac{1}{5} = \dfrac{\overset{1}{\cancel{5}}}{1} \times \dfrac{2}{\underset{1}{\cancel{3}}} \times \dfrac{\overset{2}{\cancel{6}}}{\underset{1}{\cancel{5}}} = \dfrac{4}{1} = 4$

4. $1\dfrac{4}{5} \times 2\dfrac{2}{3} \times 2\dfrac{1}{2} = \dfrac{\overset{3}{\cancel{9}}}{\underset{1}{\cancel{5}}} \times \dfrac{\overset{4}{\cancel{8}}}{\underset{1}{\cancel{3}}} \times \dfrac{\overset{1}{\cancel{5}}}{\underset{1}{\cancel{2}}} = \dfrac{12}{1} = 12$

DIVIDING FRACTIONS

To divide fractions, we first *invert* the *divisor* (turn it upside down), and then multiply the resulting fractions. Remember that when using the symbol ÷ ("divided *by*"), the divisor is the fraction on the right.

As before, we can cancel common factors in the numerators and denominators. Note, however, that this can be done only *after* the divisor is inverted and the operation is changed to multiplication.

If the divisor or dividend is a whole number or mixed number, it should first be changed to an improper fraction before proceeding.

$$\frac{a}{b} \div \frac{c}{d} = \frac{a}{b} \times \frac{d}{c}$$

$$\frac{3}{4} \div \frac{7}{8} = \frac{3}{\cancel{4}_{1}} \times \frac{\cancel{8}^{2}}{7}$$

$$= \frac{6}{7}$$

Example

Divide $3\frac{1}{2} \div 2\frac{5}{8}$.

Procedure

1. Change the mixed numbers to improper fractions.

$$3\frac{1}{2} \div 2\frac{5}{8}$$

$$= \frac{7}{2} \div \frac{21}{8}$$

2. Invert the divisor and change the division to multiplication.

$$= \frac{7}{2} \times \frac{8}{21}$$

3. Cancel the common factors in the numerators and denominators, and multiply the remaining factors.

$$= \frac{\cancel{7}^{1}}{\cancel{2}_{1}} \times \frac{\cancel{8}^{4}}{\cancel{21}_{3}}$$

$$= \frac{4}{3}$$

4. Simplify the final result.

$$= 1\frac{1}{3}$$

PRACTICE PROBLEMS

Perform the following divisions. Reduce all answers to lowest terms.

1. $\dfrac{5}{6} \div \dfrac{4}{7}$

2. $8 \div \dfrac{4}{9}$

3. $2\dfrac{2}{3} \div 1\dfrac{7}{9}$

4. $2\dfrac{2}{5} \div 6$

ANSWERS AND EXPLANATIONS

1. $\dfrac{5}{6} \div \dfrac{4}{7} = \dfrac{5}{6} \times \dfrac{7}{4} = \dfrac{35}{24} = 1\dfrac{11}{24}$

2. $8 \div \dfrac{4}{9} = \dfrac{\overset{2}{\cancel{8}}}{1} \times \dfrac{9}{\underset{1}{\cancel{4}}} = \dfrac{18}{1} = 18$

3. $2\dfrac{2}{3} \div 1\dfrac{7}{9} = \dfrac{8}{3} \div \dfrac{16}{9} = \dfrac{\overset{1}{\cancel{8}}}{\underset{1}{\cancel{3}}} \times \dfrac{\overset{3}{\cancel{9}}}{\underset{2}{\cancel{16}}} = \dfrac{3}{2} = 1\dfrac{1}{2}$

4. $2\dfrac{2}{5} \div 6 = \dfrac{12}{5} \div \dfrac{6}{1} = \dfrac{\overset{2}{\cancel{12}}}{5} \times \dfrac{1}{\underset{1}{\cancel{6}}} = \dfrac{2}{5}$

SIMPLIFYING COMPLEX FRACTIONS

A fraction that contains at least one other fraction in its numerator or denominator is called a **complex fraction**. For example:

$$\dfrac{5 - \dfrac{2}{3}}{4} \qquad \Bigg| \qquad \dfrac{\dfrac{1}{2} + 6}{\dfrac{5}{7}}$$

There are two ways of simplifying a complex fraction. The first is to combine the numbers in the numerator and denominator separately, and then divide the resulting numerator by the resulting denominator. For example:

$$\dfrac{\dfrac{1}{4} + \dfrac{1}{3}}{\dfrac{5}{6}} = \dfrac{\dfrac{7}{12}}{\dfrac{5}{6}}$$

$$= \dfrac{7}{12} \div \dfrac{5}{6}$$

$$= \dfrac{7}{\underset{2}{\cancel{12}}} \times \dfrac{\overset{1}{\cancel{6}}}{5}$$

$$= \dfrac{7}{10}$$

The second way is to multiply every term in the complex fraction by a common denominator of the fractions contained within it. As a result, all the denominators will cancel, leaving a fraction free of other fractions. For example, to simplify the complex fraction in the preceding example, we multiply every term by 12, a common denominator of $\frac{1}{4}$, $\frac{1}{3}$, and $\frac{5}{6}$, and get:

$$\frac{\frac{1}{4} + \frac{1}{3}}{\frac{5}{6}} = \frac{\overset{3}{\cancel{12}} \times \frac{1}{\cancel{4}} + \overset{4}{\cancel{12}} \times \frac{1}{\cancel{3}}}{\overset{2}{\cancel{12}} \times \frac{5}{\cancel{6}}}$$

$$= \frac{3 + 4}{10}$$

$$= \frac{7}{10}$$

PRACTICE PROBLEMS

Simplify the following complex fractions:

1. $\dfrac{\frac{2}{5}}{\frac{3}{4}}$

2. $\dfrac{4 - \frac{2}{7}}{6}$

3. $\dfrac{\frac{1}{2} + \frac{2}{3}}{5}$

4. $\dfrac{\frac{3}{4} + 2}{\frac{1}{2}}$

ANSWERS AND EXPLANATIONS

1. $\dfrac{\frac{2}{5}}{\frac{3}{4}} = \frac{2}{5} \div \frac{3}{4} = \frac{2}{5} \times \frac{4}{3} = \frac{8}{15}$

2. $\dfrac{4 - \frac{2}{7}}{6} = \dfrac{7 \times 4 - \overset{1}{\cancel{7}} \times \frac{2}{\cancel{7}}}{7 \times 6} = \frac{28 - 2}{42} = \frac{26}{42} = \frac{13}{21}$

3. $\dfrac{\frac{1}{2} + \frac{2}{3}}{5} = \dfrac{\overset{3}{\cancel{6}} \times \frac{1}{\cancel{2}} + \overset{2}{\cancel{6}} \times \frac{2}{\cancel{3}}}{6 \times 5} = \frac{3 + 4}{30} = \frac{7}{30}$

4. $\dfrac{\dfrac{3}{4}+2}{\dfrac{1}{2}} = \dfrac{\overset{1}{\cancel{4}} \times \dfrac{3}{\cancel{4}} + 2 \times 4}{\overset{2}{\cancel{4}} \times \dfrac{1}{\cancel{2}}} = \dfrac{3+8}{2} = \dfrac{11}{2} = 5\dfrac{1}{2}$

COMPARING FRACTIONS

There are several different methods of comparing the values of fractions. One method is to change the fractions to a common denominator (as in addition and subtraction), and then compare their numerators.

For example, to compare $\dfrac{4}{7}$ and $\dfrac{5}{9}$ we change each of the fractions to the common denominator 63:

$$\frac{4}{7} = \frac{36}{63} \text{ and } \frac{5}{9} = \frac{35}{63}$$

When we compare their numerators, we see that $\dfrac{36}{63}$ is greater than $\dfrac{35}{63}$, and therefore conclude that $\dfrac{4}{7}$ is greater than $\dfrac{5}{9}$.

Another method is to cross-multiply their numerators and denominators and compare the resulting products:

$$36 \underset{\dfrac{4}{7} \quad \dfrac{5}{9}}{\diagdown \diagup} 35$$

Notice that the cross-products, 36 and 35, correspond to the numerators we compared in the first method. Since 36 is greater than 35, we again conclude that $\dfrac{4}{7}$ is greater than $\dfrac{5}{9}$.

The second method is summarized below. In this summary, the symbol > means "is greater than," and the symbol < means "is less than."

To Compare Two Fractions $\dfrac{a}{b}$ and $\dfrac{c}{d}$:

1. Cross-multiply the numerators and denominators, and write the products above the fractions.

$$a \times d \qquad b \times c$$
$$\underset{\dfrac{a}{b} \quad \dfrac{c}{d}}{\diagdown \diagup}$$

2. If $a \times d > b \times c$, then $\dfrac{a}{b} > \dfrac{c}{d}$.

   If $a \times d = b \times c$, then $\dfrac{a}{b} = \dfrac{c}{d}$.

   If $a \times d < b \times c$, then $\dfrac{a}{b} < \dfrac{c}{d}$.

Remember that this method can only be used to compare two fractions at a time. When there are more than two fractions, use the process of elimination illustrated in the example on the following page.

Example

Which of the fractions $\frac{2}{5}$, $\frac{3}{7}$, or $\frac{4}{11}$ is the largest?

Procedure

1. Compare the first two fractions, $\frac{2}{5}$ and $\frac{3}{7}$, by cross-multiplying their numerators and denominators. Since 14 is less than 15, we can eliminate $\frac{2}{5}$.

$$14 \diagdown \diagup 15$$
$$\frac{2}{5} \times \frac{3}{7}$$

2. Now compare $\frac{3}{7}$ and $\frac{4}{11}$ in the same way. Since 28 is less than 33, we can eliminate $\frac{4}{11}$. Therefore, the largest fraction is $\frac{3}{7}$.

$$33 \diagdown \diagup 28$$
$$\frac{3}{7} \times \frac{4}{11}$$

The largest is $\frac{3}{7}$.

PRACTICE PROBLEMS

In each of the following groups of fractions, find the largest fraction:

1. $\frac{6}{11}$, $\frac{5}{9}$

2. $\frac{9}{13}$, $\frac{11}{15}$

3. $\frac{4}{5}$, $\frac{6}{7}$, $\frac{7}{9}$

4. $\frac{5}{7}$, $\frac{2}{3}$, $\frac{3}{4}$

ANSWERS AND EXPLANATIONS

1. 54   ⑤⑤ ← **largest**

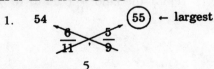

Answer: $\frac{5}{9}$

2. 135   ⑭③ ← **largest**

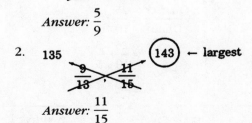

Answer: $\frac{11}{15}$

33

3.   Comparing the first two:

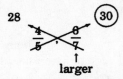

Comparing the larger with the third:

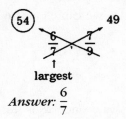

Answer: $\dfrac{6}{7}$

4.   Comparing the first two:

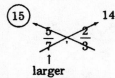

Comparing the larger with the third:

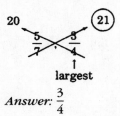

Answer: $\dfrac{3}{4}$

Finding the Missing Term of a Proportion

As previously noted, one of the ways of using a fraction is to express a ratio, or comparison, between two quantities. For example, we can use the fraction $\dfrac{25}{10}$ to express the ratio of the number of cents in a quarter to the number of cents in a dime. Like fractions, ratios can be reduced to lower terms. Therefore, the ratio $\dfrac{25}{10}$ ("25 to 10") is equivalent to the ratio $\dfrac{5}{2}$ ("5 to 2").

$$\frac{\text{Quarter}}{\text{Dime}} = \frac{25}{10}$$
$$= \frac{25 \div 5}{10 \div 5}$$
$$= \frac{5}{2}$$

When two ratios (fractions) are equal, they form a **proportion**. Thus, in the preceding example, the statement $\frac{25}{10} = \frac{5}{2}$ is a proportion. We read this statement "25 is to 10 as 5 is to 2".

Each of the four numbers in a proportion is called a **term** of the proportion. Sometimes we are given only three of the terms and are asked to find the fourth. For example, in the proportion $\frac{3}{5} = \frac{21}{N}$ we are missing the term N. To find N, we use the fact (from the preceding section) that when two fractions are equal, the cross products of their numerators and denominators are equal. Therefore:

$$3 \times N \underset{5 N}{\overset{3 21}{\times}} 5 \times 21$$

$$3 \times N = 5 \times 21$$

$$3 \times N = 105$$

Since 3 times N equals 105, N must equal 105 divided by 3. Thus, we get:

$$3 \times N = 105$$

$$N = \frac{105}{3}$$

$$N = 35$$

When we substitute this value for N back into the original proportion, we get the true statement $\frac{3}{5} = \frac{21}{35}$.

To Find the Missing Term of a Proportion:
1. Cross-multiply the numerators and denominators and set the two products equal.
2. Divide the number in the product containing the missing term into the other product.

$$\frac{7}{N} = \frac{28}{36}$$

$$28 \times N = 7 \times 36$$

$$28 \times N = 252$$

$$N = \frac{252}{28}$$

$$N = 9$$

PRACTICE PROBLEMS

Find the missing term of each of the following proportions:

1. $\dfrac{7}{9} = \dfrac{N}{72}$

2. $\dfrac{19}{12} = \dfrac{76}{N}$

3. $\dfrac{N}{16} = \dfrac{15}{20}$

4. $\dfrac{30}{N} = \dfrac{45}{27}$

ANSWERS AND EXPLANATIONS

1. $\dfrac{7}{9} = \dfrac{N}{72}$ (cross-multiply)

   $9 \times N = 7 \times 72$

   $9 \times N = 504$

   $N = \dfrac{504}{9} = 56$

2. $\dfrac{19}{12} = \dfrac{76}{N}$ (cross-multiply)

   $19 \times N = 12 \times 76$

   $19 \times N = 912$

   $N = \dfrac{912}{19} = 48$

3. $\dfrac{N}{16} = \dfrac{15}{20}$ (cross-multiply)

   $20 \times N = 16 \times 15$

   $20 \times N = 240$

   $N = \dfrac{240}{20} = 12$

4. $\dfrac{30}{N} = \dfrac{45}{27}$ (cross-multiply)

   $45 \times N = 30 \times 27$

   $45 \times N = 810$

   $N = \dfrac{810}{45} = 18$

DECIMALS

Fractions, such as $\dfrac{3}{10}$, $\dfrac{17}{100}$, and $\dfrac{9}{1000}$, whose denominators are powers of 10 (10, 100, 1000, etc.), are called **decimal fractions**, or more simply, **decimals**.

Decimal fractions are usually written in a special shorthand in which the numerator is placed to the right of a dot called a **decimal point**. The denominator is not actually written, but instead is determined in the following way: If the numerator ends one place to the right of the decimal point, the denominator is 10; if the numerator ends two places to the right of the decimal point, the denominator is 100; if the numerator ends three places to the right of the decimal point, the denominator is 1000; and so on. Note that to write $\dfrac{9}{1000}$ in this shorthand, we must use two zeros as placeholders so that the numerator ends the required three places to the right of the decimal point.

$$\frac{3}{10} = .3$$

$$\frac{17}{100} = .17$$

$$\frac{9}{1000} = .009$$

$$19\frac{7}{10} = 19.7$$

$$8\frac{3}{100} = 8.03$$

Numbers that consist of a whole number and a decimal fraction are called **mixed decimals**. As shown in the last two examples above, mixed decimals are written with the whole number to the left of the decimal point and the decimal fraction to the right of it. The values of the places in a mixed decimal are summarized below. Note that the decimal point does not occupy a place by itself, but simply separates the whole number places from the decimal places.

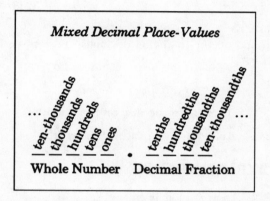

When reading mixed decimals, the decimal point is read as the word "and." This signals the separation between the whole number and the decimal fraction. For example, 347.15 is read as "three hundred forty seven *and* fifteen hundredths."

Remember that zeros have different effects on the value of a decimal, depending upon where they are placed. On the one hand, zeros placed between the decimal point and the first digit in a decimal make the value of the decimal smaller:

$$.9 = \frac{9}{10}, \ .09 = \frac{9}{100}, \text{ and } .009 = \frac{9}{1000}$$

On the other hand, zeros placed to the right of the last digit in a decimal do not change the value of the fraction at all:

$$.7 = \frac{7}{10}, \ .70 = \frac{70}{100}, \text{ and } .700 = \frac{700}{1000}$$

After reducing, each has the same value, $\frac{7}{10}$.

ROUNDING OFF DECIMALS

The procedure for rounding off decimals is very similar to the procedure for rounding off whole numbers. The only notable difference is that in rounding off decimals, the zeros to the right of the rounded off place have no value and can be dropped.

To Round Off a Decimal:
1. Circle the digit in the place being rounded off.
2. If the digit to its right is less than 5, leave the circled digit as it is.
   If the digit to its right is 5 or more, increase the circled digit by 1.
3. Drop all the digits to the right of the circled digit.

For example, round off 7.238 to the nearest hundredth.

$$7.2\,③\,8$$
$$\downarrow$$
$$7.2\,③\,8$$
$$7.2\,④\,8$$
$$7.24$$
$$7.238 \approx 7.24$$

PRACTICE PROBLEMS

Round off the following decimals to the place indicated:

1. 9.376 to the nearest hundredth

2. 0.329 to the nearest tenth

3. 12.2685 to the nearest thousandth

4. 16.998 to the nearest hundredth

ANSWERS AND EXPLANATIONS

1. $9.3\,⑦\,6 \approx 9.38$

2. $0.\,③\,29 \approx 0.3$

3. $12.26\,⑧\,5 \approx 12.269$

4. $16.9\,⑨\,8 \approx 17.00$

ADDING AND SUBTRACTING DECIMALS

To add or subtract decimals, first arrange the numbers vertically with the decimal points lined up, and then proceed as though the numbers were whole numbers (ignoring the points). After performing the operation, place a decimal point in the result directly below the other points.

$$4.79 + 5.83$$
$$\downarrow$$

$$
\begin{array}{r}
4.79 \\
+5.83 \\
\hline
10.62
\end{array}
$$

When the decimals have a different number of decimal places, it is usually helpful to fill in zeros on their right. As discussed in the preceding section, these zeros will not change the values of the decimals.

$$17.32 - 9.246$$
$$\downarrow$$

$$
\begin{array}{r}
17.320 \\
-\ \ 9.246 \\
\hline
8.074
\end{array}
$$

Example 1
Add 5.73 + 17 + 8.296.

Procedure

1. Line up the decimal points and add. Remember that the whole number, 17, has an unwritten decimal point on its right. As indicated, the zeros are optional.

$$
\begin{array}{r}
5.73 \\
17. \\
+\ 8.296 \\
\hline
31.026
\end{array}
\qquad \text{or} \qquad
\begin{array}{r}
5.730 \\
17.000 \\
+\ 8.296 \\
\hline
31.026
\end{array}
$$

Example 2
Subtract 73 − .46.

Procedure

1. Place a decimal point to the right of the whole number, 73, and line up the decimal points.

$$
\begin{array}{r}
73. \\
-\ .46 \\
\hline
\end{array}
$$

2. Fill in two zeros and subtract. Note that for subtraction, the zeros are usually not optional.

$$
\begin{array}{r}
73.00 \\
-\ \ .46 \\
\hline
72.54
\end{array}
$$

PRACTICE PROBLEMS

Perform the following additions and subtractions:

1.   4.32 + .168 + 17 =

2.   13.642 − 4.19 =

3.   5.6 − 2.931 =

4.   56 − .32 =

ANSWERS AND EXPLANATIONS

1.   4.320
          .168
       +17.000
        21.488

2.   13.642
       −4.190
        9.452

3.   5.600
       −2.931
        2.669

4.   56.00
        −.32
       55.68

MULTIPLYING DECIMALS

To multiply decimals, again proceed as though the numbers were whole numbers. This time, however, instead of lining up the decimal points, line up the right-most digits (as in whole number multiplication). After multiplying, place a decimal point in the result so that the number of places to its right is equal to the *sum* of the decimal places in the two numbers just multiplied.

          2.13   (2 places)
       × 3.4   (1 place)
          852
          639
       7.242   (3 places)

Example

Multiply $3.4 \times .007$.

Procedure

1. Arrange the numbers as though they were whole numbers (with the right most digits lined up) and multiply them.

$$
\begin{array}{r}
3.4 \\
\times .007 \\
\hline
238
\end{array}
$$

2. Since the result should have 4 decimal places $(1 + 3 = 4)$, fill in a zero in front of the 2 to act as a placeholder.

$$
\begin{array}{rl}
3.4 & \text{(1 place)} \\
\times .007 & \text{(3 places)} \\
\hline
.0238 & \text{(4 places)}
\end{array}
$$

When multiplying decimals by powers of 10 (10, 100, 1000, etc.), use the following shortcut:

To Multiply a Decimal by a Power of 10:

Move the decimal point to the *right* as many places as the number of zeros in the power of 10.

Consider the following examples:

$$
\begin{array}{r}
7.382 \\
\times 10 \\
\hline
73.820
\end{array}
\qquad\qquad
\begin{array}{r}
7.382 \\
\times 100 \\
\hline
738.200
\end{array}
$$

$$10 \times 7.382 = 73.82 \qquad\qquad 100 \times 7.382 = 738.2$$

As you can see, when we multiply by 10 (*one* zero), we move the decimal point *one* place to the right, and when we multiply by 100 (*two* zeros), we move the decimal point *two* places to the right.

PRACTICE PROBLEMS

1. 5.14×2.7

2. $6.3 \times .002$

3. 5.347×100

4. 6.23×1000

ANSWERS AND EXPLANATIONS

1.
$$
\begin{array}{r}
5.14 \\
\times\,2.7 \\
\hline
3598 \\
\underline{1028} \\
13.878
\end{array}
$$

2.
$$
\begin{array}{r}
6.3 \\
\times.002 \\
\hline
.0126
\end{array}
$$

3. $5.\underline{3}47 \times 100 = 534.7$

4. $6.\underline{230}\ \times 1000 = 6230.$

DIVIDING A DECIMAL BY A WHOLE NUMBER

When dividing a decimal by a *whole number*, first position a decimal point for the result directly above the point in the dividend. Then proceed to divide in the usual manner, treating the dividend as a whole number.

$$
\begin{array}{r}
3.12 \\
4\overline{)12.48}
\end{array}
$$

Sometimes it may be necessary to fill in zeros, to act as place-holders, between the decimal point and the first digit in the result. It is incorrect to leave these places blank.

Correct:
$$
\begin{array}{r}
.024 \\
9\overline{).216}
\end{array}
$$

Incorrect:
$$
\begin{array}{r}
.\ 24 \\
9\overline{).216}
\end{array}
$$

If the division is not exact, either express the remainder as a fraction, or continue to divide by adding zeros to the right of the last digit in the dividend. Remember, zeros added to the right of a decimal do not change its value. Both procedures are shown below.

$$
\begin{array}{r}
5.8\tfrac{3}{4} \\
4\overline{)23.5} \\
\underline{20} \\
35 \\
\underline{32} \\
3
\end{array}
\quad\text{or}\quad
\begin{array}{r}
5.875 \\
4\overline{)23.500} \\
\underline{20} \\
35 \\
\underline{32} \\
30 \\
\underline{28} \\
20 \\
\underline{20} \\
0
\end{array}
$$

Notice that by adding zeros on the right, the division eventually ends. Consequently, we call the result a **terminating decimal**. Sometimes, however, regardless of how many zeros are added, the division never ends. For example:

$$
\begin{array}{r}
2.466\cdots \\
3\overline{)7.400\cdots} \\
\underline{6} \\
1\,4 \\
\underline{1\,2} \\
20 \\
\underline{18} \\
20 \\
\underline{18} \\
2
\end{array}
$$

Since the digit 6 keeps repeating, we call the result a **repeating decimal**. In cases like these we have the following options:

1. Approximate the result by rounding it off to a given place;

2. Indicate the repeating digit by placing a bar over it; or

3. Express the remainder as a fraction.

$$2.466\cdots \approx 2.47$$

$$2.466\cdots = 2.4\overline{6}$$

$$2.466\cdots = 2.46\frac{2}{3}$$

Example

Divide $11\overline{)4}$

Procedure

1. Place a decimal point after the whole number 4, and position another point directly above it for the result.

$$11\overline{)4} = 11\overline{)4.}$$

2. By adding zeros to the right of the decimal point, keep dividing until either the division terminates, or the digits in the result start to repeat.

$$
\begin{array}{r}
.3636\cdots \\
11\overline{)4.0000} \\
\underline{33} \\
70 \\
\underline{66} \\
40 \\
\underline{33} \\
70 \\
\underline{66} \\
4
\end{array}
$$

3. Since the digits 36 are repeating, indicate them with a bar.

$$.3636\cdots = .\overline{36}$$

When dividing decimals by powers of 10 (10, 100, 1000, etc.), we can use a shortcut similar to the one for multiplying decimals by powers of 10. The main difference between the two shortcuts is that when we *multiply* by a power of 10 we move the decimal point to the *right*, and when we *divide* by a power of 10, we move the point to the *left*. Specifically,

---
To Divide a Decimal by a Power of 10:
Move the decimal point to the *left* as many places as the number of zeros in the power of 10.

Consider the examples below:

$$
\begin{array}{r}
4.27 \\
10\overline{)42.70} \\
\underline{40} \\
27 \\
\underline{20} \\
70 \\
\underline{70} \\
0
\end{array}
\qquad
\begin{array}{r}
.427 \\
100\overline{)42.700} \\
\underline{40\ 0} \\
2\ 70 \\
\underline{2\ 00} \\
700 \\
\underline{700} \\
0
\end{array}
$$

$$42.7 \div 10 = 4.27 \qquad 42.7 \div 100 = .427$$

PRACTICE PROBLEMS

1. $4\overline{).312}$

2. $8\overline{)2.5}$

3. $33\overline{)8}$

4. $100\overline{)5.42}$

ANSWERS AND EXPLANATIONS

1.
$$
\begin{array}{r}
.078 \\
4\overline{)\,.312} \\
\underline{28} \\
32 \\
\underline{32} \\
0
\end{array}
$$

2.
$$
\begin{array}{r}
.3125 \\
8\overline{)\,2.5000} \\
\underline{2\,4} \\
10 \\
\underline{8} \\
20 \\
\underline{16} \\
40 \\
\underline{40} \\
0
\end{array}
$$

3.
$$
\begin{array}{r}
.24 \\
33\overline{)\,8.00} \\
\underline{6\,6} \\
1\,40 \\
\underline{1\,32} \\
8
\end{array}
$$

4. $05.42 \div 100 = .0542$

DIVIDING A DECIMAL BY A DECIMAL

To divide a decimal by a decimal, change the problem into an equivalent problem in which the divisor is a whole number. To do this, move the decimal point in the divisor all the way to its right, and then move the decimal point in the dividend the same number of places to its right. After the decimal points are moved (and the divisor is a whole number), proceed as in the last section.

$$.2\overline{)6.84} = 2.\overline{)68.4}\;\;\overset{3\;4.2}{}$$

When the dividend has fewer decimal places than the divisor, make up the difference by adding as many zeros as necessary to the right of the dividend.

$$.23\overline{)4.6} = 23.\overline{)460.}\;\;\overset{20.}{}$$

Example 1

Divide $.4)\overline{19}$

Procedure

1. Place a decimal point and one zero after the whole number, 19, and then move both decimal points one place to the right.

$$.4)\overline{19} = .4)\overline{19.0}$$
$$= 4.)\overline{190.}$$

2. Place a decimal point directly above the decimal point in the dividend, and divide.

$$
\begin{array}{r}
47. \\
4.)\overline{190.} \\
\underline{16} \\
30 \\
\underline{28} \\
2
\end{array}
$$

3. Add one zero after the decimal point in the dividend, and continue to divide.

$$
\begin{array}{r}
47.5 \\
4.)\overline{190.0} \\
\underline{16} \\
30 \\
\underline{28} \\
20 \\
\underline{20} \\
0
\end{array}
$$

Example 2

Divide $.34)\overline{.9}$ and round off the result to the nearest tenth.

Procedure

1. Add one zero after the last digit in the dividend, and then move both decimal points two places to the right.

$$.34)\overline{.9} = 34.)\overline{90.}$$

2. Place a decimal point directly above the decimal point in the dividend, and divide.

$$
\begin{array}{r}
2. \\
34.)\overline{90.} \\
\underline{68} \\
22
\end{array}
$$

3. To round off the result to the nearest tenth, we must determine the digit in the hundredths place (one place more than asked for). Therefore, add two more zeros after the decimal point, and continue to divide.

$$
\begin{array}{r}
2.64 \\
34.\overline{)90.00} \\
\underline{68} \\
22\,0 \\
\underline{20\,4} \\
1\,60 \\
\underline{1\,36} \\
24
\end{array}
$$

4. Since the digit in the hundredths place is less than 5, drop it.

$$2.64 \approx 2.6$$

PRACTICE PROBLEMS

Perform the following divisions:

1. $.8\overline{)6.34}$

2. $.12\overline{)4.5}$

3. $.13\overline{)5.642}$

4. $.32\overline{)68}$

Perform the following divisions and round off each answer to the *nearest tenth*:

5. $.9\overline{)8.7}$

6. $.14\overline{)5.7}$

7. $.42\overline{)51}$

8. $.14\overline{)9}$

ANSWERS AND EXPLANATIONS

1.
```
           7 . 925
   ×8.  )6×3. 400
         5 6
         ─────
           7 4
           7 2
         ─────
             20
             16
         ─────
             40
             40
         ─────
              0
```

2.
```
          37 . 5
   ×12.  )4×50. 0
          3 6
         ─────
           90
           84
         ─────
            6 0
            6 0
         ─────
              0
```

3.
```
          43 . 4
   ×13.  )5×64. 2
          5 2
         ─────
           44
           39
         ─────
            5 2
            5 2
         ─────
              0
```

4.
```
          2 12 . 5
   ×32.  )68×00. 0
          64
         ─────
           4 0
           3 2
         ─────
             80
             64
         ─────
             16 0
             16 0
         ─────
                0
```

5.
```
                ↓
          9 . ⑥6  ≈ 9.7
   ×9.  )8×7. 0 0
          8 1
         ─────
           6 0
           5 4
         ─────
             6 0
             5 4
         ─────
                6
```

6.

$$
\begin{array}{r}
40.\,\textcircled{7}\,\overset{\downarrow}{1} \approx 40.7 \\
\times 14.\,\overline{)5\times 70.\,0\ 0} \\
\underline{5\ \ 6} \\
10\ \ 0 \\
\underline{9\ \ 8} \\
2\ \ 0 \\
\underline{1\ \ 4} \\
6
\end{array}
$$

7.

$$
\begin{array}{r}
1\ \ 21.\,\textcircled{4}\,\overset{\downarrow}{2} \approx 121.4 \\
\times 42.\,\overline{)51\times 00.\,0\ 0} \\
\underline{42} \\
9\ \ 0 \\
\underline{8\ \ 4} \\
60 \\
\underline{42} \\
18\ \ 0 \\
\underline{16\ \ 8} \\
1\ \ 2\ \ 0 \\
\underline{1\ \ 1\ \ 2} \\
8
\end{array}
$$

8.

$$
\begin{array}{r}
64.\,\textcircled{2}\,\overset{\downarrow}{8} \approx 64.3 \\
\times 14.\,\overline{)9\times 00.\,0\ 0} \\
\underline{8\ \ 4} \\
60 \\
\underline{56} \\
4\ \ 0 \\
\underline{2\ \ 8} \\
1\ \ 2\ \ 0 \\
\underline{1\ \ 1\ \ 2} \\
8
\end{array}
$$

COMPARING DECIMAL FRACTIONS

As you recall, one of the methods of comparing the values of fractions is to change the fractions to a common denominator, and then compare the resulting numerators.

In order to apply this method to decimal fractions, use the following procedure:

To Compare Decimal Fractions:
1. Add zeros to the right of the decimals so that all of them have the same number of decimal places (and thus the same denominator).
2. Compare the numbers to the right of the decimal points (the numerators of the decimal fractions).

For example, to compare the decimal fractions .57, .413, and .6, first add zeros to their right so that all of them are three-place decimals, having the same denominator, thousandths. Then compare their numerators by comparing the numbers to the right of the decimal points. Since 600 is the largest number, .6 is the largest decimal; since 413 is the smallest number, .413 is the smallest decimal.

$$.57 = .570$$
$$.413 = .413$$
$$.6 = .600$$

PRACTICE PROBLEMS

In each of the following groups of decimals, find the smallest decimal.

1. .5, .468, .52

2. 8.6, 9.002, 8.59

3. .09, .765, .8

4. .64, 1.002, .9

ANSWERS AND EXPLANATIONS

1. .5 = .500

    .468 = .468 ← smallest

    .52 = .520

2. 8.6 = 8.600

    9.002 = 9.002

    8.59 = 8.590 ← smallest

3. .09 = .090 ← smallest

    .765 = .765

    .8 = .800

4. .64 = .640 ← smallest

    1.002 = 1.002

    .9 = .900

CHANGING DECIMAL FRACTIONS TO COMMON FRACTIONS

Fractions written in the standard form $\dfrac{a}{b}$ are called *common fractions*. By using the definition of a decimal fraction as a fraction whose denominator is a power of 10, we can change a decimal fraction into the form of a common fraction. Specifically,

---
To Change a Decimal Fraction into a Common Fraction:
1. Form a fraction whose numerator is the number to the right of the decimal point, and whose denominator is the power of 10 corresponding to the number of decimal places in the given decimal: If the decimal has one place, make the denominator 10; if the decimal has two places, make the denominator 100; and so on.
2. Reduce the resulting fraction to lowest terms.

$$.8 = \frac{8}{10} = \frac{4}{5}$$

$$.62 = \frac{62}{100} = \frac{31}{50}$$

$$.035 = \frac{35}{1000} = \frac{7}{200}$$

A simple way of determining the correct power of 10 in the denominator is to remember that the number of zeros in the power of 10 is equal to the number of places in the decimal fraction: A one-place decimal has one zero in the denominator, a two-place decimal has two zeros in the denominator, and so on.

Example

Change the decimal fraction $.37\frac{1}{2}$ into a common fraction, reduced to lowest terms.

Procedure

1. Form a fraction whose numerator is the number to the right of the decimal point, and whose denominator is 100. (This is a two-place decimal; the $\frac{1}{2}$ does not occupy a place.)

$$.37\frac{1}{2} = \frac{37\frac{1}{2}}{100}$$

2. To simplify the complex fraction, first change the mixed number in the numerator to an improper fraction, and then divide the numerator by the denominator.

$$= \frac{\frac{75}{2}}{100}$$

$$= \frac{75}{2} \div 100$$

$$= \frac{\overset{3}{\cancel{75}}}{2} \times \frac{1}{\underset{4}{\cancel{100}}}$$

$$= \frac{3}{8}$$

PRACTICE PROBLEMS

Change the following decimal fractions to common fractions, reduced to lowest terms:

1. .048

2. 12.68

3. $.8\frac{3}{4}$

4. $9.07\frac{1}{2}$

ANSWERS AND EXPLANATIONS

1. $.048 = \dfrac{48}{1000} = \dfrac{6}{125}$

2. $12.68 = 12\dfrac{68}{100} = 12\dfrac{17}{25}$

3. $.8\dfrac{3}{4} = \dfrac{8\frac{3}{4}}{10} = 8\dfrac{3}{4} \div 10 = \dfrac{\overset{7}{\cancel{35}}}{4} \times \dfrac{1}{\underset{2}{\cancel{10}}} = \dfrac{7}{8}$

4. $.07\frac{1}{2} = \frac{7\frac{1}{2}}{100} = \overset{3}{\cancel{\frac{15}{2}}} \times \underset{20}{\frac{1}{\cancel{100}}} = \frac{3}{40}$

Thus, $9.07\frac{1}{2} = 9\frac{3}{40}$

CHANGING COMMON FRACTIONS TO DECIMAL FRACTIONS

By using the interpretation of a fraction as a quotient, we can change a common fraction into the form of a decimal fraction. Specifically,

$$\frac{a}{b} = b\overline{)a}$$

To Change a Common Fraction into a Decimal Fraction:
1. Place a decimal point and zeros to the right of the number in the numerator. The exact number of zeros depends upon the number of decimal places desired in the result.
2. Divide the denominator into the numerator.

$$\frac{3}{8} = 8\overline{)3.000} \quad \begin{array}{r} .375 \\ \hline \end{array}$$

$$\begin{array}{r} 2\ 4\ \ \\ \hline 60 \\ 56 \\ \hline 40 \\ 40 \\ \hline 0 \end{array}$$

This procedure provides us with another method for comparing the values of common fractions. For example, to compare the fractions $\frac{5}{8}, \frac{3}{5}$, and $\frac{2}{3}$, we can divide the denominators into the numerators, and then compare the resulting decimals. Since $\frac{5}{8} = .625, \frac{3}{5} = .600$, and $\frac{2}{3} = .666\frac{2}{3}$, we conclude that $\frac{2}{3}$ is the largest fraction and $\frac{3}{5}$ is the smallest fraction.

$$\frac{5}{8} = 8\overline{)5.000} \quad \begin{array}{r} .625 \\ \hline \end{array}$$

$$\frac{3}{5} = 5\overline{)3.000} \quad \begin{array}{r} .600 \\ \hline \end{array}$$

$$\frac{2}{3} = 3\overline{)2.000} \quad \begin{array}{r} .666\frac{2}{3} \\ \hline \end{array}$$

The decimal equivalents of several common fractions are summarized below. Since these fractions are used so frequently in computation, it is worthwhile to memorize them.

Common Fraction	Decimal Fraction
$\dfrac{1}{2}$	.5
$\dfrac{1}{3}$	$.33\dfrac{1}{3}$
$\dfrac{2}{3}$	$.66\dfrac{2}{3}$
$\dfrac{1}{4}$	.25
$\dfrac{3}{4}$	.75
$\dfrac{1}{5}$	.2
$\dfrac{2}{5}$	.4
$\dfrac{3}{5}$	.6
$\dfrac{4}{5}$	.8
$\dfrac{1}{6}$	$.16\dfrac{2}{3}$
$\dfrac{5}{6}$	$.83\dfrac{1}{3}$
$\dfrac{1}{8}$	.125
$\dfrac{3}{8}$	.375
$\dfrac{5}{8}$	.625
$\dfrac{7}{8}$	.875

PRACTICE PROBLEMS

Change the following common fractions to decimal fractions:

1. $\dfrac{12}{15}$

2. $9\dfrac{27}{72}$

3. $\dfrac{4}{18}$

4. $6\dfrac{12}{36}$

ANSWERS AND EXPLANATIONS

1.
$$\dfrac{12}{15} = 15\overline{)12.0}^{\;.8}$$
$$\underline{12\;0}$$
$$0$$

2.
$$\dfrac{27}{72} = 72\overline{)27.000}^{\;.375} \quad \text{Thus, } 9\dfrac{27}{72} = 9.375$$
$$\underline{21\;6}$$
$$5\;40$$
$$\underline{5\;04}$$
$$360$$
$$\underline{360}$$
$$0$$

3.
$$.22\dfrac{4}{18} = .22\dfrac{2}{9}$$
$$\dfrac{4}{18} = 18\overline{)4.00}$$
$$\underline{3\;6}$$
$$40$$
$$\underline{36}$$
$$4$$

4.
$$.33\dfrac{12}{36} = .33\dfrac{1}{3}$$
$$\dfrac{12}{36} = 36\overline{)12.00} \qquad \text{Thus, } 6\dfrac{12}{36} = 6.33\dfrac{1}{3}$$
$$\underline{10\;8}$$
$$1\;20$$
$$\underline{1\;08}$$
$$12$$

PERCENTS

Fractions whose denominators are 100, in addition to being called decimal fractions, are called **percents** ("per hundred"). Besides being written in decimal notation, percents are also denoted by the symbol %. Some examples are shown below.

Fraction	Decimal	Percent
$\dfrac{41}{100}$	.41	41%
$\dfrac{9}{100}$	.09	9%
$\dfrac{58\frac{1}{2}}{100}$	$.58\frac{1}{2}$	$58\frac{1}{2}\%$

CHANGING PERCENTS TO DECIMALS

Since a percent is a fraction whose denominator is 100, we can change a percent into the form of a decimal by dividing the percent by 100. Consider the examples below:

$$Percent \rightarrow Fraction \rightarrow Decimal$$

$$87\% \quad = \quad \frac{87}{100} \quad = \quad 100\overline{)87.00}^{\,.87}$$

$$3\% \quad = \quad \frac{3}{100} \quad = \quad 100\overline{)3.00}^{\,.03}$$

$$12.9\% \quad = \quad \frac{12.9}{100} \quad = \quad 100\overline{)12.900}^{\,.129}$$

In each example, since we are dividing by 100, the decimal point in the result is two places to the left of its original position in the percent. That is:

$$Percent \qquad \rightarrow \qquad Decimal$$

$$87\% \quad = \quad \underline{87}.\% \quad = \quad .87$$

$$3\% \quad = \quad \underline{03}.\% \quad = \quad .03$$

$$12.9\% \quad = \quad \underline{12}.9\% \quad = \quad .129$$

This leads us to the following shortcut:

To Change a Percent to a Decimal:

Move the decimal point *two* places to the *left*, and *drop* the % symbol.

To change a decimal into the form of a percent, simply reverse this procedure.

To Change a Decimal to a Percent:

Move the decimal point *two* places to the *right*, and *insert* the % symbol.

Some examples are shown below.

Decimal		$\rightarrow$		*Percent*
.93	=	.93	=	93%
.7	=	.70	=	70%
.641	=	.641	=	64.1%

In both procedures the decimal point is moved two places. A simple way of remembering the direction of moving the point is to think of the letters of the alphabet.

ABC Ⓓ EFGHIJKLMNO Ⓟ QRSTUVWXYZ

Decimal ⟺ Percent

If we change from a *Decimal* to a *Percent*, we move the point two places to the right ($D \rightarrow P$); if we change from a *Percent* to a *Decimal*, we move the point two places to the left ($D \leftarrow P$).

Example 1

Change $9\frac{1}{4}\%$ to a decimal.

Procedure

1. Change the fraction within the percent, $\frac{1}{4}$, to its decimal equivalent, .25.

$$9\frac{1}{4}\% = 9.25\%$$

2. Move the decimal point two places to the left ($D \leftarrow P$), and drop the % symbol.

$$9\frac{1}{4}\% = \underline{09}.25\% = .0925$$

Example 2

Change 1.8 to a percent.

Procedure

1. Add a zero to the right of the 8.

$$1.8 = 1.80$$

2. Move the decimal point two places to the right (D → P), and insert a % symbol.

$$1.8 = 1.\underline{80} = 180\%$$

PRACTICE PROBLEMS

Change the following percents to decimals:

1. 8.7%

2. .5%

3. $19\dfrac{1}{2}\%$

4. $16.8\dfrac{1}{4}\%$

Change the following decimals to percents:

5. .913

6. .079

7. 6.3

8. 12

ANSWERS AND EXPLANATIONS

1. $\underline{08}.7\% = .087$

2. $\underline{00}.5\% = .005$

3. $19\dfrac{1}{2}\% = \underline{19}.5\% = .195$

4. $16.8\dfrac{1}{4}\% = \underline{16}.825\% = .16825$

5. $\underline{.913} = 91.3\%$

6. $\underline{.079} = 7.9\%$

7. $6.\underline{30} = 630\%$

8. $12 = 12.\underline{00} = 1200\%$

CHANGING PERCENTS TO FRACTIONS

There are two methods of changing a percent into the form of a common fraction. In the first, we use the definition of a percent and form a fraction having a denominator of 100. In the second, we change the percent into a decimal (as in the last section), and then change the decimal into a common fraction.

To Change a Percent to a Fraction:

Method 1: Place the percent over a denominator of 100, and drop the % symbol. Reduce the resulting fraction to lowest terms.

$$28\% = \frac{28}{100} = \frac{7}{25}$$

Method 2: Change the percent into a decimal (D ← P), and then change the decimal into a common fraction. Reduce the result to lowest terms.

$$28\% = .28 = \frac{28}{100} = \frac{7}{25}$$

To change a fraction into the form of a percent, simply reverse these procedures.

To Change a Fraction to a Percent:

Method 1: Multiply the fraction by 100% and simplify the result.

$$\frac{13}{20} = \frac{13}{20} \times 100\% = 65\%$$

Method 2: Change the fraction into a decimal (by dividing the denominator into the numerator), and then change the decimal into a percent (D → P).

$$\frac{13}{20} = 20\overline{)13.00}^{\;.65} = 65\%$$

The chart below summarizes the percent equivalents of several common fractions. Remember that fractions less than 1 (proper fractions) are equivalent to percents less than 100%, and that fractions equal to or greater than 1 (improper fractions) are equivalent to percents equal to or greater than 100%.

$$100\% = \frac{100}{100} = 1$$

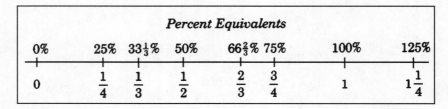

Percent Equivalents

0%	25%	33⅓%	50%	66⅔%	75%	100%	125%
0	$\frac{1}{4}$	$\frac{1}{3}$	$\frac{1}{2}$	$\frac{2}{3}$	$\frac{3}{4}$	1	$1\frac{1}{4}$

Example 1

Change $12\frac{1}{2}\%$ into a common fraction, reduced to lowest terms.

Method 1

Procedure

1. Place the percent over a denominator of 100, and drop the % symbol.

$$12\frac{1}{2}\% = \frac{12\frac{1}{2}}{100}$$

2. To simplify the complex fraction, first change the mixed number in the numerator to an improper fraction, and then divide the numerator by the denominator.

$$= \frac{\frac{25}{2}}{100}$$

$$= \frac{25}{2} \div 100$$

$$= \frac{\overset{1}{\cancel{25}}}{2} \times \frac{1}{\underset{4}{\cancel{100}}}$$

$$= \frac{1}{8}$$

Method 2

Procedure

1. Change the fraction $\frac{1}{2}$ into its decimal equivalent, .5.

$$12\frac{1}{2}\% = 12.5\%$$

2. Move the decimal point two places to the left (D ← P), and drop the % symbol.

$$12\frac{1}{2}\% = \underline{12.5}\% = .125$$

3. Change the decimal into a common fraction (3 places—thousandths), and reduce the fraction to lowest terms.

$$.125 = \frac{125}{1000}$$

$$= \frac{125 \div 125}{1000 \div 125}$$

$$= \frac{1}{8}$$

Example 2

Change 5.8% into a common fraction, reduced to lowest terms.

Method 1
Procedure

1. Place the percent over a denominator of 100, and drop the % symbol.

$$5.8\% = \frac{5.8}{100}$$

2. Simplify the complex fraction by multiplying the numerator and denominator by 10. (This eliminates the decimal point in the numerator.)

$$= \frac{5.8 \times 10}{100 \times 10}$$
$$= \frac{58}{1000}$$

3. Reduce the resulting fraction to lowest terms.

$$= \frac{58 \div 2}{1000 \div 2}$$
$$= \frac{29}{500}$$

Method 2
Procedure

1. Move the decimal point two places to the left (D ← P), and drop the % symbol.
$$5.8\% = 0\underline{5.}8\% = .058$$

2. Change the decimal into a common fraction (3 places—thousandths), and reduce the fraction to lowest terms.

$$.058 = \frac{58}{1000}$$
$$= \frac{58 \div 2}{1000 \div 2}$$
$$= \frac{29}{500}$$

Example 3

Change $\dfrac{11}{15}$ into a percent.

Method 1

Procedure

1. Multiply the fraction by 100% and simplify the result.

$$\frac{11}{15} \times 100\% = \frac{11}{\underset{3}{\cancel{15}}} \times \frac{\overset{20}{\cancel{100\%}}}{1}$$

$$= \frac{220}{3}\%$$

$$= 73\frac{1}{3}\%$$

Method 2

Procedure

1. Change the fraction to a decimal by dividing the denominator into the numerator. Stop dividing after two places.

$$\frac{11}{15} = 15\overline{\smash{)}\begin{array}{r} .73\frac{5}{15} = .73\frac{1}{3} \\ 11.00 \\ \underline{10\ 5} \\ 50 \\ \underline{45} \\ 5 \end{array}}$$

2. Move the decimal point two places to the right (D → P), and insert the % symbol.

$$\frac{11}{15} = .73\frac{1}{3} = 73\frac{1}{3}\%$$

PRACTICE PROBLEMS

Change the following percents to common fractions, reduced to lowest terms:

1. 16%

2. 125%

3. $8\frac{3}{4}\%$

4. 12.8%

Change the following fractions to percents:

5. $\frac{9}{25}$

6. $\frac{18}{30}$

7. $\frac{35}{42}$

8. $\frac{34}{51}$

ANSWERS AND EXPLANATIONS

1. $16\% = \frac{16}{100} = \frac{4}{25}$

2. $125\% = \frac{125}{100} = 1\frac{25}{100} = 1\frac{1}{4}$

3. $8\frac{3}{4}\% = \frac{8\frac{3}{4}}{100} = 8\frac{3}{4} \div 100 = \frac{\overset{7}{\cancel{35}}}{4} \times \frac{1}{\underset{20}{\cancel{100}}} = \frac{7}{80}$

4. $12.8\% = \frac{12.8}{100.0} = \frac{128}{1000} = \frac{16}{125}$

5. $\frac{9}{25} = 25\overline{)9.00}^{\;.36} \qquad .36 = 36\%$

$$\begin{array}{r} 7\,5 \\ \hline 1\,50 \\ 1\,50 \\ \hline 0 \end{array}$$

6. $\frac{18}{30} = 30\overline{)18.0}^{\;.6} \qquad .60 = 60\%$

$$\begin{array}{r} 18\,0 \\ \hline 0 \end{array}$$

7. $.83\dfrac{14}{42} = .83\dfrac{1}{3}$

$\dfrac{35}{42} = 42\overline{)35.00}$ $.83\dfrac{1}{3} = 83\dfrac{1}{3}\%$

$\underline{33\ 6}$

$1\ 40$

$\underline{1\ 26}$

14

8. $.66\dfrac{34}{51} = .66\dfrac{2}{3}$

$\dfrac{34}{51} = 51\overline{)34.00}$ $.66\dfrac{2}{3} = 66\dfrac{2}{3}\%$

$\underline{30\ 6}$

$3\ 40$

$\underline{3\ 06}$

34

SOLVING PERCENT PROBLEMS

As mentioned in the section on fractions, to find a fractional part *of* a number means *multiply* the fraction by the number. For example, to find $\dfrac{3}{4}$ of 20, multiply $\dfrac{3}{4} \times 20$ to get 15.

In general, the number we take the fractional part of (the number following the word "of") is called the **Whole**, and the result is called the **Part**. That is,

Fraction	of	*Whole*	is	*Part*
$\dfrac{3}{4}$	of	20	is	15
$\dfrac{3}{4}$	$\times$	20	$=$	15

Since a percent is also a fraction (hundredths), we can find a percent of a number in the same way. For example, to find 25% of 32, change 25% to a fraction (either in standard form or in decimal form), and multiply the fraction by 32:

Standard Form	Decimal Form
$25\% \text{ of } 32 = \dfrac{1}{4} \times 32$	$25\% \text{ of } 32 = .25 \times 32$
$= \dfrac{1}{\overset{}{\underset{1}{4}}} \times \dfrac{\overset{8}{32}}{1}$	$\downarrow$ 32 $\underline{\times .25}$ $1\ 60$ $\underline{6\ 4}$
$= 8$	$= 8.00$

As before, the number we take the percent of (following the word "of") is called the Whole, and the result is called the Part. That is,

Percent	of	*Whole*	is	*Part*
25%	of	32	is	8
$\frac{1}{4}$ or .25	×	32	=	8

When the relationship between the Percent, the Whole, and the Part, is expressed in this form, we refer to it as the **Percent Product**. Another way of expressing the relationship between these quantities is in the form of a proportion, called the **Percent Proportion**, which reads, "The Part is to the Whole as the Percent is to 100%." That is,

$$\frac{\text{Part}}{\text{Whole}} = \frac{\text{Percent}}{100\%}$$

In this proportion, the Percent is *not* changed to a fraction (or decimal) as it is in the Percent Product. For example, to find 25% of 32 by the proportion, instead of changing 25% to $\frac{1}{4}$ or .25, we write

$$\frac{\text{Part}}{\text{Whole}} = \frac{\text{Percent}}{100\%}$$
$$\frac{P}{32} = \frac{25}{100}$$

Then, to find P, we cross multiply the numerators and denominators, set the products equal, and divide. As shown below, we get the same result as before, 8.

$$100 \times P \quad\quad 32 \times 25$$
$$\frac{P}{32} \diagdown\!\!\!\!\diagup \frac{25}{100}$$
$$100 \times P = 32 \times 25$$
$$100 \times P = 800$$
$$P = \frac{800}{100}$$
$$P = 8$$

To summarize, most percent problems involve three quantities—a Percent, a Whole, and a Part. The relationship between these quantities can be expressed as the following product and proportion:

Percent Product	**Percent Proportion**
Percent × Whole = Part	$\frac{\text{Part}}{\text{Whole}} = \frac{\text{Percent}}{100\%}$

In general, we will be given the values of two of the quantities, and will be asked to find the value of the third. To do this, substitute the given values into either the product or the proportion, and then proceed accordingly. Remember that if the product is used, the percent must be changed into either a fraction or a decimal.

Both procedures will now be demonstrated. Note that in some problems the product will seem simpler to use, and in others, the proportion will seem simpler to use. This will vary from problem to problem, depending upon the specific values involved.

Example 1
Find 42.5% of 80.

Percent Product

Procedure

1. Substitute the given values into the percent product.
$$\text{Percent} \times \text{Whole} = \text{Part}$$
$$42.5\% \times 80 = P$$

2. Change the percent to a decimal (D ← P) and multiply.
$$\underline{42.5\%} \times 80 = P$$

$$
\begin{array}{r}
.425 \\
\times \quad 80 \\
\hline
34.000 = P
\end{array}
$$
$$34 = P$$

Percent Proportion

Procedure

1. Substitute the given values into the percent proportion. Remember, do *not* change the percent to a decimal.
$$\frac{\text{Part}}{\text{Whole}} = \frac{\text{Percent}}{100\%}$$
$$\frac{P}{80} = \frac{42.5}{100}$$

2. Cross-multiply the numerators and denominators, set the products equal, and divide.
$$100 \times P = 80 \times 42.5$$
$$100 \times P = 3400$$
$$P = \frac{3400}{100}$$
$$P = 34$$

Example 2

Find $66\frac{2}{3}\%$ of 24.

Percent Product

Procedure

1. Substitute the given values into the percent product.

$$\text{Percent} \times \text{Whole} = \text{Part}$$

$$66\frac{2}{3}\% \times 24 = P$$

2. Change $66\frac{2}{3}\%$ to its fractional equivalent, $\frac{2}{3}$, and multiply. In this problem it is much easier to work with the fractional equivalent $\frac{2}{3}$ than with the decimal equivalent $.66\frac{2}{3}$.

$$\frac{2}{3} \times 24 = P$$

$$\frac{2}{\cancel{3}_{1}} \times \frac{\cancel{24}^{8}}{1} = P$$

$$16 = P$$

Percent Proportion

Procedure

1. Substitute the given values into the percent proportion.

$$\frac{\text{Part}}{\text{Whole}} = \frac{\text{Percent}}{100\%}$$

$$\frac{P}{24} = \frac{66\frac{2}{3}}{100}$$

2. Cross-multiply and divide.

$$100 \times P = 24 \times 66\frac{2}{3}$$

$$100 \times P = \frac{24}{1} \times \frac{200}{3}$$

$$100 \times P = \frac{\cancel{24}^{8}}{1} \times \frac{200}{\cancel{3}_{1}}$$

$$100 \times P = 1600$$

$$P = \frac{1600}{100}$$

$$P = 16$$

Example 3

What percent of 36 is 27?

Percent Product

Procedure

1. Substitute the given values into the percent product, representing the unknown percent by N (remember that the Whole is the number following the word "of").

$$\text{Percent} \times \text{Whole} = \text{Part}$$
$$N \quad \times \quad 36 \quad = \quad 27$$

2. Divide 36 into 27, and change the resulting decimal into a percent (D → P).

$$N = \frac{27}{36} = 36\overline{)27.00}^{\,.75}$$
$$N = .\underline{75} = 75\%$$

Percent Proportion

Procedure

1. Substitute the given values into the percent proportion.

$$\frac{\text{Part}}{\text{Whole}} = \frac{\text{Percent}}{100\%}$$
$$\frac{27}{36} = \frac{N}{100}$$

2. Cross-multiply and divide.

$$36 \times N = 27 \times 100$$
$$36 \times N = 2700$$
$$N = \frac{2700}{36}$$
$$N = 75\%$$

Example 4

9% of what number is 54?

Percent Product

Procedure

1. Substitute the given values into the percent product. (Note that in this problem, we are asked to find the Whole.)

$$\text{Percent} \times \text{Whole} = \text{Part}$$
$$9\% \times W = 54$$

2. Change the percent into a decimal (D ← P), and divide.

$$.09 \times W = 54$$
$$W = \frac{54}{.09}$$
$$W = 600$$

Percent Proportion

Procedure

1. Substitute the given values into the percent proportion.

$$\frac{Part}{Whole} = \frac{Percent}{100\%}$$
$$\frac{54}{W} = \frac{9}{100}$$

2. Cross-multiply and divide.

$$9 \times W = 54 \times 100$$
$$9 \times W = 5400$$
$$W = \frac{5400}{9}$$
$$W = 600$$

PRACTICE PROBLEMS

Find the missing number or percent.

1. What is 9% of 50?

2. 64.8% of 200 is what number?

3. What is $83\frac{1}{3}$% of 18?

4. $33\frac{1}{3}$% of 57 is what number?

5. What percent of 50 is 12.5?

6. 48 is what percent of 80?

7. 21 is 37.5% of what number?

8. 17% of what number is 68?

ANSWERS AND EXPLANATIONS

1. 9% of 50 = .09 × 50 = 4.5

2. 64.8% of 200 = .648 × 200 = 129.6

3. $83\frac{1}{3}$% of 18 = $\frac{5}{6} \times 18 = 15$

4. $33\frac{1}{3}$% of 57 = $\frac{1}{3} \times 57 = 19$

5. $\dfrac{\text{Part}}{\text{Whole}} = \dfrac{\text{Percent}}{100\%}$

$\dfrac{12.5}{50} = \dfrac{N}{100}$ (cross-multiply)

$50 \times N = 12.5 \times 100$

$50 \times N = 1250$

$N = \dfrac{1250}{50} = 25\%$

6. $\dfrac{\text{Part}}{\text{Whole}} = \dfrac{\text{Percent}}{100\%}$

$\dfrac{48}{80} = \dfrac{N}{100}$ (cross-multiply)

$80 \times N = 48 \times 100$

$80 \times N = 4800$

$N = \dfrac{4800}{80} = 60\%$

7. $\dfrac{\text{Part}}{\text{Whole}} = \dfrac{\text{Percent}}{100\%}$

$\dfrac{21}{W} = \dfrac{37.5}{100}$ (cross-multiply)

$37.5 \times W = 21 \times 100$

$37.5 \times W = 2100$

$W = \dfrac{2100}{37.5} = 56$

8. $\dfrac{\text{Part}}{\text{Whole}} = \dfrac{\text{Percent}}{100\%}$

$\dfrac{68}{W} = \dfrac{17}{100}$ (cross-multiply)

$17 \times W = 68 \times 100$

$17 \times W = 6800$

$W = \dfrac{6800}{17} = 400$

PRACTICE TEST

1. What is 536,428 rounded off to the nearest ten-thousand?

   A. 536,000
   B. 530,000
   C. 537,000
   D. 540,000
   E. 500,000

2. Which of the following is closest to $\dfrac{58\times3016}{97}$?

   A. 1,700
   B. 1,800
   C. 1,900
   D. 2,000
   E. 2,100

3. The number of distinct prime divisors of 60 is

   A. 3
   B. 2
   C. 8
   D. 4
   E. 10

4. The fraction $\dfrac{450}{840}$ reduced to lowest terms is

   A. $\dfrac{4}{7}$

   B. $\dfrac{5}{8}$

   C. $\dfrac{1}{2}$

   D. $\dfrac{23}{42}$

   E. $\dfrac{15}{28}$

5. $12\dfrac{7}{8}+3\dfrac{5}{6}=$

   A. $16\dfrac{17}{24}$

   B. $15\dfrac{35}{48}$

   C. $15\dfrac{6}{7}$

   D. $15\dfrac{17}{24}$

   E. $16\dfrac{41}{48}$

6. $6\dfrac{2}{5}-2\dfrac{3}{4}=$

   A. $3\dfrac{17}{20}$

   B. $3\dfrac{13}{20}$

   C. $4\dfrac{7}{20}$

   D. $4\dfrac{5}{9}$

   E. $3\dfrac{3}{20}$

7. $2\dfrac{1}{4}\times8\times\dfrac{2}{3}=$

   A. $16\dfrac{1}{6}$

   B. $2\dfrac{2}{3}$

   C. 12

   D. $16\dfrac{3}{7}$

   E. $23\dfrac{1}{3}$

8. $6\frac{2}{3} \div 4 =$

   A. $1\frac{1}{2}$

   B. $6\frac{11}{12}$

   C. $1\frac{2}{3}$

   D. $\frac{3}{80}$

   E. $2\frac{1}{6}$

9. $\dfrac{\frac{3}{4}+\frac{5}{7}}{2} =$

   A. $1\frac{3}{14}$

   B. $\frac{8}{22}$

   C. $2\frac{13}{14}$

   D. $\frac{41}{56}$

   E. $1\frac{5}{6}$

10. Which of the following fractions is the largest?

   A. $\frac{1}{2}$

   B. $\frac{3}{4}$

   C. $\frac{7}{9}$

   D. $\frac{2}{3}$

   E. $\frac{3}{5}$

11. If $\dfrac{N}{21}=\dfrac{40}{24}$, what is the value of N?

   A.   35
   B.   43
   C.   37
   D.   33
   E.   3

12. What is 6.385 rounded off to the nearest tenth?

   A.   6.38
   B.   6.3
   C.   6
   D.   6.4
   E.   6.39

13. $7.2 + 9 - 5.413 =$

   A.   11.613
   B.   10.787
   C.   10.213
   D.   10.813
   E.   10.687

14. $8.4 \times .003 =$

   A.   2.52
   B.   .252
   C.   .00252
   D.   25.2
   E.   .0252

15. $.224 \div 7 =$

   A.   31.25
   B.   .0032
   C.   .32
   D.   .03125
   E.   .032

16. $75 \div .08 =$

   A.   9.375
   B.   .9375
   C.   9375
   D.   937.5
   E.   93.75

17. Which of the following decimals is the smallest?

   A.   1.003
   B.   .21
   C.   .1989
   D.   .5
   E.   .199

18. Change $9.6\frac{3}{4}$ to an equivalent mixed fraction reduced to lowest terms.

   A. $9\frac{27}{40}$

   B. $9\frac{67}{100}$

   C. $9\frac{2}{3}$

   D. $9\frac{63}{100}$

   E. $9\frac{63}{400}$

19. Change $15\frac{3}{8}$ to an equivalent mixed decimal fraction.

   A.   15.365
   B.   15.38
   C.   15.375
   D.   15.4
   E.   15.37

20. Change $16\frac{1}{4}\%$ to an equivalent fraction reduced to lowest terms.

   A. $\frac{4}{25}$

   B. $\frac{13}{80}$

   C. $\frac{1}{25}$

   D. $16\frac{1}{4}$

   E. $\frac{17}{80}$

21. Change $\frac{45}{72}$ to an equivalent percent.

   A.   62.5%
   B.   1.6%
   C.   .625%
   D.   16%
   E.   6.25%

22. 18.6% of 300 equals

   A.   53.3
   B.   5580
   C.   16.13
   D.   48.7
   E.   55.8

23. $66\frac{2}{3}\%$ of 18 equals

   A.   27
   B.   12
   C.   1.2
   D.   1200
   E.   13

24. 54 is what percent of 90?

   A.   62.2%
   B.   166%
   C.   54%
   D.   60%
   E.   57%

25. 27% of what number is 29.7?

   A.   80.19
   B.   120
   C.   110
   D.   113.4
   E.   8.019

ANSWERS AND EXPLANATIONS

1. **D**	6. **B**	10. **C**	14. **E**	18. **A**	22. **E**
2. **B**	7. **C**	11. **A**	15. **E**	19. **C**	23. **B**
3. **A**	8. **C**	12. **D**	16. **D**	20. **B**	24. **D**
4. **E**	9. **D**	13. **B**	17. **C**	21. **A**	25. **C**
5. **A**					

1. **The correct answer is (D).** $5\overset{\downarrow}{\underset{\bigcirc}{3}}6{,}428 \approx 540{,}000$

2. **The correct answer is (B).** $\dfrac{58 \times 3016}{97} \approx \dfrac{60 \times 3000}{100} \approx 1800$

3. **The correct answer is (A).**

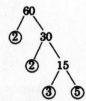

    The distinct prime divisors of 60 are 2, 3, and 5.

4. **The correct answer is (E).** $\dfrac{450}{840} = \dfrac{450 \div 10}{840 \div 10} = \dfrac{45 \div 3}{84 \div 3} = \dfrac{15}{28}$

5. **The correct answer is (A).** $12\dfrac{7}{8} = 12\dfrac{21}{24}$

    $$+3\dfrac{5}{6} = 3\dfrac{20}{24}$$

    $$15\dfrac{41}{24} = 16\dfrac{17}{24}$$

6. **The correct answer is (B).** $6\dfrac{2}{5} = \overset{5}{\cancel{6}}\,1\dfrac{8}{20} = 5\dfrac{28}{20}$

    $$-2\dfrac{3}{4} = \quad 2\dfrac{15}{20} = 2\dfrac{15}{20}$$

    $$3\dfrac{13}{20}$$

7. **The correct answer is (C).** $2\dfrac{1}{4} \times 8 \times \dfrac{2}{3} = \dfrac{\overset{3}{\cancel{9}}}{\underset{1}{\cancel{4}}} \times \dfrac{\overset{2}{\cancel{8}}}{1} \times \dfrac{2}{\underset{1}{\cancel{3}}} = 12$

8. **The correct answer is (C).** $6\dfrac{2}{3} \div 4 = \dfrac{20}{3} \div \dfrac{4}{1} = \dfrac{\overset{5}{\cancel{20}}}{3} \times \dfrac{1}{\underset{1}{\cancel{4}}} = \dfrac{5}{3} = 1\dfrac{2}{3}$

9. **The correct answer is (D).** $\dfrac{\dfrac{3}{4} + \dfrac{5}{7}}{2} = \dfrac{\overset{7}{\cancel{28}} \times \dfrac{3}{\cancel{4}} + \overset{4}{\cancel{28}} \times \dfrac{5}{\cancel{7}}}{28 \times 2} = \dfrac{21 + 20}{56} = \dfrac{41}{56}$

10. **The correct answer is (C).** $\dfrac{1}{2} = .50$

    $\dfrac{3}{4} = .75$

    $\dfrac{7}{9} \approx .78$

    $\dfrac{2}{3} \approx .66$

    $\dfrac{3}{5} = .60$

    Thus, $\dfrac{7}{9}$ is the largest.

11. **The correct answer is (A).**

    $$\dfrac{N}{21} = \dfrac{40}{24}$$
    $$24 \times N = 21 \times 40$$
    $$24 \times N = 840$$
    $$N = \dfrac{840}{24}$$
    $$N = 35$$

12. **The correct answer is (D).** $6.\overset{\downarrow}{\textcircled{3}}85 \approx 6.4$

13. **The correct answer is (B).** $\begin{array}{r} 7.2 \\ +9.0 \\ \hline 16.2 \end{array}$ $\begin{array}{r} 16.200 \\ -\ 5.413 \\ \hline 10.787 \end{array}$

14. **The correct answer is (E).** $\begin{array}{rl} 8.4 & \text{(1 place)} \\ \times .003 & \text{(3 places)} \\ \hline .0252 & \text{(4 places)} \end{array}$

15. **The correct answer is (E).** $7\overline{)\,.224}^{\,.032}$

16. **The correct answer is (D).**

$$\begin{array}{r} 9\ \ 37.5 \\ .08.)\overline{75.00.0} \\ \underline{72\ \ \ \ } \\ 30 \\ \underline{24} \\ 60 \\ \underline{56} \\ 40 \\ \underline{40} \\ 0 \end{array}$$

17. **The correct answer is (C).**

$$\begin{aligned} 1.003 &= 1.0030 \\ .21 &= .2100 \\ .1989 &= .1989 \leftarrow smallest \\ .5 &= .5000 \\ .199 &= .1990 \end{aligned}$$

18. **The correct answer is (A).**

$$.6\frac{3}{4} = \frac{6\frac{3}{4}}{10} = \frac{\frac{27}{4}}{10} = \frac{27}{4} \div 10 = \frac{27}{4} \times \frac{1}{10} = \frac{27}{40}$$

Thus, $9.6\frac{3}{4} = 9\frac{27}{40}$

19. **The correct answer is (C).**

$$\frac{3}{8} = 8)\overline{3.000}\ \ ^{.375}$$

Thus, $15\frac{3}{8} = 15.375$.

20. **The correct answer is (B).**

$$16\frac{1}{4}\% = \frac{16\frac{1}{4}}{100} = \frac{\frac{65}{4}}{100} = \frac{65}{4} \div 100 = \frac{\overset{13}{\cancel{65}}}{4} \times \frac{1}{\underset{20}{\cancel{100}}} = \frac{13}{80}$$

21. **The correct answer is (A).** $\dfrac{45}{72} = \dfrac{45}{72} \times 100\% = 62.5\%$

22. **The correct answer is (E).** 18.6% of 300 = .186 × 300 = 55.8

23. **The correct answer is (B).** $66\frac{2}{3}\%$ of $18 = \frac{2}{3} \times 18 = 12$

24. **The correct answer is (D).**

$$\frac{\text{Part}}{\text{Whole}} = \frac{\text{Percent}}{100\%}$$

$$\frac{54}{90} = \frac{N}{100}$$

$$90 \times N = 54 \times 100$$

$$90 \times N = 5400$$

$$N = \frac{5400}{90}$$

$$N = 60\%$$

25. **The correct answer is (C).**

$$\frac{\text{Part}}{\text{Whole}} = \frac{\text{Percent}}{100\%}$$

$$\frac{29.7}{W} = \frac{27}{100}$$

$$27 \times W = 29.7 \times 100$$

$$27 \times W = 2970$$

$$W = \frac{2970}{27}$$

$$W = 110$$

Chapter 3

ALGEBRA

In this chapter, we will review the procedures for:

- Evaluating numerical and algebraic expressions
- Performing operations with signed numbers
- Performing operations with polynomials
- Solving linear equations and inequalities
- Factoring polynomials and solving quadratic equations
- Performing operations with square roots
- Performing operations with algebraic fractions

The emphasis in each section will be on algebraic manipulations and techniques, not on solving word problems. That will be presented in Chapter 4.

NUMERICAL EXPRESSIONS

In algebra, as in arithmetic, numerical expressions are formed with the fundamental operations of addition, subtraction, multiplication, and division. The symbols for these operations are summarized below. Notice that multiplication and division can be denoted in several different ways.

Operations in Numerical Expressions

Addition: $8 + 3$

Subtraction: $9 - 7$

Multiplication: 5×4, $5 \cdot 4$, $(5)(4)$

Division: $2\overline{)6}$, $6 \div 2$, $\dfrac{6}{2}$

EXPONENTIAL NOTATION

As you recall, the numbers used in multiplication are called factors. When the same factor is repeated more than once, a special shorthand, called **exponential notation**, can be used. In this notation, the repeated factor, called the **base**, is written only once. Above and to the right of the base is written another number, called the **exponent** or **power** of the base, which indicates how many times the base is repeated as a factor. For example,

$$\underbrace{5 \times 5 \times 5}_{3 \text{ factors}} = 5^3 \leftarrow \text{exponent or power}$$

base

Products written in exponential notation are read by first naming the base and then the power. Some examples are given below. Note that the second power can also be read as "squared," and the third power can also be read as "cubed."

Product	Symbols	Words
8×8	8^2	8 to the second power, or 8 squared
$5 \times 5 \times 5$	5^3	5 to the third power, or 5 cubed
$7 \times 7 \times 7 \times 7$	7^4	7 to the fourth power

Since a product is always formed by at least two factors, the first power is somewhat ambiguous. Nevertheless, we define the first power to mean one "factor" of the base. For example, $6^1 = 6$, and $3^1 = 3$.

When evaluating products written in exponential notation, remember to write out as many factors of the base as indicated by the exponent, and then multiply those factors. A common mistake is to simply multiply the base by the exponent.

$$\textit{Correct}: 6^2 = 6 \times 6 = 36$$

$$\textit{Incorrect}: 6^2 = 6 \times 2 = 12$$

SQUARE ROOTS

The **square root** of a given number is a number whose square is equal to the given number. For example, the square root of 25, denoted, $\sqrt{25}$, is 5, because 5 squared is equal to 25. More examples of squares and square roots are given in the table below.

Squares	*Square Roots*
$1^2 = 1$	$\sqrt{1} = 1$
$2^2 = 4$	$\sqrt{4} = 2$
$3^2 = 9$	$\sqrt{9} = 3$
$4^2 = 16$	$\sqrt{16} = 4$
$5^2 = 25$	$\sqrt{25} = 5$
etc.	etc.

Finding the square root of a number usually involves some form of trial and error. For example, to find the square root of 289 we keep squaring numbers until we find one whose square equals 289. As shown below, we find that $17^2 = 289$ and thus conclude that $\sqrt{289} = 17$.

$$15^2 = 225$$
$$16^2 = 256$$
$$\boxed{17^2 = 289}$$
$$18^2 = 324$$

Numbers such as 1, 4, 9, and 16, whose square roots are whole numbers, are called **perfect squares**. In the example that follows, a procedure is demonstrated for finding the square roots of perfect squares. This procedure is based on the fact that if a number M divides exactly M times into a number N, then M is the square root of N. For example, since 7 divides exactly 7 times into 49, then 7 is the square root of 49.

$$7\overline{)49}^{\,7} \text{ means } \sqrt{49} = 7$$

Example

Find $\sqrt{729}$.

Procedure

1. Choose any number, say 20, as a first estimate. Divide this estimate into 729.

$$
\begin{array}{r}
36 \\
20\overline{)729} \\
\underline{60} \\
129 \\
\underline{120} \\
9
\end{array}
$$

2. Disregarding the remainder, 9, find the average of the estimate, 20, and the quotient, 36.

$$
\begin{aligned}
\text{Average} &= \frac{20+36}{2} \\
&= 28
\end{aligned}
$$

3. Using the average as a new estimate, repeat the process until the estimate is the same as the quotient (until the remainder is 0).

$$
\begin{array}{r}
26 \\
28\overline{)729} \\
\underline{56} \\
169 \\
\underline{168} \\
1
\end{array}
$$

$$
\begin{aligned}
\text{Average} &= \frac{28+26}{2} \\
&= 27
\end{aligned}
$$

$$
\begin{array}{r}
27 \\
27\overline{)729} \\
\underline{54} \\
189 \\
\underline{189} \\
0
\end{array}
$$

$$
\sqrt{729} = 27
$$

The procedures for finding the square roots of numbers that are not perfect squares are much more complicated and can only provide us with approximations, such as $\sqrt{2} \approx 1.414$ and $\sqrt{3} \approx 1.732$. These procedures will not be shown here.

PRACTICE PROBLEMS

Using the method of averaging, find the square root of each of the following perfect square numbers:

1. $\sqrt{361}$
2. $\sqrt{441}$
3. $\sqrt{1296}$
4. $\sqrt{2209}$

ANSWERS AND EXPLANATIONS

1. Choose 20 as a first estimate:

    $$\begin{array}{r} 18 \text{ Rem. } 1 \\ 20\overline{)361} \end{array}$$

    Use 19, which is the average of 18 and 20, as the new estimate:

    $$\begin{array}{r} 19 \text{ Rem. } 0 \\ 19\overline{)361} \end{array} \qquad \text{Thus, } \sqrt{361} = 19$$

2. Choose 20 as a first estimate:

    $$\begin{array}{r} 22 \text{ Rem. } 1 \\ 20\overline{)441} \end{array}$$

    Use 21, which is the average of 20 and 22, as the new estimate:

    $$\begin{array}{r} 21 \text{ Rem. } 0 \\ 21\overline{)441} \end{array} \qquad \text{Thus, } \sqrt{441} = 21$$

3. Choose 32 as a first estimate:

    $$\begin{array}{r} 40 \text{ Rem. } 16 \\ 32\overline{)1296} \end{array}$$

    Use 36, which is the average of 32 and 40, as the new estimate:

    $$\begin{array}{r} 36 \text{ Rem. } 0 \\ 36\overline{)1296} \end{array} \qquad \text{Thus, } \sqrt{1296} = 36$$

4. Choose 50 as a first estimate:

    $$\begin{array}{r} 44 \text{ Rem. } 9 \\ 50\overline{)2209} \end{array}$$

    Use 47, which is the average of 50 and 44, as the new estimate:

    $$\begin{array}{r} 47 \text{ Rem. } 0 \\ 47\overline{)2209} \end{array} \qquad \text{Thus, } \sqrt{2209} = 47$$

THE ORDER OF OPERATIONS

When numerical expressions contain more than one operation, there may be some ambiguity about the order in which the operations should be performed. For example, the expression $3+4\times2$ could either mean to add $3+4$ first, and then multiply by 2, or it could mean to multiply 4×2 first, and then add 3. Each order gives a different result:

$$3+4\times2 \qquad\qquad 3+4\times2$$
$$\overset{?}{=} 7\times2 \qquad\qquad\quad \overset{?}{=} 3\times8$$
$$\overset{?}{=} 14 \qquad\qquad\qquad \overset{?}{=} 11$$

To avoid this ambiguity, a procedure has been established which specifies the exact order in which the operations should be performed. This procedure, called the **order of operations**, is given below.

To Evaluate a Numerical Expression:
1. Perform all operations within *parentheses*, under *square root* symbols, and above and below *fraction bars*.
2. Evaluate all *powers* and *square roots*.
3. Perform all *multiplications* and *divisions* in the order they appear in the expression from left to right.
4. Perform all *additions* and *subtractions* in the order they appear in the expression from left to right.

When we apply this procedure to the above expression, $3+4\times2$, we see that we should multiply 4×2 first, and that the correct result is 11.

Example 1
What is the value of $7 + 3(8 - 3)^2$?

Procedure

1. Perform the subtraction within the parentheses.
$$7+3(8-3)^2$$
$$=7+3(5)^2$$

2. Evaluate the power.
$$= 7 + 3(25)$$

3. Multiply. (Remember that $3(25)$ means 3×25.)
$$= 7 + 75$$

4. Add.
$$= 82$$

Example 2

Evaluate the expression $3 + 2\sqrt{1 + 6(4)}$.

Procedure

1. Perform the operations under the square root sign. Remember to multiply 6(4) first.

$$3 + 2\sqrt{1 + 6(4)}$$
$$= 3 + 2\sqrt{1 + 24}$$
$$= 3 + 2\sqrt{25}$$

2. Evaluate the square root.

$$= 3 + (2)(5)$$

3. Multiply.

$$= 3 + 10$$

4. Add.

$$= 13$$

PRACTICE PROBLEMS

Evaluate the following numerical expressions:

1. $4^3 - 3(7 - 4)^2$

2. $(2^3 + 3)(6^2 - 5^2)$

3. $\dfrac{2^2 + 2^3}{3 + 3^2}$

4. $\dfrac{2 + 6\sqrt{3^2 + 4^2}}{16}$

ANSWERS AND EXPLANATIONS

1. $4^3 - 3(7 - 4)^2 = 4^3 - (3)(3^2) = 64 - (3)(9) = 64 - 27 = 37$

2. $(2^3 + 3)(6^2 - 5^2)$
    $= (8 + 3)(36 - 25) = (11) \cdot (11) = 121$

3. $\dfrac{2^2 + 2^3}{3 + 3^2} = \dfrac{4 + 8}{3 + 9} = \dfrac{12}{12} = 1$

4. $\dfrac{2 + 6\sqrt{3^2 + 4^2}}{16} = \dfrac{2 + 6\sqrt{9 + 16}}{16} = \dfrac{2 + 6\sqrt{25}}{16} =$
    $\dfrac{2 + 6(5)}{16} = \dfrac{2 + 30}{16} = \dfrac{32}{16} = 2$

ALGEBRAIC EXPRESSIONS

Mathematical expressions that contain letters or other symbols to represent numbers are called **algebraic expressions**. These symbols are called **literal numbers**, **placeholders**, **unknowns**, or most often, **variables**.

$$x^3 - y^2 + 7$$
$$\nwarrow \quad \nearrow$$
variables

As shown below, operations in algebraic expressions are denoted in essentially the same way as they are in numerical expressions. The only significant difference is that in algebraic expressions multiplication can also be denoted by placing the variables side by side, as in xy. This cannot be done in numerical expressions since placing numbers side by side would denote a new number, not multiplication. For example, placing 8 and 3 side by side would denote the number 83, not 8 times 3.

> **Operations in Algebraic Expressions**
> *Addition*: $x + y$
> *Subtraction*: $x - y$
> *Multiplication*: $x \cdot y$, $(x)(y)$, $x(y)$, xy
> *Division*: $y \overline{)x}$, $x \div y$, $\dfrac{x}{y}$

POLYNOMIALS

Algebraic expressions are formed by adding and subtracting basic units called **terms**. A term can either be a number, a variable, or the product or quotient of such quantities. The numerical factor of a term is called its **numerical coefficient** and is customarily written on the left of the term. If a numerical coefficient is not indicated, it is understood to be 1. For example, $x^2y = 1x^2y$.

$$3 + 5y^2 - \frac{7x}{y} \qquad \qquad 5a^2bx^3$$
$$\nwarrow \uparrow \nearrow \qquad \qquad \uparrow$$
$$\text{terms} \qquad \qquad \begin{array}{c} \text{numerical} \\ \text{coefficient} \end{array}$$

Algebraic expressions that do not include division by a variable or variables under square root signs are also called **polynomials**. For example, $3x^2 + 7x - 5$ and $x^2 + \dfrac{xy}{3} y$ are polynomials, while $6x^2 + \dfrac{4}{y}$ and $3x^3 - \sqrt{x}$ are not polynomials. Polynomials having exactly one term are called **monomials**; two terms, **binomials**; and three terms, **trinomials**.

Polynomials		
Monomials	*Binomials*	*Trinomials*
8	$9x - 4$	$x + y - 3$
$3x$	$x^2 - y^2$	$x^2 + 4x - 1$
$4x^2y^3$	$4x + y^3$	$x^2 - 3xy + y^2$

In the remainder of this section, we will follow the common practice of using the word "monomial" to refer to expressions containing exactly one term, and the word "polynomial" to refer to expressions containing more than one term.

EVALUATING ALGEBRAIC EXPRESSIONS

Whenever specific numerical values are given for the variables in an algebraic expression, we can determine the value of the expression by the following procedure:

> **To Evaluate an Algebraic Expression:**
> 1. Replace the variables by the given values.
> 2. Evaluate the resulting numerical expression according to the order of operations.

Remember that when substituting numbers into a product, use either parentheses or dots to indicate the product.

Example 1
If $a = 2$, $b = 3$, and $x = 1$, what is the value of $a^3 + 5b^2 - abx$?

Procedure

1. Replace the variables by their given numerical values.

$$a^3 + 5b^2 - abx$$
$$= (2)^3 + 5(3)^2 - (2)(3)(1)$$

2. Evaluate the resulting numerical expression according to the order of operations.

$$= 8 + 5(9) - (2)(3)(1)$$
$$= 8 + 45 - 6$$
$$= 47$$

Example 2

Evaluate the expression $\dfrac{\sqrt{b^2-4ac}}{2a}$ for the values $a = 6$, $b = 11$, and $c = 3$.

Procedure

1. Replace the variables by their given numerical values.

$$\frac{\sqrt{b^2 - 4ac}}{2a}$$

$$= \frac{\sqrt{11^2 - 4 \cdot 6 \cdot 3}}{2 \cdot 6}$$

2. Evaluate the resulting numerical expression according to the order of operations.

$$= \frac{\sqrt{121 - 72}}{12}$$

$$= \frac{\sqrt{49}}{12}$$

$$= \frac{7}{12}$$

PRACTICE PROBLEMS

For $a = 2$, $b = 3$, and $x = 1$, evaluate the following expressions:

1. $7a^3bx^2$

2. $b^3 - 5(a + x)$

3. $\dfrac{6x^2 + 2b^2}{4a}$

4. $\dfrac{\sqrt{b^2 + a^4}}{a + bx}$

ANSWERS AND EXPLANATIONS

1. $7a^3bx^2 = (7)(2)^3(3)(1)^2 = (7)(8)(3)(1) = 168$

2. $b^3 - 5(a + x) = (3)^3 - 5(2 + 1) = (3)^3 - (5)(3) = 27 - 15 = 12$

3. $\dfrac{6x^2 + 2b^2}{4a} = \dfrac{6(1)^2 + 2(3)^2}{4(2)} = \dfrac{6(1) + 2(9)}{4(2)} =$

   $\dfrac{6 + 18}{8} = \dfrac{24}{8} = 3$

4. $\dfrac{\sqrt{b^2 + a^4}}{a + bx} = \dfrac{\sqrt{(3)^2 + (2)^4}}{2 + 3(1)} = \dfrac{\sqrt{9 + 16}}{2 + 3(1)} =$

   $\dfrac{\sqrt{25}}{2 + 3} = \dfrac{5}{5} = 1$

EVALUATING THE SUBJECT OF A FORMULA

A **formula** is a mathematical relationship between one variable, called the **subject** of the formula, and one or more other variables. For example, the area of a trapezoid is related to its height and two bases by the formula below:

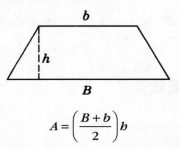

$$A = \left(\dfrac{B + b}{2}\right)h$$

To determine the value of the subject of a formula, follow the same procedure used when evaluating an algebraic expression. Replace all the other variables in the formula by specific numerical values, and then evaluate the resulting numerical expression. For example, if the height of a trapezoid is 3, and the bases are 6 and 4, then, as shown below, the area is 15.

$$A = \left(\dfrac{B + b}{2}\right)h$$

$$= \left(\dfrac{6 + 4}{2}\right)3$$

$$= \left(\dfrac{10}{2}\right)3$$

$$= 15$$

Example

For the values $b = 7$ and $h = 6$, find the volume of a pyramid given by the formula below.

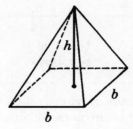

$$V = \frac{1}{3}b^2h$$

Procedure

1. Replace b and h by their given numerical values, and evaluate the resulting expression.

$$V = \frac{1}{3}b^2h$$
$$= \frac{1}{3}(7)^2(6)$$
$$= \frac{1}{3}(49)(6)$$
$$= 98$$

SIGNED NUMBERS

The $+$ and $-$ symbols, which are used to represent the **operations** of addition and subtraction, can also be used as **signs** to indicate whether a number is greater than zero or less than zero. When used in this way, the $+$ and $-$ symbols are called **positive** and **negative** signs, and the resulting numbers are called **signed numbers**.

Operations	Signs
Addition: $5 + 3$	*Positive Sign*: $+6$
Subtraction: $7 - 2$	*Negative Sign*: -4

Signed numbers can be represented graphically on a scale called the **number line**, which is constructed in the following way. An arbitrary point is chosen to represent the number 0. This point is called the **origin**. Using a specified unit of measurement, points are marked off to the right and the left of the origin. Positive whole numbers are placed at the points to the right of the origin; negative whole numbers are placed at the points to the left of the origin. (Positive numbers can be written with or without the $+$ sign.) In the diagram below, arrows are drawn at the ends of the line to indicate that the line extends indefinitely in both directions.

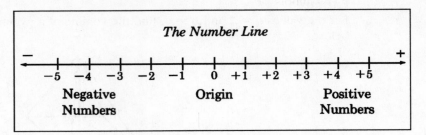

The set of numbers marked off on the number line, {..., −3, −2, −1, 0, +1, +2, +3,...}, is called the set of **integers**. Although only integers are indicated, all fractions and decimals, both positive and negative, are also on the line. Some examples are shown below.

$$-\sqrt{2} \qquad +.7 \qquad +2\tfrac{1}{4}$$

The distance from any given number on the line to the origin is called the **absolute value** of the number. For example, since +3 is 3 units from the origin, its absolute value is 3. Similarly, since −2 is 2 units from the origin, its absolute value is 2. The absolute value of a number is denoted by placing the number between two vertical bars. We would write $|+3| = 3$ and $|-2| = 2$. Notice that the absolute value of a number is simply the number without its sign.

$$|-2| = 2 \qquad\qquad |+3| = 3$$

ORDER RELATIONSHIPS ON THE NUMBER LINE

The numbers are arranged on the number line in increasing order from left to right. Consequently, if a number x lies to the left of a number y, then x is *less than y*. This is written $x < y$. Equivalently, if a number y lies to the right of a number x, then y is *greater than x*. This is written $y > x$. In addition, if a number x lies to the left of a number y ($x < y$), and the number y lies to the left of a number z ($y < z$), then y lies *between x* and z. This is written $x < y < z$.

Numbers can be related in more than one way. For example, if a number x is either less than or equal to a number y, then we can combine the symbols < and = and write $x \leq y$. Similarly, if a number x is either greater than or equal to a number y, then we can combine the symbols > and = and write $x \geq y$.

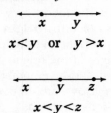

$$x < y \quad \text{or} \quad y > x$$

$$x < y < z$$

The symbols for the different order relationships are summarized below.

Order Relationships

Symbol	Words
$x = y$	x is equal to y
$x < y$	x is less than y
$x > y$	x is greater than y
$x \leq y$	x is less than or equal to y
$x \geq y$	x is greater than or equal to y

Any of these symbols can be negated simply by drawing a slash through it. For example, $x \neq y$ means x is not equal to y, and $x \not< y$ means x is *not* less than y.

ADDING SIGNED NUMBERS

The operation of addition is not performed the same with signed numbers as it is in ordinary arithmetic, where all the numbers are positive. Instead, "adding" is more like "combining," in the sense of combining profit and loss. In each of the examples below, a positive number represents a profit and a negative number represents a loss. The "sum" of the numbers is then the combined, or net, result.

+8 profit	−8 loss	+8 profit	−8 loss
+6 profit	−6 loss	−6 loss	+6 profit
+14 profit	−14 loss	+2 profit	−2 loss

In the first two examples, where the signs of the numbers are the same, the "sum" is obtained by adding the numbers. However, in the last two examples, where the signs of the numbers are different, the "sum" is obtained by subtracting the numbers. In general, we use the following procedure:

To Add (Combine) Two Signed Numbers:
1. If the signs of the numbers are the *same*, add their absolute values (the numerical parts of the numbers, without their signs), and keep the common sign.
2. If the signs of the numbers are *different*, subtract the smaller absolute value from the larger absolute value, and keep the sign of the number with the larger absolute value.

$$(+9) + (+5) = +14$$
$$(-9) + (-5) = -14$$
$$(+9) + (-5) = +4$$
$$(-9) + (+5) = -4$$

Note that when we write signed number addition horizontally, we place the signed numbers in parentheses. This is done to distinguish the positive and negative signs of the numbers from the addition symbol. The same thing will be done in subtraction of signed numbers.

$$(+9) \quad + \quad (-5)$$

positive   and   negative
sign   sign

To add more than two signed numbers, proceed step by step, adding two at a time until reaching the final result:

$$(+6)+(-5)+(+3)+(-9)$$
$$=\quad (+1)+(+3)+(-9)$$
$$=\quad (+4)+(-9)$$
$$=\quad -5$$

An alternate way of proceeding is to add the positive numbers and negative numbers separately, then combining the resulting sums:

$$(+6)+(-5)+(+3)+(-9)$$
$$=\quad (+9)+(-14)$$
$$=\quad -5$$

PRACTICE PROBLEMS

1. $(+6) + (-4) + (-7)$

2. $(-3) + (-8) + (-2)$

3. $(-5) + (-4) + (+9)$

4. $(+6) + (-2) + (+1)$

ANSWERS AND EXPLANATIONS

1. $(+6) + (-4) + (-7) = (+2) + (-7) = -5$

2. $(-3) + (-8) + (-2) = (-11) + (-2) = -13$

3. $(-5) + (-4) + (+9) = (-9) + (+9) = 0$

4. $(+6) + (-2) + (+1) = (+4) + (+1) = +5$

SUBTRACTING SIGNED NUMBERS

Subtracting signed numbers is analogous to dividing fractions in arithmetic. For example, when we divide $\frac{5}{7}$ by $\frac{3}{4}$, we don't actually divide the fractions, but instead, change the division to its inverse, multiplication, and change the divisor to its reciprocal, $\frac{4}{3}$. That is:

$$\frac{5}{7} \div \frac{3}{4}$$
$$\downarrow \downarrow$$
$$= \frac{5}{7} \times \frac{4}{3}$$
$$= \frac{20}{21}$$

Similarly, when we subtract signed numbers, we don't actually subtract the numbers, but instead, change the subtraction to its inverse, addition, and change the subtrahend (the number being subtracted) to its opposite signed number.

$(+8)-(+6)$	$(-8)-(-6)$	$(+8)-(-6)$	$(-8)-(+6)$
↓ ↓	↓ ↓	↓ ↓	↓ ↓
$=(+8)+(-6)$	$=(-8)+(+6)$	$=(+8)+(+6)$	$=(-8)+(-6)$
$=\quad +2$	$=\quad -2$	$=\quad +14$	$=\quad -14$

To Subtract Signed Numbers:
1. Change all subtractions to addition.
2. Change the sign of each number being subtracted (each number following a subtraction symbol) to its opposite sign.
3. Follow the procedure for adding (combining) signed numbers.

Example

Evaluate the expression $(+2) - (-4) + (-3) - (+1)$.

Procedure

1. Change all subtractions to addition, and change the sign of each number being subtracted to its opposite sign. Add (combine) the resulting signed numbers.

$$(+2)-(-4)+(-3)-(+1)$$

$$
\begin{aligned}
&= (+2)+(+4)+(-3)+(-1)\\
&= \quad (+6)+(-3)+(-1)\\
&= \quad\quad (+3)+(-1)\\
&= \quad\quad\quad +2
\end{aligned}
$$

PRACTICE PROBLEMS

Perform the following additions and subtractions:

1. $(-6) - (+5) - (-2) - (-1)$

2. $(+6) - (-2) - (+7) - (-4)$

3. $(-8) - (-5) + (-1) - (+3)$

4. $(4) + (-5) - (7) + (2)$

ANSWERS AND EXPLANATIONS

1. $(-6) - (+5) - (-2) - (-1) =$
    $(-6) + (-5) + (+2) + (+1) =$
    $(-11) + (+2) + (+1) = (-9) + (+1) = -8$

2. $(+6) - (-2) - (+7) - (-4) =$
    $(+6) + (+2) + (-7) + (+4) =$
    $(+8) + (-7) + (+4) = (+1) + (+4) = +5$

3. $(-8) - (-5) + (-1) - (+3) =$
    $(-8) + (+5) + (-1) + (-3) =$
    $(-3) + (-1) + (-3) = (-4) + (-3) = -7$

4. $(4) + (-5) - (7) + (2) =$
    $(4) + (-5) + (-7) + (2) =$
    $(-1) + (-7) + (2) = (-8) + (2) = -6$

MULTIPLYING AND DIVIDING SIGNED NUMBERS

Unlike addition and subtraction of signed numbers, multiplication and division are performed in almost the same manner as ordinary arithmetic.

To Multiply or Divide Two Signed Numbers:

1. Multiply or divide the absolute values of the numbers (ignoring their signs).
2. If the signs of the numbers are the *same*, make the sign of the result *positive*. That is,

$$(+)(+) \text{ or } (-)(-) = (+)$$

$$\frac{(+)}{(+)} \text{ or } \frac{(-)}{(-)} = (+)$$

Same Signs

$$(+5)(+2) = +10$$

$$(-5)(-2) = +10$$

$$\frac{(+8)}{+2} = +4$$

$$\frac{(-8)}{(-2)} = +4$$

If the signs of the numbers are *different*, make the sign of the result *negative*. That is:

$$(+)(-) \text{ or } (-)(+) = (-)$$

$$\frac{(+)}{(-)} \text{ or } \frac{(-)}{(+)} = (-)$$

Different Signs

$$(+5)(-2) = -10$$

$$(-5)(+2) = -10$$

$$\frac{(+8)}{-2} = -4$$

$$\frac{(-8)}{(+2)} = -4$$

Example

Evaluate the expression $\dfrac{(-8)}{(-2)} + (-3)(5) - \dfrac{(+6)}{(-2)}$.

Procedure

1. Multiply and divide the signed numbers.

$$\dfrac{(-8)}{(-2)} + (-3)(5) - \dfrac{(+6)}{(-2)}$$
$$= (+4) + (-15) - (-3)$$

2. Change subtraction to addition of the opposite signed number, and add (combine) the resulting numbers.

$$= (+4) + (-15) + (+3)$$
$$= \qquad (-11) + (+3)$$
$$= \qquad\qquad -8$$

To multiply more than two signed numbers, we proceed step by step, multiplying two numbers at a time, until we reach the final result:

$$(-3)(+5)(-4)(-2)$$
$$= \quad (-15)(-4)(-2)$$
$$= \quad\quad (+60)(-2)$$
$$= \quad\quad\quad -120$$

An alternate way of determining the final sign of a product of two or more signed numbers is based on the number of negative factors in the original expression. Since each pair of negative factors gives a positive result, the only way that the final sign can be negative is if the original expression contains an odd number of negative factors. Therefore,

---

To Determine the Final Sign of a Product of Signed Numbers:

1. Count the number of *negative factors*.
2. If this number is *even*, make the sign of the final result *positive*.
   If this number is *odd*, make the sign of the final result *negative*.

Two Negative Factors
$$(-2)(+5)(-3) = +30$$

Three Negative Factors
$$(-2)(-5)(-3) = -30$$

This procedure is particularly useful for determining the final sign of a signed number raised to a power:

$$(+2)^4 = \underbrace{(+2)(+2)(+2)(+2)}_{\text{no negative factors}} = +16$$

$$(-2)^4 = \underbrace{(-2)(-2)(-2)(-2)}_{\text{4 negative factors}} = +16$$

$$(-2)^5 = \underbrace{(-2)(-2)(-2)(-2)(-2)}_{\text{5 negative factors}} = -32$$

The only combination of base and power that results in a negative final sign is a *negative base* raised to an *odd power*. All other combinations result in a positive final sign.

Powers of Signed Numbers	
Positive Base	*Negative Base*
$(+)^{\text{even}} = (+)$	$(-)^{\text{even}} = (+)$
$(+)^{\text{odd}} = (+)$	$(-)^{\text{odd}} = (-)$

Note that expressions like $(-5)^2$ and -5^2 do *not* mean the same thing, as shown below. The first, $(-5)^2$, means to square the number -5. This gives $+25$. The second, -5^2, means the negative of the number 5^2. This gives -25.

$$(-5)^2 = (-5)(-5) \quad \bigg| \quad -5^2 = -(5)(5)$$
$$= +25 \qquad\qquad = -25$$

PRACTICE PROBLEMS

Evaluate the following expressions:

1. $(-3)(+4)(-2)(-7)$

2. $\dfrac{(-6)(+5)}{(-3)(-2)}$

3. $\left(\dfrac{-16}{+2}\right) + (-3)(+2)$

4. $(-5)(-2)(3) - (7)(-2)$

5. $(-3)^3$

6. $(-1)^{18}$

7. $(-2)^6$

8. -2^6

ANSWERS AND EXPLANATIONS

1. $(-3)(+4)(-2)(-7) = (-12)(-2)(-7) = (+24)(-7) = -168$

2. $\dfrac{(-6)(+5)}{(-3)(-2)} = \dfrac{-30}{+6} = -5$

3. $\left(\dfrac{-16}{+2}\right) + (-3)(+2) = (-8) + (-6) = -14$

4. $(-5)(-2)(3) - (7)(-2) = (+30) - (-14) = (+30) + (+14) = +44$

5. $(-3)^3 = (-3)(-3)(-3) = -27$

6. $(-1)^{18} = \underbrace{(-1)(-1)\cdots(-1)}_{18 \text{ factors}} = +1$

7. $(-2)^6 = (-2)(-2)(-2)(-2)(-2)(-2) = +64$

8. $-2^6 = -(2)(2)(2)(2)(2)(2) = -64$

EVALUATING ALGEBRAIC EXPRESSIONS WITH SIGNED NUMBERS

Remember, when evaluating an algebraic expression for specific values of the variables, substitute the values into the expression and then follow the order of operations. When substituting signed numbers into algebraic expressions, it is advisable to use parentheses to distinguish the positive and negative signs from the operations.

Example 1
For $a = 3$, $b = -2$, and $x = -4$, find the value of $b^3 - ax + x^2$.

Procedure

1. Substitute the given values into the expression.
$$b^3 - ax + x^2$$
$$= (-2)^3 - (3)(-4) + (-4)^2$$

2. Evaluate the powers and the product.
$$= (-8) - (-12) + (+16)$$

3. Change subtraction to addition of the opposite signed number, and add (combine) the resulting numbers.

$$= (-8) + (+12) + (+16)$$
$$= \quad (+4) + (+16)$$
$$= \quad\quad +20$$

Example 2

For $x = 3$ and $y = -2$, evaluate $x^2 - 5y$.

Procedure

1. Substitute the given values into the exprssion.

$$x^2 - 5y$$
$$= (3)^2 - 5(-2)$$

2. Evaluate the power and product.

$$= (9) - (-10)$$

3. Change subtraction to addition of the opposite signed number, and add the resulting numbers. (Note that instead of subtracting $5(-2)$, we could multiply $-5(-2)$. This would give $9 + 10$, or 19, the same result as before.)

$$= (9) + (+10)$$
$$= +19$$

PRACTICE PROBLEMS

For $a = -2$, $b = -5$, and $x = 3$, evaluate the following expressions:

1. $3a^3 - b$

2. $a^2 + b^2 - x^2$

3. $\dfrac{abx}{a + b - x}$

4. $-b^2 - 4a$

ANSWERS AND EXPLANATIONS

1. $3a^3 - b = 3(-2)^3 - (-5) = 3(-8) - (-5)$
   $= (-24) - (-5) = (-24) + (+5) = -19$

2. $a^2 + b^2 - x^2 = (-2)^2 + (-5)^2 - (3)^2 = (+4) + (+25) - (+9)$
   $= (+29) + (-9) = +20$

3. $\dfrac{abx}{a + b - x} = \dfrac{(-2)(-5)(3)}{(-2) + (-5) - (-3)} =$

   $\dfrac{30}{(-2) + (-5) + (-3)} = \dfrac{30}{-10} = -3$

4. $-b^2 - 4a = -(-5)^2 - 4(-2) = -(25) - (-8) = -25 + (+8) = -17$

POLYNOMIALS

ADDING AND SUBTRACTING ALGEBRAIC TERMS (MONOMIALS)

As you recall, algebraic terms are formed by the product and quotient of numbers and variables. Terms that have identical variable factors are called **like terms**. Some examples are given below.

Like Terms	*Unlike Terms*
$5x$ and $-7x$	$7x$ and $3y$
$-2x^2y$ and $3x^2y$	$-2ax$ and $3bx$
a^2b^3 and $-\dfrac{1}{4}a^2b^3$	$3x^2$ and $5x^3$

To add and subtract like terms, simply add and subtract (combine) their numerical coefficients. The result is a single term having the same variable factors as the original like terms.

$$3x^2y + 2x^2y - 9x^2y$$
$$= (3 + 2 - 9)x^2y$$
$$= -4x^2y$$

Terms that do not have identical variable factors (unlike terms) cannot be combined into a single term. For example, expressions such as $3x + 4y$ and $7xy^2 - 5xy$ cannot be simplified further.

PRACTICE PROBLEMS

1. $6x^3 - 2x^3 - 7x^3 + x^3$

2. $4xy^2 - 3x^2y + xy^2 - 4x^2y$

3. $(5x) + (-8x) - (-3x) + (x)$

4. $(3x) + (-5y) - (x) - (-7y)$

ANSWERS AND EXPLANATIONS

1. $6x^3 - 2x^3 - 7x^3 + x^3 = (6 - 2 - 7 + 1)x^3 = -2x^3$

2. $4xy^2 - 3x^2 + xy^2 - 4x^2y =$
   $(4 + 1)xy^2 + (-3 - 4)x^2y = 5xy^2 - 7x^2y$

3. $(5x) + (-8x) - (-3x) + (x) = (5x) + (-8x) + (+3x) + (x)$
   $= (5 - 8 + 3 + 1)x = x$

4. $(3x) + (-5y) - (x) - (-7y) =$

   $(3x) + (-5y) + (-x) + (+7y) =$
   $(3 - 1)x + (-5 + 7)y = 2x + 2y$

ADDING AND SUBTRACTING POLYNOMIALS

When adding and subtracting algebraic expressions that contain more than one term (polynomials), it is usually helpful to rearrange the expressions in a vertical format with the like terms lined up. Remember that to subtract, first change the sign of every term being subtracted to its opposite sign.

Example 1

Add $(3x^2 - 4x - 7) + (x^2 + 6x - 2)$.

Procedure

1. Rearrange the expressions vertically, with the like terms lined up. Combine the numerical coefficients of the like terms.

$$3x^2 - 4x - 7$$
$$\underline{x^2 + 6x - 2}$$
$$4x^2 + 2x - 9$$

Example 2

Subtract $(4x^2 - 5xy - y^2) - (x^2 + 3xy - 4y^2)$.

Procedure

1. Change subtraction to addition, and change the sign of each term being subtracted to its opposite sign.

$$(4x^2 - 5xy - y^2) - (x^2 + 3xy - 4y^2)$$
$$\downarrow \downarrow \searrow \searrow$$
$$= (4x^2 - 5xy - y^2) + (-x^2 - 3xy + 4y^2)$$

2. Line up the like terms, and combine the numerical coefficients.

$$4x^2 - 5xy - y^2$$
$$\underline{-x^2 - 3xy + 4y^2}$$
$$3x^2 - 8xy + 3y^2$$

PRACTICE PROBLEMS

1. $(5x^2 + 6x - 3) + (2x^2 - 8x - 5)$

2. $(y^2 - 2y + 8) - (3y^2 - 5y - 1)$

3. $(x^2 - 3xy + 5y^2) + (5x^2 - 3y^2)$

4. $(3x^2 + 5xy) - (4x^2 - 2y^2)$

ANSWERS AND EXPLANATIONS

1. $5x^2 + 6x - 3$
   $\underline{2x^2 - 8x - 5}$
   $7x^2 - 2x - 8$

2. $(y^2 - 2y + 8) - (3y^2 - 5y - 1) = (y^2 - 2y + 8) + (-3y^2 + 5y + 1)$

   $y^2 - 2y + 8$
   $\underline{-3y^2 + 5y + 1}$
   $-2y^2 + 3y + 9$

3. $x^2 - 3xy + 5y^2$
   $\underline{5x^2 \qquad - 3y^2}$
   $6x^2 - 3xy + 2y^2$

4. $(3x^2 + 5xy) - (4x^2 - 2y^2) = (3x^2 + 5xy) + (-4x^2 + 2y^2)$

   $3x^2 + 5xy$
   $\underline{-4x^2 + \qquad 2y^2}$
   $-x^2 + 5xy + 2y^2$

MULTIPLYING AND DIVIDING MONOMIALS

Although addition and subtraction can only be performed with like terms, multiplication and division can be performed with any type of terms, like or unlike. We simply regroup the numerical and variable factors, and then multiply or divide them separately:

Multiplication

$$(-5x^2)(2y^3) = (-5)(2)(x^2)(y^3)$$
$$= -10x^2y^3$$

Division

$$\frac{-6x^3}{2y} = \left(\frac{-6}{2}\right)\left(\frac{x^3}{y}\right)$$
$$= \frac{-3x^3}{y}$$

MULTIPLYING POWERS OF THE SAME BASE

When multiplying monomials that contain the same variable factor, we can simplify the result in the following way:

$$(3x^2)(2x^3)(5x^2) = (3)(2)(5)(x^2)(x^3)(x^2)$$
$$= 30\overbrace{(x \cdot x)}^{2}\overbrace{(x \cdot x \cdot x)}^{3}\overbrace{(x \cdot x)}^{2}$$
$$= 30\overbrace{(x \cdot x \cdot x \cdot x \cdot x \cdot x \cdot x)}^{7 \text{ factors}}$$
$$= 30x^7$$

By writing out all the variable factors in the product, we see that the exponent in the result is simply the *sum* of the individual exponents.

In general, when multiplying m factors of x by n factors of x, the result will contain a total of $m + n$ factors of x. In other words,

---

To Multiply Powers of the Same Base:
Keep the base and *add* the exponents.
$$x^m \cdot x^n = x^{m+n}$$
$$x^2 \cdot x^3 = x^{2+3} = x^5$$
$$y^2 \cdot y^5 \cdot y = y^{2+5+1} = y^8$$

Example
Multiply $(-3x^2y)(2x^3y^2)(5xy)$.

Procedure

1. Multiply the numerical factors and variable factors separately.

$$\left(-3x^2y\right)\left(2x^3y^2\right)(5xy)$$
$$= (-3)(2)(5)\left(x^2 \cdot x^3 \cdot x\right)\left(y \cdot y^2 \cdot y\right)$$

2. For the variables with the same base, add the exponents. Remember that when an exponent does not appear, it is understood to be 1.

$$= -30\left(x^{2+3+1}\right)\left(y^{1+2+1}\right)$$
$$= -30x^6y^4$$

PRACTICE PROBLEMS

1. $(-2x^2)(5x^3)$

2. $(-7x^3y^2)(-6xy)$

3. $(-3xy)(5xy^2)(2x)$

4. $(6a^2b)(ax)(2bx2)$

ANSWERS AND EXPLANATIONS

1. $(-2x^2)(5x^3) = (-2)(5)(x^2 \cdot x^3) = -10x^5$

2. $(-7x^3y^2)(-6xy) = (-7)(-6)(x^3 \cdot x)(y^2 \cdot y) = 42x^4y^3$

3. $(-3xy)(5xy^2)(2x) = (-3)(5)(2)(x \cdot x \cdot x)(y \cdot y^2) = -30x^3y^3$

4. $(6a^2b)(ax)(2bx^2) = (6)(2)(a^2 \cdot a)(b \cdot b)(x \cdot x^2) = 12a^3b^2x^3$

DIVIDING POWERS OF THE SAME BASE

The procedure for dividing powers of the same base is similar to the one for multiplying powers of the same base. However, instead of adding the exponents, subtract them.

Higher Power in Numerator	*Higher Power in Denominator*

$$\frac{18x^5}{3x^2} = \left(\frac{18}{3}\right)\left(\frac{x^5}{x^2}\right)$$

$$= 6\left(\frac{x \cdot x \cdot x \cdot \overset{1}{\cancel{x}} \cdot \overset{1}{\cancel{x}}}{\underset{1}{\cancel{x}} \cdot \underset{1}{\cancel{x}}}\right)$$

$$= \frac{6x^3}{1}$$

$$= 6x^3$$

$$\frac{4x^2}{8x^6} = \left(\frac{4}{8}\right)\left(\frac{x^2}{x^6}\right)$$

$$= \left(\frac{1}{2}\right)\left(\frac{\overset{1}{\cancel{x}}\,\overset{1}{\cancel{x}}}{x \cdot x \cdot x \cdot x \cdot \underset{1}{\cancel{x}} \cdot \underset{1}{\cancel{x}}}\right)$$

$$= \left(\frac{1}{2}\right)\left(\frac{1}{x^4}\right)$$

$$= \frac{1}{2x^4}$$

This time, notice that some of the factors cancel, resulting in an exponent that is the *difference* of the individual exponents. Also notice that the variable in the result is either in the numerator or denominator, depending upon which of the original factors has the higher exponent (more factors). In general,

> **To Divide Powers of the Same Base:**
> Keep the base and *subtract* the exponents.
>
> $$\frac{x^m}{x^n} = \begin{cases} x^{m-n} & , \text{for } m > n \\ 1 & , \text{for } m = n \\ \dfrac{1}{x^{n-m}} & , \text{for } m < n \end{cases}$$

$$\frac{x^5}{x^2} = x^{5-2} = x^3$$

$$\frac{x^4}{x^4} = 1$$

$$\frac{x^3}{x^7} = \frac{1}{x^{7-3}} = \frac{1}{x^4}$$

Example

Divide $\dfrac{6x^2y^6z}{8x^5y^2z^2}$.

Procedure

1. Separate the numerical and variable factors.

$$\frac{6x^2y^6z}{8x^5y^2z^2} = \left(\frac{6}{8}\right)\left(\frac{x^2 \cdot y^6 \cdot z}{x^5 \cdot y^2 \cdot z^2}\right)$$

2. Reduce the numerical fraction. For each variable factor with the same base, subtract the smaller exponent from the larger exponent.

$$= \left(\frac{\overset{3}{\cancel{6}}}{\underset{4}{\cancel{8}}} \right) \left(\frac{1 \cdot y^{6-2} \cdot 1}{x^{5-2} \cdot 1 \cdot z^{2-1}} \right)$$

$$= \frac{3y^4}{4x^3 z}$$

PRACTICE PROBLEMS

Perform the following divisions:

1. $\dfrac{-16x^3 y}{10xy}$

2. $\dfrac{2x^2 y^3}{6x^3 y^5}$

3. $\dfrac{6xy^3}{4x^2 y}$

4. $\dfrac{-2a^3 b^5 x}{8ab^2 x^3}$

ANSWERS AND EXPLANATIONS

1. $\dfrac{-16x^3 y}{10xy} = \left(\dfrac{-16}{10} \right) \left(\dfrac{x^3 y}{xy} \right) =$

    $\left(\dfrac{-8}{5} \right) \left(\dfrac{x^{3-1} \cdot 1}{1 \cdot 1} \right) = \dfrac{-8x^2}{5}$

2. $\dfrac{2x^2 y^3}{6x^3 y^5} = \left(\dfrac{2}{6} \right) \left(\dfrac{x^2 y^3}{x^3 y^5} \right) =$

    $\left(\dfrac{1}{3} \right) \left(\dfrac{1 \cdot 1}{x^{3-2} \cdot y^{5-3}} \right) = \dfrac{1}{3xy^2}$

3. $\dfrac{6xy^3}{4x^2 y} = \left(\dfrac{6}{4} \right) \left(\dfrac{xy^3}{x^2 y} \right) = \left(\dfrac{3}{2} \right) \left(\dfrac{1 \cdot y^{3-1}}{x^{2-1} \cdot 1} \right) = \dfrac{3y^2}{2x}$

4. $\dfrac{-2a^3 b^5 x}{8ab^2 x^3} = \left(\dfrac{-2}{8} \right) \left(\dfrac{a^3 b^5 x}{ab^2 x^3} \right) =$

    $\left(\dfrac{-1}{4} \right) \left(\dfrac{a^{3-1} b^{5-2} \cdot 1}{1 \cdot x^{3-1}} \right) = \dfrac{-a^2 b^3}{4x^2}$

ZERO AND NEGATIVE EXPONENTS

The procedure for dividing powers of the same base, described in the previous section, gives three possible results. The specific one you use depends upon whether the exponent in the numerator is greater than, equal to, or less than the exponent in the denominator.

$$\frac{x^m}{x^n} = \begin{cases} x^{m-n} & \text{, for } m > n \\ 1 & \text{, for } m = n \\ \dfrac{1}{x^{n-m}} & \text{, for } m < n \end{cases}$$

By defining $x^0 = 1$, and $x^{-p} = \dfrac{1}{x^p}$, we can simplify this result to:

$$\frac{x^m}{x^n} = x^{m-n}$$

For example,

$$\frac{x^5}{x^3} = x^{5-3} = x^2$$

$$\frac{x^3}{x^3} = x^{3-3} = x^0 = 1$$

$$\frac{x^3}{x^5} = x^{3-5} = x^{-2} = \frac{1}{x^2}$$

PRACTICE PROBLEMS

Perform the following divisions:

1. $\dfrac{x^5 y^7}{x^2 y^3}$

2. $\dfrac{6a^5 x^2 y^3}{2a^3 x y^7}$

3. $\dfrac{2x^2 y^2}{8x^5 y^9}$

4. $\dfrac{-3x^2 y^3}{3x^2 y^3}$

ANSWERS AND EXPLANATIONS

1. $$\frac{x^5 y^7}{x^2 y^3} = x^{5-2} y^{7-3}$$
$$= x^3 y^4$$

2. $$\frac{6a^5 x^2 y^3}{2a^3 xy^7} = 3a^{5-3} x^{2-1} y^{3-7}$$
$$= 3a^2 x^1 y^{-4}$$
$$= \frac{3a^2 x}{y^4}$$

3. $$\frac{2x^2 y^2}{8x^5 y^9} = \frac{2}{8} x^{2-5} y^{2-9}$$
$$= \frac{1}{4} x^{-3} y^{-7}$$
$$= \frac{1}{4x^3 y^7}$$

4. $$\frac{-3x^2 y^3}{3x^2 y^3} = \frac{-3}{3} x^{2-2} y^{3-3}$$
$$= -1x^0 y^0$$
$$= -1 \cdot 1 \cdot 1$$
$$= -1$$

RAISING A MONOMIAL TO A POWER

Raising a monomial to a power is a special case of multiplying monomials. In the example below, the exponent outside the parentheses indicates that we should multiply 3 factors of the monomial inside the parentheses.

$$\left(x^4 y^2\right)^3 = \left(x^4 y^2\right)\left(x^4 y^2\right)\left(x^4 y^2\right)$$
$$= \left(x^4 \cdot x^4 \cdot x^4\right)\left(y^2 \cdot y^2 \cdot y^2\right)$$
$$= \left(x^{\overbrace{4+4+4}^{4\cdot3}}\right)\left(y^{\overbrace{2+2+2}^{2\cdot3}}\right)$$
$$= x^{12} y^6$$

The exponent of each factor in the result is the product of the exponent inside the parentheses and the exponent outside the parentheses. In general,

> **To Raise a Power of a Given Base to Another Power:**
> Keep the base and *multiply* the exponents.
> $(x^m)^n = x^{m \cdot n}$

For example,

$$\left(3x^2y^5\right)^4 = 3^{1\cdot4}x^{2\cdot4}y^{5\cdot4}$$
$$= 3^4x^8y^{20}$$
$$= 81x^8y^{20}$$

PRACTICE PROBLEMS

Raise each of the following monomials to the power indicated.

1. $(3x^2y^5)^2$

2. $(-2xy^2)^3$

3. $(-x^2y^3)^2$

4. $(5x^2y^7)^3$

ANSWERS AND EXPLANATIONS

1. $(3x^2y^5)^2 = 3^{1\cdot2}x^{2\cdot2}y^{5\cdot2} = 9x^4y^{10}$

2. $(-2xy^2)^3 = (-2)^{1\cdot3}x^{1\cdot3}y^{2\cdot3} = -8xy^6$

3. $(-x^2y^3)^2 = (-1)^{1\cdot2}x^{2\cdot2}y^{3\cdot2} = x^4y^6$

4. $(5x^2y^7)^3 = 5^{1\cdot3}x^{2\cdot3}y^{7\cdot3} = 125x^6y^{21}$

MULTIPLYING POLYNOMIALS BY MONOMIALS

To multiply a polynomial by a monomial, we use the **distributive law of multiplication**.

Distributive Law of Multiplication
When multiplying a sum of terms by a single term, multiply each term in the sum by the single term, and then add the results.
$$A(B + C + ... + R) = AB + AC + ... + AR$$

For example,

$$3a(4x + 2y)$$
$$= 3a(4x) + 3a(2y)$$
$$= 12ax + 6ay$$

Example
Multiply $3x^2y(5x^3y^2 - 2xy)$.

Procedure

1. Using the distributive law, multiply each term in the parentheses by $3x^2y$. Remember that for variables with the same base, add the exponents.

$$3x^2y\left(5x^3y^2 - 2xy\right)$$
$$= 3x^2y\left(5x^3y^2\right) + 3x^2y(-2xy)$$
$$= 15x^5y^3 - 6x^3y^2$$

PRACTICE PROBLEMS

Perform the following multiplications:

1. $2x(3x^2 - 5y)$

2. $-3xy(2x + 3y)$

3. $-2xy^2(x^2 - 4y^3)$

4. $6a^2b^3(3ax + 2bx)$

ANSWERS AND EXPLANATIONS

1. $2x(3x^2 - 5y) = 2x(3x^2) + 2x(-5y) =$
   $6x^3 - 10xy$

2. $-3xy(2x + 3y) = -3xy(2x) - 3xy(3y) =$
   $-6x^2y - 9xy^2$

3. $-2xy^2(x^2 - 4y^3) = -2xy^2(x^2) - 2xy^2(-4y^3) =$
   $-2x^3y^2 + 8xy^5$

4. $6a^2b^3(3ax + 2bx) = 6a^2b^3(3ax) + 6a^2b^3(2bx) =$
   $18a^3b^3x + 12a^2b^4x$

DIVIDING POLYNOMIALS BY MONOMIALS

To divide a polynomial by a monomial, we use the **distributive law of division**.

> *Distributive Law of Division*
> When dividing a sum of terms by a single term, divide each term in the sum by the single term, and then add the results.
>
> $$\frac{B+C+\cdots+R}{A} = \frac{B}{A} + \frac{C}{A} + \cdots + \frac{R}{A}$$

For example,

$$\frac{8x+6y}{2a}$$
$$= \frac{8x}{2a} + \frac{6y}{2a}$$
$$= \frac{4x}{a} + \frac{3y}{a}$$

Example

Divide $\dfrac{6xy^4 + 15x^3 y}{3x^2 y^2}$.

Procedure

1. Using the distributive law, divide each term in the numerator by $3x^2 y^2$. Remember that for variables with the same base, subtract the exponents.

$$\frac{6xy^4 + 15x^3 y}{3x^2 y^2}$$

$$= \frac{6xy^4}{3x^2 y^2} + \frac{15x^3 y}{3x^2 y^2}$$

$$= \frac{2y^2}{x} + \frac{5x}{y}$$

PRACTICE PROBLEMS

Perform the following divisions:

1. $\dfrac{6x^2 + 4x}{2x}$

2. $\dfrac{xy^3 - x^2 y^2}{xy}$

3. $\dfrac{8x^3 y + 6x^2 y^2}{2xy}$

4. $\dfrac{5x^2 y^3 - 10xy^2}{5x^3 y^2}$

ANSWERS AND EXPLANATIONS

1. $\dfrac{6x^2 + 4x}{2x} = \dfrac{6x^2}{2x} + \dfrac{4x}{2x} = 3x + 2$

2. $\dfrac{xy^3 - x^2 y^2}{xy} = \dfrac{xy^3}{xy} - \dfrac{x^2 y^2}{xy} = y^2 - xy$

3. $\dfrac{8x^3 y + 6x^2 y^2}{2xy} = \dfrac{8x^3 y}{2xy} + \dfrac{6x^2 y^2}{2xy} = 4x^2 + 3xy$

4. $\dfrac{5x^2 y^3 - 10xy^2}{5x^3 y^2} = \dfrac{5x^2 y^3}{5x^3 y^2} - \dfrac{10xy^2}{5x^3 y^2} = \dfrac{y}{x} - \dfrac{2}{x^2}$

MULTIPLYING POLYNOMIALS BY POLYNOMIALS

The distributive law of multiplication, which we use to multiply polynomials by monomials, can also be extended to multiply polynomials by polynomials. In the examples below, the numbers indicate the order in which the terms are multiplied. Notice that when multiplying polynomials by polynomials (the second example), each term in the right polynomial is multiplied by each term in the left polynomial.

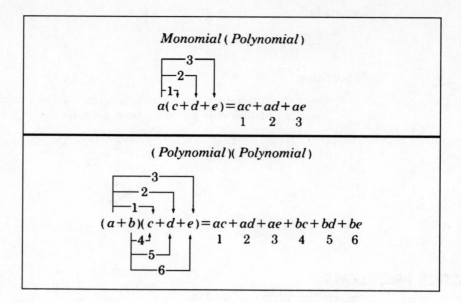

$$Monomial\,(\,Polynomial\,)$$

$$a(c+d+e)=ac+ad+ae$$

$$(\,Polynomial\,)(\,Polynomial\,)$$

$$(a+b)(c+d+e)=ac+ad+ae+bc+bd+be$$

Example

Multiply $(2x + 3y)(x - 5y)$.

Procedure

1.   Multiply each term in the right parentheses by $2x$ and $3y$. Combine like terms.

$$(2x+3y)(x-5y)$$

$$=2x(x)+2x(-5y)+3y(x)+3y(-5y)$$

$$=2x^2-10xy+3xy-15y^2$$

$$=\ 2x^2-7xy-15y^2$$

PRACTICE PROBLEMS

Perform the following multiplications:

1. $(2a + 3b)(5x - y)$

2. $(x + 2y)(3x + y)$

3. $(x + 3)(x^2 + 2x - 4)$

4. $(x^3 - 3)(x^3 + 5)$

ANSWERS AND EXPLANATIONS

1. $(2a + 3b)(5x - y) = 10ax - 2ay + 15bx - 3by$

2. $(x + 2y)(3x + y) = 3x^2 + xy + 6xy + 2y^2$
$$= 3x^2 + 7xy + 2y^2$$

3. $(x + 3)(x^2 + 2x - 4) = x^3 + 2x^2 - 4x$
$$+ 3x^2 + 6x - 12$$
$$= x^3 + 5x^2 + 2x - 12$$

4. $(x^3 - 3)(x^3 + 5) = x^6 + 5x^3 - 3x^3 - 15$
$$= x^6 + 2x^3 - 15$$

SOLVING LINEAR EQUATIONS AND INEQUALITIES

An **equation** is a mathematical statement that two quantities are equal. Equations that contain only numbers are either **true** or **false**. For example, the equation $3 + 4 = 7$ is true, while the equation $3 + 4 = 8$ is false. Equations that contain one or more variables are neither true nor false, but **open**. That is, their truth cannot be determined until all the variables are replaced by specific numerical values. For example, the equation $5x + 4 = 14$ is an open equation that is true if x is replaced by 2, and that is false if x is replaced by 3.

$$5x + 4 = 14 \quad \text{open}$$
$$5(2) + 4 = 14 \quad \text{true}$$
$$5(3) + 4 = 18 \quad \text{false}$$

The specific values of the variables that make an open equation true are called the **roots** or **solutions** of the equation. The process of finding the roots is called **solving** the equation.

The most fundamental method of solving an equation is that of trial and error. After test values are chosen for the variables and substituted into the equation, each side of the equation is evaluated separately. If both sides result in the same value, the numbers chosen are roots. If not, new values are chosen and the process is repeated.

Solving an Equation by Trial and Error

Try $x = 3$ $\qquad\qquad\qquad$ *Solve* : $5x - 2 = 3x + 8$

$$5x - 2 = 3x + 8$$
$$\overset{?}{5(3) - 2 = 3(3) + 8}$$
$$\overset{?}{15 - 2 = 9 + 8}$$
$$13 = 17$$

False

Try $x = 4$

$$5x - 2 = 3x + 8$$
$$\overset{?}{5(4) - 2 = 3(4) + 8}$$
$$\overset{?}{20 - 2 = 12 + 8}$$
$$18 = 20$$

False

Try $x = 5$

$$5x - 2 = 3x + 8$$
$$\overset{?}{5(5) - 2 = 3(5) + 8}$$
$$\overset{?}{25 - 2 = 15 + 8}$$
$$\overset{\checkmark}{23 = 23}$$

True

$x = 5$ is a root.

This method of solving an equation is obviously not very efficient, and except in the most simple cases, will probably not work at all. Instead, other, more systematic methods have been developed that will now be discussed.

SOLVING LINEAR EQUATIONS IN ONE VARIABLE

In equations that contain only one variable, the highest power of the variable is called the equation's **degree**. For example, $5x - 2 = 3x + 8$ is called a **first degree**, or linear equation, $x^2 + 2x = 10 - x$ is called a **second degree**, or **quadratic equation**, and $x^3 + 5 = x^2 + 6$ is called a **third degree**, or cubic equation.

The particular method used to solve an equation depends upon the equation's degree. For first degree (linear) equations, we use the method of **inverse operations**. The idea behind this method is to transform the given equation into an equivalent equation (an equation having the same roots) in which the variable appears alone on one side of the equation, and a number appears alone on the other. This number will be the root of the given equation.

In order to get the variable alone on one side of the equation, we must perform inverse operations to "undo" the operations on that side. Remember, addition undoes subtraction (and vice-versa), and multiplication undoes division (and vice-versa).

Since we want the new, transformed equation to have the same roots as the given equation, we must follow the equivalence principle stated on the following page.

Equivalence Principle

Whenever a number is added to, subtracted from, multiplied by, or divided into one side of an equation, the same thing must be done on the other side of the equation.

$$A = B$$
$$A + C = B + C$$
$$A - C = B - C$$
$$C \cdot A = C \cdot B$$
$$\frac{A}{C} = \frac{B}{C}$$

In each of the examples below, the equation contains one operation, and thus is solved in one step (one inverse operation).

Undo Addition	*Undo Subtraction*	*Undo Multiplication*	*Undo Division*
$x + 5 = 9$ $\underline{-5 \quad -5}$ $x = 4$ $\boxed{x = 4}$	$x - 3 = 2$ $\underline{+3 \quad +3}$ $x = 5$ $\boxed{x = 5}$	$4x = 12$ $\dfrac{\cancel{4}x}{\cancel{4}} = \dfrac{12}{4}$ $\boxed{x = 3}$	$\dfrac{x}{7} = 2$ $\cancel{7} \cdot \dfrac{x}{\cancel{7}} = 7 \cdot 2$ $\boxed{x = 14}$

To solve equations containing more than one operation, we perform the inverse operations one step at a time. Although the order of performing the inverse operations is arbitrary, it is usually preferable to undo additions and subtractions before undoing multiplications and divisions. In each of the examples that follow, we will check the root we obtain by substituting it back into the original equation.

Example 1

Solve $3x + 8 = 23$ and check the root.

Procedure

1. Subtract 8 from both sides of the equation. (Notice that if we divide both sides of the equation by 3 first, we get the fraction $\frac{23}{3}$ on the right side of the equation, which is more difficult to work with.)

$$
\begin{array}{rcl}
3x + 8 & = & 23 \\
\underline{-8} & & \underline{-8} \\
3x & = & 15
\end{array}
$$

2. Divide both sides by 3.

$$\frac{\cancel{3}x}{\cancel{3}} = \frac{15}{3}$$
$$x = 5$$

3. Check the root by substituting it back into the original equation.

$$3x + 8 = 23$$
$$3(5) + 8 \overset{?}{=} 23$$
$$15 + 8 \overset{?}{=} 23$$
$$23 \overset{\checkmark}{=} 23$$

Example 2

Solve $10 = \dfrac{x}{3} - 1$ and check the root.

Procedure

1. Add 1 to both sides of the equation.

$$10 = \frac{x}{3} - 1$$
$$\underline{+1 \qquad +1}$$
$$11 = \frac{x}{3}$$

2. Multiply both sides by 3.

$$3 \cdot 11 = \frac{x}{\cancel{3}} \cdot \cancel{3}$$
$$33 = x$$

3. Check the root by substitution.

$$10 = \frac{x}{3} - 1$$
$$10 \overset{?}{=} \frac{(33)}{3} - 1$$
$$10 \overset{?}{=} 11 - 1$$
$$10 \overset{\checkmark}{=} 10$$

Example 3

Solve $19 + 5x = 4$ and check the root.

Procedure

1. Subtract 19 from both sides of the equation.

$$
\begin{array}{rr}
19 + 5x = & 4 \\
-19 \qquad & -19 \\
\hline
5x = & -15
\end{array}
$$

2. Divide both sides by 5.

$$
\frac{\cancel{5}x}{\cancel{5}} = \frac{-15}{5}
$$
$$
x = -3
$$

3. Check the root by substitution.

$$
\begin{array}{c}
19 + 5x = 4 \\
19 + 5(-3) \overset{?}{=} 4 \\
19 - 15 \overset{?}{=} 4 \\
4 \overset{\checkmark}{=} 4
\end{array}
$$

Example 4

Solve $-2 = 22 - 4x$ and check the root.

Procedure

1. Subtract 22 from both sides of the equation.

$$
\begin{array}{rr}
-2 = & 22 - 4x \\
-22 & -22 \\
\hline
-24 = & -4x
\end{array}
$$

2. Divide both sides by -4. (Note that if we divide both sides by 4, instead, we get the equation $-6 = -x$. Then, by changing the signs on both sides, we get the same result, $6 = x$.)

$$\frac{-24}{-4} = \frac{\cancel{-4}x}{\cancel{-4}}$$
$$6 = x$$

3. Check the root by substitution.

$$-2 = 22 - 4x$$
$$-2 \overset{?}{=} 22 - 4(6)$$
$$-2 \overset{?}{=} 22 - 24$$
$$-2 \overset{\checkmark}{=} -2$$

PRACTICE PROBLEMS

Solve each of the following equations for x.

1. $x + 8 = 3$

2. $-5 = x - 9$

3. $-7x = -21$

4. $-4 = \dfrac{x}{3}$

5. $7x + 11 = 32$

6. $-6 = \dfrac{x}{2} + 1$

7. $3 = 16 + 2x$

8. $-7 - 3x = -4$

ANSWERS AND EXPLANATIONS

1. $x + 8 = 3$

   $\underline{-8 \quad -8}$

   $x = -5$

2. $-5 = x - 9$

   $\underline{+9 \quad\quad +9}$

   $+4 = x$

3. $-7x = -21$

   $\dfrac{-\cancel{7}x}{-\cancel{7}} = \dfrac{-21}{-7}$

   $x = 3$

4. $-4 = \dfrac{x}{3}$

   $-4 \cdot 3 = \dfrac{x}{\cancel{3}} \cdot \cancel{3}$

   $-12 = 3$

5. $7x + 11 = 32$

   $\underline{-11 \quad -11}$

   $7x = 21$

   $\dfrac{\cancel{7}x}{\cancel{7}} = \dfrac{21}{7}$

   $x = 3$

6. $-6 = \dfrac{x}{2} + 1$

   $\underline{-1 \quad\quad -1}$

   $-7 = \dfrac{x}{2}$

   $-7 \cdot 2 = \dfrac{x}{\cancel{2}} \cdot \cancel{2}$

   $-14 = x$

7.
$$3 = 16 + 2x$$
$$\underline{-16 \qquad -16}$$
$$-13 = \qquad 2x$$

$$\frac{-13}{2} = \frac{\cancel{2}x}{\cancel{2}}$$

$$-6\frac{1}{2} = x$$

8.
$$-7 - 3x = -4$$
$$\underline{+7 \qquad +7}$$
$$-3x = +3$$

$$\frac{-\cancel{3}x}{-\cancel{3}} = \frac{+3}{-3}$$

$$x = -1$$

SOLVING EQUATIONS CONTAINING PARENTHESES

To solve equation containing parentheses, first eliminate the parentheses by using the distributive law of multiplication.

> **Distributive Law**
> $$A(B + C) = AB + AC$$

Example 1

Solve $3(2x - 5) = 27$.

Procedure

1. Using the distributive law, multiply each term inside the parentheses by 3.

$$3(2x - 5) = 27$$
$$6x - 15 = 27$$

2. Add 15 to both sides of the equation.

$$6x - 15 = 27$$
$$\underline{\qquad +15 \quad +15}$$
$$6x \qquad = 42$$

3. Divide both sides by 6.

$$\frac{\cancel{6}x}{\cancel{6}} = \frac{42}{6}$$
$$x = 7$$

Example 2

Solve $5 - 2(3x - 1) = 25$.

Procedure

1. Multiply each term inside the parentheses by -2.

$$5 - 2(3x - 1) = 25$$
$$5 - 6x + 2 = 25$$

2. Combine the numbers on the left side of the equation, and then subtract 7 from both sides.

$$7 - 6x = 25$$
$$\underline{-7 \qquad -7}$$
$$-6x = 18$$

3. Divide both sides by -6.

$$\frac{-6x}{-6} = \frac{18}{-6}$$
$$x = -3$$

PRACTICE PROBLEMS

Solve each of the following equations for x.

1. $6(3x + 2) = 30$
2. $3 + 2(x - 9) = 6$
3. $-10 = 5(4 - 2x)$
4. $22 = 6 + 2(7 - x)$

ANSWERS AND EXPLANATIONS

1.
$$6(3x + 2) = 30$$
$$18x + 12 = 30$$
$$\underline{-12 \qquad -12}$$
$$18x = 18$$
$$\frac{18x}{18} = \frac{18}{18}$$
$$x = 1$$

2.
$$3 + 2(x - 9) = 6$$
$$3 + 2x - 18 = 6$$
$$2x - 15 = 6$$
$$\underline{+15 \qquad +15}$$
$$2x = 21$$
$$\frac{2x}{2} = \frac{21}{2}$$
$$x = 10\tfrac{1}{2}$$

3.
$$-10 = 5(4 - 2x)$$
$$-10 = 20 - 10x$$
$$\underline{-20 \quad -20}$$
$$-30 = \qquad -10x$$
$$\frac{-30}{-10} = \frac{-10x}{-10}$$
$$3 = x$$

4.
$$22 = 6 + 2(7 - x)$$
$$22 = 6 + 14 - 2x$$
$$22 = 20 - 2x$$
$$\underline{-20 \quad -20}$$
$$2 = \qquad -2x$$
$$\frac{2}{-2} = \frac{-2x}{-2}$$
$$-1 = x$$

SOLVING EQUATIONS CONTAINING LIKE VARIABLE TERMS

In some equations, the variable will appear in more than one term. If these terms are on the *same side* of the equation, we *combine* them. If they are on *opposite sides* of the equation, we use inverse operations to eliminate them from one side:

Same Side	*Opposite Sides*
$5x + 3x = 24$	$5x = 3x + 24$
	$\underline{-3x \quad -3x}$
$8x = 24$	$2x = \qquad 24$
$x = 3$	$x = 12$

Example 1

Solve $2(x - 3) + 3x = 14$.

Procedure

1. Using the distributive law, eliminate the parentheses.

$$2(x - 3) + 3x = 14$$
$$2x - 6 + 3x = 14$$

2. Combine the like variable terms, and then add 6 to both sides of the equation.

$$5x - 6 = 14$$
$$\underline{+6 \quad +6}$$
$$5x = 20$$

3.   Divide both sides by 5.

$$\frac{\cancel{5}x}{\cancel{5}} = \frac{20}{5}$$
$$x = 4$$

Example 2

Solve $5x - 12 = 3x + 4$.

Procedure

1.   To eliminate the term $3x$ on the right side of the equation, subtract $3x$ from both sides of the equation. (Note that we could eliminate the term $5x$ instead, by subtracting $5x$ from both sides of the equation. It makes no difference.)

$$
\begin{array}{rcl}
5x - 12 = & 3x + 4 \\
\underline{-3x \qquad \quad -3x} \\
2x - 12 = & 4
\end{array}
$$

2.   Add 12 to both sides of the equation.

$$
\begin{array}{rcl}
2x - 12 = & 4 \\
\underline{+12 \quad +12} \\
2x \quad = & 16
\end{array}
$$

3.   Divide both sides by 2.

$$\frac{\cancel{2}x}{\cancel{2}} = \frac{16}{2}$$
$$x = 8$$

Example 3

Solve $4x - 3 = 15 - 5x$.

Procedure

1.   Add $5x$ to both sides of the equation.

$$
\begin{array}{rcl}
4x - 3 = & 15 - 5x \\
\underline{+5x \qquad \quad +5x} \\
9x - 3 = & 15
\end{array}
$$

2.   Add 3 to both sides.

$$
\begin{array}{rcl}
9x - 3 = & 15 \\
\underline{+3 \quad +3} \\
9x \quad = & 18
\end{array}
$$

3.   Divide both sides by 9.

$$\frac{\cancel{9}x}{\cancel{9}} = \frac{18}{9}$$
$$x = 2$$

PRACTICE PROBLEMS

Solve each of the following equations for x.

1. $5(x - 4) - 2x = 3$

2. $2x - 6 = 7x + 14$

3. $15 - 3x = x + 3$

4. $17 - 2x = 9 - 6x$

ANSWERS AND EXPLANATIONS

1.
$$5(x - 4) - 2x = 3$$
$$5x - 20 - 2x = 3$$
$$3x - 20 = 3$$
$$\underline{+20 \quad +20}$$
$$3x = 23$$
$$\frac{3x}{3} = \frac{23}{3}$$
$$x = 7\tfrac{2}{3}$$

4.
$$17 - 2x = 9 - 6x$$
$$\underline{+6x \quad\quad +6x}$$
$$17 + 4x = 9$$
$$\underline{-17 \quad\quad -17}$$
$$4x = -8$$
$$\frac{4x}{4} = \frac{-8}{4}$$
$$x = -2$$

2.
$$2x - 6 = 7x + 14$$
$$\underline{-7x \quad\quad -7x}$$
$$-5x - 6 = 14$$
$$\underline{+6 \quad\quad + 6}$$
$$-5x = 20$$
$$\frac{-5x}{-5} = \frac{20}{-5}$$
$$x = -4$$

3.
$$15 - 3x = x + 3$$
$$\underline{- x \quad -x}$$
$$15 - 4x = 3$$
$$\underline{-15 \quad\quad -15}$$
$$-4x = -12$$
$$\frac{-4x}{-4} = \frac{-12}{-4}$$
$$x = 3$$

SOLVING EQUATIONS CONTAINING FRACTIONS

To solve equations containing fractions, it is usually preferable to eliminate the fractions first. This is done by multiplying both sides of the equation by a common denominator of the fractions in the equation. All the denominators will cancel, leaving an equation free of fractions. This procedure is sometimes referred to as "clearing" the equation of fractions.

Example 1

Solve $\dfrac{x}{2}+\dfrac{x}{3}=10$.

Procedure

1. Multiply both sides of the equation by 6, a common denominator of $\dfrac{x}{2}$ and $\dfrac{x}{3}$. Cancel the denominators.

$$\frac{x}{2}+\frac{x}{3}=10$$

$$6\left(\frac{x}{2}+\frac{x}{3}\right)=6(10)$$

$$\overset{3}{\cancel{6}}\cdot\frac{x}{\cancel{2}}+\overset{2}{\cancel{6}}\cdot\frac{x}{\cancel{3}}=60$$

$$3x+2x=60$$

2. Combine the like terms, and divide both sides of the equation by 5.

$$5x=60$$

$$\frac{\cancel{5}x}{\cancel{5}}=\frac{60}{5}$$

$$x=12$$

Example 2

Solve $\dfrac{4x}{5}=\dfrac{x}{2}+6$.

Procedure

1. Multiply both sides of the equation by 10, a common denominator of $\dfrac{4x}{5}$ and $\dfrac{x}{2}$. Cancel the denominators.

$$\frac{4x}{5}=\frac{x}{2}+6$$

$$10\left(\frac{4x}{5}\right)=(10)\left(\frac{x}{2}+6\right)$$

$$\overset{2}{\cancel{10}}\cdot\frac{4x}{\cancel{5}}=\overset{5}{\cancel{10}}\cdot\frac{x}{\cancel{2}}+10\cdot6$$

$$8x=5x+60$$

2. Subtract $5x$ from both sides of the equation.

$$8x = 5x + 60$$
$$\underline{-5x = -5x}$$
$$3x = 60$$

3. Divide both sides by 3.

$$\frac{\cancel{3}x}{\cancel{3}} = \frac{60}{3}$$
$$x = 20$$

Example 3

Solve $\dfrac{4x}{5} = \dfrac{x}{2} + 6$.

Procedure

1. Multiply both sides of the equation by 10, a common denominator of $\dfrac{4x}{5}$ and $\dfrac{x}{2}$. Cancel the denominators.

$$\frac{4x}{5} = \frac{x}{2} + 6$$

$$10\left(\frac{4x}{5}\right) = 10\left(\frac{x}{2} + 6\right)$$

$$\overset{2}{\cancel{10}} \cdot \frac{4x}{\cancel{5}} = \overset{5}{\cancel{10}} \cdot \frac{x}{\cancel{2}} + 10 \cdot 6$$

$$8x = 5x + 60$$

2. Subtract $5x$ from both sides of the equation.

$$8x = 5x + 60$$
$$\underline{-5x = -5x}$$
$$3x 60$$

3. Divide both sides by 3.

$$\frac{\cancel{3}x}{\cancel{3}} = \frac{60}{3}$$
$$x = 20$$

Example 4

Solve $\dfrac{3}{x} + \dfrac{3}{4x} = \dfrac{5}{8}$.

Procedure

1. Multiply both sides of the equation by $8x$, a common denominator of all the fractions. Cancel the denominators.

$$\frac{3}{x} + \frac{3}{4x} = \frac{5}{8}$$

$$8x\left(\frac{3}{x} + \frac{3}{4x}\right) = 8x\left(\frac{5}{8}\right)$$

$$8x \cdot \frac{3}{x} + \overset{2}{8}x \cdot \frac{3}{4x} = 8x \cdot \frac{5}{8}$$

$$24 + 6 = 5x$$

$$30 = 5x$$

2. Divide both sides by 5.

$$\frac{30}{5} = \frac{5x}{5}$$

$$6 = x$$

PRACTICE PROBLEMS

Solve each of the following equations for x.

1. $\dfrac{2x}{9} + \dfrac{1}{3} = 5$

2. $\dfrac{x}{5} - \dfrac{x}{3} = 1$

3. $\dfrac{2x}{3} - 2 = \dfrac{3x}{4}$

4. $\dfrac{2}{x} = \dfrac{9}{4} - \dfrac{5}{2x}$

ANSWERS AND EXPLANATIONS

1.
$$\frac{2x}{9} + \frac{1}{3} = 5$$

$$\cancel{9} \cdot \frac{2x}{\cancel{9}} + {}^{3}\cancel{9} \cdot \frac{1}{\cancel{3}} = 9 \cdot 5$$

$$2x + 3 = 45$$

$$\frac{-3 \qquad -3}{2x \quad = 42}$$

$$\frac{\cancel{2}x}{\cancel{2}} = \frac{42}{2}$$

$$x = 21$$

2.
$$\frac{x}{5} - \frac{x}{3} = 1$$

$${}^{3}\cancel{15} \cdot \frac{x}{\cancel{5}} - {}^{5}\cancel{15} \cdot \frac{x}{\cancel{3}} = 15 \cdot 1$$

$$3x - 5x = 15$$

$$-2x = 15$$

$$\frac{\cancel{-2}x}{\cancel{-2}} = \frac{15}{-2}$$

$$x = -7\frac{1}{2}$$

3.
$$\frac{2x}{3} - 2 = \frac{3x}{4}$$

$${}^{4}\cancel{12} \cdot \frac{2x}{\cancel{3}} - 12 \cdot 2 = {}^{3}\cancel{12} \cdot \frac{3x}{\cancel{4}}$$

$$8x - 24 = 9x$$

$$\frac{-8x \qquad\quad -8x}{-24 \quad = \quad x}$$

4.
$$\frac{2}{x} = \frac{9}{4} - \frac{5}{2x}$$

$$4\cancel{x} \cdot \frac{2}{\cancel{x}} = \cancel{4}x \cdot \frac{9}{\cancel{4}} - \cancel{4x} \cdot \frac{5}{\cancel{2x}}$$

$$8 = 9x - 10$$

$$\frac{+10 \qquad\quad +10}{18 = 9x}$$

$$\frac{18}{9} = \frac{\cancel{9}x}{\cancel{9}}$$

$$2 = x$$

SOLVING PROPORTIONS

As you recall, a proportion is a statement that two fractions are equal. To solve a proportion, cross-multiply the numerators and denominators of the fractions, set the products equal, and then solve the resulting equation.

For example,

$$\frac{2x}{6} = \frac{4}{3}$$

$$3 \cdot 2x = 6 \cdot 4$$
$$6x = 24$$
$$x = 4$$

Example

Solve $\dfrac{x+6}{2} = \dfrac{4x}{5}$.

Procedure

1. Cross-multiply the numerators and denominators and set them equal.

$$\frac{x+6}{2} = \frac{4x}{5}$$
$$5(x+6) = 2(4x)$$
$$5x + 30 = 8x$$

2. Subtract $5x$ from both sides of the equation.

$$\begin{array}{r} 5x + 30 = 8x \\ \underline{-5x \qquad -5x} \\ 30 = 3x \end{array}$$

3. Divide both sides by 3.

$$\frac{30}{3} = \frac{3x}{3}$$
$$10 = x$$

PRACTICE PROBLEMS

Solve each of the following proportions for x.

1. $\dfrac{2x}{9} = \dfrac{4}{3}$

2. $\dfrac{x-1}{3} = \dfrac{2x}{5}$

3. $\dfrac{5x}{6} = \dfrac{4x-3}{3}$

4. $\dfrac{2x+3}{5} = \dfrac{3x-1}{4}$

ANSWERS AND EXPLANATIONS

1.
$$\frac{2x}{9} = \frac{4}{3}$$
$$3(2x) = 9(4)$$
$$6x = 36$$
$$\frac{6x}{6} = \frac{36}{6}$$
$$x = 6$$

2.
$$\frac{x-1}{3} = \frac{2x}{5}$$
$$5(x-1) = 3(2x)$$
$$5x - 5 = 6x$$
$$\underline{-5x \qquad -5x}$$
$$-5 = x$$

3.
$$\frac{5x}{6} = \frac{4x-3}{3}$$
$$3(5x) = 6(4x-3)$$
$$15x = 24x - 18$$
$$\underline{-24x \qquad -24x}$$
$$-9x = -18$$
$$\frac{-9x}{-9} = \frac{-18}{-9}$$
$$x = 2$$

4.
$$\frac{2x+3}{5} = \frac{3x-1}{4}$$
$$4(2x+3) = 5(3x-1)$$
$$8x + 12 = 15x - 5$$
$$\underline{-15x \qquad -15x}$$
$$-7x + 12 = -5$$
$$\underline{-12 \qquad -12}$$
$$-7x = -17$$
$$\frac{-7x}{-7} = \frac{-17}{-7}$$
$$x = 2\frac{3}{7}$$

SOLVING EQUATIONS CONTAINING SQUARE ROOTS

To solve equations in which the variable appears underneath a square root sign, use inverse operations to get the square root alone on one side of the equation, and then square both sides. Since squaring is the inverse of taking a square root $((\sqrt{x})^2 = x)$, the square root sign will be eliminated from the equation.

$$\sqrt{x} + 3 = 9$$
$$\underline{-3 \quad\quad -3}$$
$$\sqrt{x} = 6$$
$$\left(\sqrt{x}\right)^2 = (6)^2$$
$$x = 36$$

Example

Solve $\sqrt{3x+1} + 2 = 6$ and check the root.

Procedure

1. Subtract 2 from both sides.

    $$\sqrt{3x+1} + 2 = 6$$
    $$\underline{-2 \quad\quad -2}$$
    $$\sqrt{3x+1} = 4$$

2. Square both sides.

    $$\left(\sqrt{3x+1}\right)^2 = (4)^2$$
    $$3x + 1 = 16$$

3. Solve the resulting equation for x.

    $$3x + 1 = 16$$
    $$\underline{-1 \quad -1}$$
    $$3x = 15$$
    $$\frac{\cancel{3}x}{\cancel{3}} = \frac{15}{3}$$
    $$x = 5$$

4. Check the root by substituting it into the original equation.

    $$\sqrt{3x+1} + 2 = 6$$
    $$\sqrt{3(5)+1} + 2 \overset{?}{=} 6$$
    $$\sqrt{15+1} + 2 \overset{?}{=} 6$$
    $$\sqrt{16} + 2 \overset{?}{=} 6$$
    $$4 + 2 \overset{?}{=} 6$$
    $$6 = 6 \quad \checkmark$$

Sometimes the root we obtain by this procedure will solve the "squared equation" (the equation after squaring both sides), but will *not* solve the original equation.

Solve: $\sqrt{2x} + 5 = 1$

Solution	*Check*
$\sqrt{2x} + 5 = 1$	$\sqrt{2x} + 5 = 1$
$\quad\underline{-5 \quad -5}$	$\sqrt{2\cdot 8} + 5 \overset{?}{=} 1$
$\sqrt{2x} \quad = -4$	$\sqrt{16} + 5 \overset{?}{=} 1$
$\left(\sqrt{2x}\right)^2 = \left(-4\right)^2$	$4 + 5 \overset{?}{=} 1$
$2x = 16$	$9 \neq 1$
$x = 8$	

As you can see, the root $x = 8$ solves the squared equation, $2x = 16$, but does not solve the original equation, $\sqrt{2x} + 5 = 1$. In cases like this, we call the root an **extraneous root** (false root) and discard it.

PRACTICE PROBLEMS

Solve each of the following equations for x, and check the root found.

1. $\sqrt{3x - 12} + 2 = 5$

2. $4\sqrt{\dfrac{2x}{3}} = 24$

3. $\sqrt{7x} = \sqrt{2x + 7}$

4. $\sqrt{2x} + 8 = 2$

ANSWERS AND EXPLANATIONS

1.
$$\sqrt{3x-12}+2 = 5$$
$$\underline{\phantom{\sqrt{3x-12}}-2 \quad\quad -2}$$
$$\sqrt{3x-12} = 3$$
$$\left(\sqrt{3x-12}\right)^2 = (3)^2$$
$$3x-12 = 9$$
$$\underline{+12 \quad\quad +12}$$
$$3x = 21$$
$$\frac{\cancel{3}x}{\cancel{3}} = \frac{21}{3}$$
$$x = 7$$

2.
$$4\sqrt{\frac{2x}{3}} = 24$$
$$\frac{\cancel{4}\sqrt{\dfrac{2x}{3}}}{\cancel{4}} = \frac{24}{4}$$
$$\left(\sqrt{\frac{2x}{3}}\right)^2 = (6)^2$$
$$\frac{2x}{3} = 36$$
$$\frac{\cancel{3}}{\cancel{2}} \cdot \frac{\cancel{2}x}{\cancel{3}} = 36 \cdot \frac{3}{2}$$
$$x = 54$$

3.
$$\sqrt{7x} = \sqrt{2x+7}$$
$$\left(\sqrt{7x}\right)^2 = \left(\sqrt{2x+7}\right)^2$$
$$7x = 2x+7$$
$$\underline{-2x \quad\quad -2x }$$
$$5x = +7$$
$$\frac{\cancel{5}x}{\cancel{5}} = \frac{7}{5}$$
$$x = 1\frac{2}{5}$$

4. $\sqrt{2x} + 8 = 2$ *Check*:

$$\underline{ -8 -8}$$
$$\sqrt{2(18)} + 8 \overset{?}{=} 2$$

$$\sqrt{2x} = -6$$
$$\sqrt{36} + 8 \overset{?}{=} 2$$

$$\left(\sqrt{2x}\right)^2 = (-6)^2$$
$$6 + 8 \overset{?}{=} 2$$

$$2x = 36$$
$$14 \neq 2$$

$$\frac{\cancel{2}x}{\cancel{2}} = \frac{36}{2}$$

$$x = 18$$

Thus, $x = 18$ is an extraneous root. The equation has no roots.

SOLVING LITERAL EQUATIONS

Equations that contain more than one variable are called **literal equations** (equations with **letters**). All formulas, for example, are literal equations. To solve a literal equation for one of its variables means to express that variable in terms of all the others. This is accomplished by treating all the other variables as though they were simply numbers, and then solving for the desired variable in the usual manner. Consider the example below. Since we are solving for the variable x, we treat the other variables, a, b, and c as though they were numbers.

Solve for x: $ax + b = c$

$$ax + b = c$$
$$\underline{ -b -b} \quad \text{(subtract } b\text{)}$$
$$ax = c - b$$
$$\frac{\cancel{a}x}{\cancel{a}} = \frac{c - b}{a} \quad \text{(divide by } a\text{)}$$
$$x = \frac{c - b}{a}$$

The method of solving literal equations for one of its variables is particularly useful for changing the subject of a formula from one of its variables to another. In the example below, we use this method to change the subject of the formula $A = \dfrac{bh}{2}$ from A, the area of the triangle to h, the height of the triangle.

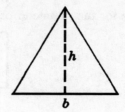

$$A = \frac{bh}{2}$$

$$2 \cdot A = 2 \cdot \frac{bh}{2} \qquad \text{(multiply by 2)}$$

$$\frac{2A}{b} = \frac{bh}{b} \qquad \text{(divide by } b\text{)}$$

$$h = \frac{2A}{b}$$

Example 1
Solve $5ax + 4a^2 = 2ax + 10a^2$ for x.

Procedure

1. Subtract $2ax$ from both sides of the equation.

$$
\begin{array}{rcl}
5ax + 4a^2 = & & 2ax + 10a^2 \\
-2ax & & -2ax \\
\hline
3ax + 4a^2 = & & 10a^2
\end{array}
$$

2. Subtract $4a^2$ from both sides of the equation.

$$
\begin{array}{rcl}
3ax + 4a^2 & = & 10a^2 \\
-4a^2 & & -4a^2 \\
\hline
3ax & = & 6a^2
\end{array}
$$

3. Divide both sides by $3a$.

$$\frac{3ax}{3a} = \frac{6a^2}{3a}$$

$$x = 2a$$

Example 2

In the formula for the perimeter of a rectangle, $P = 2(L + W)$, solve for W, the width.

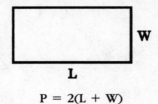

$$P = 2(L + W)$$

Procedure

1. Using the distributive law, eliminate the parentheses.

    $$P = 2(L + W)$$

    $$P = 2L + 2W$$

2. Subtract 2L from both sides of the equation.

    $$
    \begin{array}{rl}
    P & = 2L + 2W \\
    \underline{-2L} & \underline{-2L} \\
    P - 2L & = \quad\; 2W
    \end{array}
    $$

3. Divide both sides by 2.

    $$\frac{P - 2L}{2} = \frac{2W}{2}$$

    $$W = \frac{P - 2L}{2}$$

PRACTICE PROBLEMS

Solve each of the following equations for x.

1. $y = mx + b$

2. $ax + by = c$

3. $3ax + b^2 = 4b^2 - ax$

4. $\dfrac{a}{x} + \dfrac{b}{3x} = 1$

ANSWERS AND EXPLANATIONS

1.
$$y = mx + b$$
$$\underline{-b \qquad -b}$$
$$y - b = mx$$
$$\frac{y - b}{m} = \frac{mx}{m}$$
$$x = \frac{y - b}{m}$$

2.
$$ax + by = c$$
$$\underline{-by \qquad -by}$$
$$ax = c - by$$
$$\frac{ax}{a} = \frac{c - by}{a}$$
$$x = \frac{c - by}{a}$$

3.
$$3ax + b^2 = 4b^2 - ax$$
$$\underline{+ax \qquad\qquad +ax}$$
$$4ax + b^2 = 4b^2$$
$$\underline{-b^2 \qquad -b^2}$$
$$4ax = 3b^2$$
$$\frac{4ax}{4a} = \frac{3b^2}{4a}$$
$$x = \frac{3b^2}{4a}$$

4.
$$\frac{a}{x} + \frac{b}{3x} = 1$$
$$3x \cdot \frac{a}{x} + 3x \cdot \frac{b}{3x} = 3x \cdot 1$$
$$3a + b = 3x$$
$$\frac{3a + b}{3} = \frac{3x}{3}$$
$$x = \frac{3a + b}{3}$$

Solving Equations Simultaneously—Addition Method

To solve a linear equation containing two variables means to find a *pair* of numbers (one for each variable) which makes the equation true. Each pair is then called a root of the equation. For example, one root of the equation $x + y = 5$ is the pair $x = 1$, $y = 4$, and another root is the pair $x = 2$, $y = 3$.

Unlike linear equations in one variable, which have only one root, linear equations in two variables have an infinite number of roots.

Some Roots of	*Some Roots of*
$x + y = 3$	$x - y = 1$
$x = 0, y = 3$	$x = 0, y = -1$
$x = 1, y = 2$	$x = 1, y = 0$
$x = 2, y = 1$	$x = 2, y = 1$
$x = 3, y = 0$	$x = 3, y = 2$
$x = 4, y = -1$	$x = 4, y = 3$
etc.	etc.

As indicated by the dotted lines, the pair $x = 2$, $y = 1$ is a common root of both equations. This is an example of the fact that, except for a few special cases, two linear equations in two variables always have one common root. The exceptions will be discussed later.

The process of finding the common root of two equations in two variables is referred to as solving the equations **simultaneously**. There are two general methods for doing this. The idea behind the first method, called the **addition method**, is to eliminate one of the variables by adding the equations together. In our first example, note that the equations used are the same as those in the preceding example.

Example 1

Find the common root of the equations $x + y = 3$ and $x - y = 1$. Check the root in both equations.

Procedure

1. Write the equations with the like variables lined up and add them, thus eliminating the variable y.

$$\begin{array}{r} x + y = 3 \\ \underline{x - y = 1} \\ 2x \quad\;\; = 4 \end{array}$$

2. Solve the resulting equation for x.

$$\frac{\cancel{2}x}{\cancel{2}} = \frac{4}{2}$$

$$x = 2$$

3. Substitute this value for x into either one of the original equations.

$$\begin{array}{ll} x + y = 3 & \text{or} \quad x - y = 1 \\ 2 + y = 3 & \qquad\;\, 2 - y = 1 \end{array}$$

4. Solve the resulting equation for y.

$$2 + y = 3 \qquad \text{or} \qquad 2 - y = 1$$
$$\underline{-2 \qquad -2} \qquad\qquad \underline{-2 \qquad\quad -2}$$
$$y = 1 \qquad\qquad\qquad -y = -1$$
$$y = 1$$

Thus, $x = 2$, $y = 1$

5. Check the root by substituting it into both of the original equations.

$$x + y = 3 \qquad x - y = 1$$
$$? \qquad\qquad ?$$
$$2 + 1 = 3 \qquad 2 - 1 = 1$$
$$\checkmark \qquad\qquad \checkmark$$
$$3 = 3 \qquad\qquad 1 = 1$$

If adding the two equations does not eliminate one of the variables directly (as in the preceding example), then we must multiply either one or both of the equations by appropriate numbers so that one of the variables will have numerical coefficients that are opposite signed numbers (numbers with the same absolute values, but opposite signs).

Example 2

Solve the equations $3x + y = 7$ and $4x + 3y = 6$ simultaneously, and check the root in both equations.

Procedure

1. Write the equations with the like variables lined up.

$$3x + 7 = 7$$
$$4x + 3y = 6$$

2. To eliminate the variable y, multiply the top equation by -3. Leave the bottom equation as it is.

$$-3(3x + y = 7) \rightarrow -9x - 3y = -21$$
$$4x + 3y = 6 \rightarrow 4x + 3y = 6$$

3. Add the two equations.

$$-9x - 3y = -21$$
$$\underline{4x + 3y = 6}$$
$$-5x = -15$$

4. Solve the resulting equation for x.

$$\frac{-\cancel{5}x}{-\cancel{5}} = \frac{-15}{-5}$$
$$x = 3$$

135

5. Substitute this value for x into either one of the original equations, and solve the resulting equation for y.

$$3x + y = 7 \quad \text{(top equation)}$$
$$3(3) + y = 7$$
$$9 + y = 7$$
$$\underline{-9 \qquad -9}$$
$$y = -2$$

Thus, $x = 3$, $y = -2$

6. Check the root by substituting it into both of the original equations.

$$
\begin{array}{c|c}
3x + y = 7 & 4x + 3y = 6 \\
\overset{?}{3(3) + (-2) = 7} & \overset{?}{4(3) + 3(-2) = 6} \\
\overset{?}{9 - 2 = 7} & \overset{?}{12 - 6 = 6} \\
\overset{\checkmark}{7 = 7} & \overset{\checkmark}{6 = 6}
\end{array}
$$

Example 3

Solve the equations $2x = 3 - 3y$ and $2y = 13 - 5x$ simultaneously, and check the root in both equations.

Procedure

1. Using inverse operations, rewrite the equations with the variables on one side and the numbers on the other. (This is called **standard form**.)

$$
\begin{array}{c|c}
2x \quad\;\; = 3 - 3y & 2y = 13 - 5x \\
\underline{+3y \qquad +3y} & \underline{+5x \qquad\quad +5x} \\
2x + 3y = 3 & 5x + 2y = 13
\end{array}
$$

2. Write the resulting equations with the like variables lined up.

$$2x + 3y = 3$$
$$5x + 2y = 13$$

3. To eliminate the variable x (the choice is arbitrary), multiply the top equation by 5 (the coefficient of x in the bottom equation), and the bottom equation by -2 (the opposite of the coefficient of x in the top equation).

$$5(2x + 3y = 3) \rightarrow 10x + 15y = 15$$
$$-2(5x + 2y = 13) \rightarrow -10x - 4y = -26$$

4. Add the two equations, and solve the resulting equation for y.

$$10x + 15y = 15$$
$$\underline{-10x - 4y = -26}$$
$$11y = -11$$
$$\frac{\cancel{11}y}{\cancel{11}} = \frac{-11}{11}$$
$$y = -1$$

5. Substitute this value for y into either one of the original equations, and solve the resulting equation for x.

$$2x = 3 - 3y \qquad (\text{top equation})$$
$$2x = 3 - 3(-1)$$
$$2x = 3 + 3$$
$$2x = 6$$
$$\frac{\cancel{2}x}{\cancel{2}} = \frac{6}{2}$$
$$x = 3$$

Thus, $x = 3$, $y = -1$

6. Check the root by substituting it into both of the original equations.

$$
\begin{array}{c|c}
2x = 3 - 3y & 2y = 13 - 5x \\
2(3) \overset{?}{=} 3 - 3(-1) & 2(-1) \overset{?}{=} 13 - 5(3) \\
6 \overset{?}{=} 3 + 3 & -2 \overset{?}{=} 13 - 15 \\
6 \overset{\checkmark}{=} 6 & -2 \overset{\checkmark}{=} -2
\end{array}
$$

PRACTICE PROBLEMS

Solve each of the following pairs of equations simultaneously.

1. $2x + y = 8$
   $x - y = 1$

2. $3x - 2y = 17$
   $2x + y = 9$

3. $5x + 3y = 28$
   $7x - 2y = 2$

4. $3x = 2y - 18$
   $4y = 8 - x$

ANSWERS AND EXPLANATIONS

1.
$$2x + y = 8$$
$$\underline{x - y = 1}$$
$$3x \quad\ = 9$$

$$\frac{\cancel{3}x}{\cancel{3}} = \frac{9}{3}$$

$$x = 3$$

Substitute into second equation.

$$x - y = 1$$
$$3 - y = 1$$
$$\underline{-3 \qquad -3}$$
$$-y = -2$$

$$\frac{-y}{-1} = \frac{-2}{-1}$$

$$y = 2$$

Thus, $x = 3$, $y = 2$.

2.
$$3x - 2y = 17$$
$$2(2x + y = 9) \rightarrow 4x + 2y = 18$$

$$3x - 2y = 17$$
$$\underline{4x + 2y = 18}$$
$$7x \qquad = 35$$

$$\frac{\cancel{7}x}{\cancel{7}} = \frac{35}{7}$$

$$x = 5$$

Substitute into second equation.

$$2x + y = 9$$
$$2(5) + y = 9$$
$$10 + y = 9$$
$$\underline{-10 \qquad -10}$$
$$y = -1$$

Thus, $x = 5$, $y = -1$.

3. $2(5x + 3y = 28) \rightarrow 10x + 6y = 56$

   $3(7x - 2y = 2) \rightarrow 21x - 6y = 6$

   $10x + 6y = 56$

   $\underline{21x - 6y = 6}$

   $31x = 62$

   $\dfrac{\cancel{31}x}{\cancel{31}} = \dfrac{62}{31}$

   $x = 2$

   Substitute into first equation.

   $5x + 3y = 28$

   $5(2) + 3y = 28$

   $10 + 3y = 28$

   $\underline{-10 -10}$

   $3y = 18$

   $\dfrac{\cancel{3}y}{\cancel{3}} = \dfrac{18}{3}$

   $y = 6$

   Thus, $x = 2$, $y = 6$.

4. $3x = 2y - 18$ or $3x - 2y = -18$

   $4y = 8 - x$ or $x + 4y = 8$

   $2(3x - 2y = -18) \rightarrow 6x - 4y = -36$

   $6x - 4y = -36$

   $\underline{x + 4y = 8}$

   $7x = -28$

   $\dfrac{\cancel{7}x}{\cancel{7}} = \dfrac{-28}{7}$

   $x = -4$

   Substitute into second equation.

   $x + 4y = 8$

   $-4 + 4y = 8$

   $\underline{+4 +4}$

   $4y = 12$

   $\dfrac{\cancel{4}y}{\cancel{4}} = \dfrac{12}{4}$

   $y = 3$

   Thus, $x = -4$, $y = 3$.

SOLVING EQUATIONS SIMULTANEOUSLY—SUBSTITUTION METHOD

A second method of solving equations simultaneously is called the **substitution method**. The idea behind this method is to eliminate one of the variables by substituting an expression given for it by one of the equations into the other equation. This method is particularly useful when one of the equations has a form, such as $y = 2x + 1$ or $x = 3y - 5$, in which one of the variables is expressed directly in terms of the other variable.

Example

Solve $y = 2x - 1$ and $x + 3y = 11$ simultaneously, and check the roots in both equations.

Procedure

1. Substitute the expression given for y by the first equation ($y = 2 - 1$) into the second equation, thus eliminating the variable y.

$$y = 2x - 1$$
$$x + 3y = 11$$
$$x + 3(2x - 1) = 11$$

2. Solve the resulting equation for x.

$$x + 3(2x - 1) = 11$$
$$x + 6x - 3 = 11$$
$$7x - 3 = 11$$
$$\underline{\quad +3 \quad +3\quad}$$
$$7x = 14$$
$$\frac{7x}{7} = \frac{14}{7}$$
$$x = 2$$

3. To obtain y, substitute this value for x into the equation originally eliminated.

$$y = 2x - 1$$
$$y = 2(2) - 1$$
$$y = 4 - 1$$
$$y = 3$$

Thus, $x = 2$, $y = 3$

4. Check the root by substituting it into both of the original equations.

$$
\begin{array}{c|c}
y = 2x - 1 & x + 3y = 11 \\
\overset{?}{} & \overset{?}{} \\
(3) \overset{?}{=} 2(2) - 1 & (2) + 3(3) \overset{?}{=} 11 \\
3 \overset{?}{=} 4 - 1 & 2 + 9 \overset{?}{=} 11 \\
\checkmark & \checkmark \\
3 = 3 & 11 = 11
\end{array}
$$

PRACTICE PROBLEMS

Solve each of the following pairs of equations simultaneously.

1. $y = 3x$
    $x + 2y = 42$

2. $x = 2y$
    $4x - 9y = 3$

3. $y = 3x + 1$
    $x + y = 9$

4. $x = 2y - 3$
    $5x - y = 3$

ANSWERS AND EXPLANATIONS

1. $y = 3x$

    $x + 2y = 42$

    Thus, substituting:

    $$x + 2(3x) = 42$$
    $$x + \quad 6x = 42$$
    $$7x = 42$$
    $$\frac{\cancel{7}x}{\cancel{7}} = \frac{42}{7}$$
    $$x = 6$$

    Substitute into first equation.
    $y = 3x$
    $y = 3(6)$
    $y = 18$
    Thus, $x = 6$, $y = 18$.

2. $x = 2y$
    $4x - 9y = 3$
    Thus, substituting:

    $$4(2y) - 9y = 3$$
    $$8y - 9y = 3$$
    $$-y = 3$$
    $$\frac{\cancel{-}y}{-\cancel{1}} = \frac{3}{-1}$$
    $$y = -3$$

    Substitute into first equation.
    $x = 2y$
    $x = 2(-3)$
    $x = -6$
    Thus, $x = -6$, $y = -3$.

3. $y = 3x + 1$
    $x + y = 9$
    Thus, substituting:

$$x + (3x + 1) = 9$$
$$4x + 1 = 9$$
$$\underline{-1 \quad -1}$$
$$4x = 8$$
$$\frac{\cancel{4}x}{\cancel{4}} = \frac{8}{4}$$
$$x = 2$$

Substitute into first equation:
$y = 3x + 1$
$y = 3(2) + 1 = 7$
Thus, $x = 2$, $y = 7$.

4. $x = 2y - 3$
    $5x - y = 3$
    Thus, substituting:

$$5(2y - 3) - y = 3$$
$$10y - 15 - y = 3$$
$$9y - 15 = 3$$
$$\underline{+15 \qquad +15}$$
$$9y = 18$$
$$\frac{\cancel{9}y}{\cancel{9}} = \frac{18}{9}$$
$$y = 2$$

Substitute into first equation:
$x = 2y - 3$
$x = 2(2) - 3 = 1$
Thus, $x = 1$, $y = 2$.

As previously noted, there are a few special cases in which two linear equations in two variables do *not* have one common root. These special cases fall into two categories—inconsistent equations and dependent equations.

Inconsistent equations are equations, such as $x + y = 3$ and $x + y = 4$, which are impossible to solve simultaneously (the sum of x and y cannot be both 3 and 4 at the same time), and thus have *no roots* in common.

Dependent equations are equations, such as $x + y = 5$ and $2x + 2y = 10$, which are not really different from each other (one equation is simply a multiple of the other), and thus have *all their roots* in common.

SOLVING LINEAR INEQUALITIES IN ONE VARIABLE

An **inequality** is a mathematical statement in which two quantities are related by one of the following signs: > (greater than), ≥ (greater than or equal to), < (less than), or ≤ (less than or equal to).

Linear inequalities in one variable, like linear equations in one variable, are solved by the method of inverse operations. However, when solving inequalities, one additional principle must be observed.

Inequality Principle

When *multiplying* or *dividing* both sides of an inequality by a *negative number*, the direction of the inequality sign must be reversed.

This principle is demonstrated below. Notice that when we multiply or divide by 2, the direction of the inequality sign remains the same, but that when we multiply or divide by -2, the direction of the inequality sign must be reversed in order to make the resulting inequality true.

Multiply by 2	*Divide by 2*	*Multiply by -2*	*Divide by -2*
$8 > 6$	$8 > 6$	$8 > 6$	$8 > 6$
$2(8) > 2(6)$	$\dfrac{8}{2} > \dfrac{6}{2}$	$\downarrow$	$\downarrow$
$16 > 12$	$4 > 3$	$-2(8) < -2(6)$	$\dfrac{8}{-2} < \dfrac{6}{-2}$
		$-16 < -12$	$-4 < -3$

After an inequality is solved, its roots can be displayed graphically on a number line in the following way:

To Graph the Roots of an Inequality:
1. At the point representing the upper or lower limit of the roots, draw a small circle. If this number is included in the roots, blacken in the circle; if not, leave the circle empty.
2. If all the other roots are less than this number, draw an arrow from the circle to the left. If all the other roots are greater than this number, draw an arrow from the circle to the right.

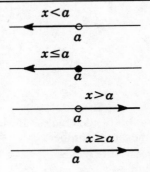

Example 1

Solve $2x - 5 < 3$, and represent the roots on a number line.

Procedure

1. Add 5 to both sides of the inequality.

$$
\begin{array}{rcl}
2x - 5 &<& 3 \\
\underline{+5} & & \underline{+5} \\
2x &<& 8
\end{array}
$$

2. Divide both sides by 2.

$$
\frac{\cancel{2}x}{\cancel{2}} < \frac{8}{2}
$$

$$
x < 4
$$

3. On a number line, draw an empty circle at 4. Draw an arrow from the circle to the left.

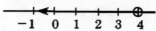

Example 2

Solve $\dfrac{x}{6} - \dfrac{x}{2} \leq 1$, and represent the roots on a number line.

Procedure

1. Multiply both sides of the inequality by 6, a common denominator of $\dfrac{x}{6}$ and $\dfrac{x}{2}$. Cancel the denominators, and combine like terms.

$$
\frac{x}{6} - \frac{x}{2} \leq 1
$$

$$
6\left(\frac{x}{6} - \frac{x}{2}\right) \leq 6(1)
$$

$$
\cancel{6} \cdot \frac{x}{\cancel{6}} - \overset{3}{\cancel{6}} \cdot \frac{x}{2} \leq 6
$$

$$
x - 3x \leq 6
$$

$$
-2x \leq 6
$$

2. Divide both sides by -2 and reverse the direction of the inequality sign (dividing by a negative number).

$$
\frac{\cancel{-2}x}{\cancel{-2}} \geq \frac{6}{-2}
$$

$$
x \geq -3
$$

3. On a number line, draw a blackened circle at -3. Draw an arrow from the circle to the right.

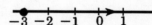

PRACTICE PROBLEMS

Solve each of the following inequalities for x.

1. $3x - 4 > 14$
2. $12 - 2x \geq 4$
3. $6x + 1 < 3(x - 2)$
4. $\dfrac{x}{3} - \dfrac{x}{2} \geq 5$

ANSWERS AND EXPLANATIONS

1. $3x - 4 > 14$

   $\underline{\quad +4 \qquad -4 \quad}$

   $3x \quad > \quad 18$

   $\dfrac{\cancel{3}x}{\cancel{3}} > \dfrac{18}{3}$

   $x > 6$

2. $12 - 2x \geq 4$

   $\underline{-12 \qquad\quad -12}$

   $-2x \geq -8$

   $\dfrac{\cancel{-2}x}{\cancel{-2}} \geq \dfrac{-8}{-2}$

   $x \leq 4$

3. $6x + 1 < 3(x - 2)$

   $6x + 1 < 3x - 6$

   $\underline{-3x \qquad\quad -3x \quad}$

   $3x - 1 < \qquad -6$

   $\underline{\quad -1 \qquad\quad -1 \quad}$

   $3x \quad < \qquad -7$

   $\dfrac{\cancel{3}x}{\cancel{3}} < \dfrac{-7}{3}$

   $x < -2\dfrac{1}{3}$

4. $\dfrac{x}{3} - \dfrac{x}{2} \geq 5$

   $^2\cancel{6} \cdot \dfrac{x}{\cancel{3}} - {}^3\cancel{6} \cdot \dfrac{x}{\cancel{2}} \geq 6 \cdot 5$

   $2x - 3x \geq 30$

   $\dfrac{\cancel{-}x}{\cancel{-1}} \geq \dfrac{30}{-1}$

   $x \leq -30$

145

FACTORING

As you recall, the numbers used in multiplication are called **factors**, and the result is called the **product**. For example, in the statement $5 \cdot 4 = 20$, 5 and 4 are factors, and 20 is the product. If we reverse this statement and write $20 = 5 \cdot 4$, we say that we have "factored" 20 into 5 times 4. In other words, **factoring** is the process of writing a number, or algebraic expression, as a product of factors.

$$\xrightarrow{\text{Multiplication}}$$
$$5 \cdot 4 = 10$$
$$\xleftarrow{\text{Factoring}}$$

The particular method used to factor an algebraic expression is based on the type of expression that is given. We will examine methods for factoring three types of expressions: 1. polynomials having a common monomial factor, 2. trinomials of the general form $ax^2 + bx + c$, and 3. binomials of the general form $A^2 - B^2$, called the difference of two squares.

FACTORING POLYNOMIALS HAVING A COMMON MONOMIAL FACTOR

To multiply a polynomial by a monomial, we use the distributive law and multiply each term in the polynomial by the monomial:

$$\boxed{\begin{array}{c} \textit{Distributive Law} \\ \underrightarrow{A(B + C)} = AB + AC \end{array}}$$

For example, $5a(x + y^3 - z^2) = 5ax + 5ay^3 - 5az^2$

The monomial, $5a$, is a common factor in each of the terms of the resulting polynomial. Therefore, to factor a polynomial whose terms have a common monomial factor, we use the distributive law in reverse, and write the polynomial as the product of the common monomial factor and another polynomial. That is,

$$5ax + 5ay^3 - 5az^2 = 5a(x + y^3 - z^2)$$

This process is sometimes referred to as "factoring out" the common monomial factor.

In general, to factor out a common monomial factor from a polynomial, use the following procedure.

To Factor a Polynomial Having a Common Monomial Factor:
1. Write the common monomial factor next to a pair of parentheses.
2. Divide this factor into each of the terms of the given polynomial, and write the resulting terms inside the parentheses.

For example,

$$6x^3 + 10xy^2$$
$$= 2x(\qquad\qquad)$$
$$= 2x(3x^2 + 5y^2)$$

$$\nearrow \qquad \nwarrow$$

$$\boxed{\dfrac{6x^3}{2x}} \quad + \quad \boxed{\dfrac{10xy^2}{2x}}$$

After completing this procedure, two checks should be made. First, multiply the common monomial factor by the polynomial inside the parentheses to verify that their product is the given polynomial. Second, look at the polynomial inside the parentheses to see if any common factors remain. If so, repeat the procedure and factor them out. If not, then the **greatest common factor** (g.c.f) has been factored out. For example, in the expression shown below, after factoring out the common monomial factor $3x$, the polynomial inside the parentheses, $x + 2x^2y$, still has a common factor of x. After factoring out x, no common factors remain, and thus $3x^2$, the greatest common factor, has been factored out.

$$3x^2 + 6x^3y$$
$$= 3x\left(x + 2x^2y\right)$$
$$= 3x^2\left(1 + 2xy\right)$$
$$\uparrow$$
$$\text{g.c.f}$$

Example
Factor $6x^2y^2 + 9xy^3 - 3xy^2$.

Procedure

1. By looking at the numerical and variable factors of each of the terms, notice that $3xy^2$ is a common factor. Write this factor next to a pair of parentheses.

$$6x^2y^2 + 9xy^3 - 3xy^2$$
$$= 3xy^2\left(\qquad\qquad\right)$$

2. Divide $3xy^2$ into each of the terms of the given polynomial, and write the resulting terms inside the parentheses.

$$= 3xy^2\left(2x + 3y - 1\right)$$
$$\nearrow \quad \uparrow \quad \nwarrow$$
$$\boxed{\dfrac{6x^2y^2}{3xy^2}} + \boxed{\dfrac{9xy^3}{3xy^2}} - \boxed{\dfrac{3xy^2}{3xy^2}}$$

PRACTICE PROBLEMS

Factor out the common monomial factor from each of the following polynomials.

1. $2a^2x + 4ab$
2. $6x^2y^3 - 9x^2y$
3. $5xy^2 + 10x^2y^2 - 15xy^3$
4. $a^2b^2 - 3a^5b^3 - a^2b$

ANSWERS AND EXPLANATIONS

1. $2a^2x + 4ab = 2a(ax + 2b)$
2. $6x^2y^3 - 9x^2y = 3x^2y(2y^2 - 3)$
3. $5xy^2 + 10x^2y^2 - 15xy^3 = 5xy^2(1 + 2x - 3y)$
4. $a^2b^2 - 3a^5b^3 - a^2b = a^2b(b - 3a^3b^2 - 1)$

FACTORING TRINOMIALS OF THE GENERAL FORM $ax^2 + bx + c$

One of the methods used to multiply binomials is called the FOIL method (First, Outer, Inner, Last). As illustrated in the example below, the first term in the result is obtained by multiplying the First terms in the binomials, A and C, the second term in the result is obtained by multiplying the Outer terms in the binomials, A and D, the third term in the result is obtained by multiplying the Inner terms of the binomials, B and C, and the fourth term in the result is obtained by multiplying the Last terms in the binomials, B and D.

$$
\textbf{\textit{The FOIL Method of Multiplying Binomials}}
$$

$$
(A+B)(C+D) = AC + AD + BC + BD
$$

$$
\text{First} \quad \text{Outer} \quad \text{Inner} \quad \text{Last}
$$

When we use the FOIL method to multiply binomials, such as $(3x + 1)$ and $(2x + 5)$, whose First terms are like variable terms, and whose Last terms are numbers, we find that the Outer and Inner products always combine, leaving a trinomial of the general form $ax^2 + bx + c$, where a, b, and c are specific signed numbers. Consider the following examples.

$$
(3x+1)(2x+5) = 6x^2 + 15x + 2x + 5
$$
$$
= 6x^2 + 17x + 5
$$

$$
(x-6)(x+4) = x^2 + 4x - 6x - 24
$$
$$
= x^2 - 2x - 24
$$

$$
(2x-3)(x-2) = 2x^2 - 4x - 3x + 6
$$
$$
= 2x^2 - 7x + 6
$$

Therefore, to factor a trinomial of the form $ax^2 + bx + c$, we must reverse the FOIL procedure and write the trinomial as the product of two binomial factors of the form $(mx + n)$ and $(rx + s)$, where m, n, r, and s are also specific signed numbers. That is, $ax^2 + bx + c = (mx + n)(rx + s)$

In general, to find the two binomial factors, $(mx + n)$ and $(rx + s)$, we use the procedure on the following page.

> **To Factor Trinomials of the Form $ax^2 + bx + c$ Having Binomial Factors of the Form $(mx + n)$ and $(rx + s)$, where a, b, c, m, n, r, and s, are Specific Signed Numbers:**
> 1. As the First terms of two binomial factors, write all possible terms, mx and rx, whose product is ax^2, the first term of the given trinomial.
> 2. As the Last terms of the binomial factors, write all possible pairs of numbers, n and s, whose product is c, the third (last) term of the given trinomial.
> 3. Combine the Outer and Inner products of all the possible binomial factors, and choose the combination that gives bx, the second (middle) term of the given trinomial.

Example 1

Factor $x^2 - 5x + 6$.

Procedure

1. Write x as the First term of two binomial factors.

$$(x \quad)(x \quad)$$

2. As the Last terms of the two binomials, write all possible pairs of numbers whose product is $+6$, the last term of the given trinomial. Note that the signs of the numbers must be the same, both $+$ or both $-$.

$$(x+1)(x+6)$$
$$(x-1)(x-6)$$
$$(x+2)(x+3)$$
$$(x-2)(x-3)$$

3. Combine the Outer and Inner products of, each possibility, and choose the combination that gives $-5x$, the middle term of the given trinomial.

$$(x+1)(x+6) \quad +6x+x = +7x$$
$$(x-1)(x-6) \quad -6x-x = -7x$$
$$(x+2)(x+3) \quad +3x+2x = +5x$$
$$(x-2)(x-3) \quad -3x-2x = \boxed{-5x}$$

$$x^2 - 5x + 6 = (x-2)(x-3)$$

Example 2

Factor $x^2 + 4x - 5$.

Procedure

1. Write x as the First term of two binomial factors.

    $$(\overset{\overbrace{\quad x^2 \quad}}{x}\quad)(x\quad)$$

2. As the Last terms of the two binomials, write all possible pairs of numbers whose product is -5, the last term of the given trinomial. Note that the signs of the numbers must be different, one $+$ and one $-$.

    $$(x+1)(x\overset{\overbrace{-5}}{-5})$$

    $$(x-1)(x\overset{\overbrace{-5}}{+5})$$

3. Combine the Outer and Inner products of each possibility, and choose the combination that gives $+4x$, the middle term of the given trinomial.

    $$(x+1)(x-5) \quad -5x+x=-4x$$

    $$(x-1)(x+5) \quad +5x-x=\boxed{+4x}$$

Example 3

Factor $x^2 - 8x + 12$.

Procedure

1. Write x as the First term of two binomial factors.

    $$(\overset{\overbrace{\quad x^2 \quad}}{x}\quad)(x\quad)$$

2. As the Last terms of the two binomials, write all possible pairs of numbers whose product is $+12$, the last term of the given trinomial. Note that the signs of the numbers must be the same, both $+$ or both $-$.

    $$(x + 1)(x + 12)$$
    $$(x - 1)(x - 12)$$
    $$(x + 2)(x + 6\ )$$
    $$(x - 2)(x - 6\ )$$
    $$(x + 3)(x + 4)$$
    $$(x - 3)(x - 4)$$

3. Combine the Outer and Inner products of each possibility, and choose the combination that gives $-8x$, the middle term of the given trinomial. (Note that only the correct combination is shown.)

    $$(x-2)(x-6) \quad -6x-2x=\boxed{-8x}$$

    $$x^2 - 8x + 12 = (x - 2)(x - 6)$$

Example 4

Factor $2x^2 + 5x + 3$.

Procedure

1. Write $2x$ as the First term of one binomial factor, and x as the First term of another binomial factor.

$$(2x \overset{\overset{\displaystyle -2x^2-}{}}{})(x \quad)$$

2. As the Last terms of the two binomials, write all possible pairs of numbers whose product is $+3$, the last term of the given trinomial. Notice that, since the First terms are not both x, we must consider each pair of numbers twice.

$$(2x+1)\overset{\overset{\displaystyle -+3-}{}}{(x+3)}$$

$$(2x+3)\overset{\overset{\displaystyle -+3-}{}}{(x+1)}$$

$$(2x-1)\overset{\overset{\displaystyle -+3-}{}}{(x-3)}$$

$$(2x-3)\overset{\overset{\displaystyle -+3-}{}}{(x-1)}$$

3. Combine the Outer and Inner products of each possibility, and choose the combination that gives $+5x$, the middle term of the given trinomial.

$$(2x+1)(x+3) \qquad +6x+x = +7x$$

$$(2x+3)(x+1) \qquad +2x+3x = \boxed{+5x}$$

$$(2x-1)(x-3) \qquad -6x-x = -7x$$

$$(2x-3)(x-1) \qquad -2x-3x = -5x$$

$$2x^2 + 5x + 3 = (2x+3)(x+1)$$

In the preceding examples, we noted certain relationships between the signs in the trinomials and the signs in the binomial factors:

> When factoring trinomials of the form $ax^2 + bx + c$, in which a is positive, look at the sign of the last term, c.
> 1. If the sign of c is *positive*, then the signs of both numbers in the binomial factors will be the *same* as bx, the middle term of the trinomial.
> 2. If the sign of c is *negative*, then the signs of the numbers in the binomial factors will be *different*, one positive and one negative.

Both Positive	*Both Negative*	*Different*
$2x^2 + 5x \,(+)\, 3$	$x^2 - 5x \,(+)\, 6$	$x^2 + 4x - 5$
$= (2x + 3)(x + 1)$	$= (x - 2)(x - 3)$	$= (x - 1)(x + 5)$

PRACTICE PROBLEMS

Factor the following trinomials.

1. $x^2 + 8x + 15$
2. $x^2 - 8x + 12$
3. $x^2 - 4x - 12$
4. $x^2 + 3x - 10$
5. $x^2 - 9x + 14$
6. $3x^2 + 7x + 2$
7. $2x^2 - 5x + 2$
8. $2x^2 + x - 3$

ANSWERS AND EXPLANATIONS

1. $x^2 + 8x + 15 =$

   ┌─ $+5x$ ─┐
   $(x + 3)(x + 5)$ $+5x + 3x = +8x$
   └─ $+3x$ ─┘

2. $x^2 - 8x + 12 =$

   ┌─ $-6x$ ─┐
   $(x - 2)(x - 6)$ $-6x - 2x = -8x$
   └─ $-2x$ ─┘

3. $x^2 - 4x - 12 =$

   ┌─ $-6x$ ─┐
   $(x + 2)(x - 6)$ $-6x + 2x = -4x$
   └─ $+2x$ ─┘

4. $x^2 + 3x - 10 =$

   ┌─ $-2x$ ─┐
   $(x + 5)(x - 2)$ $-2x + 5x = +3x$
   └─ $+5x$ ─┘

5. $x^2 - 9x + 14 =$

   ┌─ $-7x$ ─┐
   $(x - 2)(x - 7)$ $-7x - 2x = -9x$
   └─ $-2x$ ─┘

6. $3x^2 + 7x + 2 =$

   ┌─ $+6x$ ─┐
   $(3x + 1)(x + 2)$ $+6x + 1x = +7x$
   └─ $+1x$ ─┘

7. $2x^2 - 5x + 2 =$

   ┌─ $-4x$ ─┐
   $(2x - 1)(x - 2)$ $-4x - 1x = -5x$
   └─ $-1x$ ─┘

8. $2x^2 + x - 3 =$

   ┌─ $-2x$ ─┐
   $(2x + 3)(x - 1)$ $-2x + 3x = +1x$
   └─ $+3x$ ─┘

FACTORING THE DIFFERENCE OF TWO SQUARES $a^2 - b^2$

When using the FOIL method to multiply the sum of two terms, (A + B), by the difference of the same two terms, (A − B), the Outer and Inner products always cancel each other, leaving a binomial of the general form $A^2 - B^2$.

$$(x+8)\ (x-8) = x^2 - 8x + 8x - 64$$
$$= x^2 - 64$$

$$(5x+3y)(5x-3y) = 25x^2 - 15xy + 15xy - 9y^2$$
$$= 25x^2 - 9y^2$$

$$(3x+7)\ (3x-7) = 9x^2 - 21x + 21x - 49$$
$$= 9x^2 - 49$$

Therefore, to factor a binomial of the form $a^2 - b^2$, called the **difference of two squares**, again reverse the FOIL procedure and write the binomial as the product of the two factors $(a + b)$ and $(a - b)$. That is, $a^2 - b^2 = (a + b)(a - b)$.

In general, to find the two factors, $(a + b)$ and $(a - b)$, use the procedure given below.

To Factor the Difference of Two Squares: $a^2 - b^2$

1. Take the square root of the first term of the given expression, and write the result as the First term of two binomial factors.
2. Take the square root of the second term of the given expression, and write the result as the Last term of the two binomial factors.
3. In one of the binomial factors, join the terms with a + sign, and in the other binomial factor, join the terms with a − sign.

$$\text{Factor}: x^2 - 9$$
$$\sqrt{x^2} = x$$
$$(x\ \ )(x\ \ )$$
$$\sqrt{9} = 3$$
$$(x\ \ 3)(x\ \ 3)$$
$$(x + 3)(x - 3)$$
$$x^2 - 9 = (x + 3)(x - 3)$$

Example
Factor $49x^4 - 81y^2$.

Procedure

1. Take the square roots of the two given terms, and write the results as the First and Last terms of two binomial factors. In one of the binomials, join the terms with a + sign, and in the other binomial, join the terms with a − sign.

$$\sqrt{49x^4} = 7x^2$$
$$\sqrt{81y^2} = 9y$$
$$\text{Thus, } 49x^4 - 81y^2 = \left(7x^2 + 9y\right)\left(7x^2 - 9y\right)$$

PRACTICE PROBLEMS

Factor the following binomials.

1. $x^2 - 64y^2$
2. $4x^2 - 9y^2$
3. $a^2x^2 - 25b^2y^2$
4. $49x^4 - y^2$

ANSWERS AND EXPLANATIONS

1. $x^2 - 64y^2 = \left(\sqrt{x^2} + \sqrt{64y^2}\right)\left(\sqrt{x^2} - \sqrt{64y^2}\right)$
$$= (x + 8y)(x - 8y)$$

2. $4x^2 - 9y^2 = \left(\sqrt{4x^2} + \sqrt{9y^2}\right)\left(\sqrt{4x^2} - \sqrt{9y^2}\right)$
$$= (2x + 3y)(2x - 3y)$$

3. $a^2x^2 - 25b^2y^2 =$
$$\left(\sqrt{a^2x^2} + \sqrt{25b^2y^2}\right)\left(\sqrt{a^2y^2} - \sqrt{25b^2y^2}\right)$$
$$= (ax + 5by)(ax - 5by)$$

4. $49x^4 - y^2 = \left(\sqrt{49x^4} + \sqrt{y^2}\right)\left(\sqrt{49x^4} - \sqrt{y^2}\right)$
$$= \left(7x^2 + y\right)\left(7x^2 - y\right)$$

FACTORING EXPRESSIONS COMPLETELY

The three types of expressions we have factored are summarized below.

> *Polynomials Having a Common Monomial Factor:*
> $$ab + ac + ... + ar = a(b + c + ... + r)$$
>
> *Trinomials of the Form:* $ax^2 + bx + c$
> $$ax^2 + bx + c = (mx + n)(rx + s)$$
> where a, b, c, m, n, r, and s are
> specific signed numbers.
>
> *The Difference of Two Squares:* $a^2 - b^2$
> $$a^2 - b^2 = (a + b)(a - b)$$

Sometimes, after an expression has been factored, one or more of its resulting polynomial factors can be factored further. This is illustrated in the example below. Notice that after factoring out a common monomial factor of $5x$, the resulting polynomial factor, $x^2 - 16$, is the difference of two squares, which can be factored further.

$$5x^3 - 80x = 5x\left(x^2 - 16\right)$$
$$= 5x\left(x + 4\right)\left(x - 4\right)$$

When an expression cannot be factored further, like the final result above, it is said to be **factored completely**.

Example 1
Factor $x^4y + 2x^3y - 15x^2y$ completely.

Procedure

1. Factor out the common monomial factor, x^2y.
$$x^2y + 2x^3y - 15x^2y$$
$$= x^2y(x^2 + 2x - 15)$$

2. Factor the trinomial in the parentheses.
$$= x^2y(x + 5)(x - 3)$$

Example 2
Factor $x^4 - y^4$ completely.

Procedure

1. Factor the difference of two squares.
$$x^4 - y^2$$
$$= (x^2 + y^2)(x^2 - y^2)$$

2. Factor the expression in the right parentheses, which is also the difference of two squares.
$$= (x^2 + y^2)(x + y)(x - y)$$

PRACTICE PROBLEMS

Factor the following expressions completely.

1. $3x^2y + 9xy + 6y$

2. $x^3 - 16x$

3. $5x^3 + 5x^2 - 30x$

4. $50x^2 - 8y^2$

ANSWERS AND EXPLANATIONS

1. $3x^2y + 9xy + 6y = 3y\left(x^2 + 3x + 2\right)$
    $$= 3y(x+1)(x+2)$$

2. $x^3 - 16x = x\left(x^2 - 16\right)$
    $$= x(x+4)(x-4)$$

3. $5x^3 + 5x^2 - 30x = 5x\left(x^2 + x - 6\right)$
    $$= 5x(x-2)(x+3)$$

4. $50x^2 - 8y^2 = 2\left(25x^2 - 4y^2\right)$
    $$= 2(5x + 2y)(5x - 2y)$$

SOLVING QUADRATIC EQUATIONS BY FACTORING

Equations such as $x^2 = 2x + 3$ and $5x - 6 = x^2$, in which the highest power of the variable is *two*, are called **second degree**, or **quadratic equations**.

When a quadratic equation is written in a form such that one side of the equation is 0, and the other side of the equation has the variable terms arranged in descending order of their powers, the equation is said to be written in **standard form**.

> *Standard Form*
> $ax^2 + bx + c = 0$

There are several methods of solving quadratic equations. One method is based on the following principle:

> *Zero Product Principle*
> If the product of two factors is equal to 0, then at least one of the factors is equal to 0. If $A \cdot B = 0$, then $A = 0$, $B = 0$, or A and B = 0.

To demonstrate the method, let us solve the quadratic equation $x^2 + 2 = 3x$. First, by using inverse operations, rewrite the equation in standard form. The purpose of this step is to get 0 on one side of the equation. Thus,

$$
\begin{array}{rcr}
x^2 + 2 & = & 3x \\
-3x & & -3x \\
\hline
x^2 - 3x + 2 & = & 0
\end{array}
$$

Then, by factoring the expression on the left side of the equation, transform the equation into a product of factors equal to 0. That is,

$$x^2 - 3x + 2 = 0$$
$$(x-1)(x-2) = 0$$

Finally, by using the zero product principle stated above, set each factor equal to 0, and solve for x. Since the values of x that make the factors equal to 0, also make the product equal to 0, these values will also be the roots of the original quadratic equation. Therefore,

$$x^2 - 3x + 2 = 0$$
$$(x-1)(x-2) = 0$$

$$
\begin{array}{c|c}
x - 1 = 0 & x - 2 = 0 \\
\underline{+1 \quad +1} & \underline{+2 \quad +2} \\
x \quad = 1 & x \quad = 2
\end{array}
$$

$$x = 1, \ x = 2$$

To check the roots obtained, substitute each one separately into the original equation:

$$\underline{x = 1}$$
$$x^2 + 2 \overset{?}{=} 3x$$
$$(1)^2 + 2 \overset{?}{=} 3(1)$$
$$1 + 2 \overset{\checkmark}{=} 3$$
$$3 = 3$$

$$\underline{x = 2}$$
$$x^2 + 2 \overset{?}{=} 3x$$
$$(2)^2 + 2 \overset{?}{=} 3(2)$$
$$4 + 2 \overset{\checkmark}{=} 6$$
$$6 = 6$$

As this example demonstrates, most quadratic equations have two distinct roots. There are, however, some quadratic equations which have only one root. For example, consider the equation $x^2 - 6x + 9 = 0$. When we factor this equation, we get $(x - 3)(x - 3) = 0$. Since both factors are the same, they both lead to the same root, $x = 3$.

The method just demonstrated for solving quadratic equations by factoring is summarized below. Not all quadratic equations are factorable, and thus other methods must be used. These methods, however, will not be discussed here.

To Solve a Quadratic Equation by Factoring:
1. Rewrite the equation in standard form: $ax^2 + bx + c = 0$.
2. Factor the expression on the left side of the equation.
3. Set each factor equal to 0, and solve the resulting linear equations.

Example 1

Solve $3x^2 - 12 = x(1 + 2x)$, and check the roots.

Procedure

1. Using the distributive law, eliminate the parentheses. Rewrite the equation in standard form.

$$3x^2 - 12 = x(1 + 2x)$$
$$3x^2 - 12 = x + 2x^2$$
$$\underline{-2x^2 \qquad \qquad -2x^2}$$
$$x^2 - 12 = x$$
$$\underline{\quad -x \qquad -x \quad}$$
$$x^2 - x - 12 = 0$$

2. Factor the expression on the left side of the equation.

$$x^2 - x - 12 = 0$$
$$(x - 4)(x + 3) = 0$$

3. Set each factor equal to 0, and solve the resulting linear equations for x.

$$
\begin{array}{c|c}
x - 4 = 0 & x + 3 = 0 \\
\underline{+4 \quad +4} & \underline{-3 \quad -3} \\
x \quad = 4 & x \quad = -3
\end{array}
$$

$$x = 4, \ x = -3$$

4. Check each root separately by substituting it into the original equation.

$$\textit{Check } x = 4$$
$$3x^2 - 12 = x(1 + 2x)$$
$$3(4)^2 - 12 \overset{?}{=} 4(1 + 2(4))$$
$$3(16) - 12 \overset{?}{=} 4(1 + 8)$$
$$48 - 12 \overset{?}{=} 4(9)$$
$$\overset{\checkmark}{36 = 36}$$

$$\textit{Check } x = -3$$
$$3x^2 - 12 = x(1 + 2x)$$
$$3(-3)^2 - 12 \overset{?}{=} -3(2(-3) + 1)$$
$$3(9) - 12 \overset{?}{=} -3(-6 + 1)$$
$$27 - 12 \overset{?}{=} -3(-5)$$
$$\overset{\checkmark}{15 = 15}$$

Example 2

Solve $2x^2 + 3x = 9x$, and check the roots.

Procedure

1. Rewrite the equation in standard form.

$$
\begin{aligned}
2x^2 + 3x &= 9x \\
-9x \quad &\quad -9x \\
\hline
2x^2 - 6x &= 0
\end{aligned}
$$

2. Factor out the common factor $2x$.

$$2x(x - 3) = 0$$

3. Set each factor equal to 0, and solve the resulting linear equations for x.

$$
\begin{array}{c|c}
2x = 0 & x - 3 = 0 \\
\dfrac{2x}{2} = \dfrac{0}{2} & \begin{aligned} +3 \quad &+3 \\ x \quad &= 3 \end{aligned} \\
x = 0 &
\end{array}
$$

$$x = 0, x = 3$$

4. Check each root separately by substituting it into the original equation.

$$
\begin{aligned}
\textbf{\textit{Check }} x &= 0 \\
2x^2 + 3x &= 9x \\
2(0)^2 + 3(0) &\overset{?}{=} 9(0) \\
0 &\overset{\checkmark}{=} 0 \\
\textbf{\textit{Check }} x &= 3 \\
2x^2 + 3x &= 9x \\
2(3)^2 + 3(3) &\overset{?}{=} 9(3) \\
2(9) + 9 &\overset{?}{=} 27 \\
27 &\overset{\checkmark}{=} 27
\end{aligned}
$$

Example 3

Solve $5x^2 = 36 + x^2$, and check the roots.

Procedure

1. Rewrite the equation in standard form.

$$
\begin{aligned}
5x^2 &= 36 + x^2 \\
\underline{-x^2} \quad &\underline{\quad -x^2} \\
4x^2 &= 36 \\
\underline{-36} \quad &\underline{-36} \\
4x^2 - 36 &= 0
\end{aligned}
$$

2. Factor the difference of two squares.

$$4x^2 - 36 = 0$$
$$(2x + 6)(2x - 6) = 0$$

3. Set each factor equal to 0 and solve the resulting linear equations for x.

$$
\begin{array}{c|c}
\begin{aligned}
2x + 6 &= 0 \\
\underline{-6} \quad &\underline{-6} \\
2x &= -6 \\
\frac{2x}{2} &= \frac{-6}{2} \\
x &= -3
\end{aligned}
&
\begin{aligned}
2x - 6 &= 0 \\
\underline{+6} \quad &\underline{+6} \\
2x &= 6 \\
\frac{2x}{2} &= \frac{6}{2} \\
x &= 3
\end{aligned}
\end{array}
$$

$$x = -3, x = 3$$

4. Check each root separately by substituting it into the original equation.

$$
\begin{aligned}
\textbf{\textit{Check }} x &= -3 \\
5x^2 &\overset{?}{=} 36 + x^2 \\
5(-3)^2 &\overset{?}{=} 36 + (-3)^2 \\
5(9) &\overset{\checkmark}{=} 36 + 9 \\
45 &= 45
\end{aligned}
$$

$$
\begin{aligned}
\textbf{\textit{Check }} x &= 3 \\
5x^2 &\overset{?}{=} 36 + x^2 \\
5(3)^2 &\overset{?}{=} 36 + (3)^2 \\
5(9) &\overset{\checkmark}{=} 36 + 9 \\
45 &= 45
\end{aligned}
$$

PRACTICE PROBLEMS

Solve each of the following quadratic equations for x.

1. $x^2 - 7x + 12 = 0$

2. $x^2 - 18x + 81 = 0$

3. $x^2 - 18 = 3x$

4. $x^2 + x = 30$

5. $3x^2 + 12x = 0$

6. $2x^2 - 5x = x$

7. $2x^2 - 50 = 0$

8. $4x^2 = x^2 + 48$

ANSWERS AND EXPLANATIONS

1. $x^2 - 7x + 12 = 0$

    $(x-3)(x-4) = 0$

    $\begin{array}{c|c} x - 3 = 0 & x - 4 = 0 \\ x = 3 & x = 4 \end{array}$

2. $x^2 - 18x + 81 = 0$

    $(x-9)(x-9) = 0$

    $\begin{array}{c|c} x - 9 = 0 & x - 9 = 0 \\ x = 9 & x = 9 \end{array}$

3. $\begin{aligned} x^2 \qquad -18 &= \quad 3x \\ \underline{-3x \qquad\quad} & \underline{\quad -3x} \\ x^2 - 3x - 18 &= \quad 0 \end{aligned}$

    $(x-6)(x+3) = 0$

    $\begin{array}{c|c} x - 6 = 0 & x + 3 = 0 \\ x = 6 & x = -3 \end{array}$

4. $\begin{aligned} x^2 + x \qquad &= 30 \\ \underline{\qquad -30} & \underline{\quad -30} \\ x^2 + x - 30 &= \quad 0 \end{aligned}$

    $(x+6)(x-5) = 0$

    $\begin{array}{c|c} x + 6 = 0 & x - 5 = 0 \\ x = -6 & x = 5 \end{array}$

5. $3x^2 + 12x = 0$

    $3x(x + 4) = 0$

    $\begin{array}{c|c} 3x = 0 & x + 4 = 0 \\ x = 0 & x = -4 \end{array}$

6. $\begin{aligned} 2x^2 - 5x &= \quad x \\ \underline{\quad -x} & \underline{\quad -x} \\ 2x^2 - 6x &= \quad 0 \end{aligned}$

    $2x(x - 3) = 0$

    $\begin{array}{c|c} 2x = 0 & x - 3 = 0 \\ x = 0 & x = 3 \end{array}$

7. $2x^2 - 50 = 0$

        $2(x^2 - 25) = 0$

        $2(x + 5)(x - 5) = 0$

        $x + 5 = 0$ | $x - 5 = 0$

            $x = -5$ | $x = 5$

8. $4x^2 = \quad x^2 + 48$

        $\underline{-x^2 \quad\quad -x^2}$

        $3x^2 \quad = \quad\quad 48$

        $\underline{\quad\quad -48 \quad\quad -48}$

        $3x^2 - 48 = \quad 0$

        $3(x^2 - 16) = 0$

        $3(x + 4)(x - 4) = 0$

        $x + 4 = 0$ | $x - 4 = 0$

            $x = -4$ | $x = 4$

SOLVING INCOMPLETE QUADRATIC EQUATIONS

Quadratic equations such as $x^2 - 9 = 0$, which when written in standard form do not contain a middle term, bx, are called **incomplete quadratic equations.**

$$ax^2 + c = 0$$

One way of solving incomplete quadratic equations is by the factoring method described in the last section. Note that in general, the expression on the left side of the equation will be the difference of two squares. For example,

$$x^2 - 9 = 0$$
$$(x + 3)(x - 3) = 0$$

$$x + 3 = 0 \quad\Big|\quad x - 3 = 0$$
$$\underline{-3 \quad -3} \quad\Big|\quad \underline{+3 \quad +3}$$
$$x \quad = -3 \quad\Big|\quad x \quad = \quad 3$$

$$x = -3, \ x = 3$$

Another way of solving incomplete quadratic equations is to rewrite the equation in the form $x^2 = n$, where n is some positive number, and then take the square root of both sides. That is,

$$x^2 - 9 = \quad 0$$
$$\underline{\quad +9 \quad +9}$$
$$x^2 \quad = \quad 9$$

$$x^2 \quad = \quad 9$$
$$\sqrt{x^2} = +\sqrt{9} \quad \text{or} \quad \sqrt{x^2} = -\sqrt{9}$$
$$x = +3 \quad \text{or} \quad x = -3$$

Notice that we must consider both $+\sqrt{9}$ and $-\sqrt{9}$, since both of these numbers squared equal 9. This second procedure is summarized on the following page.

> **To Solve an Incomplete Quadratic Equation:**
> 1. Rewrite the equation in the form $x^2 = n$, where n is some positive number.
> 2. Take the square root of n. The two roots are $x = +\sqrt{n}$ or $x = -\sqrt{n}$, which is sometimes denoted $x = \pm\sqrt{n}$.

Example
Solve $5x^2 = 3x^2 + 32$, and check the roots.

Procedure

1. Rewrite the equation in the form $x^2 = n$.

$$5x^2 = 3x^2 + 32$$
$$\underline{-3x^2 \qquad -3x^2}$$
$$2x^2 = \qquad 32$$
$$\frac{\cancel{2}x^2}{\cancel{2}} = \frac{32}{2}$$
$$x^2 = 16$$

2. Take the positive and negative square roots of 16.

$$x = +\sqrt{16} \text{ and } x = -\sqrt{16}$$
$$x = +4, x = -4$$

3. Check each root separately by substituting it into the original equation.

$$\textit{Check } x = 4$$
$$5x^2 = 3x^2 + 32$$
$$5(4)^2 \overset{?}{=} 3(4)^2 + 32$$
$$5(16) \overset{?}{=} 3(16) + 32$$
$$80 = 80$$
$$\textit{Check } x = -4$$
$$5x^2 = 3x^2 + 32$$
$$5(-4)^2 \overset{?}{=} 3(-4)^2 + 32$$
$$5(16) \overset{?}{=} 3(16) + 32$$
$$80 = 80$$

PRACTICE PROBLEMS

Solve each of the following incomplete quadratic equations for x.

1. $x^2 - 49 = 0$
2. $4x^2 = 100$
3. $3x^2 - 32 = x^2$
4. $2x^2 + 18 = 3x^2 - 7$

ANSWERS AND EXPLANATIONS

1. $x^2 - 49 = 0$

   $\underline{ +49 \quad +49}$

   $x^2 \quad = \quad 49$

   $x = +\sqrt{49} \text{ or } -\sqrt{49}$

   $x = +7 \text{ or } -7$

2. $4x^2 = 100$

   $\dfrac{\cancel{4}x^2}{\cancel{4}} = \dfrac{100}{4}$

   $x^2 = 25$

   $x = +\sqrt{25} \text{ or } -\sqrt{25}$

   $x = +5 \text{ or } -5$

3. $3x^2 - 32 = \quad x^2$

   $\underline{-x^2 \quad -x^2}$

   $2x^2 - 32 = \quad 0$

   $\underline{ +32 \quad +32}$

   $2x^2 = \quad 32$

   $\dfrac{\cancel{2}x^2}{\cancel{2}} = \dfrac{32}{2}$

   $x^2 = 16$

   $x = +\sqrt{16} \text{ or } -\sqrt{16}$

   $x = +4 \text{ or } -4$

4. $2x^2 + 18 = \quad 3x^2 - 7$

   $\underline{-3x^2 \quad -3x^2}$

   $-x^2 + 18 = \quad -7$

   $\underline{ -18 \quad -18}$

   $-x^2 \quad = \quad -25$

   $\dfrac{-x^2}{-1} = \dfrac{-25}{-1}$

   $x^2 = 25$

   $x = +\sqrt{25} \text{ or } -\sqrt{25}$

   $x = +5 \text{ or } -5$

OPERATIONS WITH SQUARE ROOTS

SIMPLIFYING SQUARE ROOTS OF NUMBERS

As you recall, numbers such as 4, 9, and 16, whose square roots are whole numbers, are called **perfect squares**. To **simplify** a square root means to remove any perfect square factors from under the square root sign. The method we use to do this is based on the following principle.

Multiplication Principle of Square Roots
The square root of a product is equal to the product of the square roots.

$$\sqrt{a \cdot b} = \sqrt{a} \cdot \sqrt{b}$$

To demonstrate the method, let us simplify $\sqrt{18}$. First, by writing $18 = 9 \cdot 2$, transform the number under the square root sign into a product containing a perfect square factor, 9:

$$\sqrt{18} = \sqrt{9 \cdot 2}$$

Then, by using the multiplication principle just stated, write the square root of the product as the product of the square roots.

$$\sqrt{18} = \sqrt{9 \cdot 2}$$
$$= \sqrt{9} \cdot \sqrt{2}$$

Finally, take the square root of the perfect square factor and get

$$\sqrt{18} = \sqrt{9 \cdot 2}$$
$$= \sqrt{9} \cdot \sqrt{2}$$
$$= 3\sqrt{2}$$

To Simplify Square Roots:
1. Express the number under the square root sign as the product of two factors, one of which is a perfect square.
2. Rewrite the square root of the product as the product of the square roots.
3. Take the square root of the perfect square factor.
4. Repeat the process until all the perfect square factors have been removed from under the square root sign.

$$\sqrt{720} = \sqrt{36 \cdot 20}$$
$$= \sqrt{36} \cdot \sqrt{20}$$
$$= 6\sqrt{20}$$
$$= 6\sqrt{4 \cdot 5}$$
$$= 6\sqrt{4} \cdot \sqrt{5}$$
$$= 6 \cdot 2\sqrt{5}$$
$$= 12\sqrt{5}$$

Note that this procedure depends on the number being expressed as a *product*. As the examples below illustrate, the same procedure cannot be used if the number is expressed as a *sum* or a *difference*. That is, $\sqrt{a+b} \neq \sqrt{a} + \sqrt{b}$, and $\sqrt{a-b} \neq \sqrt{a} - \sqrt{b}$.

Square Root of Sum	*Square Root of Difference*
$\sqrt{9+16} \overset{?}{=} \sqrt{9} + \sqrt{16}$	$\sqrt{100-36} \overset{?}{=} \sqrt{100} - \sqrt{36}$
$\sqrt{25} \overset{?}{=} 3 + 4$	$\sqrt{64} \overset{?}{=} 10 - 6$
$5 \neq 7$	$8 \neq 4$

PRACTICE PROBLEMS

Simplify completely.

1. $\sqrt{75}$

2. $\sqrt{128}$

3. $\sqrt{40}$

4. $\sqrt{63}$

ANSWERS AND EXPLANATIONS

1. $\sqrt{75} = \sqrt{25 \cdot 3} = 5\sqrt{3}$

2. $\sqrt{128} = \sqrt{64 \cdot 2} = 8\sqrt{2}$

3. $\sqrt{40} = \sqrt{4 \cdot 10} = 2\sqrt{10}$

4. $\sqrt{63} = \sqrt{9 \cdot 7} = 3\sqrt{7}$

SIMPLIFYING SQUARE ROOTS OF VARIABLES

To simplify square roots containing variable factors, use the following general principle:

> The square root of a variable raised to an *even power* is the variable raised to one-half that even power.
>
> $$\sqrt{x^m} = x^{\frac{1}{2}m}$$

$$\sqrt{x^2} = x$$
$$\sqrt{x^6} = x^3$$
$$\sqrt{x^{10}} = x^5$$

If the variable is raised to an *odd power*, rewrite it as the product of two factors, one with a power of 1 less than the given odd power, and the other with a power of 1. For example,

$$\sqrt{x^7} = \sqrt{x^6 \cdot x^1}$$
$$= \sqrt{x^6} \cdot \sqrt{x^1}$$
$$= x^3 \sqrt{x}$$

Example
Simplify $\sqrt{75x^2 y^7 z^3}$.

Procedure

1. Express 75 as the product of the perfect square factor 25 and the factor 3.

$$\sqrt{75x^2 y^7 z^3}$$
$$= \sqrt{25 \cdot 3 x^2 y^7 z^3}$$

2. Rewrite y^7 as $y^6 \cdot y$, and z^3 as $z^2 \cdot z$.

$$= \sqrt{25 \cdot 3 \cdot x^2 \cdot y^6 \cdot y \cdot z^2 \cdot z}$$

3. Group all the perfect square factors together.

$$= \sqrt{25x^2 y^6 z^2 \cdot 3yz}$$

4. Use the multiplication principle to separate the two groups.

$$= \sqrt{25x^2 y^6 z^2} \cdot \sqrt{3yz}$$

5. Take the square root of the perfect square factors.

$$= 5xy^3 z \sqrt{3yz}$$

PRACTICE PROBLEMS
Simplify completely.

1. $\sqrt{50x^2 y^4}$

2. $\sqrt{80x^5}$

3. $\sqrt{700x^6 y^7}$

4. $\sqrt{12x^3 y^3}$

ANSWERS AND EXPLANATIONS

1. $\sqrt{50x^2y^4} = \sqrt{25x^2y^4 \cdot 2} = 5xy^2\sqrt{2}$

2. $\sqrt{80x^5} = \sqrt{16 \cdot 5 \cdot x^4 \cdot x} = 4x^2\sqrt{5x}$

3. $\sqrt{700x^6y^7} = \sqrt{100 \cdot 7 \cdot x^6 \cdot y^6 \cdot y} = 10x^3y^3\sqrt{7y}$

4. $\sqrt{12x^3y^3} = \sqrt{4 \cdot 3 \cdot x^2 \cdot x \cdot y^2 \cdot y} = 2xy\sqrt{3xy}$

ADDING AND SUBTRACTING SQUARE ROOTS

Square roots that have identical expressions under the square root signs are called **like square roots**. To add and subtract like square roots, simply add and subtract (combine) their coefficients. Note how this is similar to adding and subtracting like algebraic terms:

$$2\sqrt{7} + 4\sqrt{7} - 9\sqrt{7}$$
$$= (2 + 4 - 9)\sqrt{7}$$
$$= -3\sqrt{7}$$

$$3\sqrt{xy} - \sqrt{xy} + 2\sqrt{xy}$$
$$= (3 - 1 + 2)\sqrt{xy}$$
$$= 4\sqrt{xy}$$

In general, square roots that do not have identical expressions under their square root signs (unlike square roots) cannot be combined into a single term. For example, expressions such as $\sqrt{5} + \sqrt{3}$ and $\sqrt{x} - \sqrt{y}$ cannot be simplified further. In some cases, however, it may be possible to change unlike square roots into like square roots by simplifying them (removing perfect square factors):

$$\sqrt{20} + 6\sqrt{5}$$
$$= \sqrt{4 \cdot 5} + 6\sqrt{5}$$
$$= \sqrt{4} \cdot \sqrt{5} + 6\sqrt{5}$$
$$= 2\sqrt{5} + 6\sqrt{5}$$
$$= 8\sqrt{5}$$

Example

Simplify and combine $\sqrt{2x^3} + 3x\sqrt{8x} - x\sqrt{2x}$.

Procedure

1. Using the multiplication principle, remove all the perfect square factors from under the square root signs.

$$\sqrt{2x^3} + 3x\sqrt{8x} - x\sqrt{2x}$$
$$= \sqrt{x^2 \cdot 2x} + 3x\sqrt{4 \cdot 2x} - x\sqrt{2x}$$
$$= \sqrt{x^2} \cdot \sqrt{2x} + 3x\sqrt{4} \cdot \sqrt{2x} - x\sqrt{2x}$$
$$= x\sqrt{2x} + 3x \cdot 2\sqrt{2x} - x\sqrt{2x}$$
$$= x\sqrt{2x} + 6x\sqrt{2x} - x\sqrt{2x}$$

2. Combine the coefficients.

$$= (x + 6x - x)\sqrt{2x}$$
$$= 6x\sqrt{2x}$$

PRACTICE PROBLEMS

Perform the following additions and subtractions:

1. $5\sqrt{2x} - 9\sqrt{2x} + \sqrt{2x}$

2. $\sqrt{45} + 7\sqrt{125}$

3. $\sqrt{12} - 6\sqrt{3} + 2\sqrt{48}$

4. $6\sqrt{3x^5} - x^2\sqrt{12x}$

ANSWERS AND EXPLANATIONS

1. $5\sqrt{2x} - 9\sqrt{2x} + \sqrt{2x} =$
   $(5 - 9 + 1)\sqrt{2x} = -3\sqrt{2x}$

2. $\sqrt{45} + 7\sqrt{125} = \sqrt{9 \cdot 5} + 7\sqrt{25 \cdot 5}$
   $$= 3\sqrt{5} + 7 \cdot 5\sqrt{5}$$
   $$= 3\sqrt{5} + 35\sqrt{5}$$
   $$= 38\sqrt{5}$$

3. $\sqrt{12} - 6\sqrt{3} + 2\sqrt{48} =$

    $\sqrt{4 \cdot 3} - 6\sqrt{3} + 2\sqrt{16 \cdot 3} =$

    $2\sqrt{3} - 6\sqrt{3} + 2 \cdot 4\sqrt{3} =$

    $2\sqrt{3} - 6\sqrt{3} + 8\sqrt{3} = 4\sqrt{3}$

4. $6\sqrt{3x^5} - x^2\sqrt{12x} =$

    $6\sqrt{3x^4 \cdot x} - x^2\sqrt{4 \cdot 3x} =$

    $6x^2\sqrt{3x} - 2x^2\sqrt{3x} = 4x^2\sqrt{3x}$

MULTIPLYING SQUARE ROOTS

The multiplication principle used to simplify square roots can be stated in reverse to multiply square roots.

> A product of square roots is equal to the square root of the product.
>
> $$\sqrt{a} \cdot \sqrt{b} = \sqrt{a \cdot b}$$

Consider the following examples:

$$\sqrt{18} \cdot \sqrt{2} = \sqrt{18 \cdot 2}$$
$$= \sqrt{36}$$
$$= 6$$

$$\sqrt{2xy} \cdot \sqrt{32xy} = \sqrt{2xy \cdot 32xy}$$
$$= \sqrt{64x^2 y^2}$$
$$= 8xy$$

Remember that when square roots have coefficients other than 1, the square roots and coefficients must be multiplied separately:

$$\left(3\sqrt{5}\right)\left(7\sqrt{2}\right) = \left(3 \cdot 7\right)\left(\sqrt{5} \cdot \sqrt{2}\right)$$
$$= 21\sqrt{5 \cdot 2}$$
$$= 21\sqrt{10}$$

A common mistake that is made at this point is to continue multiplying and write $21\sqrt{10} = \sqrt{210}$. This is an error, however, because the number outside the square root *cannot* be multiplied by the number underneath the square root.

Example

Multiply $\left(2\sqrt{6xy}\right)\left(5\sqrt{3x^3y}\right)\left(3\sqrt{y}\right)$.

Procedure

1. Multiply the numerical coefficients and square roots separately.

$$\left(2\sqrt{6xy}\right)\left(5\sqrt{3x^3y}\right)\left(3\sqrt{y}\right)$$
$$= 2\cdot 5\cdot 3\sqrt{(6xy)(3x^3y)(y)}$$
$$= 30\sqrt{18x^4y^3}$$

2. Simplify the square root by removing perfect square factors.

$$= 30\sqrt{9\cdot 2\cdot x^4\cdot y^2\cdot y}$$
$$= 30\sqrt{9x^4y^2\cdot 2y}$$
$$= 30\sqrt{9x^4y^2}\cdot\sqrt{2y}$$
$$= 30\cdot 3x^2y\sqrt{2y}$$
$$= 90x^2y\sqrt{2y}$$

PRACTICE PROBLEMS

Multiply and simplify completely.

1. $\left(3\sqrt{32}\right)\left(5\sqrt{2}\right)$

2. $\left(-2\sqrt{3}\right)\left(6\sqrt{27}\right)$

3. $\sqrt{18x^3}\cdot\sqrt{2x}$

4. $\sqrt{3x^3y}\cdot\sqrt{15xy}$

ANSWERS AND EXPLANATIONS

1. $\left(3\sqrt{32}\right)\left(5\sqrt{2}\right) = 15\sqrt{64} = 15 \cdot 8 = 120$

2. $\left(-2\sqrt{3}\right)\left(6\sqrt{27}\right) = -12\sqrt{81} = -12 \cdot 9 = -108$

3. $\sqrt{18x^3} \cdot \sqrt{2x} = \sqrt{36x^4} = 6x^2$

4. $\sqrt{3x^3y} \cdot \sqrt{15xy} = \sqrt{45x^4y^2} = \sqrt{9 \cdot 5x^4y^2} = 3x^2y\sqrt{5}$

DIVIDING SQUARE ROOTS

To divide square roots, we use a principle similar to the one used in the last section for multiplying square roots.

The quotient of two square roots is equal to the square root of the quotient.

$$\frac{\sqrt{a}}{\sqrt{b}} = \sqrt{\frac{a}{b}}$$

Consider these examples:

$$\frac{\sqrt{45}}{\sqrt{5}} = \sqrt{\frac{45}{5}}$$
$$= \sqrt{9}$$
$$= 3$$

$$\frac{\sqrt{48x^3}}{\sqrt{3x}} = \sqrt{\frac{48x^3}{3x}}$$
$$= \sqrt{16x^2}$$
$$= 4x$$

As before, remember that when square roots have coefficients other than 1, the square roots and coefficients must be divided separately:

$$\frac{12\sqrt{75}}{2\sqrt{3}} = \frac{12}{2}\sqrt{\frac{75}{3}}$$
$$= 6\sqrt{25}$$
$$= 6 \cdot 5$$
$$= 30$$

Example

Divide and simplify completely.

$$\frac{6\sqrt{56xy^4}}{2\sqrt{7x^5y}}$$

Procedure

1. Divide the numerical coefficients and square roots separately.

$$\frac{6\sqrt{56xy^4}}{2\sqrt{7x^5y}}$$

$$= \frac{6}{2}\sqrt{\frac{56xy^4}{7x^5y}}$$

$$= 3\sqrt{\frac{8y^3}{x^4}}$$

2. Simplify the square root by removing perfect square factors.

$$= 3\sqrt{\frac{4y^2 \cdot 2y}{x^4}}$$

$$= 3\sqrt{\frac{4y^2}{x^4}} \cdot \sqrt{2y}$$

$$= 3 \cdot \frac{2y}{x^2}\sqrt{2y}$$

$$= \frac{6y}{x^2}\sqrt{2y}$$

PRACTICE PROBLEMS

Divide and simplify completely.

1. $\dfrac{6\sqrt{75}}{2\sqrt{3}}$

2. $\dfrac{\sqrt{98x^3}}{\sqrt{2x}}$

3. $\dfrac{7\sqrt{54x^5}}{\sqrt{2x^2}}$

4. $\dfrac{15\sqrt{8x^5y^5}}{5\sqrt{2xy^3}}$

ANSWERS AND EXPLANATIONS

1. $\dfrac{6\sqrt{75}}{2\sqrt{3}} = 3\sqrt{25} = 3\cdot 5 = 15$

2. $\dfrac{\sqrt{98x^3}}{\sqrt{2x}} = \sqrt{49x^2} = 7x$

3. $\dfrac{7\sqrt{54x^5}}{\sqrt{2x^2}} = 7\sqrt{27x^3} = 7\sqrt{9\cdot 3\cdot x^2\cdot x}$
$$= 7\cdot 3x\sqrt{3x}$$
$$= 21x\sqrt{3x}$$

4. $\dfrac{15\sqrt{8x^5 y^5}}{5\sqrt{2xy^3}} = 3\sqrt{4x^4 y^2} = 3\cdot 2x^2\cdot y = 6x^2 y$

ALGEBRAIC FRACTIONS

Fractions that contain variables, such as $\dfrac{x}{4}, \dfrac{3x}{2y}$, and $\dfrac{7}{3x-4}$ are called **algebraic fractions**. Any algebraic expression can be put into the form of an algebraic fraction by placing it over a denominator of 1. For example, $3x = \dfrac{3x}{1}$, and $2x^3 - 5 = \dfrac{2x^3 - 5}{1}$.

Since division by 0 is undefined, we must be careful not to replace any variables in the denominator of an algebraic fraction by numbers that would make its value 0. For example, the fraction $\dfrac{5x}{x-2}$ has no meaning for $x = 2$.

$$\frac{5x}{x-2} = \frac{5\cdot 2}{2-2}$$
$$= \frac{10}{0}??$$

REDUCING ALGEBRAIC FRACTIONS TO LOWEST TERMS

We know from arithmetic that to reduce a fraction to lowest terms means to divide the numerator and denominator by common factors until no common factors remain. As shown below, this is equivalent to expressing the numerator and denominator as a product, and then cancelling the common factors.

$$\frac{10}{2} = \frac{5\cdot \cancel{2}}{6\cdot \cancel{2}} = \frac{5}{6}$$

When both the numerator and denominator of an algebraic fraction are monomials, we can cancel common factors by using the rules that follow for dividing powers of the same base.

$$\frac{x^m}{x^n} = \begin{cases} x^{m-n}, & m > n \\ 1, & m = n \\ \dfrac{1}{x^{n-m}}, & m < n \end{cases}$$

For example,

$$\frac{6x^3y^2}{8xy^3} = \frac{\overset{3}{\cancel{6}} \cdot x \cdot x \cdot x \cdot \cancel{y} \cdot \cancel{y}}{\underset{4}{\cancel{8}} \cdot x \cdot y \cdot \cancel{y} \cdot \cancel{y}}$$

$$= \frac{3x^{3-1}}{4y^{3-2}}$$

$$= \frac{3x^2}{4y}$$

When the expressions in the numerator or denominator are polynomials (more than one term), we cannot cancel common factors until the expressions are rewritten in factored form:

$$\frac{3x^2 + 6x}{12x} = \frac{\overset{1}{\cancel{3x}}\,(x+2)}{\underset{4}{\cancel{12x}}}$$

$$= \frac{x+2}{4}$$

$$\frac{x^2 - 9}{5x + 15} = \frac{\overset{1}{\cancel{(x+3)}}(x-3)}{5\underset{1}{\cancel{(x+3)}}}$$

$$= \frac{x-3}{5}$$

A common mistake in reducing fractions containing polynomials is to reduce common terms before the expressions are rewritten in factored form. Some typical errors are shown below.

Errors in Cancelling

$$\frac{x+3}{y+3} = \frac{x+\cancel{3}}{y+\cancel{3}}$$

$$= \frac{x}{y} \quad \textit{False}$$

$$\frac{x^2 + 6}{x+3} = \frac{\overset{x}{\cancel{x^2}} + \overset{3}{\cancel{6}}}{x+2}$$

$$= x+3 \quad \textit{False}$$

Remember that the only correct way of reducing fractions by cancelling is to cancel common *factors*, *not* common *terms*.

Example

Reduce the fraction $\dfrac{x^2 - 3x - 10}{x^2 - 25}$.

Procedure

1. Factor the expressions in the numerator and denominator.

$$\frac{x^2 - 3x - 10}{x^2 - 25}$$

$$= \frac{(x+2)(x-5)}{(x+5)(x-5)}$$

2. Cancel the common factor, $(x - 5)$.

$$= \frac{(x+2)\cancel{(x-5)}^{1}}{(x+5)\cancel{(x-5)}_{1}}$$

$$= \frac{x+2}{x+5}$$

PRACTICE PROBLEMS

Reduce each of the following fractions to lowest terms.

1. $\dfrac{4x^3 y^2}{8xy^5}$

2. $\dfrac{6x^3 + 2x}{4x}$

3. $\dfrac{x^2 + 7x + 12}{2x + 6}$

4. $\dfrac{x^2 - 64}{3x - 24}$

ANSWERS AND EXPLANATIONS

1. $\dfrac{4x^3y^2}{8xy^5} = \dfrac{x^{3-1}}{2y^{5-2}} = \dfrac{x^2}{2y^3}$

2. $\dfrac{6x^3 + 2x}{4x} = \dfrac{\overset{1}{\cancel{2x}}\left(3x^2 + 1\right)}{\underset{2}{\cancel{4x}}} = \dfrac{3x^2 + 1}{2}$

3. $\dfrac{x^2 + 7x + 12}{2x + 6} = \dfrac{\overset{1}{\cancel{(x+3)}}(x+4)}{2\underset{1}{\cancel{(x+3)}}} = \dfrac{x+4}{2}$

4. $\dfrac{x^2 - 64}{3x - 24} = \dfrac{(x+8)\overset{1}{\cancel{(x-8)}}}{3\underset{1}{\cancel{(x-8)}}} = \dfrac{x+8}{3}$

ADDING AND SUBTRACTING LIKE ALGEBRAIC FRACTIONS

To add or subtract algebraic fractions having the same denominator (*like* algebraic fractions), add or subtract their numerators, and place the result over the common denominator. In each case, reduce the resulting fraction to lowest terms:

$$\frac{a}{c} + \frac{b}{c} = \frac{a+b}{c}$$
$$\frac{a}{c} - \frac{b}{c} = \frac{a-b}{c}$$

For example,

$$\frac{3x^2}{8y} + \frac{7x^2}{8y} - \frac{4x^2}{8y} = \frac{3x^2 + 7x^2 - 4x^2}{8y}$$
$$= \frac{6x^2}{8y}$$
$$= \frac{3x^2}{4y}$$

Example 1

Add $\dfrac{x+1}{4x+6} + \dfrac{x+2}{4x+6}$.

Procedure

1. Add the numerators, and place the result over the common denominator.

$$\dfrac{x+1}{4x+6} + \dfrac{x+2}{4x+6}$$
$$= \dfrac{x+1+x+2}{4x+6}$$
$$= \dfrac{2x+3}{4x+6}$$

2. Factor the expression in the denominator, and then cancel the common factor $(2x + 3)$.

$$= \dfrac{\overset{1}{\cancel{2x+3}}}{2\underset{1}{\cancel{(2x+3)}}}$$
$$= \dfrac{1}{2}$$

Example 2

Subtract $\dfrac{5x-2}{2xy} - \dfrac{3x-7}{2xy}$.

Procedure

1. Subtract the numerators, and place the result over the common denominator. Remember to change the sign of each term being subtracted to its opposite sign.

$$\dfrac{5x-2}{2xy} - \dfrac{3x-7}{2xy}$$
$$= \dfrac{(5x-2)-(3x-7)}{2xy}$$
$$= \dfrac{5x-2-3x+7}{2xy}$$
$$= \dfrac{2x+5}{2xy}$$

PRACTICE PROBLEMS

Perform the following additions and subtractions. Reduce all answers to lowest terms.

1. $\dfrac{2x}{3a} + \dfrac{8x}{3a} - \dfrac{x}{3a}$

2. $\dfrac{6x-4}{y} + \dfrac{2x+3}{y}$

3. $\dfrac{7x+3}{ab} - \dfrac{2x-5}{ab}$

4. $\dfrac{4x+1}{x-2} - \dfrac{x+7}{x-2}$

ANSWERS AND EXPLANATIONS

1. $\dfrac{2x}{3a} + \dfrac{8x}{3a} - \dfrac{x}{3a} = \dfrac{2x+8x-x}{3a} = \dfrac{9x}{3a} = \dfrac{3x}{a}$

2. $\dfrac{6x-4}{y} + \dfrac{2x+3}{y} = \dfrac{(6x-4)+(2x+3)}{y}$

   $= \dfrac{8x-1}{y}$

3. $\dfrac{7x+3}{ab} - \dfrac{2x-5}{ab} = \dfrac{(7x+3)-(2x-5)}{ab}$

   $= \dfrac{7x+3-2x+5}{ab}$

   $= \dfrac{5x+8}{ab}$

4. $\dfrac{4x+1}{x-2} - \dfrac{x+7}{x-2} = \dfrac{(4x+1)-(x+7)}{x-2}$

   $= \dfrac{4x+1-x-7}{x-2}$

   $= \dfrac{3x-6}{x-2}$

   $= \dfrac{3(x-2)}{x-2} = 3$

ADDING AND SUBTRACTING UNLIKE ALGEBRAIC FRACTIONS

To add or subtract algebraic fractions having different denominators (*unlike* algebraic fractions), first change them to equivalent fractions having a common denominator, and then proceed as in the last section. Remember that a simple way of obtaining a common denominator is to multiply the given denominators.

For example, to add $\dfrac{a}{b} + \dfrac{c}{d}$ first change the fractions to equivalent fractions having the common denominator bd (the product of the denominators). As demonstrated below, to change the fractions to this denominator, multiply $\dfrac{a}{b}$ by $\dfrac{d}{d}$ and $\dfrac{c}{d}$ by $\dfrac{b}{b}$.

$$\frac{a}{b} + \frac{c}{d} = \frac{a}{b} \cdot \frac{d}{d} + \frac{c}{d} \cdot \frac{b}{b}$$

$$= \frac{ad}{bd} + \frac{bc}{bd}$$

$$= \frac{ad + bc}{bd}$$

The following shortcut can be used to obtain the same result:

To Add or Subtract Two Unlike Fractions:

Cross multiply the numerators and denominators, and place their sum or difference over the product of the denominators (the common denominator).

$$\overset{ad \qquad bc}{\underset{b d}{a \times c}} = \frac{ad + bc}{bd} \qquad \Bigg| \qquad \overset{ad \qquad bc}{\underset{b d}{a \times c}} = \frac{ad - bc}{bd}$$

Example 1

Add $\dfrac{2x}{5} + \dfrac{3x}{7}$.

Procedure

1. Cross-multiply the numerators and denominators, and place their sum over the product of the denominators.

$$\frac{2x}{5} + \frac{3x}{7}$$

$$= \frac{7(2x) + 5(3x)}{5 \cdot 7}$$

$$= \frac{14x + 15x}{35}$$

$$= \frac{29x}{35}$$

Example 2

Add $\dfrac{5x}{x+3} + \dfrac{2x}{x-3}$.

Procedure

1. Cross-multiply the numerators and denominators, and place their sum over the product of the denominators.

$$\frac{5x}{x+3} + \frac{2x}{x-3}$$

$$= \frac{5x(x-3) + 2x(x+3)}{(x+3)(x-3)}$$

$$= \frac{5x^2 - 15x + 2x^2 + 6x}{x^2 - 9}$$

$$= \frac{7x^2 - 9x}{x^2 - 9}$$

Example 3

Subtract $\dfrac{7}{xy^2} - \dfrac{3}{x^2 y}$.

Procedure

1. Cross-multiply the numerators and denominators, and place their difference over the product of the denominators.

$$\frac{7}{xy^2} - \frac{3}{x^2 y}$$

$$= \frac{7(x^2 y) - 3(xy^2)}{(xy^2)(x^2 y)}$$

$$= \frac{7x^2 y - 3xy^2}{x^3 y^3}$$

2. Factor the expression in the numerator, and cancel the common factor xy.

$$= \frac{\overset{1}{\cancel{xy}}(7x - 3y)}{\underset{x^2 y^2}{\cancel{x^3 y^3}}}$$

$$= \frac{7x - 3y}{x^2 y^2}$$

PRACTICE PROBLEMS

Perform the following additions and subtractions. Reduce all answers to lowest terms.

1. $\dfrac{3x}{8} + \dfrac{4x}{9}$

2. $\dfrac{8}{x^2} - \dfrac{5}{x}$

3. $\dfrac{4}{x+5}+\dfrac{3}{x-5}$

4. $\dfrac{7}{x+1}-\dfrac{3}{x+2}$

ANSWERS AND EXPLANATIONS

1. $\dfrac{3x}{8}+\dfrac{4x}{9}=\dfrac{9(3x)+8(4x)}{8\cdot9}=\dfrac{27x+32x}{72}=\dfrac{59x}{72}$

2. $\dfrac{8}{x^2}-\dfrac{5}{x}=\dfrac{8(x)-5(x^2)}{x^2\cdot x}=\dfrac{8x-5x^2}{x^3}$

$=\dfrac{\overset{1}{\cancel{x}}(8-5x)}{\underset{x^2}{\cancel{x^3}}}$

$=\dfrac{8-5x}{x^2}$

3. $\dfrac{4}{x+5}+\dfrac{3}{x-5}=\dfrac{4(x-5)+3(x+5)}{(x+5)(x-5)}$

$=\dfrac{4x-20+3x+15}{x^2-25}$

$=\dfrac{7x-5}{x^2-25}$

4. $\dfrac{7}{x+1}-\dfrac{3}{x+2}=\dfrac{7(x+2)-3(x+1)}{(x+1)(x+2)}$

$=\dfrac{7x+14-3x-3}{x^2+3x+2}$

$=\dfrac{4x+11}{x^2+3x+2}$

MULTIPLYING ALGEBRAIC FRACTIONS

To multiply algebraic fractions, multiply the numerators by the numerators and the denominators by the denominators:

$$\frac{a}{b} \cdot \frac{c}{d} = \frac{a \cdot c}{b \cdot d}$$

$$\frac{3x}{y} \cdot \frac{2x^2}{5y} = \frac{3x \cdot 2x^2}{y \cdot 5y}$$

$$= \frac{6x^3}{5y^2}$$

If the numerators and denominators contain common factors, they can be cancelled before multiplying:

$$\frac{12x^2}{y} \cdot \frac{5}{4x} = \frac{\overset{3x}{\cancel{12x^2}}}{y} \cdot \frac{5}{\underset{1}{\cancel{4x}}}$$

$$= \frac{3x \cdot 5}{y \cdot 1}$$

$$= \frac{15x}{y}$$

Remember that if the numerators or denominators are polynomials (more than one term), they must first be factored before common factors can be cancelled.

Example

Multiply $\dfrac{2x-10}{x-3} \cdot \dfrac{x^2-9}{8x-40}.$

Procedure

1. Factor the expressions in the numerator and denominator.

    $$\frac{2x-10}{x-3} \cdot \frac{x^2-9}{8x-40}$$

    $$= \frac{2(x-5)}{x-3} \cdot \frac{(x+3)(x-3)}{8(x-5)}$$

2. Cancel the common factors.

    $$= \frac{\overset{1}{\cancel{2}}\,\overset{1}{(\cancel{x-5})}}{\underset{1}{\cancel{x-3}}} \cdot \frac{(x+3)\overset{1}{(\cancel{x-3})}}{\underset{4}{\cancel{8}}\,\underset{1}{(\cancel{x-5})}}$$

3. Multiply the remaining factors.

    $$= \frac{x+3}{4}$$

PRACTICE PROBLEMS

Perform the following multiplications. Reduce all answers to lowest terms.

1. $\dfrac{4x^2}{y} \cdot \dfrac{3x}{y^3}$

2. $\dfrac{5x^3}{2y^4} \cdot \dfrac{4y}{x}$

3. $\dfrac{8y}{4x-4} \cdot \dfrac{x^2-1}{y^2}$

4. $\dfrac{3x+6}{x+1} \cdot \dfrac{x^2-4x-5}{7x+14}$

ANSWERS AND EXPLANATIONS

1. $\dfrac{4x^2}{y} \cdot \dfrac{3x}{y^3} = \dfrac{12x^3}{y^4}$

2. $\dfrac{5x^3}{2y^4} \cdot \dfrac{4y}{x} = \dfrac{5 \overset{x^2}{\cancel{x^3}} \cdot \overset{2}{\cancel{4}} \cancel{y}}{\underset{1}{\cancel{2}} \underset{y^3}{\cancel{y^4}} \cdot \underset{1}{\cancel{x}}} = \dfrac{10x^2}{y^3}$

3. $\dfrac{8y}{4x-4} \cdot \dfrac{x^2-1}{y^2} = \dfrac{\overset{2}{\cancel{8}} \cancel{y}}{\underset{1}{\cancel{4}} \underset{1}{(\cancel{x-1})}} \cdot \dfrac{(x+1)\overset{1}{(\cancel{x-1})}}{\underset{y}{\cancel{y^2}}}$

   $= \dfrac{2(x+1)}{y} = \dfrac{2x+2}{y}$

4. $\dfrac{3x+6}{x+1} \cdot \dfrac{x^2-4x-5}{7x+14} = \dfrac{3\overset{1}{(\cancel{x+2})}}{\underset{1}{\cancel{x+1}}} \cdot \dfrac{(x-5)\overset{1}{(\cancel{x+1})}}{7\underset{1}{(\cancel{x+2})}}$

   $= \dfrac{3(x-5)}{7} = \dfrac{3x-15}{7}$

DIVIDING ALGEBRAIC FRACTIONS

To divide algebraic fractions, first invert the divisor (the fraction following the division symbol), and then multiply the resulting fractions as in the last section. Remember that if the divisor is not a fraction, first place it over a denominator of 1 before inverting it:

$$\frac{a}{b} \div \frac{c}{d} = \frac{a}{b} \cdot \frac{d}{c}$$

$$\frac{2x}{3y} \div 5y = \frac{2x}{3y} \div \frac{5y}{1}$$

$$= \frac{2x}{3y} \cdot \frac{1}{5y}$$

$$= \frac{2x}{15y^2}$$

Example

Divide $\dfrac{x^2}{2x-8} \div \dfrac{x^3}{x^2-16}$.

Procedure

1. Invert the divisor, and change the division to multiplication.

$$\frac{x^2}{2x-8} \div \frac{x^3}{x^2-16}$$

$$= \frac{x^2}{2x-8} \cdot \frac{x^2-16}{x^3}$$

2. Factor the expressions in the numerator and denominator.

$$= \frac{x^2}{2(x-4)} \cdot \frac{(x+4)(x-4)}{x^3}$$

3. Cancel the common factors.

$$= \frac{\overset{1}{\cancel{x^2}}}{2\underset{1}{\cancel{(x-4)}}} \cdot \frac{(x+4)\cancel{(x-4)}}{\underset{x}{\cancel{x^3}}}$$

4. Multiply the remaining factors.

$$= \frac{x+4}{2x}$$

PRACTICE PROBLEMS

Perform the following divisions. Reduce all answers to lowest terms.

1. $\dfrac{x^2}{3} \div \dfrac{x^3}{6}$

2. $\dfrac{8x^2}{3y^3} \div \dfrac{2x}{9y}$

3. $\dfrac{x^2-9}{x^2} \div \dfrac{2x+6}{x}$

4. $\dfrac{x^2-5x+6}{3x} \div \dfrac{x-2}{9x}$

ANSWERS AND EXPLANATIONS

1. $\dfrac{x^2}{3} \div \dfrac{x^3}{6} = \dfrac{x^2}{3} \cdot \dfrac{6}{x^3} = \dfrac{2}{x}$

2. $\dfrac{8x^2}{3y^3} \div \dfrac{2x}{9y} = \dfrac{8x^2}{3y^3} \cdot \dfrac{9y}{2x} = \dfrac{12x}{y^2}$

3. $\dfrac{x^2-9}{x^2} \div \dfrac{2x+6}{x} = \dfrac{x^2-9}{x^2} \cdot \dfrac{x}{2x+6}$

$= \dfrac{(x+3)(x-3)}{x^2} \cdot \dfrac{x}{2(x+3)}$

$= \dfrac{x-3}{2x}$

4. $\dfrac{x^2-5x+6}{3x} \div \dfrac{x-2}{9x} = \dfrac{x^2-5x+6}{3x} \cdot \dfrac{9x}{x-2}$

$= \dfrac{(x-2)(x-3)}{3x} \cdot \dfrac{9x}{x-2}$

$= 3(x-3) = 3x-9$

SIMPLIFYING COMPLEX ALGEBRAIC FRACTIONS

An algebraic fraction that contains at least one other fraction in its numerator or denominator is called a **complex algebraic fraction**.

To simplify a complex algebraic fraction, multiply every term in the fraction by a common denominator of the fractions contained within it. For example, to simplify the complex fraction shown below, multiply every term by $2x$, a common denominator of the fractions $\frac{3}{x}$ and $\frac{z}{2}$. As a result, all the denominators cancel, leaving a fraction free of other fractions.

$$\frac{y+\dfrac{3}{x}}{\dfrac{z}{2}} = \frac{2x\cdot y + 2x\cdot \dfrac{3}{x}}{2x\cdot \dfrac{z}{2}}$$

$$= \frac{2xy+6}{xz}$$

Example

Simplify $\dfrac{x+\dfrac{2}{x}}{y+\dfrac{3}{y}}$.

Procedure

1. Multiply every term in the fraction by xy, a common denominator of $\frac{2}{x}$ and $\frac{3}{y}$. Cancel the denominators.

$$\frac{x+\dfrac{2}{x}}{y+\dfrac{3}{y}}$$

$$= \frac{xy\cdot x + xy\cdot \dfrac{2}{x}}{xy\cdot y + xy\cdot \dfrac{3}{y}}$$

$$= \frac{x^2 y + 2y}{xy^2 + 3x}$$

PRACTICE PROBLEMS

Simplify the following complex fractions:

1. $\dfrac{\dfrac{x}{y}}{\dfrac{a}{b}}$

2. $\dfrac{5+\dfrac{2}{x}}{6}$

3. $\dfrac{\dfrac{2}{x}-\dfrac{3}{y}}{5}$

4. $\dfrac{4+\dfrac{3}{x}}{\dfrac{7}{x^2}}$

ANSWERS AND EXPLANATIONS

1. $\dfrac{\dfrac{x}{y}}{\dfrac{a}{b}} = \dfrac{x}{y} \div \dfrac{a}{b} = \dfrac{x}{y} \cdot \dfrac{b}{a} = \dfrac{bx}{ay}$

2. $\dfrac{5+\dfrac{2}{x}}{6} = \dfrac{x \cdot 5 + \cancel{x} \cdot \dfrac{2}{\cancel{x}}}{x \cdot 6}$

   $= \dfrac{5x+2}{6x}$

3. $\dfrac{\dfrac{2}{x}-\dfrac{3}{y}}{5} = \dfrac{\cancel{x}\,y \cdot \dfrac{2}{\cancel{x}} - x\cancel{y} \cdot \dfrac{3}{\cancel{y}}}{xy \cdot 5} = \dfrac{2y-3x}{5xy}$

4. $\dfrac{4+\dfrac{3}{x}}{\dfrac{7}{x^2}} = \dfrac{x^2 \cdot 4 + \cancel{x^2} \cdot \dfrac{\overset{x}{3}}{\cancel{x}}}{\cancel{x^2} \cdot \dfrac{7}{\underset{1}{\cancel{x^2}}}} = \dfrac{4x^2+3x}{7}$

PRACTICE TEST

1. $5^2 + 3(7 - 5)^3 =$

   A. 224
   B. 28
   C. 49
   D. 78
   E. 241

2. For $a = 2$, $b = 1$, and $x = -3$, what is the value of $\dfrac{\sqrt{b^2 - 4ax}}{a - x}$?

   A. $\dfrac{3\sqrt{2}}{5}$
   B. 5
   C. -5
   D. 1
   E. $\dfrac{2\sqrt{6}}{5}$

3. $(4x^2 + y^2) + (x^2 - 5y^2) - (2x^2 - y^2) =$

   A. $3x^2 - 4y^2$
   B. $x^2 y^2$
   C. $3x^6 - 3y^6$
   D. $3x^2 - 3y^2$
   E. $-8x^2 - 5y^2$

4. $(-2x^2 y)(-4xy^3)(x^2 y^2) =$

   A. $8x^5 y^6$
   B. $-6x^5 y^6$
   C. $-5x^4 y^6$
   D. $8x^4 y^6$
   E. $-5x^5 y^6$

5. $(2a^2 b^3)^5 =$

   A. $10a^7 b^8$
   B. $32a^{10} b^{15}$
   C. $10a^{10} b^{15}$
   D. $10a^2 b^3$
   E. $32a^7 b^8$

6. $8a^2 b - 2ab(4b + a) =$

   A. $10a^2 b - 8ab^2$
   B. $-2a^2 b$
   C. $8a^2 b - 8ab^2 + a$
   D. $-2a^5 b^4$
   E. $6a^2 b - 8ab^2$

7. $\dfrac{8x^5 y^{-2}}{4x^{-2} y^{-5}} =$

   A. $2x^7 y^3$
   B. $2x^3 y^3$
   C. $2x^7 y^{-7}$
   D. $2x^3 y^{-7}$
   E. $\dfrac{x^7 y^3}{2}$

8. If $2x + 5 = 3$, then $x + 6$ equals

   A. 7
   B. 2
   C. 5
   D. $2\dfrac{1}{2}$
   E. 10

9. Solve for x: $4(2x - 1) = 6x + 2$

   A. $1\dfrac{1}{2}$
   B. -3
   C. 5
   D. 3
   E. 7

10. Solve for x: $\dfrac{3}{4}x + \dfrac{x}{3} = 13$

    A. $30\dfrac{1}{3}$
    B. 13
    C. 39
    D. 24
    E. 12

11. Solve for x: $\dfrac{2x}{3} = \dfrac{3x-1}{4}$

   A. $-\dfrac{1}{4}$

   B. 3

   C. 1

   D. $\dfrac{1}{4}$

   E. 0

12. Solve for x: $\sqrt{2x-1} = 5$

   A. $5\dfrac{1}{2}$

   B. 18

   C. 13

   D. 3

   E. 12

13. Solve for x in terms of a, b, and c: $a = \dfrac{b}{1+cx}$

   A. $\dfrac{b-a}{ac}$

   B. $b - a - ac$

   C. $\dfrac{b}{a+ac}$

   D. $\dfrac{b}{a+c}$

   E. $\dfrac{a-b}{ac}$

14. If $5x - 2y = 4$ and $x + y = 5$, then $x^2 + y$ equals

   A. 5

   B. 25

   C. 3

   D. 49

   E. 7

15. If $\dfrac{x}{5} - \dfrac{x}{2} > 6$ then a possible value of x is

   A. 20

   B. -20

   C. -21

   D. -19

   E. 19

16. Factor $x^2 - 5x - 6$

   A. $(x - 3)(x + 2)$

   B. $(x - 6)(x + 1)$

   C. $(x - 6)(x - 1)$

   D. $(x + 6)(x - 1)$

   E. $(x - 5)(x + 1)$

17. Factor $9a^2 - 25b^4$

   A. $(9a - 25b^2)^2$

   B. $(9a - 25b^2)(9a + 25b^2)$

   C. $(3a - 5b^2)^2$

   D. $9(a - 5b^2)(a + 5b^2)$

   E. $(3a + 5b^2)(3a - 5b^2)$

18. Factor $2x^3 + 10x^2 - 48x$

   A. $2x(x + 8)(x - 3)$

   B. $2x(x - 12)(x + 2)$

   C. $2(x - 2)(x + 8)(x - 3)$

   D. $2x(x - 12)(x + 4)$

   E. $2x(x - 8)(x + 3)$

19. Solve for x: $x^2 + 2x = 35$

   A. $8\dfrac{3}{4}$ or $-8\dfrac{3}{4}$

   B. -5 or 7

   C. $\sqrt{33}$ or $-\sqrt{33}$

   D. -7 or 5

   E. -5 or -7

20. $\sqrt{50x^2 y^3} =$

   A. $5x^2 y^2 \sqrt{2xy}$

   B. $5xy\sqrt{2y}$

   C. $5x^3 y^3 \sqrt{2}$

   D. $25xy\sqrt{y}$

   E. $10xy\sqrt{5y}$

21. $\sqrt{2x} + \sqrt{32x} - \sqrt{18x} =$

A. $4\sqrt{x}$

B. $8\sqrt{2x}$

C. $2\sqrt{2x}$

D. $4\sqrt{2x}$

E. $4x\sqrt{x}$

22. $\dfrac{\sqrt{5xy} \cdot \sqrt{15x^3 y}}{\sqrt{3}} =$

A. $5x^2 y$

B. $5x^4 y^2$

C. $\dfrac{2xy\sqrt{5}}{\sqrt{3}}$

D. $\dfrac{5x^2 y}{\sqrt{3}}$

E. $10xy$

23. $\dfrac{5}{x-2} - \dfrac{2}{x+2} =$

A. $\dfrac{3}{4}$

B. $\dfrac{3}{2x}$

C. $\dfrac{3x+6}{x^2-4}$

D. $\dfrac{3x}{x^2-4}$

E. $\dfrac{3x+14}{x^2-4}$

24. $\dfrac{x^2-25}{x^2} \div \dfrac{3x+15}{x} =$

A. $\dfrac{x-5}{6x}$

B. $\dfrac{x-5}{3x}$

C. $\dfrac{x+5}{3}$

D. $\dfrac{3x}{x-5}$

E. $\dfrac{6x}{x-5}$

25. $\dfrac{\dfrac{3}{x} + \dfrac{5}{y}}{2} =$

A. $\dfrac{6x+10y}{xy}$

B. $\dfrac{4}{x+y}$

C. $\dfrac{16}{x+y}$

D. $\dfrac{3y+5x}{2xy}$

E. $\dfrac{4}{xy}$

ANSWERS AND EXPLANATIONS

1. C	6. E	10. E	14. E	18. A	22. A
2. D	7. A	11. B	15. C	19. D	23. E
3. D	8. C	12. C	16. B	20. B	24. B
4. A	9. D	13. A	17. E	21. C	25. D
5. B					

1. The correct answer is (C).

$$5^2 + 3(7-5)^3$$
$$= 5^2 + 3(2)^3$$
$$= 25 + 3(8)$$
$$= 25 + 24$$
$$= 49$$

2. The correct answer is (D).

$$\frac{\sqrt{b^2 - 4ax}}{a - x}$$
$$= \frac{\sqrt{(1)^2 - 4(2)(-3)}}{(2) - (-3)}$$
$$= \frac{\sqrt{1 + 24}}{2 + 3}$$
$$= \frac{\sqrt{25}}{5}$$
$$= \frac{5}{5}$$
$$= 1$$

3. The correct answer is (D).

$$\left(4x^2 + y^2\right) + \left(x^2 - 5y^2\right) - \left(2x^2 - y^2\right)$$
$$= \left(4x^2 + y^2\right) + \left(x^2 - 5y^2\right) + \left(-2x^2 + y^2\right)$$

$$4x^2 + y^2$$
$$x^2 - 5y^2$$
$$\frac{-2x^2 + y^2}{3x^2 - 3y^2}$$

4. The correct answer is (A).

$$\left(-2x^2 y\right)\left(-4xy^3\right)\left(x^2 y^2\right)$$
$$= (-2)(-4)\left(x^2 \cdot x \cdot x^2\right)\left(y \cdot y^3 \cdot y^2\right)$$
$$= 8x^5 y^6$$

5. **The correct answer is (B).**

$$\left(2a^2b^3\right)^5$$
$$= 2^5 a^{2 \cdot 5} b^{3 \cdot 5}$$
$$= 32a^{10}b^{15}$$

6. **The correct answer is (E).**

$$8a^2b - 2\overbrace{ab(4b+a)}$$
$$= 8a^2b - 8ab^2 - 2a^2b$$
$$= 6a^2b - 8ab^2$$

7. **The correct answer is (A).**

$$\frac{8x^5y^{-2}}{4x^{-2}y^{-5}} = \frac{8}{4}x^{5-(-2)}y^{-2-(-5)}$$
$$= 2x^{5+2}y^{-2+5}$$
$$= 2x^7y^3$$

8. **The correct answer is (C).**

$$
\begin{array}{rcr}
2x - 5 = & & 3 \\
-5 & & -5 \\
\hline
2x = & & -2 \\
\end{array}
$$

$$\frac{2x}{2} = \frac{-2}{2}$$
$$x = -1$$

Thus, $x + 6 = -1 + 6$
$$= 5$$

9. **The correct answer is (D).**

$$
\begin{array}{rcr}
\overbrace{4(2x-1)} = & & 6x+2 \\
8x - 4 = & & 6x+2 \\
-6x & & -6x \\
\hline
2x - 4 = & & +2 \\
+4 & & +4 \\
\hline
2x = & & 6 \\
\end{array}
$$

$$\frac{2x}{2} = \frac{6}{2}$$
$$x = 3$$

10. **The correct answer is (E).**

$$\frac{3}{4}x + \frac{x}{3} = 13 \text{ (multiply by 12)}$$

$$\cancel{12} \cdot \frac{3}{4}x + \cancel{12} \cdot \frac{x}{\cancel{3}} = 12 \cdot 13$$

$$9x + 4x = 156$$

$$\frac{\cancel{13}x}{\cancel{13}} = \frac{156}{13}$$

$$x = 12$$

11. **The correct answer is (B).**

$$\frac{2x}{3} = \frac{3x-1}{4} \text{ (cross-multiplying)}$$

$$4(2x) = 3(3x-1)$$

$$8x = 9x - 3$$

$$\underline{-9x \qquad -9x}$$

$$-x = -3$$

$$x = 3$$

12. **The correct answer is (C).**

$$\sqrt{2x-1} = 5 \text{ (square both sides)}$$

$$\left(\sqrt{2x-1}\right)^2 = (5)^2$$

$$2x - 1 = 25$$

$$\underline{ +1 \quad +1}$$

$$2x = 26$$

$$\frac{\cancel{2}x}{\cancel{2}} = \frac{26}{2}$$

$$x = 13$$

13. **The correct answer is (A).**

$$a = \frac{b}{1+cx}$$

$$\frac{a}{1} = \frac{b}{1+cx} \text{ (cross-multiply)}$$

$$a(1+cx) = 1(b)$$

$$a + acx = b$$

$$\underline{-a \qquad -a}$$

$$acx = b - a$$

$$\frac{\cancel{acx}}{\cancel{ac}} = \frac{b-a}{ac}$$

$$x = \frac{b-a}{ac}$$

14. **The correct answer is (E).**

$$5x - 2y = 4 \rightarrow 5x - 2y = 4$$
$$2(x + y = 5) \rightarrow \underline{2x + 2y = 10}$$
$$7x \quad\quad = 14$$

$$\frac{7x}{7} = \frac{14}{7}$$
$$x = 2 \text{ (substitute into } x + y = 5)$$
$$x + y = 5$$
$$2 + y = 5$$
$$\underline{-2 \quad\quad -2}$$
$$y = 3$$

Thus, $x^2 + y = 2^2 + 3$
$$= 4 + 3$$
$$= 7$$

15. **The correct answer is (C).**

$$\frac{x}{5} - \frac{x}{2} > 6 \text{ (multiply by 10)}$$

$$\overset{2}{\cancel{10}} \cdot \frac{x}{\cancel{5}} - \overset{5}{\cancel{10}} \cdot \frac{x}{\cancel{2}} > 10 \cdot 6$$

$$2x - 5x > 60$$

$$-3x > 60$$

$$\frac{-3x}{-3} < \frac{60}{-3} \text{ (reverse inequality)}$$

$$x < -20$$

16. **The correct answer is (B).**

$$x^2 - 5x - 6$$
$$= (x \quad)(x \quad)$$
$$= (x - 6)(x + 1) \quad\quad +x - 6x = -5x$$

17. **The correct answer is (E).**

$$9a^2 - 25b^4$$
$$= \left(\sqrt{9a^2} + \sqrt{25b^4}\right)\left(\sqrt{9a^2} - \sqrt{25b^4}\right)$$
$$= \left(3a + 5b^2\right)\left(3a - 5b^2\right)$$

18. **The correct answer is (A).**

$$2x^3 + 10x^2 - 48x$$
$$= 2x(x^2 + 5x - 24)$$
$$= 2x(x+8)(x-3) \qquad -3x + 8x = +5x$$

The factor $x+8$ comes from $+8x$ and $x-3$ comes from $-3x$.

19. **The correct answer is (D).**

$$
\begin{aligned}
x^2 + 2x &= 35 \\
-35 &= -35 \\
\hline
x^2 + 2x - 35 &= 0 \\
(x+7)(x-5) &= 0
\end{aligned}
$$

$$
\begin{array}{c|c}
x + 7 = 0 & x - 5 = 0 \\
\underline{-7 \quad -7} & \underline{+5 \quad +5} \\
x = -7 & x = +5
\end{array}
$$

20. **The correct answer is (B).**

$$\sqrt{50x^2y^3}$$
$$= \sqrt{25x^2y^2 \cdot 2y}$$
$$= \sqrt{25x^2y^2} \cdot \sqrt{2y}$$
$$= 5xy\sqrt{2y}$$

21. **The correct answer is (C).**

$$\sqrt{2x} + \sqrt{32x} - \sqrt{18x}$$
$$= \sqrt{2x} + \sqrt{16 \cdot 2x} - \sqrt{9 \cdot 2x}$$
$$= \sqrt{2x} + \sqrt{16} \cdot \sqrt{2x} - \sqrt{9} \cdot \sqrt{2x}$$
$$= \sqrt{2x} + 4\sqrt{2x} - 3\sqrt{2x}$$
$$= (1 + 4 - 3)\sqrt{2x}$$
$$= 2\sqrt{2x}$$

22. **The correct answer is (A).**

$$\frac{\sqrt{5xy} \cdot \sqrt{15x^3y}}{\sqrt{3}}$$
$$= \sqrt{\frac{5xy \cdot 15x^3y}{3}}$$
$$= \sqrt{25x^4y^2}$$
$$= 5x^2y$$

23. **The correct answer is (E).**

$$\frac{5}{x-2} - \frac{2}{x+2} \quad \text{(cross-multiply)}$$

$$= \frac{5(x+2) - 2(x-2)}{(x-2)(x+2)}$$

$$= \frac{5x + 10 - 2x + 4}{x^2 - 4}$$

$$= \frac{3x + 14}{x^2 - 4}$$

24. **The correct answer is (B).**

$$\frac{x^2 - 25}{x^2} \div \frac{3x + 15}{x} \quad \text{(invert and multiply)}$$

$$= \frac{x^2 - 25}{x^2} \cdot \frac{x}{3x + 15}$$

$$= \frac{\overset{1}{\cancel{(x+5)}}(x-5)}{\underset{x}{\cancel{x^2}}} \cdot \frac{\overset{1}{\cancel{x}}}{3\underset{1}{\cancel{(x+5)}}}$$

$$= \frac{x - 5}{3x}$$

25. **The correct answer is (D).**

$$\frac{\dfrac{3}{x} + \dfrac{5}{y}}{2} \quad \text{(multiply by } xy\text{)}$$

$$= \frac{\cancel{x}\,y \cdot \dfrac{3}{\cancel{x}} + x\,\cancel{y} \cdot \dfrac{5}{\cancel{y}}}{xy \cdot 2}$$

$$= \frac{3y + 5x}{2xy}$$

Chapter 4
WORD PROBLEMS

In this chapter we will discuss various types of word problems, most of which have algebraic solutions. The problems discussed include:

- Arithmetic problems
- Number, integer, and age problems
- Average and mixture problems
- Motion problems
- Work problems
- Set problems

In general, problem-solving involves four basic steps:

1. Understanding the problem

2. Formulating a plan

3. Carrying out the plan

4. Checking the solution

Understanding the problem involves reading the problem carefully to determine what is given, what relationships and conditions must be satisfied, and, most important, what is unknown. In some problems, it may help to draw a diagram. Once it is determined what is unknown, suitable notation should be introduced. For example, an unknown number might be represented by the letter n or x, an unknown time by the letter t, an unknown distance by the letter d, and so on.

Formulating a plan involves recognizing some essential element in the problem that reminds you of another problem you have seen and solved before. Needless to say, the more problems you have solved of a similar nature, the easier it will be to make the appropriate connection. In some problems, it may help to focus on the unknown and to write down any formulas you know involving this type of quantity. In other problems, it may help to write equations that translate into symbolic form the relationships and conditions stated in words.

Carrying out the plan involves performing the specific operations and procedures necessary to obtain the solution. Whether multiplying fractions, or factoring quadratic equations, this step should be done carefully and accurately.

Checking the solution involves returning to the original problem with the solution obtained to determine whether or not it satisfies the given relationships and conditions.

ARITHMETIC PROBLEMS

FRACTION WORD PROBLEMS

In order to find a fractional part of a number, we multiply the fraction times the number.

For example, to find $\dfrac{2}{3}$ of 18, we multiply $\dfrac{2}{3} \times 18$ and get the result 12.

As discussed previously (see *Solving Percent Problems* p. 63), the number we take the fractional part *of* is called the **Whole**, and the result is called the **Part**.

$$\text{Fraction} \times \text{Whole} = \text{Part}$$

In most fraction word problems, we will be given values for two of the quantities in this equation, and will be asked to find the third. Note that, if we are given the Part and the Whole, and are asked to find the Fraction, we usually use the alternate form of the equation:

$$\text{Fraction} = \frac{\text{Part}}{\text{Whole}}$$

Example 1
A team played M games and won N of them. What fraction of its games did it lose?

Procedure

1. To find the number of games the team lost, subtract the number of games it won from the total number of games.
    $$\text{Games Lost} = M - N$$

2. Form a fraction by placing the number of games lost over the total number of games played.

    $$\text{Fraction} = \frac{\text{Part}}{\text{Whole}}$$
    $$= \frac{M - N}{M}$$

    The team lost $\dfrac{M - N}{M}$ of its games.

Example 2

If a woman paints $\frac{2}{3}$ of her apartment one weekend, and her roommate paints $\frac{3}{4}$ of what remains the following weekend, what fraction still remains to be painted?

Procedure

1. After the first weekend, $\frac{1}{3}$ of the apartment remains to be painted $\left(1 - \frac{2}{3}\right)$. To find the fraction painted by the roommate, multiply this remaining fraction by $\frac{3}{4}$.

$$\frac{3}{4} \text{ of } \frac{1}{3} = \frac{\cancel{3}}{4} \times \frac{1}{\cancel{3}}$$

$$= \frac{1}{4} \text{ painted by roomate}$$

2. Add the fractions painted by the woman and her roommate, and subtract the result from 1.

$$\frac{2}{3} = \frac{8}{12} \text{ painted by woman}$$

$$+\frac{1}{4} = \frac{3}{12} \text{ painted by roommate}$$

$$\frac{11}{12} \text{ painted together}$$

$$1 - \frac{11}{12} = \frac{1}{12} \text{ remains}$$

$$\frac{1}{12} \text{ remains to be painted}$$

Example 3

An automobile gasoline gauge reads $\frac{1}{8}$ full. After the gas tank is filled with 15 gallons, the gauge reads $\frac{7}{8}$ full. What is the capacity of the tank?

Procedure

1. Represent the capacity of the tank by C.

    Let C = the capacity of the tank.

2. To obtain the fraction of the tank filled, subtract the original gauge reading from the final gauge reading.

$$\frac{7}{8}$$

$$-\frac{1}{8}$$

$$\frac{6}{8} = \frac{3}{4} \text{ of the tank was filled}$$

3. Write an equation expressing the fact that $\frac{3}{4}$ of the capacity of the tank equals 15 gallons. Solve this equation for C.

$$\text{Fraction} \times \text{Whole} = \text{Part}$$

$$\frac{3}{4} \times C = 15$$

$$\cancel{4} \cdot \frac{3}{\cancel{4}} C = 15 \cdot 4$$

$$3C = 60$$

$$\frac{\cancel{3}C}{\cancel{3}} = \frac{60}{3}$$

$$C = 20 \text{ gallons}$$

The capacity of the tank is 20 gallons.

Example 4

A student spends $\frac{3}{4}$ of his money on tuition, and $\frac{1}{3}$ of what remains on books. If he has $50 left, how much money did he start with?

Procedure

1. Represent the student's money at the start by S.

Let S = the student's money at the start.

2. After tuition, $\frac{1}{4}$ of the original amount of money remains $\left(1 - \frac{3}{4}\right)$. To find the fraction spent on books, multiply this remaining fraction by $\frac{1}{3}$.

$$\frac{1}{3} \text{ of } \frac{1}{4} = \frac{1}{3} \times \frac{1}{4}$$

$$= \frac{1}{12} \text{ spent on books}$$

3. Add the fractions spent on tuition and books, and subtract the result from 1.

$$\frac{3}{4} = \frac{9}{12} \quad \text{tuition}$$

$$+\frac{1}{12} = \frac{1}{12} \quad \text{books}$$

$$\frac{10}{12} = \frac{5}{6} \quad \text{spent together}$$

$$1 - \frac{5}{6} = \frac{1}{6} \quad \text{remains}$$

4. Write an equation expressing the fact that the fraction remaining times the original amount of money equals $50. Solve this equation for S.

$$\frac{1}{6}S = 50$$

$$\cancel{6} \cdot \frac{1}{\cancel{6}}S = 50 \cdot 6$$

$$S = 300$$

The student started with $300.

PRACTICE PROBLEMS

1. On a certain bus there are M men and W women. If 2 men and 1 woman get off the bus, what fraction of the remaining passengers are men?

2. Five friends decide to rent a summer house at a total cost of D dollars. They agree to share the rent equally. Before the summer begins, 1 of the friends has to drop out. By how many dollars does the cost to each of the other friends increase?

3. In company X, $\frac{1}{4}$ of the employees earn under $12,000 per year. If $\frac{3}{5}$ of the remaining employees earn between $12,000 and $18,000, what fraction of the employees earn more than $18,000?

4. After traveling 220 miles, Hilda completed $\frac{4}{5}$ of her trip. How far does she still have to travel?

5. A family budgets $\frac{1}{3}$ of its monthly income for rent, $\frac{1}{4}$ for food, and $\frac{1}{6}$ for clothing. If, after paying these items, the family has $420 left, what is the monthly income?

ANSWERS AND EXPLANATIONS

1. $\text{Men} = M - 2$ (2 men leave)

   $\underline{\text{Women} = W - 1}$ (1 woman leaves)

   $\text{Total} = M + W - 3$

   $\text{Fraction of Men} = \dfrac{\text{Men}}{\text{Total}}$

   $= \dfrac{M - 2}{M + W - 3}$

2. The initial cost to each friend $= \dfrac{D}{5}$

   The final cost to each friend $= \dfrac{D}{4}$

   Thus, the increase to each friend $= \dfrac{D}{4} - \dfrac{D}{5} = \dfrac{5D - 4D}{20} = \dfrac{D}{20}$

3. $\frac{1}{4}$ of the employees earn under $12,000. Thus, $\frac{3}{4}$ remain.

   $\frac{3}{5}$ of the remaining employees, or $\frac{3}{5}$ of $\frac{3}{4} = \frac{3}{5} \times \frac{3}{4} = \frac{9}{20}$, earn between $12,000 and $18,000.

The total of these two groups is $\frac{1}{4} + \frac{9}{20} = \frac{14}{20} = \frac{7}{10}$. Thus, the fraction of remaining employees (those earning more than \$18,000) is $1 - \frac{7}{10} = \frac{3}{10}$.

4. Let x = the total trip.

$$\frac{4}{5} \cdot x = 220$$

$$\cancel{5} \cdot \frac{4}{\cancel{5}} \cdot x = 220 \cdot 5$$

$$4x = 1100$$

$$x = 275 \text{ miles}$$

Thus, Hilda still has $275 - 220 = 55$ miles to travel.

5. The fraction of money spent $= \frac{1}{3} + \frac{1}{4} + \frac{1}{6} = \frac{4}{12} + \frac{3}{12} + \frac{2}{12} = \frac{9}{12} = \frac{3}{4}$

Thus, $1 - \frac{3}{4} = \frac{1}{4}$ of the monthly income is left.

Let x = the monthly income.

$$\frac{1}{4} x = 420$$

$$\cancel{4} \cdot \frac{1}{\cancel{4}} x = 420 \cdot 4$$

$$x = \$1680$$

PROPORTION PROBLEMS

In proportion problems, we are told the rate at which two quantities vary, and are asked to find the value of one of them, given the value of the other.

For example, suppose we are told that a certain item costs \$5 per dozen, and we are asked to find out how much 84 of them would cost. By expressing the cost rate as a ratio, we can write the following proportion: \$5 is to 12 items (per dozen) as \$$x$ is to 84 items, where x represents the unknown cost. That is,

$$\frac{\text{Cost} \rightarrow}{\text{\# Item} \rightarrow} \quad \frac{\$5}{12} = \frac{\$x}{84}$$

Notice that the order of the quantities on both sides of the proportion is the same—cost to number of items.

In order to find the unknown cost, x, we cross-multiply the numerators and denominators, set the products equal, and divide. Thus, we get:

$$5 \cdot 84 \qquad 12 \cdot x$$

$$\frac{5}{12} \diagup\!\!\!\!\diagdown \frac{x}{84}$$

$$5 \cdot 84 = 12 \cdot x$$

$$420 = 12x$$

$$\frac{420}{12} = \frac{\cancel{12}x}{\cancel{12}}$$

$$\$35 = x$$

In other words, at the rate of \$5 per dozen, 84 items would cost \$35.

Example 1

A recipe calls for M cups of water for every N cups of rice. How many cups of water are needed to make Q cups of rice?

Procedure

1. Represent the unknown number of cups of water by x.
   Let $x =$ the number of cups of water needed to make Q runs of rice.

2. Write a proportion in which the number of cups of water is compared to the number of cups of rice. Remember to keep the order of the two quantities the same on both sides of the proportion. Solve this proportion for x by cross-multiplying and dividing.

$$\frac{\text{Water} \rightarrow \text{M}}{\text{Rice} \rightarrow \text{N}} = \frac{x}{\text{Q}}$$

$$\text{Q} \cdot \text{M} = \text{N} \cdot x$$

$$\frac{\text{QM}}{\text{N}} = \frac{\cancel{\text{N}} x}{\cancel{\text{N}}}$$

$$\frac{\text{QM}}{\text{N}} = x$$

Example 2

In a certain class, 4 out of every 5 students passed an exam. If 20 students passed the exam, how many failed?

Procedure

1. Represent the total number of students in the class by T.
   Let T = the total number of students in the class.

2. Write a proportion in which the number of people that passed the exam are compared to the total number of students. Solve this proportion for T by cross-multiplying and dividing.

$$\frac{\text{Passed} \rightarrow 4}{\text{Total} \rightarrow 5} = \frac{20}{\text{T}}$$

$$4 \cdot \text{T} = 5 \cdot 20$$

$$\frac{\cancel{4}\text{T}}{\cancel{4}} = \frac{100}{4}$$

$$\text{T} = 25$$

3. To find the number of students that failed the exam, subtract the number of students that passed the exam, 20, from this total.

$$\text{Failed} = \text{Total} - \text{Passed}$$

$$\text{Failed} = 25 - 20 = 5$$

The number of students that failed the exam is 5.

PRACTICE PROBLEMS

1. A team wins M out of every N games played. If the team wins 45 games, how many games does it play?

2. The scale on a map is $\frac{3}{4}$ inch $=$ 15 miles. If the distance between two cities is represented by $4\frac{1}{2}$ inches on the map, what is the actual distance between the cities?

3. If N dozen apples cost D dollars, what is the cost, in *cents*, of R apples at the same rate?

4. Mary can read P pages in M minutes. At the same rate, how many *hours* will it take her to read a book of 300 pages?

5. In a recent survey, R out of S people said they walked to work. If 50 people said they walked to work, how many people said they did not walk to work?

ANSWERS AND EXPLANATIONS

1. Let $x =$ the number of games played.

$$\frac{\text{wins} \rightarrow M}{\text{plays} \rightarrow N} = \frac{45}{x} \ (\text{cross-multiply})$$

$$Mx = 45N$$

$$x = \frac{45N}{M}$$

2. Let $x =$ the distance between the cities.

$$\frac{\text{inches} \rightarrow \frac{3}{4}}{\text{miles} \rightarrow 15} = \frac{4\frac{1}{2}}{x} \ (\text{cross-multiply})$$

$$\frac{3}{4}x = 4\frac{1}{2} \cdot 15$$

$$\frac{3}{4}x = \frac{9}{2} \cdot 15$$

$$\cancel{4} \cdot \frac{3}{\cancel{4}}x = \frac{135}{\cancel{2}} \cdot \cancel{4}^2$$

$$3x = 270$$

$$x = 90 \text{ miles}$$

3. Let $x =$ the cost of R apples.
   Also, N dozen apples $=$ $12N$ apples, and D dollars $=$ $100D$ cents.

$$\frac{\text{cents} \rightarrow 100D}{\text{apples} \rightarrow 12N} = \frac{x}{R} \ (\text{cross-multiply})$$

$$12Nx = 100DR$$

$$x = \frac{100DR}{12N}$$

$$x = \frac{25DR}{3N}$$

4. Let x = the number of hours needed to read 300 pages.

    Also, M minutes = $\dfrac{M}{60}$ hours.

$$\frac{\text{pages} \rightarrow}{\text{hours} \rightarrow} \frac{P}{\dfrac{M}{60}} = \frac{300}{x} \quad (\text{cross-multiply})$$

$$Px = \frac{M}{\cancel{60}} \cdot \cancel{300}^{5}$$

$$Px = 5M$$

$$x = \frac{5M}{P}$$

5. Let x = the number of people that said they did not walk to work.
    If R out of S people said they walked to work, then $S - R$ said they did not walk to work.

$$\frac{\text{walked} \rightarrow}{\text{did not walk} \rightarrow} \frac{R}{S - R} = \frac{50}{x} (\text{cross-multiply})$$

$$Rx = 50(S - R)$$

$$x = \frac{50(S - R)}{R}$$

Percent Word Problems—General

As discussed previously (see *Solving Percent Problems* p. 63), most percent problems involve three quantities—a *Percent*, a *Whole*, and a *Part*. These quantities are related by the following product and proportion:

Percent Product	*Percent Proportion*
Percent $\times$ Whole = Part	$\dfrac{\text{Part}}{\text{Whole}} = \dfrac{\text{Percent}}{100\%}$

In percent word problems, we will be given values for two of these quantities, and will be asked to find the value of the third. Either the product or the proportion can be used. Remember that if the product is used, the Percent must be changed to either a fraction or a decimal.

Example 1

Of its net monthly income, a family budgets 25% for rent, and 20% for food. If its net monthly income is $1200, how much money is budgeted for things other than rent and food?

Procedure

1. Represent the amount of money budgeted for other things by N.
   Let N = the amount of money budgeted for things other than rent and food.

2. To find the percent budgeted for other things, add the two given percents and subtract the result from 100%.

$$25\% \text{ rent}$$
$$+20\% \text{ food}$$
$$45\%$$

$$100\% - 45\% = 55\% \text{ budgeted for other things.}$$

3. Using either the product or the proportion, solve for N. With the product, remember to change the percent to a decimal (D ← P). With the proportion, cross-multiply and divide.

Product	*Proportion*

$$\% \times \text{Whole} = \text{Part}$$
$$.55 \times 1200 = N$$
$$660 = N$$

$$\frac{\text{Part}}{\text{Whole}} = \frac{\%}{100\%}$$
$$\frac{N}{1200} = \frac{55}{100}$$
$$100 \cdot N = 55 \cdot 1200$$
$$100N = 66000$$
$$\frac{\cancel{100}N}{\cancel{100}} = \frac{66000}{100}$$
$$N = 660$$

The amount budgeted for things other than rent and food is $660.

Example 2

On a certain test, 18 students passed and 7 students failed. What percent passed the test?

Procedure

1. Represent the percent that passed by P.
   Let P = the percent that passed.

2. Using either the product or the proportion, solve for P. In both methods, the Whole is 25 (18 + 7). With the product, remember to move the decimal point in the result two places to the right (D → P).

Product	*Proportion*
$\% \times \text{Whole} = \text{Part}$	$\dfrac{\text{Part}}{\text{Whole}} = \dfrac{\%}{100\%}$
$P \times 25 = 18$	
$\dfrac{25P}{25} = \dfrac{18}{25}$	$\dfrac{18}{25} = \dfrac{P}{100}$
$P = .72$	$25 \cdot P = 18 \cdot 100$
$P = 72\%$	$\dfrac{25P}{25} = \dfrac{1800}{25}$
	$P = 72\%$

72% passed the test.

Example 3

A woman gave $115 as a deposit on a stereo system. If this represents 20% of the total cost, how much does she still owe?

Procedure

1. Represent the total cost of the stereo system by C.
   Let C = the total cost of the stereo system.

2. Using either the product or the proportion, solve for C. With the product, remember to change the percent to a decimal (D ← P).

Product	*Proportion*
$\% \times \text{Whole} = \text{Part}$	$\dfrac{\text{Part}}{\text{Whole}} = \dfrac{\%}{100\%}$
$.20 \times C = 115$	
$\dfrac{.20C}{.20} = \dfrac{115}{.20}$	$\dfrac{115}{C} = \dfrac{20}{100}$
$C = 575$	$20 \cdot C = 115 \cdot 100$
	$\dfrac{20C}{20} = \dfrac{11500}{20}$
	$C = 575$

3. To find the amount still owed, subtract the amount deposited from the total cost.

$$\begin{array}{r} \$575 \text{ total cost} \\ -\$115 \text{ deposit} \\ \hline \$460 \end{array}$$

The woman still owes $460.

PRACTICE PROBLEMS

1. Rachel invests $3000 at 8% simple annual interest. How much interest is earned after 3 months?

2. In an election, only R, S, and T received votes. If S received twice as many votes as R, and T received three times as many votes as S, what percent of the total vote was received by T?

3. In a class of 40 students, 80% are men. Of the 24 students that pass the midterm, 75% are men. What percent of the women in the class pass the midterm?

4. After having dinner at a restaurant, Anna leaves $6.30 as a tip for the waiter. If this represents 15% of the total bill, how much was the bill?

5. A manufacturer finds that, on the average, .2% of his items must be rejected. If, in a certain month, 5 items are rejected, how many items pass the inspection?

6. A car dealer advertises two different payment plans for a new car. If the buyer pays cash, the car costs $5700. If the buyer pays on the installment plan, he pays 20% of the cash cost as a down payment, and then $200 a month for 24 months. How much more money must a buyer pay on the installment plan than on the cash plan?

7. R percent of what number is Q?

8. In a certain high school graduating class, there are 200 boys and 300 girls. If 60% of the boys and 70% of the girls go to college, what percent of the entire graduating class go to college?

9. After traveling 480 miles, Steve completed 80% of his trip. How much further must he still travel?

10. If 30% of 50% of $70x$ equals 21, what is the value of x?

ANSWERS AND EXPLANATIONS

1. The interest earned in one year is 8% of $3000 = .08 \times \$3000 = \$240$.

    Since 3 months is $\dfrac{3}{12}$, or $\dfrac{1}{4}$ of a year, the interest earned after 3 months is

    $\dfrac{1}{4} \times \$240 = \$60$.

2. Let $n =$ the number of votes received by R, 2n = the number of votes received by S, and $3(2n) = 6n =$ the number of votes received by T.

    Thus, the total number of votes is $n + 2n + 6n = 9n$. If $x =$ the % of votes received by T,

    $$\frac{\text{Part}}{\text{Whole}} = \frac{\%}{100\%}$$

    $$\frac{6n}{9n} = \frac{n}{100} \text{ (cross-multiply)}$$

    $$9n = 600$$

    $$n = 66\frac{2}{3}\%$$

3.

$$.8 \times 40 = 32 \quad \boxed{.2 \times 40 = 8} \qquad .75 \times 24 = 18 \quad \boxed{.25 \times 24 = 6}$$

40 students → Men | Women   24 pass midterm → Men | Women

Let x = the % of women in the class that pass the midterm

$$\frac{\text{Part}}{\text{Whole}} = \frac{\%}{100\%}$$

$$\frac{6}{8} = \frac{x}{100} \ (\text{cross-multiply})$$

$$8x = 600$$

$$x = 75\%$$

4. Let x = the total bill.

$$\frac{\text{Part}}{\text{Whole}} = \frac{\%}{100\%}$$

$$\frac{\$6.30}{x} = \frac{15}{100} \ (\text{cross-multiply})$$

$$15x = 630$$

$$x = \$42$$

5. Let x = the total number of items.

$$\frac{\text{Part}}{\text{Whole}} = \frac{\%}{100\%}$$

$$\frac{5}{x} = \frac{.2}{100} \ (\text{cross-multiply})$$

$$.2x = 500$$

$$x = 2500$$

Since 5 items are rejected, $2500 - 5 = 2495$ pass the inspection.

6. On the installment plan, the downpayment is 20% of \$5700, or $.2 \times \$5700 = \$1140$. Then, the payments each month total $24 \times \$200 = \$4800$. Thus, the total payment is $\$1140 + \$4800 = \$5940$, which is \$240 more than the full cash payment of \$5700.

7.

$$\frac{\text{Part}}{\text{Whole}} = \frac{\%}{100\%}$$

$$\frac{Q}{x} = \frac{R}{100} \ (\text{cross-multiply})$$

$$Rx = 100Q$$

$$x = \frac{100Q}{R}$$

8. The number of boys going to college is $.6 \times 200 = 120$.
    The number of girls going to college is $.7 \times 300 = 210$.
    Thus, the total number of boys and girls going to college is $120 + 210 = 330$.
    Let x = the percent of boys and girls going to college.

    $$\frac{Part}{Whole} = \frac{\%}{100\%}$$

    $$\frac{330}{500} = \frac{x}{100} \quad (\text{cross-multiply})$$

    $$500x = 33,000$$

    $$x = 66\%$$

9. Let x = the total length of the trip.

    $$\frac{Part}{Whole} = \frac{\%}{100\%}$$

    $$\frac{480}{x} = \frac{80}{100} \quad (\text{cross-multiply})$$

    $$80x = 48,000$$

    $$x = 600 \text{ miles}$$

    Since Steve has already traveled 480 miles, $600 - 480 = 120$ miles remain.

10. 30% of 50% of 70x equals 21.

    $$(.3)(.5)(70x) = 21$$

    $$10.5x = 21$$

    $$x = 2$$

PERCENT WORD PROBLEMS—PERCENT OF INCREASE OR DECREASE

Sometimes, we are asked to find the percent of *change* (increase or decrease) from one number to another number. In these problems, we use the special forms of the percent product and proportion shown below. Notice that in both forms, the *Part* is represented by the *Amount of Change*, and the *Whole* is represented by the *Original Value*.

Percent of Change Product
% of Change $\times$ Original Value = Amount of Change

Percent of Change Proportion

$$\frac{\text{Amount of Change}}{\text{Original Value}} = \frac{\% \text{ of Change}}{100\%}$$

Example

A class increased in size from 20 students to 25 students. What was the percent of increase?

Procedure

1. Represent the percent of increase by P.
    Let P = the percent of increase

2. To find the amount of increase, subtract the original class size from the new class size.
    Amount of Increase = 25 − 20 = 5

3. Using either the product or proportion, solve for P.

Product	Proportion
% Inc. × Orig. = Inc.	$\dfrac{\text{Inc.}}{\text{Orig.}} = \dfrac{\text{\% Inc.}}{100\%}$
P × 20 = 5	$\dfrac{5}{20} = \dfrac{P}{100}$
$\dfrac{20P}{20} = \dfrac{5}{20}$	$20 \cdot P = 5 \cdot 100$
P = .25	$\dfrac{20P}{20} = \dfrac{500}{20}$
P = 25%	P = 25%

The class increased 25% in size.

PRACTICE PROBLEMS

1. Before starting a diet, Norm weighed 180 pounds. After the diet, he weighed 153 pounds. What was his percent of weight loss?

2. The number of employees at company X increases from 50 to 60. What is the percent of increase?

3. Patty sold her camera for $300, thus making a $60 profit. What was her percent of profit?

4. A piano, which normally sells for $800, is marked down to $700. What is the percent of markdown?

5. Marta buys a house for C dollars, and later sells it for R dollars, where R is greater than C. What is her percent of profit?

ANSWERS AND EXPLANATIONS

1. Let x = the % of weight loss.

$$\frac{\text{loss}}{\text{orig. value}} = \frac{\% \text{ loss}}{100\%}$$

$$\frac{27}{180} = \frac{x}{100} \, (\text{cross-multiply})$$

$$180x = 2700$$

$$x = 15\% \text{ weight loss}$$

2. Let x = the percent of increase.

$$\frac{\text{increase}}{\text{orig. value}} = \frac{\% \text{ increase}}{100\%}$$

$$\frac{10}{50} = \frac{x}{100} \, (\text{cross-multiply})$$

$$50x = 1000$$

$$x = 20\% \text{ increase}$$

3. The original cost was $300 − $60 = $240. Let x = the percent of profit.

$$\frac{\text{profit}}{\text{orig. cost}} = \frac{\% \text{ profit}}{100\%}$$

$$\frac{60}{240} = \frac{x}{100} \, (\text{cross-multiply})$$

$$240x = 6000$$

$$x = 25\% \text{ profit}$$

4. Let x = the percent of markdown.

$$\frac{\text{markdown}}{\text{orig. price}} = \frac{\% \text{ markdown}}{100\%}$$

$$\frac{100}{800} = \frac{x}{100} \, (\text{cross-multiply})$$

$$800x = 10,000$$

$$x = 12\frac{1}{2}\% \text{ markdown}$$

5. The profit is the revenue minus the cost, or $R − C$.
Let x = the percent of profit.

$$\frac{\text{profit}}{\text{orig. cost}} = \frac{\% \text{ profit}}{100\%}$$

$$\frac{R - C}{C} = \frac{x}{100} \, (\text{cross-multiply})$$

$$Cx = 100(R - C)$$

$$x = \frac{100(R - C)}{C}$$

When we are given the original value of a quantity, and the percent of increase or decrease, we can find the new value by two different methods.

Method 1: We use the percent product to find the amount of increase or decrease, and then add it to (in the case of an increase), or subtract it from (in the case of a decrease), the original value.

> % *Increase*: New Value = Original Value + Amount of Increase
> % *Decrease*: New Value = Original Value − Amount of Decrease

Method 2: We add the percent of increase to 100%, or subtract the percent of decrease from 100%, and then multiply the resulting percent by the original value.

> % *Increase*: New Value = (100% + % Increase) × Original Value
> % *Decrease*: New Value = (100% − % Decrease) × Original Value

For example, if the value of an item is increased by 25%, then its new value is 100% + 25%, or 125%, of its original value. Similarly, if the value of an item is reduced by 25%, then its new value is 100% − 25%, or 75% of its original value.

> % *Profit*: Selling Price = (100% + % Profit) × Cost
> % *Discount*: Selling Price = (100% − % Discount) × List Price

Example 1

A certain stock decreased in value by 15%. If it was originally selling at $80 a share, what is its value after the decrease?

Method 1

Procedure

1. To find the amount of decrease, multiply the percent of decrease by the original value.

$$\text{Amount of Decrease} = \% \text{ Dec.} \times \text{Orig. Value}$$
$$= .15 \times \$80$$
$$= \$12$$

2. Subtract the amount of decrease from the original value.

$$\text{New Value} = \text{Orig. Value} - \text{Amount of Decrease}$$
$$= \$80 - \$12$$
$$= \$68$$

Method 2

Procedure

1. Subtract the percent of decrease from 100%, and multiply the resulting percent by the original value.

$$\text{New Value} = (100\% - 15\%) \times \$80$$
$$= (85\%) \times \$80$$
$$= .85 \times \$80$$
$$= \$68$$

The new value of the stock is $68.

Example 2

A music store sells a guitar for $480, thus making a profit of 20% of their cost. What did the guitar cost the store?

Procedure

1. Represent the cost by C.
    Let C = the cost of the guitar for the store.

2. Write an equation expressing the fact that the selling price is equal to 120% of the cost. Solve this equation for C.

$$\text{S. Price} = (100\% + 20\%) \times \text{Cost}$$
$$\$480 = (120\%) \times C$$
$$\$480 = 1.20C$$
$$\frac{\$480}{1.20} = \frac{1.20C}{1.20}$$
$$\$400 = C$$

The guitar cost the store $400.

Example 3

During a sale, a camera is marked 25% off the list price. If the camera is on sale for $330, what is the list price?

Procedure

1. Represent the list price by L.
    Let L = the list price of the camera.

2. Write an equation expressing the fact that the sales price is 75% of the list price. Solve this equation for L.

$$\text{S. Price} = (100\% - 25\%) \text{ List Price}$$
$$\$330 = (75\%) \text{ L}$$
$$\$330 = .75L$$
$$\frac{\$330}{.75} = \frac{75L}{75}$$
$$\$440 = L$$

The list price of the camera is $440.

PRACTICE PROBLEMS

1. If a $300 typewriter loses 10% of its value each year, what is its value after three years?

2. Stu sold his cassette deck for $600, thus making a profit of 25%. What did the cassette deck originally cost Stu?

3. The population of a certain city is 44,800, an increase of 12% from the previous year. What was the population in the previous year?

4. An airline offers a special night flight at a 30% discount off the day flight fare. If the night flight costs $280, what is the day flight fare?

5. A store buys an item for $40. At what price should the store list the price of the item in order to give its customers a 20% discount off the list price, and still make a 10% profit on the cost?

ANSWERS AND EXPLANATIONS

1. At the end of each year, the value of the typewriter is $100\% - 10\% = 90\%$ of its value of the previous year.
After one year, its value is $.9(\$300) = \$270$.
After two years, its value is $.9(\$270) = \$243$.
After three years, its value is $.9(\$243) = \$218.70$.

2. Let C = the original cost of the deck.

$$\text{Selling Price} = (100\% + \% \text{ Profit}) \times \text{Cost}$$
$$\$600 = (100\% + 25\%) \times C$$
$$\$600 = 1.25C$$
$$\$480 = C$$

3. Let P = the population the previous year.

$$\text{New Value} = (100\% + \% \text{ Increase}) \times \text{Orig. Value}$$
$$44,800 = (100\% + 12\%) \times P$$
$$44,800 = 1.12P$$
$$40,000 = P$$

4. Let D = the dayflight fare.

$$\text{Night Fare} = (100\% - \% \text{ Discount}) \times \text{Day Fare}$$
$$\$280 = (100\% - 30\%) \times D$$
$$\$280 = .7D$$
$$\$400 = D$$

5. Since the store makes a 10% profit on the cost, it sells the item for $40 + 10\% \times \$40$, or $44.
Let L = the List Price of the item.

$$\text{Selling Price} = (100\% - \% \text{ Discount}) \times \text{List Price}$$
$$\$44 = (100\% - 20\%) \times L$$
$$\$44 = .8L$$
$$\$55 = L$$

NUMBER PROBLEMS

NUMBER PROBLEMS INVOLVING ONE UNKNOWN

In number problems involving one unknown quantity, we are asked to find a number that satisfies a given condition. This condition can usually be expressed as an algebraic equation by translating the words and phrases in the condition into symbolic form.

Following are the most common words and phrases, along with their translations into symbolic form:

Word or Phrase	Symbolic Form
the *sum* of x and 5, x *plus* 5, x increased by 5, 5 more than x	$x + 5$
the *difference* of x and 2, x *minus* 2, x *decreased* by 2, x *less* 2, 2 *less than* x (note the reversal)	$x - 2$
the *product* of 7 and x, 7 *times* x	$7x$
$\frac{3}{4}$ *of* x (a fraction of x), 75% *of* x (a percent of x)	$\frac{3}{4}x$, $.75x$
the *quotient* of x and 3, x *divided by* 3, 3 *divided into* x (note the reversal)	$\frac{x}{3}$
x equals 9, x *is the same* as 9, x *is* 9	$x = 9$

Example 1

If 4 times a number is increased by 7, the result is 1 less than 6 times the same number. What is the number?

Procedure

1. Represent the unknown number by n.
   Let n = the number.

2. Translate the given condition into symbolic form. Note that "1 *less than* 6n" is written $6n - 1$.

"If 4 times a number is increased by 7,	$4n + 7$
the result is	=
1 less than 6 times the same number"	$6n - 1$

3. Solve the resulting equation for n.

$$4n + 7 = 6n - 1$$
$$\underline{-4n \qquad -4n}$$
$$7 = 2n - 1$$
$$\underline{+1 \qquad +1}$$
$$8 = 2n$$
$$\frac{8}{2} = \frac{2n}{2}$$
$$4 = n$$

The number is 4.

Example 2

If 9 more than a number equals 3 times the sum of the number and 1, find the number.

Procedure

1. Represent the unknown number by n.
   Let n = the number.

2. Translate the given condition into symbolic form. Note that "3 times the sum" must be written with parentheses.

"If 9 more than a number	$n + 9$
equals	=
3 times the sum of the number and 1"	$3(n + 1)$

3. Solve the resulting equation for n.

$$n + 9 = 3(n + 1)$$
$$n + 9 = 3n + 3$$
$$\underline{-n \qquad -n}$$
$$9 = 2n + 3$$
$$\underline{-3 \qquad -3}$$
$$6 = 2n$$
$$\frac{6}{2} = \frac{2n}{2}$$
$$3 = n$$

The number is 3.

PRACTICE PROBLEMS

1. If 6 times a number is decreased by 4, the result is the same as when 3 times the number is increased by 2. What is the number?

2. The sum of a number and twice the same number is equal to 8 less than 5 times the number. What is the number?

3. Five less than twice a number is equal to one-half the difference of the number and 1. What is the number?

4. If the quotient of a number and 3 is decreased by 2, the result is equal to 1 more than the quotient of the number and 4. What is the number?

5. If $\frac{3}{4}$ of a number is decreased by 5, the result is equal to $\frac{1}{3}$ of the same number. What is the number?

ANSWERS AND EXPLANATIONS

1. $6x - 4 = 3x + 2$
$$3x = 6$$
$$x = 2$$

2. $x + 2x = 5x - 8$
$$3x = 5x - 8$$
$$-2x = -8$$
$$x = 4$$

3.
$$2x - 5 = \frac{1}{2}(x - 1) \quad [\text{multiply by 2}]$$
$$2 \cdot 2x - 2 \cdot 5 = \cancel{2} \cdot \frac{1}{\cancel{2}}(x - 1)$$
$$4x - 10 = x - 1$$
$$3x = 9$$
$$x = 3$$

4.
$$\frac{x}{3} - 2 = \frac{x}{4} + 1 \quad [\text{multiply by 12}]$$
$$\overset{4}{\cancel{12}} \cdot \frac{x}{\cancel{3}} - 12 \cdot 2 = \overset{3}{\cancel{12}} \cdot \frac{x}{\cancel{4}} + 12 \cdot 1$$
$$4x - 24 = 3x + 12$$
$$x = 36$$

5.
$$\frac{3}{4}x - 5 = \frac{1}{3}x \quad [\text{multiply by 12}]$$
$$\overset{3}{\cancel{12}} \cdot \frac{3}{\cancel{4}}x - 12 \cdot 5 = \overset{4}{\cancel{12}} \cdot \frac{1}{\cancel{3}}x$$
$$9x - 60 = 4x$$
$$5x = 60$$
$$x = 12$$

NUMBER PROBLEMS INVOLVING MORE THAN ONE UNKNOWN

In number problems involving more than one unknown, we are asked to find several numbers that satisfy a given condition. By using information given in the problem, we can usually represent all of the unknowns in terms of one variable, instead of using a different variable for each.

Example 1

The larger of two numbers is 3 more than twice the smaller. If their sum is 18, what are the numbers?

Procedure

1. Represent the smaller number by s, and the larger number by $2s + 3$ ("3 more than twice the smaller").
   Let s = the smaller number, and $2s + 3$ = the larger number.

2. Translate the given condition into symbolic form.

"If their sum	$s + (2s + 3)$
is	=
18"	18

3. Solve the equation for s, and substitute the result into the expression for the larger number.

$$s + (2s + 3) = 18$$
$$3s + 3 = 18$$
$$\underline{\quad -3 \quad -3 \quad}$$
$$3s \quad = 15$$
$$\frac{3s}{\cancel{3}} = \frac{15}{3}$$
$$s = 5$$

$$\text{Thus, } 2s + 3 = 2(5) + 3$$
$$= 13$$

The smaller number is 5, and the larger number is 13.

Example 2

A class has 38 students. If 3 less than the number of men equals 5 more than twice the number of women, how many women are in the class?

Procedure

1. Represent the number of men by M. Since there are a total of 38 people in the class, this leaves 38 − M women.
   Let M = the number of men,
   and 38 − M = the number of women.

2. Translate the given condition into symbolic form.

"If 3 less than the number of men	M − 3
equals	=
5 more than twice the number of women"	2(38 − M) + 5

3. Solve the equation for M, and substitute the result into the expression for the number of women.

$$M - 3 = 2(38 - M) + 5$$
$$M - 3 = 76 - 2M + 5$$
$$M - 3 = 81 - 2M$$

$$\underline{+2M \qquad\qquad +2M}$$
$$3M - 3 = 81$$

$$\underline{\qquad +3 \quad +3}$$
$$3M \quad = 84$$

$$\frac{\cancel{3}M}{\cancel{3}} = \frac{84}{3}$$

$$M = 28$$

Thus, $33 - M = 10$

The number of women is 10.

PRACTICE PROBLEMS

1. The smaller of two numbers is 12 less than three times the larger. If their difference is 2, what is the larger number?

2. A carpenter cuts a board, 36 inches long, into two pieces, such that twice the longer piece is 2 inches more than three times the shorter piece. How many inches is the longer piece?

3. An inheritance of $18,000 is divided among three children in the ratio of 2:3:4. How much is the largest share?

4. Nancy invested part of $3000 at 12% simple annual interest, and the rest at 9% simple annual interest. If the total interest earned after one year was $330, how much did she invest at the 12% rate?

5. At the 5 P.M. showing of a recent hit movie, 300 tickets were sold for a total of $1000. If people with student discount tickets paid one-half the regular price of $5.00, how many student discount tickets were sold?

ANSWERS AND EXPLANATIONS

1. Let x = the larger number, and $3x - 12$ = the smaller number.

$$x - (3x - 12) = 2$$
$$-2x + 12 = 2$$
$$-2x = -10$$
$$x = 5$$

2. Let x = the longer piece, and $36 - x$ = the shorter piece.

$$2x = 3(36 - x) + 2$$
$$2x = 108 - 3x + 2$$
$$2x = 110 - 3x$$
$$5x = 110$$
$$x = 22$$

3. Let $2x$ = the smallest share, $3x$ = the second share, and $4x$ = the largest share.

$$2x + 3x + 4x = 18,000$$
$$9x = 18,000$$
$$x = 2,000$$

Thus, the largest share is $4x = 4(\$2,000) = \$8,000$.

4. Let x = the amount invested at 12%, and $3000 - x$ = the amount invested at 9%.

$$.12x + .09(3000 - x) = 330$$
$$.12x + 270 - .09x = 330$$
$$.03x + 270 = 330$$
$$.03x = 60$$
$$x = \$2,000$$

5. Let x = the number of student tickets, and $300 - x$ = the number of regular tickets.

The regular tickets are sold at \$5 each, and the student discount tickets are sold at one-half that price, or \$2.50 each.

$$2.50x + 5(300 - x) = 1000$$
$$2.50x + 1500 - 5x = 1000$$
$$-2.5x = -500$$
$$x = 200$$

CONSECUTIVE INTEGER PROBLEMS

Consecutive integers are integers (positive whole numbers, negative whole numbers, and 0) that differ by 1. Algebraically, we can represent them by N, N + 1 , N + 2 , etc., where N is any integer.

Consecutive even integers and **consecutive odd integers** are integers that differ by 2. Algebraically, we can represent them both by N, N + 2, N + 4, etc. Note that for consecutive *even* integers, N must be *even*, and for consecutive *odd* integers, N must be *odd*.

Consecutive Integers
..., −2, −1, 0, 1, 2,...

Consecutive Even
..., −4, −2, 0, 2, 4,...

Consecutive Odd
..., −3, −1, 1, 3, 5,...

Example 1

Find three consecutive integers whose sum is 21.

Procedure

1. Represent the three consecutive integers algebraically.
   Let N = the first integer,
   N + 1 = the second integer,
   and N + 2 = the third integer.

2. Translate the given condition into symbolic form.

"Their sum	N + (N + 1) + (N + 2)
is	=
21"	21

3. Solve the equation for N, and substitute the result into the expressions for the other two integers.

$$N + (N+1) + (N+2) = 21$$
$$3N + 3 = 21$$
$$\underline{-3 = -3}$$
$$3N \quad = 18$$
$$\frac{\cancel{3}N}{\cancel{3}} = \frac{18}{3}$$
$$N = 6$$

Thus, N + 1 = 7, and N + 2 = 8
The integers are 6, 7, and 8.

Example 2

Find three consecutive even integers such that 5 times the first, minus twice the second, equals the third.

Procedure

1. Represent the three consecutive *even* integers algebraically.
   Let N = the first even integer,
   N + 2 = the second even integer,
   and N + 4 = the third even integer.

2. Translate the given condition into symbolic form.

"5 times the first, minus twice the second	$5N - 2(N + 2)$
equals	=
the third"	$N + 4$

3. Solve the equation for N, and substitute the result into the expressions for the other two integers.

$$5N - 2(N + 2) = N + 4$$
$$5N - 2N - 4 = N + 4$$
$$3N - 4 = N + 4$$
$$\underline{-N \qquad -N}$$
$$2N - 4 = \quad 4$$
$$\underline{+4 \quad +4}$$
$$2N = \quad 8$$
$$\frac{2N}{2} = \frac{8}{2}$$
$$N = 4$$

Thus, N + 2 = 6, and N + 4 = 8.
The even integers are 4, 6, and 8.

PRACTICE PROBLEMS

1. Find the smallest of three consecutive even integers whose sum is 48.

2. If the sum of three consecutive integers is 13 more than the smallest, what is their sum?

3. Find the smallest of three consecutive odd integers such that the sum of the first and the second is 27 less than 3 times the third.

4. Find the smallest of three consecutive integers such that 8 more than the product of the first and the second is equal to the product of the second and the third.

5. If the product of two consecutive *positive* odd integers is 63, what is their sum?

ANSWERS AND EXPLANATIONS

1. Let x = the 1st even integer, $x + 2$ = the 2nd even integer, and $x + 4$ = the 3rd even integer.

$$x + x + 2 + x + 4 = 48$$
$$3x + 6 = 48$$
$$3x = 42$$
$$x = 14$$

2. Let x = the 1st integer, $x + 1$ = the 2nd integer, and $x + 2$ = the 3rd integer.

$$x + x + 1 + x + 2 = x + 13$$
$$3x + 3 = x + 13$$
$$2x = 10$$
$$x = 5$$

Thus, their sum is $5 + 6 + 7 = 18$.

3. Let x = the 1st odd integer, $x + 2$ = the 2nd odd integer, and $x + 4$ = the 3rd odd integer.

$$x + x + 2 = 3(x + 4) - 27$$
$$2x + 2 = 3x + 12 - 27$$
$$2x + 2 = 3x - 15$$
$$-x = -17$$
$$x = 17$$

4. Let x = the 1st integer, $x + 1$ = the 2nd integer, and $x + 2$ = the 3rd integer.

$$x(x + 1) + 8 = (x + 1)(x + 2)$$
$$x^2 + x + 8 = x^2 + 3x + 2$$
$$x + 8 = 3x + 2$$
$$-2x = -6$$
$$x = 3$$

5. Let x = the 1st odd integer, and $x + 2$ = the 2nd odd integer.

$$x(x + 2) = 63$$
$$x^2 + 2x = 63$$
$$x^2 + 2x - 63 = 0$$
$$(x + 9)(x - 7) = 0$$
$$x + 9 = 0 \quad | \quad x - 7 = 0$$
$$x = -9 \quad | \quad x = 7$$

Since the integers are *positive*, the value $x = -9$ cannot be a solution.
Thus, the two consecutive positive odd integers are 7 and 9, and their sum is $7 + 9 = 16$.

AGE PROBLEMS

In age problems, we are asked to find the present ages of certain people, given information comparing their ages in the present, as well as their ages at a specified time in the future or the past.

Remember that to represent an age N years in the future, we add N to the present age, and to represent an age N years in the past, we subtract N from the present age.

> Age N years in the future = Present age + N
> Age N years in the past = Present age − N

Example 1

A father is now 3 times as old as his daughter. In 12 years he will be twice as old as his daughter will be then. What are their present ages?

Procedure

1. Represent the daughter's present age by D, and the father's present age by 3D ("3 times as old").

$$\text{Let } D = \text{the daughter's present age,}$$
$$\text{and } 3D = \text{the father's present age.}$$

2. To represent their ages 12 years in the future, add 12 to their present ages.

$$D + 12 = \text{the daughter's age in 12 years.}$$
$$3D + 12 = \text{the father's age in 12 years.}$$

3. Translate the given condition into symbolic form.

"In 12 years he	$3D + 12$
will be	$=$
twice as old as his daughter will be then"	$2(D + 12)$

4. Solve the equation for D, and substitute the result into the expression for the father's present age.

$$3D + 12 = 2(D + 12)$$
$$3D + 12 = 2D + 24$$
$$\underline{-2D \qquad -2D}$$
$$D + 12 = \qquad +24$$
$$\underline{\quad -12 \qquad -12}$$
$$D \quad = \qquad 12$$
$$D = 12$$

Thus, $3D = 36$

The daughter's present age is 12, and the father's present age is 36.

Example 2

A man is now 42 years old and his friend is 33 years old. How many years ago was the man twice as old as his friend was then.

Procedure

1. Represent the "number of years ago" by N.
    Let N = the number of years ago.

2. To represent the ages of the man and his friend N years ago, subtract N from their present ages.

    $$42 - N = \text{the age of the man N years ago.}$$

    $$33 - N = \text{the age of the friend N years ago.}$$

3. Translate the given condition into symbolic form.

"the man	$42 - N$
was	=
twice as old as his friend was then"	$2(33 - N)$

4. Solve the equation for N.

    $$42 - N = 2(33 - N)$$
    $$42 - N = 66 - 2N$$
    $$\underline{ +2N = +2N}$$
    $$42 + N = 66$$
    $$\underline{-42 -42}$$
    $$N = 24$$

    The number of years ago is 24.

PRACTICE PROBLEMS

1. Sara is now 3 times as old as Kristin. Four years ago, Sara was 5 times as old as Kristin was then. How old is Sara now?

2. Eileen is now 24 years older than her daughter. In 8 years, Eileen will be twice as old as her daughter will be then. How old is her daughter now?

3. James is now 3 years older than Lynette. If 7 years from now the sum of their ages will be 79, how old is Lynette now?

4. Anne is 25 years old, and Francis is 21 years old. How many years ago was Anne 3 times as old as Francis was then?

5. The sum of Hank's age and Eloise's age is 60. If Hank's age 8 years from now will be 3 times Eloise's age 4 years ago, how old is Hank now?

ANSWERS AND EXPLANATIONS

1. Let x = Kristin's age now, and $3x$ = Sara's age now.
   Then, $x - 4$ = Kristin's age 4 years ago, and $3x - 4$ = Sara's age 4 years ago.

   $$3x - 4 = 5(x - 4)$$
   $$3x - 4 = 5x - 20$$
   $$-2x = -16$$
   $$x = 8$$

   Thus, Sara is now $3x = (3)(8)$
   $$= 24 \text{ years old.}$$

2. Let x = Eileen's daughter's age now, and $x + 24$ = Eileen's age now.
   Then, $x + 8$ = Eileen's daughter's age in 8 years, and $x + 24 + 8$ = Eileen's age in 8 years.

   $$x + 24 + 8 = 2(x + 8)$$
   $$x + 32 = 2x + 16$$
   $$-x = -16$$
   $$x = 16$$

   Thus, the daughter is now 16 years old.

3. Let x = Lynette's age now, and $x + 3$ = James' age now.
   Then, $x + 7$ = Lynette's age in 7 years, and $x + 3 + 7$ = James' age in 7 years.

   $$(x + 7) + (x + 3 + 7) = 79$$
   $$2x + 17 = 79$$
   $$2x = 62$$
   $$x = 31$$

   Thus, Lynette is now 31 years old.

4. Let x = the number of years ago.
   Then $25 - x$ = Anne's age x years ago, and $21 - x$ = Francis' age x years ago.

   $$25 - x = 3(21 - x)$$
   $$25 - x = 63 - 3x$$
   $$2x = 38$$
   $$x = 19$$

   Thus, the number of years ago is 19.

5. Since the sum of their ages is 60:
   Let x = Hank's age now, and $60 - x$ = Eloise's age now.
   Then, $x + 8$ = Hank's age in 8 years, and $60 - x - 4$ = Eloise's age 4 years ago.

   $$x + 8 = 3(60 - x - 4)$$
   $$x + 8 = 180 - 3x - 12$$
   $$x + 8 = 168 - 3x$$
   $$4x = 160$$
   $$x = 40$$

   Thus, Hank is now 40 years old.

AVERAGE PROBLEMS

SIMPLE AVERAGE

The **average**, or **mean**, of a set of numbers is equal to the sum of the numbers divided by the number of terms in the set. In other words, the average of the set of N numbers, a_1, a_2, a_3,...,a_N, is given by the equation

$$\text{Average} = \frac{a_1 + a_2 + a_3 + \cdots + a_N}{N}$$

Example 1

If a woman bowls scores of 187, 193, and 211 in her first three games, what must she score in her final game in order to average 200 overall?

Procedure

1. Represent the score of her final game by S.
    Let S = the score of the final game.

2. Using the definition of average, divide the sum of the scores by the number of scores. Solve the resulting equation for S.

$$\text{Average} = \frac{\text{Sum}}{N}$$

$$200 = \frac{187 + 193 + 211 + S}{4}$$

$$200 = \frac{591 + S}{4}$$

$$4(200) = \cancel{4}\left(\frac{591 + S}{\cancel{4}}\right)$$

$$800 = 591 + S$$

$$\frac{-591 \qquad -591}{209 = \qquad S}$$

$$209 = S$$

The final score must be 209.

Example 2

During a one week period in January there were 4 days of snow. If the average daily snowfall for those 4 days was .35 inches, what was the average daily snowfall for the entire week?

Procedure

1. Represent the total snowfall by T.
    Let T = the total number of inches of snowfall during the 4 days.

2. Using the definition of average, divide the total snowfall, T, by the number of days it snowed, 4. Solve the resulting equation for T.

$$\text{Average} = \frac{\text{Sum}}{\text{N}}$$

$$.35 = \frac{T}{4}$$

$$4(.35) = \cancel{4}\left(\frac{T}{\cancel{4}}\right)$$

$$1.40 \text{ in.} = T$$

3. To find the average for the entire week, divide the total snowfall by 7 (7 days in a week).

$$\text{Average} = \frac{\text{Sum}}{\text{N}}$$

$$= \frac{1.40}{7}$$

$$= .2$$

The average daily snowfall for the week was .2 inches.

PRACTICE PROBLEMS

1. Barbara has marks of 92%, 86%, and 89% on her first three tests. What mark must she get on her next test in order to have a 90% average overall?

2. The average weight of Don, Pat, and Jennifer is 135 lbs. How much does Adrian weigh if the average weight of all four people is 120 lbs?

3. In the first game of a bowling tournament, a three-person team averaged 190. If, in the second game, one person's score increased by 7, another person's score increased by 15, and the third person's score decreased by 4, what was the teams's average score in the second game?

4. The average of two numbers is A. If one of the numbers is P, what is the other number?

5. The average of four numbers is what percent of the sum of the four numbers?

ANSWERS AND EXPLANATIONS

1. Let x = the mark Barbara must get.

    $$\text{Average} = \frac{\text{Sum}}{\text{N}}$$
    $$90 = \frac{92 + 86 + 89 + x}{4}$$
    $$90 = \frac{267 + x}{4}$$
    $$360 = 267 + x$$
    $$93 = x$$

2. Since the average weight of Don, Pat, and Jennifer is 135 lbs., their total weight is $3(135) = 405$ lbs.
    Let x = Adrian's weight.

    $$\text{Average} = \frac{\text{Sum}}{\text{N}}$$
    $$120 = \frac{405 + x}{4}$$
    $$480 = 405 + x$$
    $$75 = x$$

3. Since the average score in the first game was 190, the total of the scores was $3(190) = 570$.
    The total of the scores in the second game was $570 + 7 + 15 - 4 = 588$.
    Thus, the average score in the second game is

    $$\text{Average} = \frac{\text{Sum}}{\text{N}}$$
    $$= \frac{588}{3}$$
    $$= 196$$

4. Let x = the other number.

    $$\text{Average} = \frac{\text{Sum}}{\text{N}}$$
    $$A = \frac{P + x}{2}$$
    $$2A = P + x$$
    $$2A - P = x$$

5. If A is the average of 4 numbers, then 4A is the sum of the 4 numbers.
    Let x = the % that the average of the 4 numbers is of the sum of the 4 numbers.

$$\frac{\text{Part}}{\text{Whole}} = \frac{\%}{100\%}$$

$$\frac{\text{Average}}{\text{Sum}} = \frac{x}{100}$$

$$\frac{\overset{1}{\cancel{A}}}{\cancel{4}A} = \frac{x}{100} \quad \text{(cross-multiply)}$$

$$4x = 100$$

$$x = 25\%$$

MEDIAN AND MODE

Another way to measure the average of a set of numbers is to list the numbers in increasing order and choose the middle number in the list. This value is called the **median** of the set of numbers.

For example, to find the median of the set of numbers 6, 4, 7, 2, and 1, first list the numbers in increasing order:

$$1, 2, 4, 6, 7$$

Then the median is the middle number, 4.

When the number of numbers in the set is an even number, there is no middle number. In this case, the median is defined to be the simple average, or mean, of the two middle numbers.

For example, since the set of numbers, 6, 4, 9, 3, 2, 8 has six numbers (an even number), we see that when we list them in increasing order, there is no middle number:

$$2, 3, 4, 6, 8, 9$$

In this case, we find the median by taking the simple average of the two middle numbers 4 and 6.

$$\text{median} = \frac{4+6}{2} = 5$$

One other way to measure the average of a set of numbers is to find the number in the set that occurs most frequently. This number is called the **mode** of the set of numbers.

For example, in the set of numbers, 6, 5, 4, 5, 6, 2, and 6, the number 2 occurs once, the number 4 occurs once, the number 5 occurs twice, and the number 6 occurs three times. Thus, 6, which occurs most frequently, is the mode of the set of numbers.

The three different averages are summarized below.

Average of a Set of Numbers

The **mean** is the sum of the numbers divided by the number of numbers in the set.

The **median** is the middle number in the set after the numbers are arranged in increasing order. If there are an even number of numbers in the set, then the median is the simple average (the mean) of the two middle numbers.

The **mode** is the number that occurs most frequently.

PRACTICE PROBLEMS

1. The daily high temperatures, in degrees Fahrenheit, for the first week in June were 58, 62, 54, 61, 63, 70, and 52. What was the mean and median temperatures for the week?

2. The diameters, in centimeters, of six pipes are 22, 14, 15, 22, 22, and 15. What is the mode of these diameters?

ANSWERS AND EXPLANATIONS

1. $\text{mean} = \dfrac{\text{sum of temperatures}}{\text{number of temperatures}}$

   $= \dfrac{58 + 62 + 54 + 61 + 63 + 70 + 52}{7}$

   $= \dfrac{420}{7}$

   $= 60 \text{ degrees}$

   To find the median, list the temperatures in increasing order:
   52, 54, 58, 61, 62, 63, 70
   The median is the middle number, 61 degrees.

2. The diameter that occurs most frequently, 22 centimeters, is the mode.

RANGE OF A SET OF NUMBERS

The **range** of a set of numbers measures the amount of spread between the numbers. It is determined by subtracting the smallest number in the set from the largest number in the set.

> Range = Largest Number − Smallest Number

For example, if the height, in inches, of a group of students in a class are 62, 61, 65, 60, and 54, then:

$$\text{Range} = 65 - 54 = 11 \text{ inches}$$

PRACTICE PROBLEMS

For each of the following sets of numbers, what is the range?

1. 12, 36, 8, 15, 19

2. −2, 9, 27, −12, 0

ANSWERS AND EXPLANATIONS

1. Range = Largest Number − Smallest Number

   $= 36 - 8$

   $= 28$

2. Range = Largest Number − Smallest Number

   $= 27 - (-12)$

   $= 27 + 12$

   $= 39$

WEIGHTED AVERAGE

To combine the averages of different sets of numbers, the average of each set must be "weighted" (multiplied) by the number of terms in that set. For example, if a class of 12 students has an average of 80% on a test, and another class of 18 students has an average of 90% on the same test, then the average of the two classes combined is the sum of all the scores (12 with an average of 80% and 18 with an average of 90%) divided by the total number of scores (12 + 18 = 30).

$$\text{Combined Avg.} = \frac{12(80\%) + 18(90\%)}{12 + 18}$$
$$= \frac{2580\%}{30}$$
$$= 86\%$$

In this example, the numbers 12 and 18 are referred to as the weights for the averages 80% and 90%, respectively. Notice that, since there are more scores averaging 90% than 80%, the combined average is higher than 85%, the simple average of 80% and 90%.

> In general, the **combined (weighted) average** of a group of N1 numbers, having an average of A1, and another group of N2 numbers, having an average of A2, is
>
> $$\text{Combined Avg.} = \frac{N_1 \cdot A_1 + N_2 \cdot A_2}{N_1 + N_2}$$

Example

According to the table below, what is the average number of credits taken per semester by the freshmen and sophomores combined, rounded off to the nearest tenth?

	Number of Students	Avg No. of Credits/Semester
Freshmen	300	12.5
Sophomores	200	14.8

Procedure

1. Multiply each average by the corresponding number of students, and add the results together. Divide the sum by the total number of students. Round off the result to the nearest tenth.

$$\text{Combined Avg.} = \frac{300(12.5) + 200(14.8)}{300 + 200}$$
$$= \frac{6710}{500}$$
$$= 13.42$$
$$\approx 13.4$$

The average number of credits taken per semester by the freshmen and sophomores combined is 13.4, rounded off to the nearest tenth.

PRACTICE PROBLEMS

1. In a certain school, 2 teachers earn $16,000 per year, 3 teachers earn $17,000 per year, and 5 teachers earn $18,000 per year. What is the average annual salary of these teachers?

2. On the midterm exam, the average grade of a class was 86. If 20% of the class averaged 95, and 30% of the class averaged 90, what was the average grade of the rest of the class?

3. The average temperature for the first 4 days of a week was 50°. If the average temperature for the next 3 days was 43°, what was the average temperature for the entire week?

4. The average age of 10 friends is 32 years. If 3 of them average 28 years, and 5 others average 34 years, what is the average age of the remaining 2 people?

5. The average of 8 scores is Q. If the average of 3 of the scores is Z, what is the average of the other 5 scores?

ANSWERS AND EXPLANATIONS

1.
$$\text{Average} = \frac{2(16,000)+3(17,000)+5(18,000)}{10}$$
$$= \frac{32,000+51,000+90,000}{10}$$
$$= \frac{173,000}{10}$$
$$= \$17,300$$

2. Let x = the average grade of the remaining 50% of the class.
   If we choose the class size to be 100 people, we get

$$86 = \frac{20(95)+30(90)+50(x)}{100}$$
$$86 = \frac{1900+2700+50x}{100}$$
$$86 = \frac{4600+50x}{100} \quad (\text{cross-multiply})$$
$$8600 = 4600+50x$$
$$4000 = 50x$$
$$80 = x$$

3.
$$\text{Average} = \frac{4(50°)+3(43°)}{7}$$
$$= \frac{200+129}{7}$$
$$= \frac{329}{7}$$
$$= 47°$$

4. Let x = the average of the remaining two people.

$$32 = \frac{3(28) + 5(34) + 2(x)}{10}$$

$$32 = \frac{84 + 170 + 2x}{10}$$

$$32 = \frac{254 + 2x}{10} \quad (\text{cross-multiply})$$

$$320 = 254 + 2x$$

$$66 = 2x$$

$$33 = x$$

5. Let x = the average of the other 5 scores.

$$Q = \frac{3Z + 5x}{8} \quad (\text{cross-multiply})$$

$$8Q = 3Z + 5x$$

$$8Q - 3Z = 5x$$

$$\frac{8Q - 3Z}{5} = x$$

MIXTURE PROBLEMS

In mixture problems, we are given the unit value of several different items and are asked to determine the number of units that should be used of each to obtain a mixture having a specified value.

The *value of each item* in a mixture is equal to the number of units of that item multiplied by the value per unit (the unit value). For example, the value of 3 pounds of coffee, worth $2.25 per pound, is 3($2.25), or $6.75. In general,

> The Value of Each Item = (Number of Units) · (Unit Value)

The *value of the mixture* is equal to the *sum* of the values of the items within it. For example, the value of a mixture of 5 pounds of nuts, worth $2.00 per pound, and 4 pounds of candy, worth $3.00 per pound, is 5($2.00) + 4($3.00), or $22.00.

> In general, if N_1 units of an item having a unit value of U_1 are mixed with N_2 units of an item having a unit value of U_2, then
>
> The Value of the Mixture = $N_1 \cdot U_1 + N_2 \cdot U_2$

Example

A grocer wishes to mix one type of coffee worth $2.70 per pound with another type of coffee worth $1.95 per pound in order to make a 40 pound mixture worth $2.25 per pound. How many pounds of each type should he use?

Procedure

1. Represent the number of pounds of $2.70 coffee by P, and the number of pounds of $1.95 coffee by 40 − P. (The total weight of the mixture is 40 pounds.)
    Let P = the number of pounds of $2.70 coffee, and
    40 − P = the number of pounds of $1.95 coffee.

2. To obtain the value of each type of coffee, and the value of the mixture, multiply the number of pounds of each by the corresponding price per pound.
   Values
   $2.70 coffee: 2.70P
   $1.95 coffee: 1.95(40 − P)
   mixture: 2.25(40)

3. Write an equation expressing the fact that the value of the mixture is equal to the sum of the values of the two coffees. Solve this equation for P, and substitute the result into the expression for the number of pounds of $1.95 coffee.

$$\frac{\text{value of}}{\text{mixture}} = \begin{array}{c}\text{value of}\\ \$2.70\\ \text{coffee}\end{array} + \begin{array}{c}\text{value of}\\ \$1.95\\ \text{coffee}\end{array}$$

$$2.25(40) = 2.70P + 1.95(40 - P)$$
$$90 = 2.70P + 1.95(40) - 1.95(P)$$
$$90 = 2.70P + 78 - 1.95P$$
$$90 = .75P + 78$$
$$\underline{-78 = \qquad -78}$$
$$12 = .75P$$
$$\frac{12}{.75} = \frac{\cancel{.75}P}{\cancel{.75}}$$
$$16 = P$$

Thus, 40 − P = 24.
The grocer should use 16 pounds of the $2.70 coffee, and 24 pounds of the $1.95 coffee.

PRACTICE PROBLEMS

1. What is the total value of a mixture of tea consisting of 20 pounds of tea worth 65 cents per pound and 10 pounds of tea worth 75 cents per pound?

2. A 50 pound mixture of coffee consists of 35 pounds of coffee worth $4.00 per pound, and the rest of the coffee worth D dollars per pound. What is the total value of the mixture, in dollars?

3. Kathy wishes to mix candy worth 80 cents per pound with another type of candy worth 50 cents per pound in order to make 30 pounds of candy worth 75 cents per pound. How many pounds of the 80 cent candy should she use?

4. Robin has one type of coffee worth $3.10 per pound, and another type of coffee worth $3.50 per pound. How many pounds of the $3.50 coffee should she use in order to make a 20 pound mixture of the two coffees worth $3.40 per pound?

5. How many pounds of nuts worth 65 cents per pound must be mixed with 10 pounds of nuts worth 90 cents per pound in order to make a mixture worth 70 cents per pound?

ANSWERS AND EXPLANATIONS

1. $$\begin{aligned} \text{Value of Mixture} &= \text{Value of } 65\text{¢ tea} + \text{Value of } 75\text{¢ tea} \\ &= 20(.65) + 10(.75) \\ &= 13 + 7.50 \\ &= \$20.50 \end{aligned}$$

2. $$\begin{aligned} \text{Value of Mixture} &= \text{Value of } \$4 \text{ coffee} + \text{Value of } \$D \text{ coffee} \\ &= 35(4) + 15(D) \\ &= 140 + 15D \end{aligned}$$

3. Let $x =$ the # lbs. of 80¢ candy, and $30 - x =$ the # lbs. of 50¢ candy.

    $$\begin{aligned} \text{Value of Mixture} &= \text{Value of } 80\text{¢ candy} + \text{Value of } 90\text{¢ candy} \\ 30(.75) &= .80(x) + .50(30 - x) \\ 22.5 &= .80x + 15 - .50x \\ 22.5 &= .30x + 15 \\ 7.5 &= .30x \\ 25 \text{ lbs.} &= x \end{aligned}$$

4. Let $x =$ the # lbs. of \$3.50 coffee, and $20 - x =$ the # lbs. of \$3.10 coffee.

    $$\begin{aligned} \text{Value of Mixture} &= \text{Value of } \$3.50 \text{ coffee} + \text{Value of } \$3.10 \text{ coffee} \\ 20(\$3.40) &= 3.50(x) + 3.10(20 - x) \\ 68 &= 3.50x + 62 - 3.10x \\ 6 &= .40x \\ 15 \text{ lbs.} &= x \end{aligned}$$

5. Let $x =$ the # lbs. of 65¢ nuts.
    Thus, there are $x + 10$ lbs. total in the mixture.

    $$\begin{aligned} \text{Value of Mixture} &= \text{Value of } 65\text{¢ nuts} + \text{Value of } 90\text{¢ nuts} \\ 70(x + 10) &= 65(x) + 90(10) \\ 70x + 700 &= 65x + 900 \\ 5x &= 200 \\ x &= 40 \text{ lbs.} \end{aligned}$$

MOTION PROBLEMS

BASIC FORMULA

The distance traveled by a moving object is equal to its rate of speed multiplied by the time traveled. For example, an object traveling at the rate of 200 miles per hour (m.p.h.), for a period of 3 hours, will cover a distance of (200) · (3), or 600 miles. In this example, note that the rate can either mean a *constant* rate of 200 m.p.h., or an *average* rate of 200 m.p.h. It makes no difference.

In general, we have the following formula:

$$\text{Distance} = \text{Rate} \cdot \text{Time}$$
$$D = R \cdot T$$

By dividing both sides of this formula by R, we can change the subject of the formula to the time, T. Similarly, by dividing both sides of this formula by T, we can change the subject of the formula to the rate, R. Thus, we have the following alternate formulas:

$$D = R \cdot T \qquad\qquad D = R \cdot T$$
$$\frac{D}{R} = \frac{\cancel{R} \cdot T}{\cancel{R}} \qquad\qquad \frac{D}{T} = \frac{R \cdot \cancel{T}}{\cancel{T}}$$
$$\boxed{T = \frac{D}{R}} \qquad\qquad \boxed{R = \frac{D}{T}}$$

When using these formulas, remember that the units of measurement must match. For example, if the rate is measured in *miles per hour*, then the distance must be measured in *miles*, and the time must be measured in *hours*.

Example 1

A car traveled 78 miles in 98 minutes. If it traveled the first 42 miles in 50 minutes, what was its average rate of speed, in miles per hour, the rest of the way?

Procedure

1. Draw a diagram indicating the given information.

    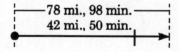

2. To find the distance and time of the second part of the trip, subtract the distance and time of the first part of the trip from the total distance and time.

Distance		*Time*
78 miles		98 minutes
− 42 miles		− 50 minutes
36 miles		48 minutes

3. Change the 48 minutes to hours by placing it over a denominator of 60 (60 minutes in 1 hour).

    $$48 \text{ minutes} = \frac{48}{60} \text{ hours}$$
    $$= \frac{4}{5} \text{ hours}$$

4. Using the formula for the average rate, divide the distance of the second part of the trip, by the time of the second part of the trip.

$$R = \frac{D}{T}$$

$$R = \frac{36 \text{ miles}}{\frac{4}{5} \text{ hours}}$$

$$= 36 \div \frac{4}{5}$$

$$= \frac{\overset{9}{\cancel{36}}}{1} \times \frac{5}{\underset{1}{\cancel{4}}}$$

$$= 45 \text{ m.p.h.}$$

Its average rate the rest of the way was 45 m.p.h.

Example 2

A man runs a race in S seconds, running at an average rate of 14Y yards per second. If a woman runs the same race in $\frac{7}{8}$S seconds, what is her average rate, in yards per second?

Procedure

1. Draw a diagram indicating the given information.

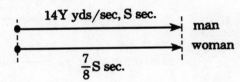

2. Represent the woman's rate by W.
   Let W = the woman's rate.

3. Using the formula for the distance, multiply each runner's rate by their time.

$$D = R \cdot T$$
$$D_{man} = 14Y \cdot S = 14YS$$
$$D_{woman} = W \cdot \frac{7}{8}S = \frac{7}{8}WS$$

4. Since the distance of both runners is the same, set these expressions equal and solve for W.

$$D_{man} = D_{woman}$$

$$14YS = \frac{7}{8}WS$$

$$8 \cdot 14YS = \cancel{8} \cdot \frac{7}{\cancel{8}}WS$$

$$112YS = 7WS$$

$$\frac{112Y\cancel{S}}{7\cancel{S}} = \frac{\cancel{7}W\cancel{S}}{\cancel{7}\cancel{S}}$$

$$16Y = W$$

The woman's rate is 16Y yds/sec.

Example 3

A train travels 120 miles at an average rate of 40 m.p.h. and returns along the same route at an average rate of 60 m.p.h. What is its average rate of speed for the entire trip?

Procedure

1. Draw a diagram indicating the given information.

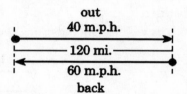

2. Using the formula for the time, find the time in each direction. Add the results.

$$T = \frac{D}{R}$$

$$T_{out} = \frac{120}{40} \quad \bigg| \quad T_{out} = \frac{120}{60}$$

$$= 3 \text{ hr.} \quad \bigg| \quad = 2 \text{ hr.}$$

$$T_{total} = T_{out} + T_{back}$$

$$= 3 \text{ hr.} + 2 \text{ hr.}$$

$$= 5 \text{ hr.}$$

3. Using the formula for the average rate, divide the total distance (twice the one way distance) by the total time. (Note that the average rate we obtain is less than 50 m.p.h., the simple average of the two rates 40 m.p.h. and 60 m.p.h. The reason for this is that the train traveled more time at the slower rate, thus weighting the overall rate in that direction.)

$$R = \frac{D}{T}$$

$$= \frac{240 \text{ miles}}{5 \text{ hours}}$$

$$= 48 \text{ m.p.h.}$$

The average rate for the entire trip is 48 m.p.h.

PRACTICE PROBLEMS

1. From 10:30 A.M. to 11:45 A.M., Rick travels a total distance of 50 miles. What is his average rate of speed, in miles per hour?

2. Michele can swim Y yards in S seconds. If in 20 seconds more time, Tim can swim twice as far as Michele does in S seconds, what is Tim's average rate, in yards per second?

3. Deirdre runs a race in S seconds, running at an average rate of 10Y yards per second. If Maud finishes the race 3 seconds after Deirdre, what is Maud's average rate, in yards per second?

4. Emmanuelle travels the first 60 miles of a trip at an average rate of 30 miles per hour. For the next 120 miles she averages 40 miles per hour. What is her average rate for the entire trip?

5. On a trip of 408 miles, Dennis travels the first 160 miles in 4 hours. At what rate must he travel for the remainder of the trip in order to average 34 miles per hour for the entire trip?

ANSWERS AND EXPLANATIONS

1. The amount of time from 10:30 to 11:45 is $1\frac{1}{4}$ hours.

    $$R = \frac{D}{T}$$
    $$R = \frac{50}{1\frac{1}{4}} = 50 \div 1\frac{1}{4} = 50 \div \frac{5}{4}$$
    $$= 50 \times \frac{4}{5} = 40 \text{ m.p.h.}$$

2. Since Tim can swim twice as far, his distance is 2Y. Also, since it takes him 20 seconds more time, his time is $S + 20$. Thus, his average rate is

    $$R = \frac{D}{T}$$
    $$R = \frac{2Y}{S + 20}$$

3. The distance run by Deirdre is $D = R \cdot T = (10Y)(S) = 10YS$. Since Maud runs the same race, her distance is also $10YS$. Also, since she finishes 3 seconds after Deirdre, her time is $S + 3$. Thus, Maud's average rate is

    $$R = \frac{D}{T}$$
    $$R = \frac{10YS}{S + 3}$$

4.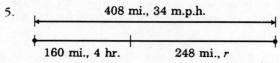

The time for the first part of the trip is $T = \dfrac{D}{R} = \dfrac{60}{30} = 2$ hrs. The time for the second part of the trip is $T = \dfrac{D}{R} = \dfrac{120}{40} = 3$ hrs. Thus, the total time for the trip is 2 hrs + 3 hrs. = 5 hrs. Therefore, the average rate for the entire trip is

$$R = \dfrac{D}{T}$$
$$R = \dfrac{180}{5} = 36 \text{ m.p.h.}$$

5.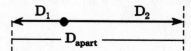

The time for the total trip is $T = \dfrac{D}{R} = \dfrac{408}{34} = 12$ hrs. Since the time for the first 160 mi. is 4 hrs., the time for the remaining 248 mi. is 12 hrs. − 4 hrs. = 8 hrs. Thus, the rate for the remaining 248 mi. is

$$r = \dfrac{D}{T}$$
$$r = \dfrac{248}{8} = 31 \text{ m.p.h.}$$

SPECIAL SITUATIONS

The situations described below are typical of many motion problems. In each of them, we can write an equation based on a relationship between certain distances. These relationships are derived from the accompanying diagrams.

Separation Situation: Two objects start from the same place and travel in opposite directions. After a given amount of time, they are a certain distance apart.

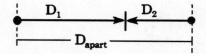

The sum of the distances traveled by the two objects is equal to the final distance apart.

$$\boxed{D_1 + D_2 = D_{apart}}$$

Meeting Situation: Two objects start at a given distance apart and travel towards each other until they meet.

The sum of the distances traveled by the two objects is equal to the original distance apart.

$$\boxed{D_1 + D_2 = D_{apart}}$$

Overtake Situation: One object starts at a given place and travels in a certain direction. Some time later a second objects starts from the same place and travels at a faster rate in the same direction. The second object eventually overtakes the first object.

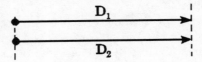

The distance traveled by the first object equals the distance traveled by the second object.

$$\boxed{D_1 = D_2}$$

Round-Trip Situation: One object travels out and back along the same path.

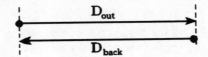

The distance out equals the distance back.

$$\boxed{D_{out} = D_{back}}$$

Example 1

A freight train and a passenger train leave from the same station at 2:00 P.M. and travel in opposite directions. The freight train averages 52 m.p.h. and the passenger train averages 84 m.p.h. At what time are the trains 340 miles apart?

Procedure

1. Represent the number of hours traveled by each train by h. (They both travel the same amount of time.)
    Let h = the number of hours traveled by each train.

2. Using the distance formula, multiply each rate by h.

    $$D = R \cdot T$$
    $$D_{freight} = 52h$$
    $$D_{passenger} = 84h$$

3. Draw a diagram showing all distances.

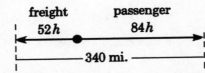

4. Write an equation expressing the fact that the sum of the distances traveled by the two trains equals the final distance apart. Solve this equation for h.

    $$52h + 84h = 340$$
    $$136h = 340$$
    $$\frac{\cancel{136}h}{\cancel{136}} = \frac{340}{136}$$

$$h = 2\frac{1}{2} \text{ hours}$$

5. Add the time traveled to the starting time, 2:00 P.M.

$$2{:}00 \text{ P.M.} + 2\frac{1}{2} \text{ hrs.} = 4{:}30 \text{ P.M.}$$

The trains are 340 mi. apart at 4:30 P.M.

Example 2

Two cars start traveling towards each other at the same time from cities 416 miles apart. The average rate of one car is 10 m.p.h. faster than the other car. If they pass each other in 4 hours, what is the average rate of each car?

Procedure

1. Represent the rate of the slower car by s and the rate of the faster car by $s + 10$ ("10 m.p.h. faster").
   Let s = the rate of the slower car,
   and $s + 10$ = the rate of the faster car.

2. Using the distance formula, multiply each rate by 4 hrs. (Since both cars leave at the same time, they both travel the same amount of time.)

$$D = R \cdot T$$
$$D_{slower} = s \cdot 4 = 4s$$
$$D_{faster} = (s + 10) \cdot 4 = 4s + 40$$

3. Draw a diagram showing all distances.

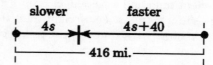

4. Write an equation expressing the fact that the sum of the distances traveled by the two cars equals the original distance apart. Solve this equation for s, and substitute the result into the expression for the rate of the faster car.

$$
\begin{aligned}
4s + (4s + 40) &= 416 \\
8s + 40 &= 416 \\
-40 &\quad -40 \\
8s &= 376 \\
\frac{8s}{8} &= \frac{376}{8} \\
s &= 47
\end{aligned}
$$

Thus, $s + 10 = 57$

The slower car averages 47 m.p.h., and the faster car averages 57 m.p.h.

Example 3

A man leaves his home and starts jogging at an average rate of 8 m.p.h. Fifteen minutes later his wife leaves home and starts bicycling after him at an average rate of 11 m.p.h. How long after the wife leaves does she catch up with her husband?

Procedure

1. Represent the time of the wife (in hours) by h, and the time of the husband by $h + \dfrac{1}{4}$. (The husband leaves 15 min., or $\dfrac{1}{4}$ hour, earlier than his wife.)

   Let h = the number of hours traveled by the wife,

   and $h + \dfrac{1}{4}$ = the number of hours traveled by the husband.

2. Using the distance formula, multiply each rate by its respective time.

$$D = R \cdot T$$
$$D_{wife} = 11 \cdot h = 11h$$
$$D_{husband} = 8 \cdot \left(h + \frac{1}{4} \right) = 8h + 2$$

3. Draw a diagram showing all distances.

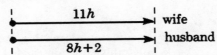

4. Write an equation expressing the fact that the distance traveled by the wife and the husband is the same. Solve this equation for h.

$$11h = 8h + 2$$
$$\underline{-8h \quad -8h}$$
$$3h = \quad 2$$
$$\frac{\cancel{3}h}{\cancel{3}} = \frac{2}{3}$$
$$h = \frac{2}{3} \text{ hr., or 40 min.}$$

The wife catches up with the husband in 40 min.

Example 4

A plane makes a round trip flight from the San Francisco airport, which lasts 5 hours. If the average rate out is 200 m.p.h. and the average rate back is 300 m.p.h., what is the plane's greatest distance from the airport?

Procedure

1. Represent the time flying out by h, and the time flying back by $5 - h$. (The total flight time is 5 hours.)
    Let h = the number of hours flying out,
    and $5 - h$ = the number of hours flying back.

2. Using the distance formula, multiply each rate by its respective time.

    $$D = R \cdot T$$
    $$D_{out} = 200h$$
    $$D_{back} = 300(5 - h)$$

3. Draw a diagram showing all distances.

    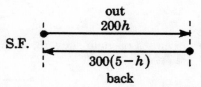

4. Write an equation expressing the fact that the distance out equals the distance back. Solve this equation for h.

    $$200h = 300(5 - h)$$
    $$200h = 1500 - 300h$$
    $$\underline{+300h \qquad\qquad +300h}$$
    $$500h = 1500$$
    $$\frac{\cancel{500}h}{\cancel{500}} = \frac{1500}{500}$$
    $$h = 3 \text{ hours}$$

5. Substitute this value into the expression for the distance out.

    $$D_{out} = 200h$$
    $$D_{out} = 200(3)$$
    $$= 600 \text{ miles}$$

    The plane's greatest distance from the airport is 600 mi.

PRACTICE PROBLEMS

1. Two trains start at the same time from the same station and travel in opposite directions. One travels at the rate of 50 m.p.h., and the other travels at the rate of 60 m.p.h. In how many hours are the trains 440 miles apart?

2. Maria took a trip of 370 miles by bus and train. She traveled 3 hours by bus and 4 hours by train. If the train averaged 19 m.p.h. more than the bus, what was the rate of the train?

3. At 5 P.M., Jill leaves New York City and travels toward Boston at an average rate of 56 m.p.h. At 6 P.M., Billy leaves Boston and travels toward New York, on the same road as Jill, at an average rate of 50 m.p.h. If they were initially 215 miles apart, at what time do Billy and Jill pass each other?

4. An airplane leaves LaGuardia Airport at 3 P.M. and flies west at an average rate of 200 m.p.h. At 3:30 P.M., another airplane leaves the airport and flies west at an average rate of 250 m.p.h. At what time does the second plane overtake the first plane?

5. A helicopter makes a round trip flight that lasts $4\frac{1}{2}$ hours. If the average rate out was 80 m.p.h., and the average rate back was 100 m.p.h., what was the helicopter's greatest distance from the airport?

ANSWERS AND EXPLANATIONS

1. Let x = the no. hours traveled by each train.
    Using the distance formula, $D = R \cdot T$, the distance traveled by one train is $60x$, and the distance traveled by the other train is $50x$.

    $$50x + 60x = 440$$
    $$110x = 440$$
    $$x = 4 \text{ hrs.}$$

2. Let x = the average rate of the bus, and $x + 19$ = the average rate of the train. Using the distance formula, $D = R \cdot T$, the distance traveled on the bus is $3x$ and the distance traveled on the train is $4(x + 19)$.

    $$3x + 4(x + 19) = 370$$
    $$3x + 4x + 76 = 370$$
    $$7x + 76 = 370$$
    $$7x = 294$$
    $$x = 42 \text{ m.p.h.}$$

    Thus, the average rate of the train is $x + 19 = 42 + 19 = 61$ m.p.h.

3. Let x = the no. hours traveled by Jill, and $x - 1$ = the no. hours traveled by Billy (he starts 1 hr. later).

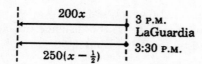

$$56x + 50(x - 1) = 215$$
$$56x + 50x - 50 = 215$$
$$106x - 50 = 215$$
$$106x = 265$$
$$x = 2\frac{1}{2} \text{ hrs.}$$

Since Jill started at 5 P.M., she passes Billy at $5 + 2\frac{1}{2} = 7{:}30$ P.M

4. Let x = the no. hours traveled by the first plane, and $x - \frac{1}{2}$ = the no. hours traveled by the second plane (it starts $\frac{1}{2}$ hour later).

Using the distance formula, $D = R \cdot T$, the distance traveled by the first plane is $200x$, and the distance traveled by the second plane is $250\left(x - \frac{1}{2}\right)$

```
        200x          3 P.M.
    |----------->|    LaGuardia
    |----------->|    3:30 P.M.
       250(x - ½)
```

$$200x = 250\left(x - \frac{1}{2}\right)$$
$$200x = 250x - 125$$
$$-50x = -125$$
$$x = 2\frac{1}{2} \text{ hrs.}$$

Since the first plane started at 3 P.M., the second plane overtakes the first plane at $3 + 2\frac{1}{2} = 5{:}30$ P.M.

5. Let x = the no. hours flying out, and $4\frac{1}{2} - x$ = the no. hours flying back.

Using the distance formula, $D = R \cdot T$, the distance out is $80x$, and the distance back is $100\left(4\frac{1}{2} - x\right)$.

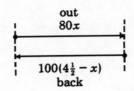

$$80x = 100\left(4\frac{1}{2} - x\right)$$

$$80x = 450 - 100x$$

$$180x = 450$$

$$x = 2\frac{1}{2} \text{ hrs.}$$

Thus, the distance traveled out is $80x = 80\left(2\frac{1}{2}\right) = 200$ miles.

WORK PROBLEMS

INDIVIDUALS

In work problems involving individuals (individual people, individual machines, etc.), we are told how long it takes several individuals working alone to complete a job, and are asked to determine how long it would take the same individuals to complete the job, working together.

If an individual can complete a job in 5 hours, then after 1 hour he will complete $\frac{1}{5}$ of the job, after 2 hours he will complete $\frac{2}{5}$ of the job, after 3 hours he will complete $\frac{3}{5}$ of the job, and so on. (This assumes, of course, that the individual works at a constant rate.) In general:

> The Fractional Part of the Job Completed =
>
> $$\frac{\text{Actual Time Worked}}{\text{Total Time Required}}$$

When individuals work together, the fractional part of the job they complete as a group is simply the *sum* of the fractional parts they complete as individuals within the group (assuming that they work independently of each other). For example, if one individual can complete a job in 6 hours alone, and another individual can complete the same job in 12 hours alone, then after working together for 1 hour they complete $\frac{1}{6} + \frac{1}{12}$, or $\frac{1}{4}$ of the job, after working together for 2 hours they complete $\frac{2}{6} + \frac{2}{12}$, or $\frac{1}{2}$ of the job, and so on.

In order for them to complete the job, the sum of the fractional parts must equal 1 (1 whole job). Thus, if we let T represent the amount of time required to complete the job together, we get the equation

$$\frac{T}{6} + \frac{T}{12} = 1$$

To solve this equation for T, we multiply both sides by the common denominator 12, and get

$$12\left(\frac{T}{6} + \frac{T}{12}\right) = 12(1)$$
$$2T + T = 12$$
$$3T = 12$$
$$T = 4 \text{ hours}$$

In other words, the two individuals would complete the job in 4 hours working together.

In general, if one individual can complete a job in H_1 hours alone, and another individual can complete the same job in H_2 hours alone, then the amount of hours it would take them to complete the job working together, T, is given by the equation

$$\frac{T}{H_1} + \frac{T}{H_2} = 1$$

Example 1

If used alone, one pipe can fill a tank in 8 minutes, a second pipe can fill the tank in 12 minutes, and a third pipe can fill the tank in 24 minutes. How long would it take all three pipes, operating together, to fill the tank?

Procedure

1. Represent the number of minutes required to fill the tank by M.
   Let M = the number of minutes required by the three pipes to fill the tank together.

2. For each pipe, write a fraction indicating the part of the job it completes in M minutes. (Each pipe operates for M minutes.)

$$8 \text{ min. pipe: } \frac{M}{8}$$

$$12 \text{ min. pipe: } \frac{M}{12}$$

$$24 \text{ min. pipe: } \frac{M}{24}$$

3. Write an equation expressing the fact that, since the job is completed, the sum of the fractional parts must equal 1. Solve this equation for M.

$$\frac{M}{8} + \frac{M}{12} + \frac{M}{24} = 1$$

$$24\left(\frac{M}{8} + \frac{M}{12} + \frac{M}{24}\right) = 24(1)$$

$$3M + 2M + M = 24$$

$$6M = 24$$

$$\frac{\cancel{6}M}{\cancel{6}} = \frac{24}{6}$$

$$M = 4 \text{ min.}$$

The three pipes, operating together, will fill the tank in 4 minutes.

Example 2

Operating together, two copy machines can reproduce a report in 30 minutes. If one machine is twice as fast as the other, how long would it take each machine, operating alone, to do the same job?

Procedure

1. Represent the time of the faster machine by T, and the time of the slower machine by 2T. (The slower machine requires twice as much time.)
   Let T = the time required by the faster machine to complete the job alone,
   and 2T = the time required by the slower machine to complete the job alone

2. For each machine, write a fraction indicating the part of the job completed in 30 minutes.

Faster Machine: $\dfrac{30}{T}$

Slower Machine: $\dfrac{30}{2T}$

253

3. Write an equation expressing the fact that when the job is completed, the sum of the fractions must be 1. Solve this equation for T, and substitute the result into the expression for the time of the slower machine.

$$\frac{30}{T} + \frac{30}{2T} = 1$$

$$2T\left(\frac{30}{T} + \frac{30}{2T}\right) = 2T(1)$$

$$2\cancel{T}\left(\frac{30}{\cancel{T}}\right) + \cancel{2}\,\cancel{T}\left(\frac{30}{\cancel{2}\,\cancel{T}}\right) = 2T$$

$$60 + 30 = 2T$$

$$90 = 2T$$

$$\frac{90}{2} = \frac{\cancel{2}T}{\cancel{2}}$$

$$45 = T$$

Thus, 2T = 90

The faster machine would take 45 min. operating alone, and the slower machine would take 90 min. operating alone.

PRACTICE PROBLEMS

1. Working alone, Danny can paint a room in 4 hours and Cindy can paint the same room in 5 hours. After working together for 2 hours, what fraction of the room remains to be painted?

2. Brita can rake a lawn in 45 minutes by herself, and Denise can rake the same lawn in 90 minutes by herself. How long would it take the two of them working together to rake the lawn?

3. Working alone, Fritz can build a bookcase in 8 hours, and Holly can build the same bookcase in 10 hours. After working together for 3 hours, Fritz had to leave. How long will it take Holly to complete the bookcase by herself?

4. Working together, Nora, Weedy, and Daphne can set the Thanksgiving table in 4 minutes. If Nora, alone, can set the table in 7 minutes, and Weedy, alone, can set the table in 28 minutes, how long would it take Daphne to set the table by herself?

5. One printing press is three times faster than another. If together the two presses can print a newspaper in 6 hours, how long would it take the faster press to print the newspaper by itself?

ANSWERS AND EXPLANATIONS

1. In 2 hours, Danny paints $\frac{2}{4}$ of the room and Cindy paints $\frac{2}{5}$ of the room. Therefore, together they paint $\frac{2}{4} + \frac{2}{5} = \frac{18}{20} = \frac{9}{10}$ of the room. Thus, the fraction remaining is $1 - \frac{9}{10} = \frac{1}{10}$.

2. Let x = the no. minutes needed to rake the lawn together.

$$\frac{x}{45} + \frac{x}{90} = 1 \quad \left(\text{multiply by } 90\right)$$
$$90\left(\frac{x}{45} + \frac{x}{90}\right) = 90(1)$$
$$2x + x = 90$$
$$3x = 90$$
$$x = 30 \text{ min.}$$

3. Let x = the no. hours needed by Holly to complete the bookcase by herself. After working together for 3 hours, Fritz has completed $\frac{3}{8}$ of the bookcase and Holly has completed $\frac{3}{10}$ of the bookcase. Thus,

$$\frac{3}{8} + \frac{3}{10} + \frac{x}{10} = 1 \quad \left(\text{multiply by } 80\right)$$
$$80\left(\frac{3}{8} + \frac{3}{10} + \frac{x}{10}\right) = 80(1)$$
$$30 + 24 + 8x = 80$$
$$54 + 8x = 80$$
$$8x = 26$$
$$x = 3\frac{1}{4} \text{ hrs.}$$

4. Let x = the no. minutes Daphne needs to set the table by herself.

$$\frac{4}{7} + \frac{4}{28} + \frac{4}{x} = 1 \quad \left(\text{multiply by } 28x\right)$$
$$28x\left(\frac{4}{7} + \frac{4}{28} + \frac{4}{x}\right) = 28x(1)$$
$$16x + 4x + 112 = 28x$$
$$20x + 112 = 28x$$
$$-8x = -112$$
$$x = 14 \text{ min.}$$

5. Let x = the no. hours needed by the faster press by itself and $3x$ = the no. hours needed by the slower press by itself.

$$\frac{6}{x} + \frac{6}{3x} = 1 \quad \text{(multiply by } 3x\text{)}$$

$$3x\left(\frac{6}{x} + \frac{6}{3x}\right) = 3x(1)$$

$$18 + 6 = 3x$$

$$24 = 3x$$

$$8 \text{ hrs.} = x$$

GROUPS

In work problems involving groups, we are told how long it takes a group of a certain size to complete a job, and are asked to determine how long it would take a group of a different size to complete the same job. For example:

Suppose a group of 4 machines requires 6 hours to complete a job. If the number of machines is doubled to 8, the number of hours would be cut in half to 3. If, on the other hand, the number of machines is cut in half to 2, the number of hours would be doubled to 12. In other words, the more machines, the less time; the fewer machines, the more time.

In each case, the product of the number of machines and the number of hours is the same, 24. That is, each combination must produce the same amount of work to complete the job, 24 "machine-hours."

# of machines		# of hours	
4	×	6	= 24
8	×	3	= 24
2	×	12	= 24

In general, if a group of size N_1 completes a job in H_1 hours, and another group of size N_2 completes the same job in H_2 hours, then
$$N_1 \cdot H_1 = N_2 \cdot H_2$$

Note that this principle assumes that the individual workers in one group work at the same rate as the individual workers in the other group.

Example

Eight machines can complete a job in 5 hours. If only 6 of these machines are working, how long will it take them to complete the same job?

Procedure

1. Represent the number of hours required by the smaller group by h.
   Let h = the number of hours required by the group of 6 machines to complete the job.

2. Write an equation expressing the fact that the product of the number of machines and the number of hours must be the same for both groups. Solve this equation for h.

$$N_1 \cdot H_1 = N_2 \cdot H_2$$
$$8 \cdot 5 = 6 \cdot h$$
$$40 = 6h$$
$$\frac{40}{6} = \frac{\cancel{6}h}{\cancel{6}}$$
$$6\frac{2}{3} = h$$

The group of 6 machines will take $6\frac{2}{3}$ hours to complete the job.

PRACTICE PROBLEMS

1. Five tractors can plow a certain field in 12 hours. How long would it take 6 of these tractors to plow the same field?

2. If Q machines can complete a job in D days, how many of these machines are required to complete the same job in 2 days less time?

3. M machines can complete a job in H hours. If N machines break down before starting the job, how many hours will it take the remaining number of machines to do the same job?

4. Four people can build a fence in 12 days. How much less time would be required by 6 people working at the same rate?

5. If 4 pipes can fill a pool in 15 hours, how many more of these pipes are required to fill the same pool in only 10 hours?

ANSWERS AND EXPLANATIONS

1. Let x = the no. hours needed by 6 tractors.

$$5 \cdot 12 = 6 \cdot x$$
$$60 = 6x$$
$$10 \text{ hrs.} = x$$

2. Let x = the no. machines needed to complete the job in 2 days less time. Two days less time is $D - 2$ days. Thus,

$$Q \cdot D = x(D - 2)$$
$$x = \frac{QD}{D - 2}$$

3. After N machines break down, $M - N$ machines remain.
   Let $x =$ the no. hrs. needed by the remaining $M - N$ machines.

   $$M \cdot H = x(M - N)$$

   $$\frac{MH}{M - N} = x$$

4. Let $x =$ the no. days needed by 6 people.

   $$4 \cdot 12 = 6 \cdot x$$

   $$48 = 6x$$

   8 days $= x$

   This is $12 - 8 = 4$ days less time.

5. Let $x =$ the no. pipes needed to fill the pool in 10 hours.

   $$15 \cdot 4 = 10 \cdot x$$

   $$60 = 10x$$

   6 pipes $= x$

   This is $6 - 4 = 2$ more pipes.

SET PROBLEMS

A collection of things (numbers, people, attributes, etc.) is called a **set**. Each member of a set is called an **element** of the set. For example, the set of odd numbers less than 10 consists of the elements 1, 3, 5, 7, and 9.

VENN DIAGRAM

A common way of depicting the relationship between sets is by a diagram, called a **Venn diagram**, in which each set is represented by a circle. All the possible Venn diagrams for two sets are shown below. In the diagram on the left, set A and set B have *no elements* in common and are said to be **disjoint**; in the next diagram, set A and set B have *some elements* in common (but not all) and are said to be **overlapping**; in the next diagram, set A has *all its elements* in set B and is said to be a **subset** of set B; in the last diagram, set B has all its elements in set A and is thus a subset of set A.

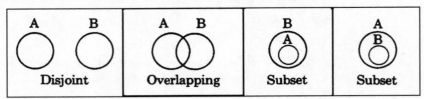

Venn diagrams are particularly useful in solving problems involving *overlapping* sets. For example, suppose we are told that in a class of 25 students, 15 students have brown hair, 12 students have blue eyes, and 8 students have *both* brown hair *and* blue eyes. This information can be organized into a Venn diagram, as shown below. The overlapping section contains the 8 students who have both brown hair and blue eyes. This leaves 7 students ($15 - 8 = 7$) in the section of brown hair, but not blue eyes, and 4 students ($12 - 8 = 4$) in the section of blue eyes, but not brown hair.

By organizing the information this way, we can then determine, for example, how many students have *neither* brown hair *nor* blue eyes. This is simply the number of students outside the two circles. Since there are 19 students inside the two circles ($7 + 8 + 4 = 19$) and 25 students in the entire class, we can conclude that there are 6 students ($25 - 19 = 6$) who have neither brown hair nor blue eyes.

Remember that, in general, it is best to fill in the number of elements in the overlapping section first. This will help avoid the common error of counting the same element more than once.

Example

In a survey, 60% of the people said that they had tried brand X, 50% said that they had tried brand Y, and 20% said that they had tried both. What percent said that they had tried neither?

Procedure

1. Draw a Venn diagram depicting brand X and brand Y.

2. Place the 20% that had tried both brands in the overlapping section. This leaves 40% in the brand X, but not brand Y section, and 30% in the brand Y, but not brand X section.

$$(60\% - 20\% = 40\%) \qquad (50\% - 20\% = 30\%)$$

3. To obtain the percent outside the two circles (the percent that had tried neither), subtract the sum of the percents inside the two circles from 100%.

$$40\% + 20\% + 30\% = 90\%$$

$$
\begin{array}{r}
100\% \\
-90\% \\
\hline
10\%
\end{array}
$$

10% said that they had tried neither brand.

PRACTICE PROBLEMS

1. In a group of 30 students, 18 are taking calculus, 15 are taking physics, and 11 are taking both calculus and physics. How many students in the group are taking neither calculus nor physics?

2. In a recent survey, 40% of the people said they read newspaper X, 50% said they read newspaper Y, and 10% said they read both newspapers. What percent of the people said they read neither newspaper?

3. At a party of 100 people, 75 people wore bluejeans, 30 people wore sweaters, and 20 people wore both. How many people at the party wore neither bluejeans nor sweaters?

4. At a wedding reception of 50 people, 37 people had an appetizer and 30 people had a dessert. If 10 people had neither an appetizer nor a dessert, how many people at the reception had both?

5. In a foreign language school, 64% of the students are studying Spanish, 52% are studying French, and 28% are studying a language other than Spanish or French. What percent of the students at the school are studying both Spanish and French?

ANSWERS AND EXPLANATIONS

1. Let x = the number of students who take neither calculus nor physics.

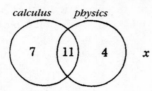

$$7 + 11 + 4 + x = 30$$
$$x = 8$$

2. Let $x\%$ = the % that read neither X nor Y.

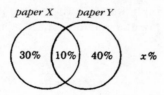

$$30\% + 10\% + 40\% + x\% = 100\%$$
$$x\% = 20\%$$

3. Let x = the number of people who wore neither blue jeans nor sweaters.

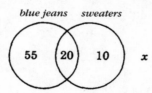

$$55 + 20 + 10 + x = 100$$
$$x = 15$$

4. Let x = the number of people who had both an appetizer and dessert.

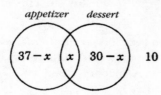

$$37 - x + x + 30 - x + 10 = 50$$
$$-x + 77 = 50$$
$$-x = -27$$
$$x = 27$$

5.   Let x = the % studying both Spanish and French.

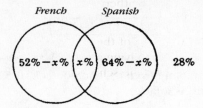

$$52\% - x\% + x\% + 64\% - x\% + 28\% = 100\%$$
$$-x\% + 144\% = 100\%$$
$$-x\% = -44\%$$
$$x\% = 44\%$$

PROBABILITY

BASIC FORMULA

The **probability** that an event occurs is defined to be the ratio of the number of outcomes in which the event occurs to the total number of possible outcomes. For example, when you flip a coin, there are a total of two possible outcomes, a head or a tail. The number of outcomes in which you get a head is one. Therefore, the probability of getting a head when you flip it once is the ratio 1 to 2, or $\frac{1}{2}$.

If we denote an event by E, and the probability of the event occurring by P(E), we have:

$$P(E) = \frac{\text{Number of outcomes in which E occurs}}{\text{Total number of possible outcomes}}$$

Let us look at another example. Suppose a drawer contains 2 white socks, 1 black sock, and 4 brown socks, and you pull out one sock randomly. Let us compute the probabilities of getting a white sock, a black sock, and a brown sock. Since there are 7 socks in the drawer, the total number of possible outcomes is 7.

$$P(\text{white sock}) = \frac{2}{7}$$

$$P(\text{black sock}) = \frac{1}{7}$$

$$P(\text{brown sock}) = \frac{4}{7}$$

Notice that when you add the three fractions, you get the number 1. In other words, since it is certain that when you pull out a sock from this drawer it will either be white, black, or brown, the probability of a **certain event** is 1. Similarly, since it is impossible to pull out a red sock from this draw, we say that the probability of an **impossible event** is 0. In other words, the probability that an event occurs is always a number between 0 and 1.

$$0 \leq P(E) \leq 1$$

Finally, note that to compute the probability that an event does NOT occur, simply subtract the probability that the event does occur from 1. For example, if the probability

that it will rain tomorrow is 85%, or .85, then the probability that it will not rain is
$1 - .85 = .15$, or 15%.

$$P(\text{Not } E) = 1 - P(E)$$

PRACTICE PROBLEMS

1. If a card is selected randomly from a standard deck of 52 playing cards, what is the probability that the card is a Jack?

2. If a coin is flipped twice, what is the probability that you get two heads?

3. A drawer contains 4 black socks, 6 brown socks, and 2 red socks. If you pull out one sock randomly, what is the probability of getting a black sock or a red sock?

4. A box contains 20 electrical parts, of which 3 are defective. If you pull out one of these parts randomly from the box, what is the probability that the part is not defective?

ANSWERS AND EXPLANATIONS

1. In general, the probability that an event occurs is

$$P(E) = \frac{\text{Number of outcomes in which E occurs}}{\text{Total number of possible outcomes}}$$

In this case, there are 4 Jacks in the deck, and any one of 52 cards can be selected. Therefore the probability of getting a Jack is:

$$P(\text{Jack}) = \frac{4}{52} = \frac{1}{13}$$

2. When you flip a coin twice there are 4 possible outcomes, HH, HT, TH, TT. Of these, only 1 outcome has 2 heads, HH. Therefore:

$$P(2 \text{ Heads}) = \frac{1}{4}$$

3. When you pull out one sock from the drawer, there are $4 + 6 + 2 = 12$ possible outcomes. Of these, there are $4 + 2 = 6$ outcomes in which you get either a black sock or a red sock. Therefore:

$$P(\text{black sock or red sock}) = \frac{6}{12} = \frac{1}{2}$$

4. The probability of selecting a defective part is $\frac{3}{20}$. Therefore:

$$P(\text{Not Defective}) = 1 - P(\text{Defective})$$

$$= 1 - \frac{3}{20}$$

$$= \frac{17}{20}$$

PRACTICE TEST

1. At a party there are S men and T women. If 3 more men arrive, and 2 women leave, what fraction of the party are now women?

   A. $\dfrac{T-2}{S-T+5}$

   B. $\dfrac{T-S}{S+T}$

   C. $\dfrac{T-2}{S+T+1}$

   D. $\dfrac{T}{S+T+1}$

   E. $\dfrac{T-2}{S+3}$

2. A traveler spends $\dfrac{2}{5}$ of his money on a plane ticket and $\dfrac{1}{3}$ of his money on lodging. If he is left with $160, how much money did he start with?

   A. $600
   B. $200
   C. $1,200
   D. $218
   E. $540

3. On a driving test, 4 out of 5 applicants passed the written test. Of every 4 that passed the written test, 1 failed the road test. What fraction of all the applicants passed both tests?

   A. $\dfrac{3}{4}$

   B. $\dfrac{4}{15}$

   C. $\dfrac{5}{8}$

   D. $\dfrac{3}{5}$

   E. $\dfrac{8}{15}$

4. If M calculators can be bought for D dollars, how many calculators can be bought for G dollars, at the same rate?

   A. $\dfrac{M}{DG}$

   B. $M(D-G)$

   C. $\dfrac{MG}{D}$

   D. $\dfrac{MD}{G}$

   E. $\dfrac{DG}{M}$

5. In a school debating team, there are three times as many juniors as sophomores, and twice as many seniors as juniors. What percent of the debating team are juniors?

   A. 60%
   B. 30%
   C. 10%
   D. 22.2%
   E. 16%

6. In a recent election, only three candidates, A, B, and C, received votes. If A received $\frac{1}{5}$ of the votes, B received 35% of the votes, and C received 900 votes, how many votes did A receive?

   A. 700
   B. 2,000
   C. 782
   D. 400
   E. 1,100

7. The price of an airline ticket increases from $240 to $300. What is the percent of increase?

   A. 80%
   B. 25%
   C. 30%
   D. 120%
   E. 20%

8. Nikki sells her house for $50,000, thus making a profit of 25% of the cost. What did the house cost?

   A. $40,000
   B. $37,500
   C. $30,000
   D. $42,500
   E. $20,000

9. If a selling price of $24 results in a 20% discount off the list price, what selling price would result in a 30% discount off the list price?

   A. $9
   B. $20
   C. $27
   D. $18
   E. $21

10. A markup of 10%, followed by a discount of 30%, is equivalent to a single discount of what percent?

    A. 28%
    B. 20%
    C. 23%
    D. 25%
    E. 37%

11. Four times the sum of a number and 2 is equal to 11 more than the number. What is the number?

    A. 1
    B. $4\frac{1}{3}$
    C. 3
    D. 2
    E. $1\frac{4}{5}$

12. Joe has 20 coins consisting only of dimes and quarters. If the number of dimes is 5 more than twice the number of quarters, what is the total value of the coins?

    A. $3.20
    B. $3.75
    C. $2.75
    D. $4.25
    E. $4.50

13. If the sum of three consecutive even integers is twice the largest, what is the largest?

    A. 8
    B. 6
    C. 7
    D. 2
    E. 10

14. Ann is now twice as old as Jerry. Four years ago she was three times as old as Jerry was then. How old is Ann now?

    A. 4
    B. 16
    C. 24
    D. 8
    E. 10

15. A basketball team averages 98 points in its first three games. How many points must it score in the next game in order to have a 100 point average overall?

 A. 102
 B. 104
 C. 108
 D. 112
 E. 106

16. The daily low temperatures, in degrees Fahrenheit, for the first five days in February were 28, 32, 27, 25, and 28. What was the mean temperature for those days?

 A. 25
 B. 26
 C. 27
 D. 28
 E. 29

17. What is the range of the following set of numbers: 3, −7, 8, −12, and 13,?

 A. 25
 B. 10
 C. 6
 D. 1
 E. −25

18. Maureen runs a 26 mile marathon in 5.4 hours. If she runs the first half of the race in 2.8 hours, what is her average rate, in miles per hour, for the second half of the race?

 A. 2
 B. 2.6
 C. 6
 D. 5
 E. 4.8

19. Rick travels 120 miles at an average rate of 20 m.p.h., and returns along the same route at an average rate of 30 m.p.h. What is his average rate, in miles per hour, for the entire round trip?

 A. 26
 B. 25
 C. 22
 D. 24
 E. 23

20. A train leaves a station at 6 P.M. and travels east at an average rate of 80 m.p.h. At 8 P.M. another train leaves the same station and travels west at an average rate of 90 m.p.h. At what time are the two trains 415 miles apart?

 A. 9:38 P.M.
 B. 10:44 P.M.
 C. 11:30 P.M.
 D. 10:30 P.M.
 E. 9:30 P.M.

21. Tom leaves a roadside diner and travels south at an average rate of 45 m.p.h. One hour later, Rosemary leaves the same diner and travels south along the same road at an average rate of 60 m.p.h. How many miles are the two people from the diner when Rosemary catches up with Tom?

 A. 180
 B. 120
 C. 135
 D. 360
 E. 240

22. Working alone, Allen can build a fence in 8 hours, and Danny can build the same fence in 16 hours. If after working alone for 2 hours, Allen is joined by Danny, how many more hours will it take the two of them to complete the fence?

 A. 2
 B. $3\frac{1}{3}$
 C. 6
 D. 10
 E. 4

23. Five printing presses can print a newspaper in 6 hours. If only 3 of the presses are operating, how long will it take them to do the same job?

 A. 8
 B. 9
 C. 10
 D. 11
 E. 12

24. In a group of 15 married couples, 16 people have brown hair, 12 people have blue eyes, and 9 people have both brown hair and blue eyes. How many people have neither brown hair nor blue eyes?

    A. 2
    B. 11
    C. 14
    D. 16
    E. 19

25. A box contains 30 light bulbs, of which 5 are defective. If you pull out one of these light bulbs randomly from the box, what is the probability that the light bulb is not defective?

    A. $\dfrac{1}{6}$

    B. $\dfrac{1}{5}$

    C. $\dfrac{1}{3}$

    D. $\dfrac{2}{3}$

    E. $\dfrac{5}{6}$

ANSWERS AND EXPLANATIONS

1. C	6. D	10. C	14. B	18. D	22. E
2. A	7. B	11. A	15. E	19. D	23. C
3. D	8. A	12. C	16. D	20. E	24. B
4. C	9. E	13. B	17. A	21. A	25. E
5. B					

1. **The correct answer is (C).**

$$\text{Men} = S + 3 \quad (3 \text{ men arrive})$$
$$\underline{\text{Women} = T - 2} \quad (2 \text{ women leave})$$
$$\text{Total} = S + T + 1$$

$$\text{Fraction of women} = \frac{\text{Women}}{\text{Total}}$$
$$= \frac{T-2}{S+T+1}$$

2. **The correct answer is (A).** The fraction of money spent $= \frac{2}{5} + \frac{1}{3} = \frac{11}{15}$

Thus, the fraction of money left is $1 - \frac{11}{15} = \frac{4}{15}$

Let S = the amount of money started with. Thus,

$$\frac{4}{15}S = \$160$$

$$\cancel{15} \cdot \frac{4}{\cancel{15}}S = 15 \cdot 160$$

$$4S = 2400$$

$$S = \$600$$

3. **The correct answer is (D).** $\frac{4}{5}$ passed the written test.

$\frac{3}{4}$ of those that passed the written test also passed the road test.

Thus, the fraction that passed both tests is

$$\frac{3}{4} \text{ of } \frac{4}{5} = \frac{3}{\cancel{4}} \times \frac{\cancel{4}}{5} = \frac{3}{5}$$

4. **The correct answer is (C).** Let x = the number of calculators that can be bought for G dollars.

$$\frac{\text{calculators} \to \text{M}}{\text{dollars} \to \text{D}} = \frac{x}{\text{G}} \quad \text{(cross-multiply)}$$
$$\text{D}x = \text{MG}$$
$$x = \frac{\text{MG}}{\text{D}}$$

5.   The correct answer is (B).

Let So = the number of sophomores,

Jr = the number of juniors,

and Se = the number of seniors.

$$Jr = 3So \quad \text{or} \quad So = \frac{Jr}{3}$$

$$Se = 2Jr$$

$$\text{Fraction of juniors} = \frac{Jr}{So + Jr + Se}$$

$$\left(\text{substitute } So = \frac{Jr}{3} \text{ and } Se = 2Jr \right)$$

$$= \frac{Jr}{\frac{Jr}{3} + Jr + 2Jr} \quad \left(\text{multiply by 3} \right)$$

$$= \frac{3 \cdot Jr}{3 \cdot \frac{Jr}{3} + 3 \cdot Jr + 3 \cdot 2Jr}$$

$$= \frac{3Jr}{Jr + 3Jr + 6Jr}$$

$$= \frac{3\,Jr}{10\,Jr}$$

$$= \frac{3}{10}$$

Thus, the percent of juniors = $\frac{3}{10} \times 100\% = 30\%$.

6.   The correct answer is (D). A received $\frac{1}{5}$, or 20%, of the vote.

B received 35% of the vote.

Thus, C received $100\% - (20\% + 35\%) = 45\%$ of the vote.

Let T = the total number of votes cast.

Since C received 900 votes,

$$\frac{\text{Part}}{\text{Whole}} = \frac{\text{Percent}}{100\%}$$

$$\frac{900}{T} = \frac{45}{100} \quad \left(\text{cross-multiply} \right)$$

$$45T = 90000$$

$$T = 2000 \text{ total votes}$$

Thus, A received $\frac{1}{5}$ of 2000 = $\frac{1}{5} \times 2000 = 400$ votes.

7. **The correct answer is (B).**

$$\frac{\text{amount of increase}}{\text{original value}} = \frac{\% \text{ of increase}}{100\%}$$

$$\frac{\$300 - \$240}{\$240} = \frac{x}{100}$$

$$\frac{60}{240} = \frac{x}{100} \quad (\text{cross-multiply})$$

$$240x = 6000$$

$$x = 25\% \text{ increase}$$

8. **The correct answer is (A).**

Let C = the cost of the house.

$$\text{Selling Price} = (100\% + \% \text{ of Profit}) \times \text{Cost}$$

$$\$50,000 = (\$100\% + 25\%) \times C$$

$$50,000 = 1.25C$$

$$\frac{50,000}{1.25} = \frac{\cancel{1.25}C}{\cancel{1.25}}$$

$$\$40,000 = C$$

9. **The correct answer is (E).**

Let L = the list price for a 20% discount.

$$\text{Selling Price} = (100\% - \% \text{ of Discount}) \times \text{List Price}$$

$$\$24 = (100\% - 20\%) \times L$$

$$24 = .80L$$

$$\frac{24}{.80} = \frac{\cancel{.80}L}{\cancel{.80}}$$

$$\$30 = L$$

Let S = the selling price for a 30% discount.

$$\text{Selling Price} = (100\% - \% \text{ of Discount}) \times \text{List Price}$$

$$S = (100\% - 30\%) \times \$30$$

$$= .70 \times 30$$

$$= \$21$$

10. **The correct answer is (C).** After a 10% markup, the selling price is 110% of the original value.
After a 30% discount, the selling price is 70% of 110% of the original value.
Thus, a 10% markup followed by a 30% discount means

$$.70 \times 1.10 \times \text{original value}$$

$$= .77 \times \text{original value}$$

This is equivalent to a single discount of 23% off the original value.

11. The correct answer is (A).

Let n = the number.

$$4(n+2) = n+11$$
$$4n+8 = n+11$$
$$3n+8 = 11$$
$$3n = 3$$
$$n = 1$$

12. The correct answer is (C).

Let Q = the number of quarters,

and $2Q+5$ = the number of dimes.

Since there are a total of 20 coins,

$$Q+2Q+5 = 20$$
$$3Q+5 = 20$$
$$3Q = 15$$
$$Q = 5 \text{ quarters}$$
$$\text{and } 2Q+5 = 2(5)+5$$
$$= 15 \text{ dimes}$$

Thus, the total value $= 5(\$.25)+15(\$.10) = \$2.75$

13. The correct answer is (B).

Let N = the first even integer,

N + 2 = the second even integer,

and N + 4 = the third even integer.

$$N+N+2+N+4 = 2(N+4)$$
$$3N+6 = 2N+8$$
$$N+6 = 8$$
$$N = 2$$

Thus, the largest, N + 4 = 2 + 4 = 6

14. The correct answer is (B).

Let J = Jerry's age now,

and 2J = Ann's age now.

Thus, J − 4 = Jerry's age 4 years ago,

and 2J − 4 = Ann's age 4 years ago.

$$2J-4 = 3(J-4)$$
$$2J-4 = 3J-12$$
$$-4 = J-12$$
$$8 = J$$

Thus, 2J = 16 = Ann's age now.

15. **The correct answer is (E).** Let S = the score of the next game.

$$\text{Average} = \frac{\text{Sum}}{N}$$

$$100 = \frac{3(98)+S}{4}$$

$$100 = \frac{294+S}{4}$$

$$400 = 294+S$$

$$106 = S$$

16. **The correct answer is (D).**

$$\text{mean} = \frac{\text{sum of temperatures}}{\text{number of temperatures}}$$

$$= \frac{28+32+27+25+28}{5}$$

$$= \frac{140}{5}$$

$$= 28 \text{ degrees}$$

17. **The correct answer is (A).**

$$\text{Range} = \text{Largest Number} - \text{Smallest Number}$$

$$= 13 - (-12)$$

$$= 13 + 12$$

$$= 25$$

18. **The correct answer is (D).**

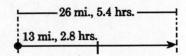

The distance in the second half = 26 mi. − 13 mi. = 13 mi.
The time in the second half = 5.4 hrs. − 2.8 hrs. = 2.6 hrs.

$$\text{Rate} = \frac{\text{Distance}}{\text{Time}}$$

$$R = \frac{13 \text{ mi.}}{2.6 \text{ hrs.}}$$

$$= 5 \text{ mi./hr. in second half}$$

19. **The correct answer is (D).**

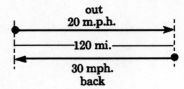

$$\text{Time} = \frac{\text{Distance}}{\text{Rate}}$$

$$T_{out} = \frac{120}{20} \quad \bigg| \quad T_{back} = \frac{120}{30}$$

$$= 6 \text{ hrs.} \quad \bigg| \quad = 4 \text{ hrs.}$$

$$T_{total} = T_{out} + T_{back}$$

$$= 6 \text{ hrs.} + 4 \text{ hrs.}$$

$$= 10 \text{ hrs.}$$

$$\text{Rate}_{round\ trip} = \frac{D_{total}}{T_{total}}$$

$$= \frac{240 \text{ mi.}}{10 \text{ hrs.}}$$

$$= 24 \text{ m.p.h.}$$

20. **The correct answer is (E).** Let h = the number of hours traveled by the train that leaves at 6 P.M., and $h - 2$ = the number of hours traveled by the train that leaves at 8 P.M.

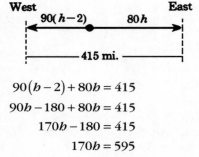

$$90(h-2) + 80h = 415$$

$$90h - 180 + 80h = 415$$

$$170h - 180 = 415$$

$$170h = 595$$

$$h = 3.5 \text{ hrs}$$

Thus, the trains are 415 miles apart at 6 P.M. + 3.5 hrs = 9:30 P.M.

21. **The correct answer is (A).** Let h = the number of hours traveled by Tom, and $h - 1$ = the number of hours traveled by Rosemary.

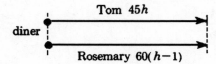

$$45h = 60(h-1)$$
$$45h = 60h - 60$$
$$-15h = -60$$
$$h = 4 \text{ hrs.}$$

Thus, the number of miles from the diner = $45h = (45)(4) = 180$ mi.

22. **The correct answer is (E).** Let h = the number of hours worked together to complete the fence.

Allen alone   Allen   Danny

$$\frac{2}{8} \quad + \quad \frac{h}{8} \quad + \quad \frac{h}{16} = 1 \ (\text{multiply by } 16)$$

$$\cancel{16}^{2} \cdot \frac{2}{\cancel{8}} + \cancel{16}^{2} \cdot \frac{h}{\cancel{8}} \ \cancel{16}^{1} + \frac{h}{\cancel{16}} = 16 \cdot 1$$

$$4 + 2h + h = 16$$
$$4 + 3h = 16$$
$$3h = 12$$
$$h = 4 \text{ hrs.}$$

23. **The correct answer is (C).** Let h = the number of hours required by the group of 3 presses to print the newspaper.

$$5 \text{ presses} \cdot 6 \text{ hours} = 3 \text{ presses} \cdot h$$
$$30 = 3h$$
$$10 \text{ hrs.} = h$$

24. **The correct answer is (B).**

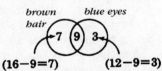

$$(16-9=7) \qquad (12-9=3)$$

Since there are a total of 30 people (15 couples), the number of people that have neither brown hair nor blue eyes is $30 - (7 + 9 + 3) = 30 - 19 = 11$.

25. **The correct answer is (E).** The probability of selecting a defective part is $\frac{5}{30}$.

Therefore:

$$P(\text{Not Defective}) = 1 - P(\text{Defective})$$
$$= 1 - \frac{5}{30}$$
$$= \frac{25}{30}$$
$$= \frac{5}{6}$$

Chapter 5

GEOMETRY

Geometry, as developed by the Greeks, is divided into general categories: **plane geometry**—the study of figures in a flat, two-dimensional surface, called a plane, and **solid geometry**—the study of figures in three-dimensional space. In this unit, we will primarily review the basic definitions, concepts, and formulas found in plane geometry. The topics included are:

- Points, lines, and angles
- Polygons
- Triangles
- Quadrilaterals
- Perimeter and area
- Circles
- Coordinate geometry
- Volume

POINTS, LINES, AND ANGLES

The most fundamental concepts in plane geometry are those of a point and a line. A **point** has no size (no dimensions), only position. As illustrated below, points are represented by dots, and are denoted by capital letters.

A **line** is a continuous set of points having one-dimension—length. Lines can either be straight or curved, although generally, they are assumed to be straight. Most geometric figures are made up of parts of lines, called **line segments**. A line can be denoted in two different ways: by a small letter placed next to it, or by two capital letters naming two of its points. Line segments are usually denoted by their endpoints.

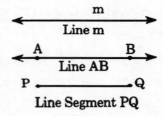

DENOTING ANGLES

When two lines (or line segments) meet at a point, they form a figure called an **angle**. The two lines are called the **sides** of the angle, and the point is called the **vertex**. The symbol for angle is ∠.

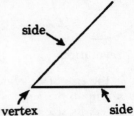

Angles can be denoted in three different ways: 1. by a capital letter naming its vertex, 2. by a small letter, or number, placed inside the vertex, or 3. by three capital letters naming three of its points—a point on one side, the point at the vertex, and a point on the other side.

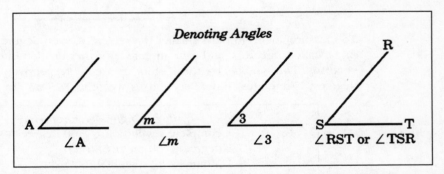

Denoting Angles

∠A   ∠m   ∠3   ∠RST or ∠TSR

Note that the method of naming three points, see below, is most often used when there are more than one angle at the same vertex.

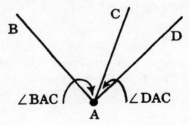

∠BAC   ∠DAC

MEASURING ANGLES

The size of an angle is determined by the amount of **rotation** needed to make one of its sides coincide with the other. The basic unit for measuring rotation is the **degree**, which has the symbol °. By defining the amount of rotation needed to make one complete revolution of a circle as 360 degrees (360°), each angle can then be measured as a fractional part of one revolution. For example, an angle that is $\frac{1}{4}$ of a revolution measures $\frac{1}{4}$ of 360° or 90°, and an angle that is $\frac{1}{3}$ of a revolution measures $\frac{1}{3}$ of 360°, or 120°.

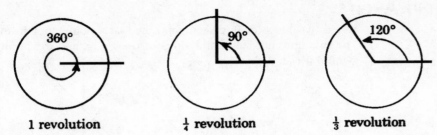

| 1 revolution | ¼ revolution | ⅓ revolution |

Remember that the size of an angle depends only upon the amount of rotation between its sides, and *not* upon the lengths of its sides. In other words, even if the sides of an angle are extended, its size remains the same.

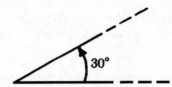

To measure angles in units smaller than degrees, each degree is divided into 60 equal parts, called **minutes**, and each minute is further divided into 60 equal parts, called **seconds**. The symbols for these units are ' and " respectively. For example, an angle of 52 degrees, 17 minutes, and 42 seconds is written 52°17'42". In summary,

---

Units of Angle Measurement
1 complete revolution = 360 degrees (360°)
1 degree = 60 minutes (60')
1 minute = 60 seconds (60")

Example
How many degrees are there between the hands of a clock at 1:30?

Procedure

1. Draw a clock, indicating the position of the hands at 1:30. Note that the hour hand is exactly half way between the 1 and the 2.

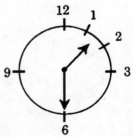

2. To find the number of degrees between each hour, divide the total number of degrees, 360°, by the total number of hours, 12.

$$\frac{360°}{12} = 30° \text{ between each hour}$$

3. Multiply the result by $4\frac{1}{2}$, the number of hours between the hands at 1:30.

$$4\frac{1}{2} \times 30° = 135°$$

The number of degrees between the hands of the clock is 135°.

PRACTICE PROBLEMS

1. Through how many degrees does the hour hand of a clock turn from 9 A.M. to 5 P.M.?

2. How many spokes are on a circular wheel, if every two spokes form an angle of 12°?

ANSWERS AND EXPLANATIONS

1.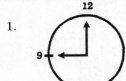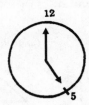

    From 9 A.M. to 5 P.M. the hour hand moves 8 hours. Since there are 30° between each hour, the hour hand moves 8 × 30°, or 240°.

2. Since there are 360° in the wheel, there are a total of 360° ÷ 12, or 30 spokes.

TYPES OF ANGLES

Angles are classified into five different categories according to size: 1. **acute angles**—angles less than 90°, 2. **right angles**—angles equal to 90°, 3. **obtuse angles**—angles greater than 90° but less than 180°, 4. **straight angles**—angles equal to 180°, and 5. **reflex angles**—angles greater than 180° and less than 360°. An example of each type is shown in the table that follows. Note that right angles are usually indicated by placing a small square at the vertex.

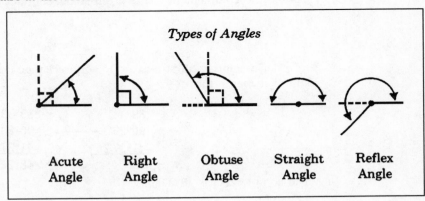

Types of Angles

Acute Angle   Right Angle   Obtuse Angle   Straight Angle   Reflex Angle

ANGLE RELATIONSHIPS

Two angles that have a common vertex and share a common side are called **adjacent angles**. In the following example, ∠BAC and ∠DAC are adjacent angles.

If the sum of two angles is 90°, the angles are said to be **complementary**. Each angle is called the **complement** of the other. Complementary angles, when placed adjacent, form a right angle.

If the sum of two angles is 180°, the angles are said to be **supplementary**. Each angle is called the **supplement** of the other. Supplementary angles, when placed adjacent, form a straight angle.

Complementary Angles

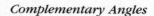

$$x° + y° = 90°$$

Supplementary Angles

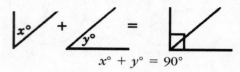

$$x° + y° = 180°$$

Example 1

What is the complement of an angle measuring 41°37'26"?

Procedure

1. To find the complement of the given angle, subtract the angle from 90°.

$$90°$$
$$-41°37'26''$$

2. In order to subtract, first borrow 1° and exchange it for 60', and then borrow 1' and exchange it for 60".

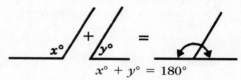

The complement is 48°22'34".

Example 2

How many degrees are in an angle that is 20° less than 4 times its supplement?

Procedure

1. Represent the number of degrees in the angle by x, and the number of degrees in the supplement of the angle by $180 - x$.

Translate the given condition into symbolic form. Solve the resulting equation for x.

Let x = the number of degrees in the angle,

and $180 - x$ = the number of degrees in the supplement of the angle.

$$x = 4(180 - x) - 20$$
$$x = 720 - 4x - 20$$
$$x = 700 - 4x$$
$$\underline{+4x = \quad\quad +4x}$$
$$5x = 700$$
$$\frac{\cancel{5}x}{\cancel{5}} = \frac{700}{5}$$
$$x = 140$$

The number of degrees in the angle is 140°.

PRACTICE PROBLEMS

1. What is the supplement of an angle measuring 113°15'40"?

2. Find the number of degrees in an angle that is 36° more than twice its complement.

3. Two supplementary angles are in the ratio of 3:7. How many degrees are in the smaller angle?

4. If the supplement of an angle is 3 times the complement of the same angle, how many degrees are in the angle?

ANSWERS AND EXPLANATIONS

1. Subtract from 180°. In order to subtract, first borrow 1° and exchange it for 60', then borrow 1' and exchange it for 60".

$$
\begin{array}{rrr}
179° & 59' & \\
\cancel{180°} & \cancel{60'} & \cancel{60''} \\
-113° & 15' & 40'' \\
\hline
66° & 44' & 20''
\end{array}
$$

2. Let x = the number of degrees in the angle, and $90 - x$ = the number of degrees in the complement of the angle.

$$x = 2(90 - x) + 36$$
$$x = 180 - 2x + 36$$
$$x = 216 - 2x$$
$$3x = 216$$
$$x = 72°$$

3. Let $3x$ = the number of degrees in one angle, and $7x$ = the number of degrees in the other angle.

$$3x + 7x = 180$$
$$10x = 180$$
$$x = 18°$$

Thus, the smaller angle is $3x$, or $3(18°) = 54°$.

4. Let x = the number of degrees in the angle, $90 - x$ = the number of degrees in the complement of the angle, and $180 - x$ = the number of degrees in the supplement of the angle.

$$180 - x = 3(90 - x)$$
$$180 - x = 270 - 3x$$
$$2x = 90$$
$$x = 45°$$

INTERSECTING LINES

When two lines intersect, we have the following angle relationships:

Angle Relationships for Intersecting Lines

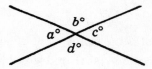

1. The angles opposite each other are equal: $a° = c°$, $b° = d°$. Each pair is called a pair of **vertical angles**.
2. The angles adjacent to each other are supplementary: $a° + b° = 180°$, $b° + c° = 180°$, $c° + d° = 180°$, $a° + d° = 180°$.

For example,

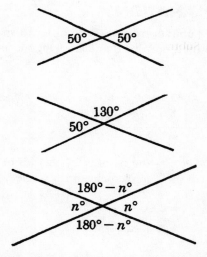

Note that knowing the value of any one of the angles allows us to determine the values of the other three.

Two lines that intersect at right angles are said to be **perpendicular**. In the example below, AB is perpendicular to CD. This is denoted AB ⊥ CD.

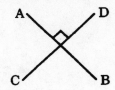

Example 1

In the diagram below, what is the value of y?

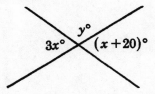

Procedure

1. Set the opposite angles equal, and solve the resulting equation for x.

$$3x = \qquad x + 20$$
$$\underline{-x \qquad -x}$$
$$2x = \qquad\quad 20$$
$$\frac{\cancel{2}x}{\cancel{2}} = \frac{20}{2}$$
$$x = \quad 10$$

2. Substitute the value of x into the expressions in the diagram.

$$3x = 30, \; x + 20 = 30$$

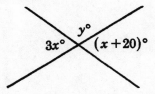

3. Subtract 30° from 180°. (y is the supplement of 30°.)

$$y° = 180° - 30°$$
$$y° = 150°$$

y equals 150.

Example 2

In the diagram below, DB ⊥ BE and ∠ABD = 145°. What is the value of *x*?

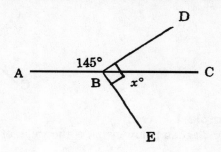

Procedure

1. To find ∠DBC, subtract 145° from 180° (∠DBC is the supplement of 145°).

$$\angle DBC = 180° - 145°$$
$$= 35°$$

2. Since DB ⊥ BE, subtract the result, 35°, from 90°.

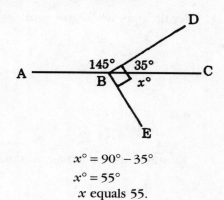

$$x° = 90° - 35°$$
$$x° = 55°$$
$$x \text{ equals } 55.$$

PRACTICE PROBLEMS

In each of the following diagrams, what is the value of *x*?

1.

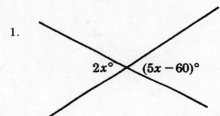

2.

3.

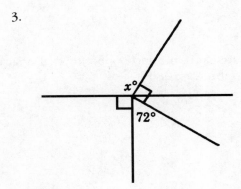

4.

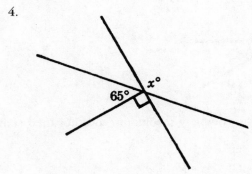

ANSWERS AND EXPLANATIONS

1.

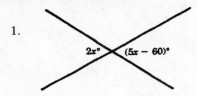

Since vertical angles are equal,

$$2x = 5x - 60$$
$$60 = 3x$$
$$20 = x$$

2.

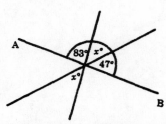

Since vertical angles are equal, the angle opposite $x°$ also measures $x°$. The sum of the three angles that form AB is 180°.

$$83 + x + 47 = 180$$
$$x + 130 = 180$$
$$x = 50$$

3.

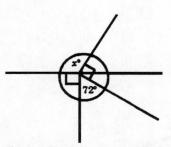

The angles form one complete revolution, and thus their sum is 360°.

$$x + 90 + 72 + 90 = 360$$
$$x + 252 = 360$$
$$x = 108$$

4.

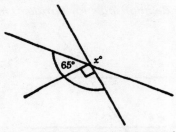

Since vertical angles are equal,

$$x = 65 + 90$$
$$x = 155$$

PARALLEL LINES

Lines that never intersect, no matter how far extended, are called **parallel lines**. In the example below, AB is parallel to CD. This is denoted AB ∥ CD.

A———B
C———D

When a third line, called a **transversal**, crosses a pair of parallel lines, we have the following angle relationships:

Angle Relationships for Parallel Lines

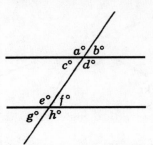

1. The angles in corresponding positions, relative to the points of intersection, are equal: $a° = e°$, $b° = f°$, $c° = g°$, $d° = h°$. Each pair is called a pair of **corresponding angles**.

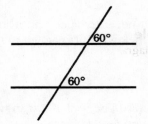

2. The angles between the parallel lines, on opposite sides of the transversal, are equal: $c° = f°$, $d° = e°$. Each pair is called a pair of **alternate interior angles**.

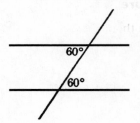

3. The angles between the parallel lines, on the same side of the transversal, are supplementary: $c° + e° = 180°$, $d° + f° = 180°$.

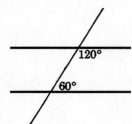

These relationships can be combined in the following general diagram:

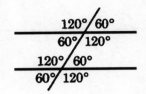

Note that knowing the value of any one of the angles allows us to determine the values of the other seven. For example:

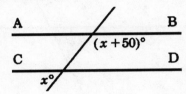

Example

In the diagram below, AB ∥ CD. What is the value of x?

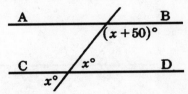

Procedure

1. In the diagram, indicate that the angle opposite $x°$ also measures $x°$.

2. Since the interior angles on the same side of the transversal are supplementary, set their sum equal to 180. Solve the resulting equation for x.

$$x + (x + 50) = 180$$
$$2x + 50 = 180$$
$$\underline{\quad -50 \quad -50}$$
$$2x \quad = 130$$
$$\frac{2x}{2} = \frac{130}{2}$$
$$x = 65$$

x equals 65.

PRACTICE PROBLEMS

In each of the following diagrams AB ∥ CD. What is the value of x?

1.

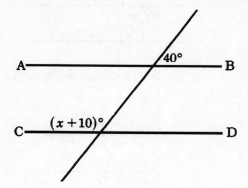

2.

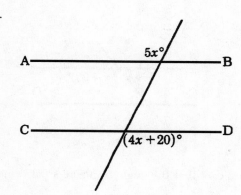

3.

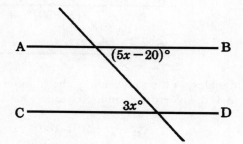

4.

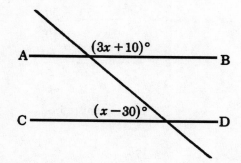

ANSWERS AND EXPLANATIONS

1.

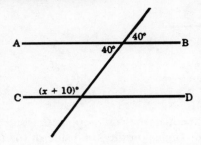

Since vertical angles are equal, the angle opposite 40° is also 40° The interior angles on the same side of the transversal are supplementary. Thus,

$$x + 10 + 40 = 180$$
$$x + 50 = 180$$
$$x = 130$$

2.

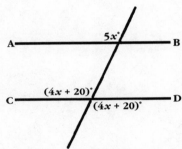

Since vertical angles are equal, the angle opposite $(4x + 20)°$ also measures $(4x + 20)°$. Corresponding angles are equal. Thus,

$$5x = 4x + 20$$
$$x = 20$$

3.

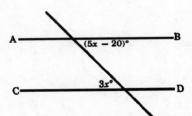

Since alternate interior angles are equal,

$$5x - 20 = 3x$$
$$2x = 20$$
$$x = 10$$

4.

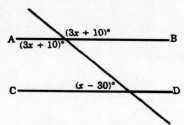

Since vertical angles are equal, the angle opposite $(3x + 10)°$ also measures $(3x + 10)°$. The interior angles on the same side of the transversal are supplementary. Thus,

$$(3x + 10) + (x - 30) = 180$$
$$4x - 20 = 180$$
$$4x = 200$$
$$x = 50$$

POLYGONS

A **polygon** is a plane (flat) closed figure made up of straight line segments. Polygons are denoted by the capital letters at their vertices. For example, the polygon in the diagram below can be denoted ABCDE.

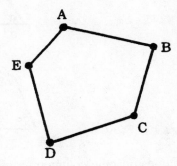

Polygons are classified into different categories according to their number of sides. Some examples are given in the following table.

Number of Sides	Type of Polygon	Example
3	Triangle	
4	Quadrilateral	
5	Pentagon	
6	Hexagon	

The sum of the angles inside each type of polygon is given by the formula below. In this formula, N represents the number of sides.

$$\text{Sum of Angles} = (N - 2) \times 180°$$

For example, the sum of the angles inside a triangle equals $(3 - 2) \times 180°$, or $180°$, and the sum of the angles inside a quadrilateral equals $(4 - 2) \times 180°$, or $360°$.

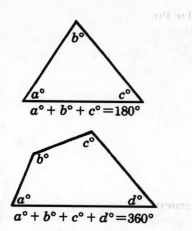

$$a° + b° + c° = 180°$$

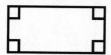

$$a° + b° + c° + d° = 360°$$

The definitions of some common terms associated with polygons are given below. An example of each term is shown below the definition.

Equilateral Polygon: A polygon having all equal sides.

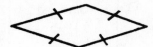

Equiangular Polygon: A polygon having all equal angles.

Regular Polygon: A polygon that is both equilateral and equiangular.

Altitude or Height of a polygon: A line segment drawn from any vertex of the polygon, perpendicular to the opposite side. In some cases, the opposite side has to be extended to meet the altitude.

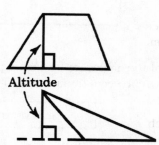

Altitude

Similar Polygons: Polygons having their corresponding angles equal, and their corresponding sides in proportion—having the same shape, but not necessarily the same size. The symbol for similar is ∼. In the following example, ABC ∼ RST.

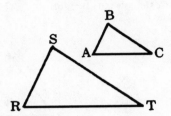

Congruent Polygons: Polygons having their corresponding angles equal, and their corresponding sides equal—having the same shape and the same size. The symbol for congruent is ≅. In the following example, ABCD ≅ RSTU.

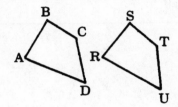

Example
How many degrees are in each angle of a regular pentagon?

Procedure

1. To determine the total number of degrees inside the pentagon, substitute N = 5 (5 sides in a pentagon) into the formula for the sum of angles inside a polygon.

$$
\begin{aligned}
\text{Sum} &= (N - 2) \times 180° \\
&= (5 - 2) \times 180° \\
&= 3 \times 180° \\
&= 540°
\end{aligned}
$$

2. Since the pentagon is regular, all its angles are equal. Therefore, divide the total number of degrees by 5.

$$
\begin{aligned}
\text{Eagle angle} &= \frac{540°}{5} \\
&= 108°
\end{aligned}
$$

Each angle measures 108°.

TRIANGLES

A **triangle** is a polygon having three sides. The symbol for a triangle is △. Triangles, like all polygons, are denoted by the capital letters at their vertices. For example, the triangle in the diagram below can be denoted △RST.

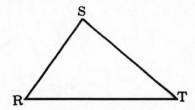

Triangles are classified into three different categories according to the equality of their sides: 1. **scalene** triangles—triangles having no sides equal, 2. **isosceles** triangles—triangles having two sides equal, and 3. **equilateral** triangles—triangles having all three sides equal.

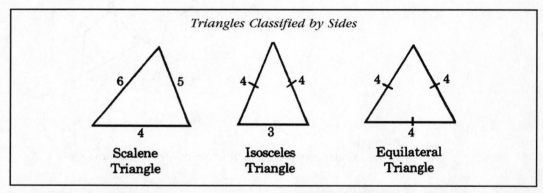

In an isosceles triangle the two equal sides are called the **legs**, and the third side is called the **base**. The angle formed by the legs is called the **vertex angle**, and the angles opposite the legs are called the **base angles**.

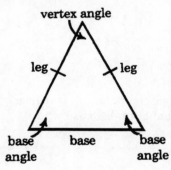

Triangles are also classified into three different categories according to the size of their angles: 1. **acute** triangles—triangles having all acute angles, 2. **right** triangles—triangles having a right angle, and 3. **obtuse** triangles—triangles having an obtuse angle.

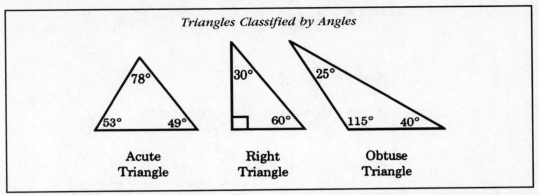

Triangles Classified by Angles

Acute Triangle   **Right Triangle**   **Obtuse Triangle**

In a right triangle, the two sides that form the right angle are called the **legs**, and the side opposite the right angle (the longest side of the triangle) is called the **hypotenuse**.

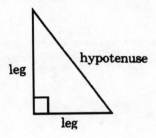

PROPERTIES OF TRIANGLES

All triangles have the following general properties:

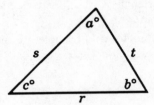

Properties of Triangles

1. The sum of the angles is 180°: $a° + b° + c° = 180°$.
2. The longest side is opposite the largest angle; the shortest side is opposite the smallest angle: If $a° > b° > c°$, then $r > s > t$.
3. The sum of the lengths of any two sides is greater than the length of the third: $r + s > t, s + t > r, t + r > s$.

Example

The angles of a triangle are in the ratio of 2:3:7. How many degrees are in the smallest angle?

Procedure

1. Represent the number of degrees in the angles by $2x°$, $3x°$, and $7x°$, where x is some factor common to all three angles.

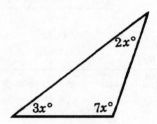

2. Write an equation expressing the fact that the sum of the angles is 180°. Solve this equation for x, and substitute the result into the expression for the smallest angle.

$$2x + 3x + 7x = 180$$
$$12x = 180$$

$$x = \frac{180°}{12} = 15°$$

The smallest angle is $2x° = 30°$.

PRACTICE PROBLEMS

1. In triangle ABC, $\angle B$ is twice $\angle A$, and $\angle C$ is 30° more than $\angle B$. How many degrees are in $\angle A$?

2. The angles of a triangle are in the ratio of 1:3:5. How many degrees are in the largest angle?

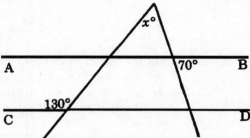

3. In the figure above, AB∥CD. What is the value of x?

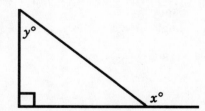

4. In the figure above, what is x in terms of y?

ANSWERS AND EXPLANATIONS

1. Let x = the number of degrees in $\angle A$, $2x$ = the number of degrees in $\angle B$, and $2x + 30$ = the number of degrees in $\angle C$.
    Since the sum of the angles in a triangle is 180°,

    $$x + 2x + 2x + 30 = 180$$
    $$5x + 30 = 180$$
    $$5x = 150$$
    $$x = 30°$$

2. Represent the number of degrees in the angles by $x°$, $3x°$, and $5x°$. Since the sum of the angles in a triangle is 180°,

    $$x + 3x + 5x = 180$$
    $$9x = 180$$
    $$x = 20$$

    Thus, the largest angle is $5x = 5(20°) = 100°$.

3.

    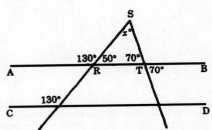

    Corresponding angles are equal. Thus, $\angle ARS$ is also 130°.
    Since $\angle SRT$ is the supplement of $\angle ARS$, $\angle SRT$ is $180° - 130° = 50°$.
    Since vertical angles are equal, $\angle RTS$ is also 70°.
    The sum of the angles in $\triangle SRT$ is 180°. Thus,

    $$x + 50 + 70 = 180$$
    $$x + 120 = 180$$
    $$x = 60$$

4.

    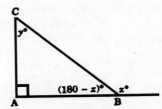

    Since $\angle ABC$ is the supplement of $x°$, represent it by $(180 - x)°$. The sum of the angles in $\triangle BAC$ is 180°. Thus,

    $$(180 - x) + 90 + y = 180$$
    $$270 - x + y = 180$$
    $$-x = -y - 90$$
    $$x = y + 90$$

Besides the general properties just described, certain triangles have additional special properties:

Properties of Isosceles Triangles

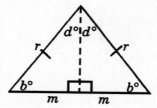

1. The base angles are equal: $b° = b°$.
2. The altitude from the vertex angle to the base bisects (cuts in half) both the vertex angle and the base: $d° = d°$, $m = m$.

Properties of Equilateral Triangles

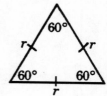

1. All the angles are equal, each measuring 60°.

Properties of Right Triangles

1. The acute angles are complementary: $a° + b° = 90°$.
2. The sum of the squares of the two legs is equal to the square of the hypotenuse: $r^2 + s^2 = h^2$. This is called the **Pythagorean theorem**.
3. In a 30°−60°−90° right triangle, the leg opposite the 30° angle is exactly one-half the hypotenuse: If $a° = 30°$, and $b° = 60°$, then $s = \frac{1}{2}h$.

Example 1

In the diagram below, what is the value of x?

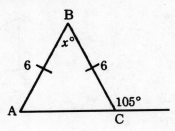

Procedure

1. To determine $\angle BCA$, subtract 105° from 180°. ($\angle BCA$ is the supplement of 105°.)

    $$\angle BCA = 180° - 105°$$
    $$= 75°$$

2. Since $\triangle ABC$ is isosceles, $\angle BAC$ is also 75°. Indicate this in the diagram.

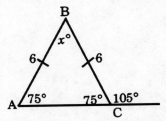

3. To find x, add the two base angles, and subtract the sum from 180°. (The sum of the angles of a triangle is 180°.)

    $$x° = 180° - (75° + 75°)$$
    $$= 180° - 150°$$
    $$= 30°$$

    x is 30.

Example 2

In right triangle RST below, what is the length of leg x?

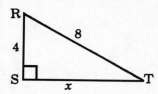

Procedure

1. Using the Pythagorean theorem, write an equation expressing the fact that the sum of the squares of the legs is equal to the square of the hypotenuse. Solve this equation for x, and then simplify the square root.

$$\text{leg}^2 + \text{leg}^2 = \text{hypotenuse}^2$$
$$x^2 + 4^2 = 8^2$$
$$x^2 + 16 = 64$$
$$\underline{-16 \quad -16}$$
$$x^2 = 48$$
$$x = \sqrt{48}$$
$$x = \sqrt{16 \cdot 3}$$
$$x = 4\sqrt{3}$$

Leg x is $4\sqrt{3}$.

PRACTICE PROBLEMS

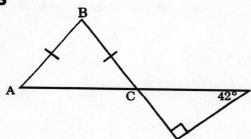

1. In isosceles triangle ABC above, how many degrees are in $\angle$B?

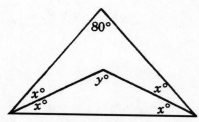

2. In the figure above, what is the value of y?

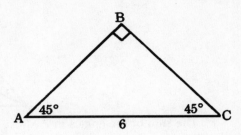

3. In right triangle ABC above, what is the length of leg AB? Simplify all square roots.

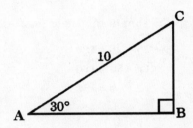

4. In right triangle ABC above, what is the length of leg AB? Simplify all square roots.

ANSWERS AND EXPLANATIONS

1.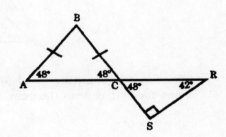

The sum of the angles in △RSC is 180°. Thus,

$$\angle RCS + 90 + 42 = 180$$
$$\angle RCS + 132 = 180$$
$$\angle RCS = 48$$

Since ∠BCA and ∠RCS are vertical angles, ∠BCA also measures 48°.
Since the base angles of an isosceles triangle are equal, ∠BAC is also 48°.
The sum of the angles of ∠ABC is 180°. Thus,

$$\angle B + 48 + 48 = 180$$
$$\angle B + 96 = 180$$
$$\angle B = 84°$$

2.

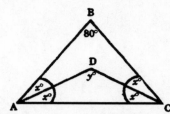

The sum of the angles in $\triangle ABC$ is 180°. Since $\angle BAC$ is $2x°$ and $\angle BCA$ is $2x°$,

$$80 + 2x + 2x = 180$$
$$80 + 4x = 180$$
$$4x = 100$$
$$x = 25$$

The sum of the angles in $\triangle ADC$ is 180°. Thus,

$$y + 25 + 25 = 180$$
$$y + 50 = 180$$
$$y = 130$$

3.

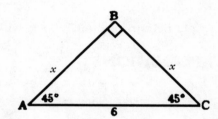

Since $\angle A = \angle C$, $\triangle ABC$ is an isosceles triangle. Represent sides AB and BC by x. Using the Pythagorean theorem,

$$x^2 + x^2 = 6^2$$
$$2x^2 = 36$$
$$x^2 = 18$$
$$x = \sqrt{18}$$
$$x = \sqrt{9 \cdot 2} = 3\sqrt{2}$$

4.

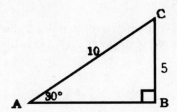

Since the side opposite the 30° angle in a 30°−60°−90° right triangle is one-half the hypotenuse, side CB is 5. Using the Pythagorean theorem:

$$\left(AB\right)^2 + 5^2 = 10^2$$
$$\left(AB\right)^2 + 25 = 100$$
$$\left(AB\right)^2 = 75$$
$$AB = \sqrt{75}$$
$$AB = \sqrt{25 \cdot 3} = 5\sqrt{3}$$

PYTHAGOREAN TRIPLES

Any set of whole numbers, x, y, and z, which form the sides of a right triangle, and thus satisfy the Pythagorean relationship, $x^2 + y^2 = z^2$, is called a **Pythagorean triple**. Each triple is denoted $x−y−z$, where x and y represent the two legs of the right triangle, and z represents the hypotenuse. Some common triples are 3−4−5 ($3^2 + 4^2 = 5^2$), 5−12−13 ($5^2 + 12^2 = 13^2$), and 8−15−17 ($8^2 + 15^2 = 17^2$). Other triples can be obtained from these basic ones by taking their multiples. For example, if we multiply each number in the triple 3−4−5 by 2, we obtain the new triple 6−8−10 ($6^2 + 8^2 = 10^2$). Similarly if we multiply each number in the triple 5−12−13 by 3, we obtain the new triple 15−36−39 ($15^2 + 36^2 = 39^2$). In general, if $x−y−z$ is a Pythagorean triple, then so is $mx−my−mz$, where m is any positive whole number.

Recognizing Pythagorean triples can save a lot of time in solving problems involving right triangles. Suppose that in the right triangle shown below we are asked to find side S. Instead of writing the Pythagorean equation $6^2 + S^2 = 10^2$, and then solving for S, we can simply recognize that S is the middle number of the Pythagorean triple 6−8−10.

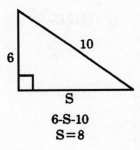

6-S-10
S=8

PRACTICE PROBLEMS

1. A plane starts at point P, flies 300 miles north to point Q, and then flies 400 miles west to point R. What is the straight line distance from point P to point R?

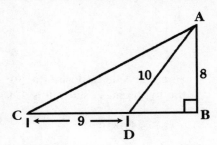

2. In the figure above, what is the length of AC?

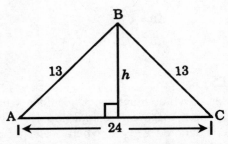

3. In isosceles triangle ABC above, what is the length of altitude h?

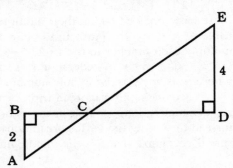

4. In the figure above, if AE = 10, what is the length of BD?

ANSWERS AND EXPLANATIONS

1.

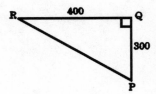

Side PR is the hypotenuse of the Pythagorean triple 300−400−PR. Thus, PR is 500 miles.

2.

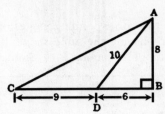

Since DB is one of the legs of the Pythagorean triple DB−8−10, DB must be 6. In △ABC, AC is the hypotenuse of the Pythagorean triple 8−15−AC. Thus, AC must be 17.

3.

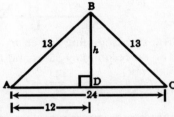

The altitude of isosceles triangle ABC bisects side AC. Thus, AD is 12. Since, in right triangle ADB, h is one of the legs of the Pythagorean triple h−12−13, h must be 5.

4.

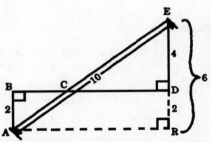

Draw line AR parallel to BD. Draw line DR parallel to BA. In right triangle ARE, leg AR is one of the legs of the Pythagorean triple 6−AR−10. Thus, AR must be 8, and BD, which is parallel and equal to AR, must also be 8.

SIMILAR TRIANGLES

When the corresponding angles of two triangles are equal, the triangles are said to be similar—having the same shape, but not necessarily the same size. As mentioned before, the symbol for similar is $\sim$. Similar triangles have the following properties.

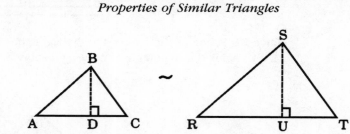

Properties of Similar Triangles

1. The corresponding angles are equal: $\angle A = \angle R$, $\angle B = \angle S$, $\angle C = \angle T$
2. The corresponding sides and the corresponding altitudes are in proportion:
$$\frac{AB}{RS} = \frac{BC}{ST} = \frac{AC}{RT} = \frac{BD}{SU}.$$

Example 1

A vertical pole, 5 ft. tall, casts a shadow 3 ft. At the same time, a nearby tree casts a shadow 12 ft. How tall is the tree?

Procedure

1. Draw a diagram, representing the height of the tree by x. Notice that at the same time of day, nearby objects and their shadows form similar triangles.

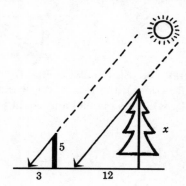

2. Write a proportion between the corresponding sides of the triangles, and solve the proportion for x. (Cross-multiply and divide.)

$$\frac{5}{x} = \frac{3}{12}$$
$$3 \cdot x = 5 \cdot 12$$
$$\frac{\cancel{3}x}{\cancel{3}} = \frac{60}{3}$$
$$x = 20$$

The tree is 20 ft. tall.

Example 2

In the diagram below, what is the length of side x?

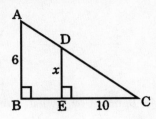

Procedure

1. Since the corresponding angles in $\triangle ABC$ and $\triangle DEC$ are equal, the triangles are similar. Therefore, write a proportion between the corresponding sides, and solve for x.

$$\frac{AB}{DE} = \frac{BC}{EC}$$

$$\frac{6}{x} = \frac{15}{10}$$

$$15 \cdot x = 6 \cdot 10$$

$$\frac{\cancel{15}x}{\cancel{15}} = \frac{60}{15}$$

$$x = 4$$

Side x is 4.

PRACTICE PROBLEMS

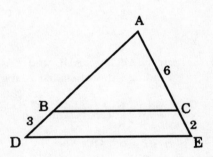

1. In the figure above, BC‖DE. What is the length of AB?

2. A person, 6 feet tall, casts a shadow of 4 feet at the same time a nearby flagpole casts a shadow of 10 feet. What is the height of the flagpole?

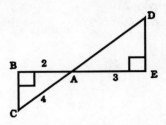

3. In the figure above, what is the length of AD?

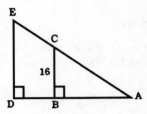

4. In the figure above, if AB is twice the length of BD, what is the length of DE?

ANSWERS AND EXPLANATIONS

1.

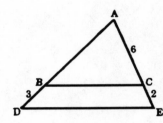

Since ∠ABC = ∠ADE, and ∠ACB = ∠AED, △ABC is similar to △ADE. The corresponding sides of similar triangles are in proportion. Thus,

$$\frac{AB}{AB+3} = \frac{6}{8} \text{ (cross-multiply)}$$

$$8 \cdot AB = 6 \cdot (AB + 3)$$

$$8 \cdot AB = 6 \cdot AB + 18$$

$$2 \cdot AB = 18$$

$$AB = 9$$

2.

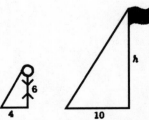

At the same time of the day, nearby objects and their shadows form similar triangles. Thus, the corresponding sides are in proportion.

$$\frac{h}{6} = \frac{10}{4} \text{ (cross-multiply)}$$

$$4h = 60$$

$$h = 15$$

3.

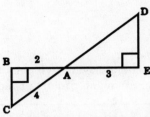

Since ∠BAC and ∠DAE are vertical angles, and thus are equal, right triangle ABC is similar to right triangle AED. Thus, their corresponding sides are in proportion.

$$\frac{AD}{4} = \frac{3}{2} \text{ (cross-multiply)}$$

$$2 \cdot AD = 12$$

$$AD = 6$$

4.

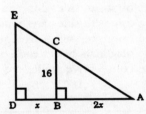

Represent BD by x and AB by $2x$. Since ∠A is one of the angles of both triangles, right triangle ABC is similar to right triangle ADE. Thus, their corresponding sides are in proportion.

$$\frac{DE}{16} = \frac{3x}{2x} \quad \text{(cross-multiply and cancel out the } x\text{'s)}$$

$$2 \cdot DE = 48$$

$$DE = 24$$

QUADRILATERALS

A **quadrilateral** is a polygon having four sides. The sum of the angles inside a quadrilateral is 360°.

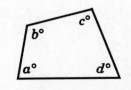

$$a° + b° + c° + d° = 360°$$

A quadrilateral having one pair of parallel sides is called a **trapezoid**. The parallel sides are called the **bases**, and the non-parallel sides are called the **legs**. In the example below, the parallel sides are indicated by arrows.

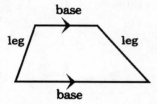

A quadrilateral having two pairs of parallel sides is called a **parallelogram**. Parallelograms have the following general properties:

Properties of Parallelograms

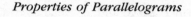

1. The opposite sides are parallel: AB‖CD, AC‖BD.
2. The opposite sides are equal: AB = CD, AC = BD.
3. The opposite angles are equal: ∠A = ∠D, ∠B = ∠C.
4. The diagonals bisect each other: AE = ED, CE = EB.
5. The consecutive angles are supplementary:
   ∠A + ∠B = 180°, ∠B + ∠D = 180°, ∠D + ∠C = 180°, ∠C + ∠A = 180°.

By adding certain conditions to parallelograms, we get the following special cases: a **rectangle** is a parallelogram having four equal angles, each measuring 90°; a **rhombus** is a parallelogram having four equal sides; a **square** is a parallelogram having four equal angles and four equal sides.

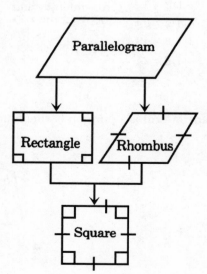

These figures also have the following special properties concerning their diagonals:

Diagonal Property of Rectangles

1. The diagonals are equal: AD = BC.

Diagonal Properties of Rhombuses

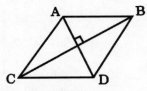

1. The diagonals are perpendicular: AD⊥BC.
2. The diagonals bisect the angles they join: AD bisects ∠A and ∠D; BC bisects ∠B and ∠C.

Diagonal Properties of Squares

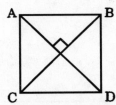

1. The diagonal properties of both the rectangle and the rhombus: AD = BC, AD⊥BC, AD bisects ∠A and ∠D, BC bisects ∠B and ∠C.

PERIMETER

The **perimeter** of a plane closed figure is the **length** around its boundary. Perimeters are measured in units such as inches, feet, and yards.

Perimeter

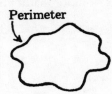

Since a polygon is made up of straight line segments, its perimeter is simply the sum of its sides.

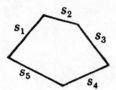

$$P = s_1 + s_2 + s_3 + s_4 + s_5$$

Based on this principle, we have the following two formulas:

Perimeter Formulas

The perimeter of a *rectangle* is equal to twice its length plus twice its width.

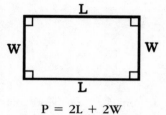

$$P = 2L + 2W$$

The perimeter of a *square* is equal to four times its side.

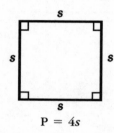

$$P = 4s$$

Example 1

The perimeter of a rectangle is 50 feet. If the length of the rectangle is 4 more than twice its width, what are the dimensions of the rectangle?

Procedure

1. Draw a diagram of the rectangle, representing its width by x, and its length by $2x + 4$ ("4 more than twice its width").

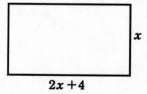

2. Using the formula for the perimeter of a rectangle, write an equation setting the perimeter equal to 50 feet. Solve this equation for x, and substitute the result into the expression for the length.

$$P_{rect.} = 2L + 2W$$
$$50 = 2(2x + 4) + 2(x)$$
$$50 = 4x + 8 + 2x$$
$$50 = 6x + 8$$
$$\underline{-8 \qquad\qquad -8}$$
$$42 = 6x$$
$$\frac{42}{6} = \frac{\cancel{6}x}{\cancel{6}}$$
$$7 = x$$

Thus, $2x + 4 = 18$

The length of the rectangle is 18 feet, and its width is 7 feet.

Example 2

What is the length of the diagonal of a square whose perimeter is 20 feet.

Procedure

1. Using the formula for the perimeter of a square, write an equation setting the perimeter equal to 20 feet. Solve this equation for S, the side of the square.

$$P_{sq.} = 4S$$
$$20 = 4S$$
$$\frac{20}{4} = \frac{\cancel{4}S}{\cancel{4}}$$
$$5 = S$$

2. Draw a diagram of the square, representing the length of the diagonal by D. Since D is the hypotenuse of a right triangle, use the Pythagorean theorem and solve for D. Simplify the square root in the result.

$$leg^2 + leg^2 = hypotenuse^2$$
$$5^2 + 5^2 = D^2$$
$$25 + 25 = D^2$$
$$50 = D^2$$
$$\sqrt{50} = D$$
$$\sqrt{25 \cdot 2} = D$$
$$5\sqrt{2} = D$$

The length of the diagonal is $5\sqrt{2}$ feet.

PRACTICE PROBLEMS

1. The second side of a triangle is 3 inches less than the first side, and the third side is 2 inches more than the first side. If the perimeter of the triangle is 17 inches, what is the length of the shortest side of the triangle?

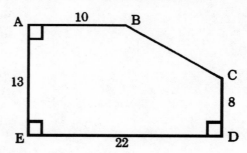

2. What is the perimeter of figure ABCDE above?

3. The side of a square is 5 feet longer than the side of an equilateral triangle. If the perimeter of the square is 30 feet longer than the perimeter of the triangle, what is the length of the side of the triangle?

4. The length of a rectangle is twice its width. If the length is increased by 4 inches and the width is decreased by 3 inches, a new rectangle is formed whose perimeter is 62 inches. What is the length of the original rectangle?

ANSWERS AND EXPLANATIONS

1.

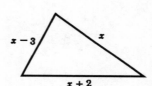

Represent the three sides as shown in the diagram above. Since the perimeter is the sum of the sides,

$$x + x + 2 + x - 3 = 17$$
$$3x - 1 = 17$$
$$3x = 18$$
$$x = 6$$

Thus, the shortest side is $x - 3 = 6 - 3 = 3$ in.

2.

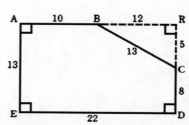

Draw right triangle BRC. Since AR = ED, BR must be $22 - 10 = 12$. Similarly, since RD = AE, RC must be $13 - 8 = 5$. Therefore, BC must be 13, the hypotenuse of the Pythagorean triple, 5−12−BC. The perimeter of ABCDE is the sum of its sides, or $10 + 13 + 8 + 22 + 13 = 66$.

3.

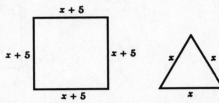

Represent the sides of the equilateral triangle and square as indicated in the diagram above. Since the perimeter of the square is 30 feet longer than that of the triangle,

$$4(x+5) = 3x + 30$$
$$4x + 20 = 3x + 30$$
$$x = 10$$

4.

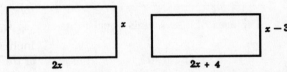

Represent the sides of the rectangles as indicated in the diagram above. Since the perimeter of the new rectangle is 62,

$$2(2x+4) + 2(x-3) = 62$$
$$4x + 8 + 2x - 6 = 62$$
$$6x + 2 = 62$$
$$6x = 60$$
$$x = 10$$

Thus, the length of the original rectangle is $2x = (2)(10) = 20$ in.

AREA

The **area** of a plane closed figure is the amount of *surface* contained within its boundary. Areas are measured in units such as square inches, square feet, and square yards. As shown below, 1 square inch is defined to be the amount of surface contained within a square having a side of 1 inch. The other square units are defined in a similar way.

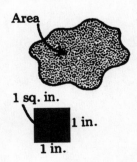

Area Formulas

The area of a *rectangle* is equal to its length times its width.

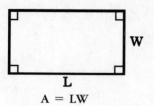

$$A = LW$$

$A = LW$
$A = (6)(4)$
$A = 24$

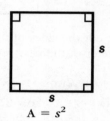

The area of a *square* is equal to its side squared.

$$A = s^2$$

$A = s^2$
$A = (4)^2$
$A = 16$

The area of a *parallelogram* is equal to a side (called the base) multiplied by the height to that side.

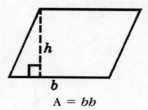

$$A = bh$$

$$A = bh$$
$$A = (5)(3)$$
$$A = 15$$

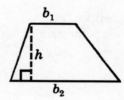

The area of a *trapezoid* is equal to the average of the two bases multiplied by the height between the bases.

$$A = \left(\frac{b_1 + b_2}{2}\right)h$$

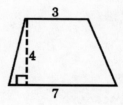

$$A = \left(\frac{b_1 + b_2}{2}\right)h$$

$$A = \left(\frac{3 + 7}{2}\right)4$$

$$A = 20$$

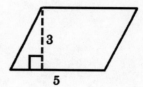

The area of a *triangle* is equal to one-half a side (called the base) multiplied by the height to that side. For right triangles, the base is one of the legs, and the height is the other. For obtuse triangles, the base must be extended to meet the height.

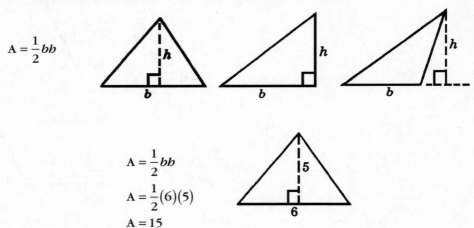

$$A = \frac{1}{2}bh$$

$$A = \frac{1}{2}bh$$
$$A = \frac{1}{2}(6)(5)$$
$$A = 15$$

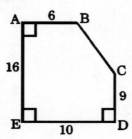

Example 1

What is the area of figure ABCDE below?

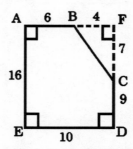

Procedure

1. In the diagram, complete a rectangle by drawing in right triangle BFC.

2. Using the formula for the area of a rectangle, determine the area of AFDE.

$$A_{rect.} = LW$$
$$\text{Area of AFDE} = (10)(16)$$
$$= 160$$

3. Using the formula for the area of a triangle, determine the area of BFC.

$$A_{\text{tri.}} = \frac{1}{2}bh$$

$$\text{Area of BFC} = \frac{1}{2}(4)(7)$$

$$= 14$$

4. To find the area of ABCDE, subtract the area of triangle BFC from the area of rectangle AFDE.

$$\text{ABCDE} = \text{AFDE} - \text{BFC}$$

$$= 160 - 14$$

$$= 146$$

The area of ABCDE is 146.

Example 2

If one side of a square is increased by 20% and the other side is decreased by 15%, by what percent does the area change?

Procedure

1. Draw a diagram of the original square, representing its side by s. Draw a diagram of the new figure (a rectangle), representing one of its sides by 1.20s ("increased by 20%"), and the other side by .85s ("decreased by 15%").

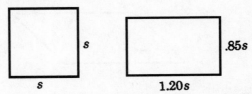

2. Using the appropriate area formulas, write expressions for the areas of the two figures. To find the change in area, subtract the area of the original square from the area of the rectangle.

$$A_{\text{sq.}} = s^2$$

$$A_{\text{rect.}} = (1.20s)(.85s) = 1.02s^2$$

$$\text{Change} = A_{\text{rect.}} - A_{\text{sq.}}$$

$$= 1.02s^2 - s^2$$

$$= +.02s^2$$

The area increases by .02, or 2%.

PRACTICE PROBLEMS

1. The longer base of a trapezoid is three times the shorter base. If the height of the trapezoid is 3, and the area is 42, what is the length of the shorter base?

2. If the base of a parallelogram decreases by 10%, and its height increases by 30%, by what percent does its area increase?

3. If the side of a square is increased by 3 ft., its area is increased by 39 sq. ft. What is the length of the side of the original square?

4. The area of an isosceles right triangle is 8. What is the length of its hypotenuse? Simplify all square roots.

ANSWERS AND EXPLANATIONS

1.

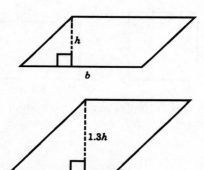

The area of a trapezoid is given by the formula

$$A = \left(\frac{b_1 + b_2}{2}\right) \cdot h$$

$$42 = \left(\frac{x + 3x}{2}\right) \cdot 3$$

$$42 = \left(\frac{4x}{2}\right) \cdot 3$$

$$42 = (2x) \cdot 3$$

$$42 = 6x$$

$$7 = x$$

2.

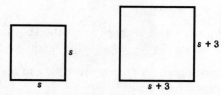

Since the base decreases by 10%, its new value is $(100\% - 10\%) \cdot b$, or $.9b$. Also, since the height increases by 30%, its new value is $(100\% + 30\%) \cdot h$, or $1.3h$. The area of the original parallelogram is bh, and the area of the new parallelogram is $(.9b)(1.3h) = 1.17bh$. Thus, the increase in area is $1.17bh - 1bh = .17bh$, or 17%.

3.

The area of the original square is s^2; the area of the new square is $(s + 3)^2$. Since the area of the new square is 39 square feet more than that of the original square,

$$(s+3)^2 = s^2 + 39$$
$$s^2 + 6s + 9 = s^2 + 39$$
$$6s + 9 = 39$$
$$6s = 30$$
$$s = 5 \text{ ft.}$$

4.

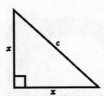

The area of a triangle is given by the formula

$$A = \frac{1}{2}b \cdot h$$
$$8 = \frac{1}{2}x \cdot x$$
$$16 = x^2$$
$$4 = x$$

By the Pythagorean theorem,

$$4^2 + 4^2 = c^2$$
$$16 + 16 = c^2$$
$$32 = c^2$$
$$\sqrt{32} = c$$
$$\sqrt{16 \cdot 2} = c$$
$$4\sqrt{2} = c$$

When one plane closed figure is completely contained within another plane closed figure, we can find the area between them by subtracting the area of the inner figure from the area of the outer figure:

Outer Figure

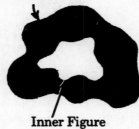

Inner Figure

Example

A rectangular photograph, 11" by 14", is surrounded by a 3" wide mat. What is the area of the mat?

Procedure

1. Draw a diagram of the photograph and mat. Notice that the outer dimensions of the mat are 6" longer than the dimensions of the photograph (20" = 14" + 3" + 3" and 17" = 11" + 3" + 3").

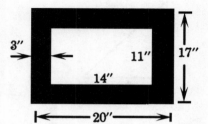

2. Find the area of the inner rectangle and the area of the outer rectangle.

$$A_{rect.} = LW$$
$$\text{Inner Area} = (14'')(11'')$$
$$= 154 \text{ sq. in.}$$

$$\text{Outer Area} = (20'')(17'')$$
$$= 340 \text{ sq. in.}$$

3. To find the area of the mat (the shaded area), subtract the inner area from the outer area.

$$\text{Area of mat} = \frac{\text{Outer}}{\text{Area}} - \frac{\text{Inner}}{\text{Area}}$$
$$= 340 - 154$$
$$= 186$$

The area of the mat is 186 sq. in.

PRACTICE PROBLEMS

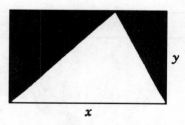

1. In the rectangle above, what is the area of the shaded part?

2. A 4 ft. wide cement walk is built around a rectangular swimming pool. If the outer dimensions of the walk are 50 ft. long by 40 ft. wide, what is the area of the walk?

ANSWERS AND EXPLANATIONS

1.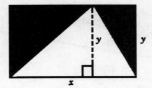

The area of the rectangle is xy. The area of the triangle is $\frac{1}{2}xy$. Thus, the area of the shaded part is $xy - \frac{1}{2}xy = \frac{1}{2}xy$.

2.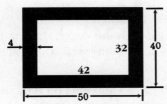

The length of the swimming pool is $50 - 4 - 4 = 42$ ft. The width of the swimming pool is $40 - 4 - 4 = 32$ ft. The area of the outer rectangle is $50 \times 40 = 2000$ sq. ft., and the area of the inner rectangle is $42 \times 32 = 1344$ sq. ft. Thus, the area of the walk is 2000 sq. ft. $- 1344$ sq. ft. $= 656$ sq. ft.

CIRCLES

A **circle** is a plane closed figure formed by a set of points equidistant from a fixed point called the **center**. The boundary of the circle is called the **circumference**, and the distance from the center to any point on the circumference is called the **radius**. Circles are usually denoted by a capital letter at the center. The circle below is denoted as circle O.

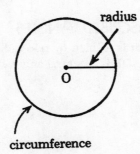

323

The definitions of some common terms associated with circles are given below.

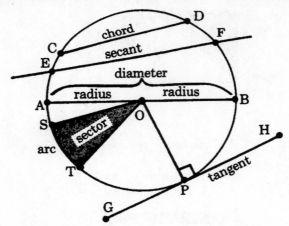

Diameter: A line segment passing through the center, having both points on the circumference (diameter AB). A circle has an infinite number of diameters, each measuring twice the radius.

Chord: A line segment having both of its endpoints on the circumference (chord CD). Chords vary in length, the longest of which is a diameter.

Secant: A line passing through the circle, intersecting it at two points (secant EF).

Tangent: A line intersecting the circle at exactly one point (tangent GH). A radius drawn to the point of intersection is perpendicular to the tangent line (OP ⊥ GH).

Arc: A part of the circumference. Arcs are denoted by the symbol ⌢ (arc $\overset{\frown}{ST}$).

Semi-circle: An arc measuring half the circumference (semi-circle $\overset{\frown}{AB}$).

Sector: The interior part of a circle bounded by two radii and the arc they intercept (sector SOT).

CENTRAL ANGLES AND INSCRIBED ANGLES

An angle that is formed by two radii of a circle is called a **central angle**. In the following example, ∠AOB is a central angle.

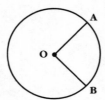

An angle that is formed by two chords having a common endpoint on the circumference of a circle is called an **inscribed angle**. In the following example, ∠RST is an inscribed angle.

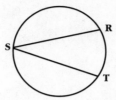

If an inscribed angle and a central angle intercept the same arc, the inscribed angle will measure exactly half the central angle. Two examples are shown below.

 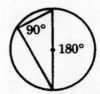

Notice that, in the special case of both angles intercepting a semicircle (the diagram above right), the central angle will measure 180°, and the inscribed angle half of that, or 90°, Since, in this case, a right triangle is always formed, we have the following general principle:

All triangles inscribed in a semi-circle are right triangles having the diameter as their hypotenuse.

For example, in the diagram below, △ARB, △ASB, and △ATB are all right triangles.

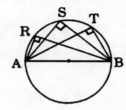

Example

In the circle below, chord AB = 6, and chord BC = 8. If AC is a diameter of the circle, what is the length of the radius?

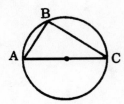

Procedure

1. Since ABC is inscribed in a semi-circle, ABC is a right triangle. Therefore, using the Pythagorean theorem, find the length of the diameter, AC.

$$\text{leg}^2 + \text{leg}^2 = \text{hypotenuse}^2$$
$$6^2 + 8^2 = (AC)^2$$
$$36 + 64 = (AC)^2$$
$$100 = (AC)^2$$
$$\sqrt{100} = AC$$
$$10 = AC$$

2. To find the radius, take half of the diameter.

$$\text{radius} = \frac{1}{2} \, (\text{diameter})$$
$$= \frac{1}{2}(10)$$
$$= 5$$

The radius is 5.

PRACTICE PROBLEMS

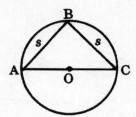

1. In the figure above, isosceles triangle ABC is inscribed in circle O. What is the length of radius OC in terms of *s*? Simplify all square roots.

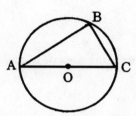

2. In the figure above, triangle ABC is inscribed in circle O. If diameter AC = 10, and AB is twice BC, what is the area of the triangle?

ANSWERS AND EXPLANATIONS

1.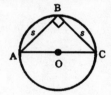

Since triangle ABC is inscribed in a semi-circle, $\angle B$ is a right angle. Using the Pythagorean theorem,

$$s^2 + s^2 = \left(\text{AC}\right)^2$$
$$2s^2 = \left(\text{AC}\right)^2$$
$$\sqrt{2s^2} = \text{AC}$$
$$\sqrt{2}s = \text{AC}$$

Thus, the radius is $\frac{1}{2}\text{AC}$, or $\frac{\sqrt{2}s}{2}$.

2.

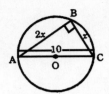

Since triangle ABC is inscribed in a semi-circle, ∠B is a right angle. Using the Pythagorean theorem,

$$x^2 + (2x)^2 = 10^2$$
$$x^2 + 4x^2 = 100$$
$$5x^2 = 100$$
$$x^2 = 20$$
$$x = \sqrt{20}$$

Thus, the area of triangle ABC is

$$\text{Area} = \frac{1}{2}(\text{AB}) \cdot (\text{BC})$$
$$= \frac{1}{2}(2x) \cdot (x)$$
$$= \frac{1}{2}(2\sqrt{20})(\sqrt{20})$$
$$= \frac{1}{2}(2 \cdot 20)$$
$$= \frac{1}{2}(40)$$
$$= 20$$

CIRCUMFERENCE AND AREA

The ratio of the circumference of a circle to its diameter is the same for all circles. This special ratio has the value $3.14159\cdots$ and is denoted by the Greek letter π (pi). If we represent the circumference of a circle by C, and the diameter by d, then for all circles, $\frac{C}{d} = \pi$. By multiplying both sides of this equation by d, we get the formula below for the circumference of a circle.

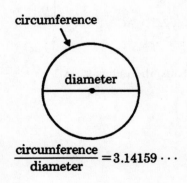

$$\frac{\text{circumference}}{\text{diameter}} = 3.14159\cdots$$

Circumference Formula
The **circumference** of a circle is equal to π times its diameter.

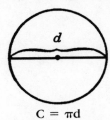

C = πd

The formula for the area of a circle also contains the number π. Specifically,

Area Formula
The area of a circle is equal to π times its radius squared.

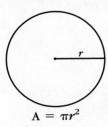

$A = \pi r^2$

When solving problems involving these formulas, π can either be approximated by values such as 3.1, 3.14, and $3\frac{1}{7}$, or it can be left in symbolic form.

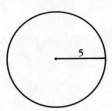

$$A = \pi r^2$$
$$A = \pi(5)^2$$
$$A = 25\pi$$

Example 1

In circle O below, if the length of arc $\overset{\frown}{PR}$ is 5π, what is the area of square OPQR?

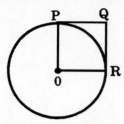

Procedure

1. To find the length of the circumference, multiply arc $\overset{\frown}{PR}$ by 4. (Arc $\overset{\frown}{PR}$ is $\frac{1}{4}$ of the circumference.)

    $$C = 4(\overset{\frown}{PR})$$
    $$= 4(5\pi)$$
    $$= 20\pi$$

2. Using the formula for the circumference, write an equation setting the circumference equal to 20π. Solve this equation for the diameter, d.

    $$C = \pi d$$
    $$20\pi = \pi d$$
    $$\frac{20\cancel{\pi}}{\cancel{\pi}} = \frac{\cancel{\pi}d}{\cancel{\pi}}$$
    $$20 = d$$

3. To find the side of the square, which is also the radius of the circle, take half the diameter.

    $$\text{side OR} = \frac{1}{2}d$$
    $$= \frac{1}{2}(20)$$
    $$= 10$$

4. Using the result, find the area of the square.

    $$A_{sq.} = s^2$$
    $$= (10)^2$$
    $$= 100$$

The area of square OPQR is 100.

Example 2

In the diagram below, circle O is inscribed in square ABCD. What is the area of the shaded part?

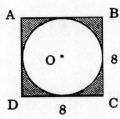

Procedure

1. Find the area of the square.

$$A_{sq.} = s^2$$
$$= (8)^2$$
$$= 64$$

2. Since the diameter of the circle is the same length as the side of the square, 8, its radius is half that, or 4. Using this value, find the area of the circle.

$$A_{sq.} = \pi r^2$$
$$= \pi (4)^2$$
$$= 16\pi$$

3. To find the area of the shaded part, subtract the area of the circle from the area of the square.

$$A_{shaded} = A_{sq.} - A_{cir.}$$
$$= 64 - 16\pi$$

The area of the shaded part is $64 - 16\pi$.

PRACTICE PROBLEMS

1. What is the circumference of a circle whose area is 25π? Leave answer in terms of π.

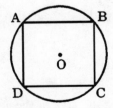

2. In the figure above, square ABCD is inscribed in circle O. If the circumference of the circle is 8π, what is the area of the square?

3. A circular path is bounded by two concentric circles (circles having the same center). If the smaller circle has a diameter of 50 feet, and the larger circle has a diameter of 60 feet, what is the area of the path? Leave answer in terms of π.

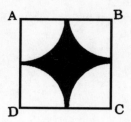

4. In square ABCD above, the four unshaded parts are quarter circles, each having the same radius. If the side of the square is 16, what is the area of the shaded part? Leave answer in terms of π.

ANSWERS AND EXPLANATIONS

1. The area of a circle is given by the formula

$$A = \pi r^2$$
$$25\pi = \pi r^2 \; (\text{divide by } \pi)$$
$$25 = r^2$$
$$5 = r$$

Since the radius is 5, the diameter is 10. The circumference of the circle is given by the formula

$$C = \pi d$$
$$C = 10\pi$$

2.

Draw diameter BD. Using the formula for the circumference of a circle.

$$C = \pi d$$
$$8\pi = \pi (BD)$$
$$8 = BD$$

Using the Pythagorean theorem,

$$s^2 + s^2 = 8^2$$
$$2s^2 = 64$$
$$s^2 = 32$$

Since the area of the square is also s^2, the area of the square is 32.

3.

The radius of the smaller circle is $\frac{1}{2}$(50 ft.), or 25 ft., and the radius of the larger

circle is $\frac{1}{2}$(60 ft.) = 30 ft.

The area of the larger circle is $\pi(30)^2 = 900\pi$.

The area of the smaller circle is $\pi(25)^2 = 625\pi$.

Thus, the area of the path is $900\pi - 625\pi = 275\pi$ sq. ft.

4.

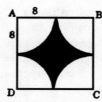

Since the quarter-circles bisect each side of the square, the radius of each quarter-circle is 8.

The area of the square is $(16)^2 = 256$. The area of the four quarter-circles is the same as the area of one full circle of radius 8, or $\pi(8)^2 = 64\pi$. Thus, the area of the shaded part is the area of the square − the area of the four quarter-circles, or $256 - 64\pi$.

COORDINATE GEOMETRY

CARTESIAN COORDINATE SYSTEM

In order to locate the position of geometric figures in a plane, we use a reference system, called the **Cartesian coordinate system**, named after the French mathematician René Descartes.

This system consists of two number lines, which are perpendicular to each other, and that cross each other at their respective origins (0 on each number line). The horizontal line is called the **x-axis** and is ordered in the usual way, with the positive numbers increasing to the right, and the negative numbers decreasing to the left. The vertical line is called the **y-axis** and is ordered in a similar way, with the positive numbers increasing upwards, and the negative numbers decreasing downwards. The two axes divide the plane into four regions, called **quadrants**, which are numbered I, II, III, and IV in counter-clockwise order.

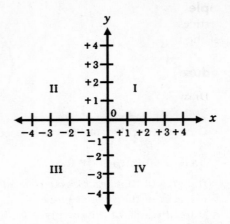

To locate a point in reference to the two axes, we use an **ordered** pair of signed numbers, called **coordinates**. The first number in the pair is called the **x-coordinate**. This number tells us how far in the x direction (horizontally) the point is from the origin. If the number is positive, the point is to the right of the origin; if negative, the point is to the left of the origin. The second number in the pair is called the **y-coordinate**, which tells us how far in the y direction (vertically) the point is from the origin. If the number is positive, the point is above the origin; if negative, the point is below the origin.

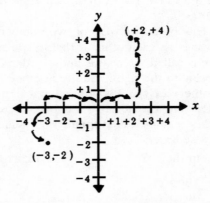

For example, to locate the point whose coordinates are $(+2, +4)$, start at the origin, go 2 units to the right (the x-coordinate is $+2$), and then 4 units up (the y-coordinate is $+4$). Similarly, to locate the point whose coordinates are $(-3, -2)$, start at the origin, go 3 units to the left (the x-coordinate is -3), and then go 2 units down (the y-coordinate is -2).

Remember that the order in which the coordinates are given is very important: the x-coordinate must be given first, and the y-coordinate must be given second. If the order is reversed, the location of the point usually changes. For example, the point whose coordinates are $(+3, -2)$ is located in quadrant IV, while the point whose coordinates are $(-2, +3)$ is located in quadrant II.

Example

The vertices of a triangle are located at the points $(2, -1)$, $(5, -1)$, and $(5, 3)$. What is the area of the triangle?

Procedure

1. Draw a diagram of the triangle, indicating the lengths of the base and the height. Note that the triangle is a right triangle.

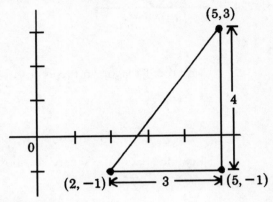

2. Find the area of the triangle.

$$A_{tri.} = \frac{1}{2}bh$$
$$= \frac{1}{2}(3)(4)$$
$$= 6$$

The area of the triangle is 6.

PRACTICE PROBLEMS

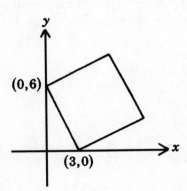

1. In the figure above, what is the area of the square?

2. The vertices of a triangle are located at the points $(1, 2)$, $(1, 6)$ and $(4, 6)$. What is the perimeter of the triangle?

ANSWERS AND EXPLANATIONS

1.

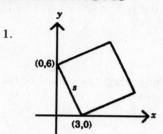

Using the Pythagorean theorem,

$$6^2 + 3^2 = s^2$$
$$36 + 9 = s^2$$
$$45 = s^2$$

Since the area of the square is also s^2, the area of the square is 45.

2.

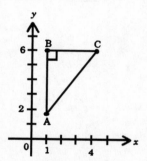

The triangle formed, $\triangle ABC$, is a right triangle with leg AB = 4 and leg BC = 3. Thus, the hypotenuse AC is 5, the hypotenuse of the Pythagorean triple 3−4−5. Therefore, the perimeter of the triangle is the sum of the sides, or 3 + 4 + 5 = 12.

DISTANCE FORMULA

The **distance** between two points located at (x_1, y_1) and (x_2, y_2) is given by the formula below. As indicated in the accompanying diagram, the formula is derived by applying the Pythagorean theorem to a right triangle whose hypotenuse is the desired distance, D.

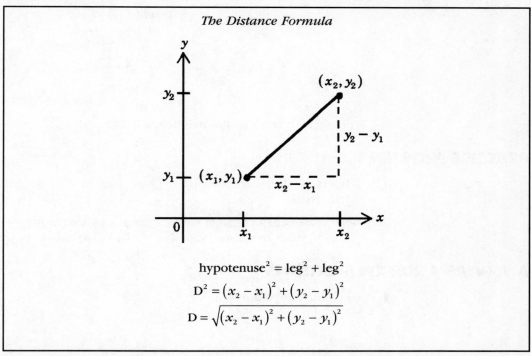

The Distance Formula

$$\text{hypotenuse}^2 = \text{leg}^2 + \text{leg}^2$$
$$D^2 = (x_2 - x_1)^2 + (y_2 - y_1)^2$$
$$D = \sqrt{(x_2 - x_1)^2 + (y_2 - y_1)^2}$$

If we use the symbol Δx ("delta x") to represent the difference between the x-coordinates, and Δy ("delta y") to represent the difference between the y-coordinates, then we can write the distance formula in the following simplified form:

$$D = \sqrt{(\Delta x)^2 + (\Delta y)^2}$$
$$\Delta x = x_2 - x_1$$
$$\Delta y = y_2 - y_1$$

Example
What is the distance between the points located at $(-2, 1)$ and $(4, 9)$?

Procedure
1. Find the difference between the x-coordinates, Δx, and the difference between the y-coordinates, Δy.

$$\Delta x = x_2 - x_1 \qquad\qquad \Delta y = y_2 - y_1$$
$$= (4) - (-2) \qquad\qquad = (9) - (1)$$
$$= 4 + 2 \qquad\qquad\quad = 9 - 1$$
$$= 6 \qquad\qquad\qquad\quad = 8$$

2. Using the distance formula, square the differences, add them, and take the square root of the result. (Note that the choice of $(-2, 1)$ as (x_1, y_1) and $(4, 9)$ as (x_2, y_2) is purely arbitrary. If we reverse this choice, we find that $\Delta x = -6$ and $\Delta y = -8$. When we square these differences, we get 36 and 64, the same as before.)

$$D = \sqrt{(\Delta x)^2 + (\Delta y)^2}$$
$$= \sqrt{(6)^2 + (8)^2}$$
$$= \sqrt{36 + 64}$$
$$= \sqrt{100}$$
$$= 10$$

The distance between the two points is 10.

PRACTICE PROBLEMS

1. What is the distance between the points located at $(3, 1)$ and $(5, -7)$? Simplify all square roots.

2. What is the area of a circle whose center is located at the point $(2, 1)$, and that passes through the point located at $(5, 4)$? Leave answer in terms of π.

ANSWERS AND EXPLANATIONS

1. Using the midpoint formula.

$$D = \sqrt{(x_2 - x_1)^2 + (y_2 - y_1)^2}$$
$$D = \sqrt{(5 - 3)^2 + (-7 - 1)^2}$$
$$D = \sqrt{(2)^2 + (-8)^2}$$
$$D = \sqrt{4 + 64}$$
$$D = \sqrt{68}$$
$$D = \sqrt{4 \cdot 17} = 2\sqrt{17}$$

2.

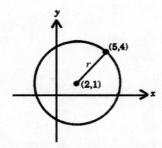

The radius of the circle, r, is the distance from the center $(2, 1)$ to the point $(5, 4)$.

Using the distance formula,

$$D = \sqrt{\left(x_2 - x_1\right)^2 + \left(y_2 - y_1\right)^2}$$

$$r = \sqrt{\left(5 - 2\right)^2 + \left(4 - 1\right)^2}$$

$$r = \sqrt{\left(3\right)^2 + \left(3\right)^2}$$

$$r = \sqrt{9 + 9}$$

$$r = \sqrt{18}$$

The area of the circle is given by the formula

$$A = \pi r^2$$

$$A = \pi\left(\sqrt{18}\right)^2$$

$$A = 18\pi$$

MIDPOINT FORMULA

The coordinates of the **midpoint** of a line segment joining the points located at (x_1, y_1) and (x_2, y_2) are given by the formula below. The x-coordinate, x_m, is the average of the x-coordinates of the endpoints, and the y-coordinate, y_m, is the average of the y-coordinates of the endpoints.

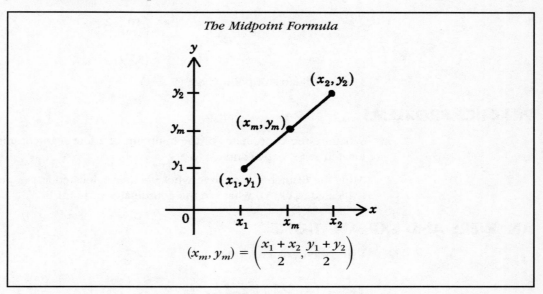

The Midpoint Formula

$$(x_m, y_m) = \left(\frac{x_1 + x_2}{2}, \frac{y_1 + y_2}{2}\right)$$

Example

In the circle below, AB is a diameter. What are the coordinates of point C, the center of the circle?

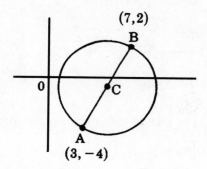

Procedure

1. Since the center of the circle is the midpoint of the diameter, substitute the coordinates of points A and B into the midpoint formula.

$$(x_C, y_C) = \left(\frac{x_A + x_B}{2}, \frac{y_A + y_B}{2} \right)$$

$$= \left(\frac{3+7}{2}, \frac{-4+2}{2} \right)$$

$$= \left(\frac{10}{2}, \frac{-2}{2} \right)$$

$$= (5, -1)$$

The coordinates of point C are (5, −1).

PRACTICE PROBLEMS

1. What are the coordinates of the midpoint of a line segment joining the points located at (−5, −2) and (3, 8)?

2. AB is the diameter of a circle whose center is located at the point (3, 1). If point A is located at (1, 5), what are the coordinates of point B?

ANSWERS AND EXPLANATIONS

1. Using the distance formula,

$$(x_m, y_m) = \left(\frac{x_1 + x_2}{2}, \frac{y_1 + y_2}{2} \right)$$

$$(x_m, y_m) = \left(\frac{-5+3}{2}, \frac{-2+8}{2} \right)$$

$$(x_m, y_m) = \left(\frac{-2}{2}, \frac{6}{2} \right)$$

$$(x_m, y_m) = (-1, 3)$$

2.

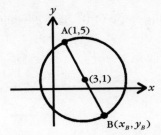

Since the center of the circle (3, 1) is the midpoint of diameter AB,

$$\left(x_m, y_m\right) = \left(\frac{x_A + x_B}{2}, \frac{y_A + y_B}{2}\right)$$

$$(3,1) = \left(\frac{1 + x_B}{2}, \frac{5 + y_B}{2}\right)$$

or

$$3 = \frac{1 + x_B}{2}$$

$$6 = 1 + x_B$$

$$5 = x_B$$

$$1 = \frac{5 + y_B}{2}$$

$$2 = 5 + y_B$$

$$-3 = y_B$$

Thus, point B is at (5, −3).

SLOPE OF A LINE

If you connect two points located at (x_1, y_1) and (x_2, y_2) with a straight line, the **slope** of that line is defined to be the ratio of the difference between the y-coordinates to the difference between the x-coordinates. In the formula below, the slope is denoted by the letter m.

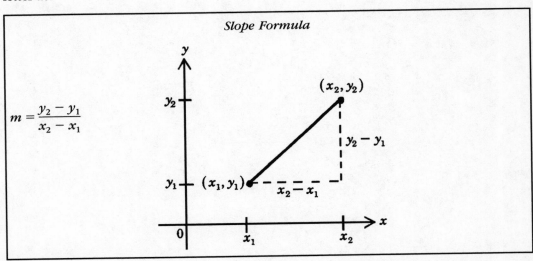

Slope Formula

PRACTICE PROBLEMS

For each of the following, what is the slope of the line passing through the two given points?

1. (1, 3) and (3, 6)
2. (2, 5) and (4, 3)
3. (−3, 4) and (−8, 4)
4. (1, 3) and (6, −5)

ANSWERS AND EXPLANATIONS

1. $$m = \frac{y_2 - y_1}{x_2 - x_1}$$
   $$= \frac{6 - 3}{3 - 1}$$
   $$= \frac{3}{2}$$

2. $$m = \frac{y_2 - y_1}{x_2 - x_1}$$
   $$= \frac{3 - 5}{4 - 2}$$
   $$= \frac{-2}{2}$$
   $$= -1$$

3. $$m = \frac{y_2 - y_1}{x_2 - x_1}$$
   $$= \frac{4 - 4}{-8 - (-3)}$$
   $$= \frac{0}{-5}$$
   $$= 0$$

4. $$m = \frac{y_2 - y_1}{x_2 - x_1}$$
   $$= \frac{-5 - 3}{6 - 1}$$
   $$= \frac{-8}{5}$$

SLOPE-INTERCEPT EQUATION OF A LINE

As indicated in the diagram below, the point $(0, b)$ represents the point where a line crosses the y-axis. This point is called the **y-intercept**. If m represents the slope of the line, then the equation of all points on that line is $y = mx + b$.

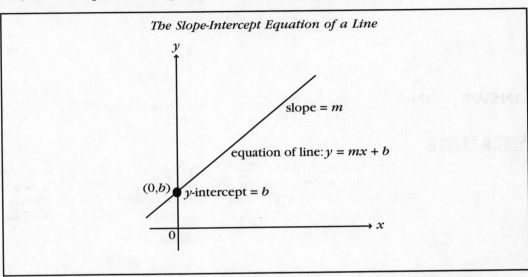

The Slope-Intercept Equation of a Line

slope = m

equation of line: $y = mx + b$

$(0, b)$ y-intercept = b

For example, the straight line with the equation $y = 2x + 5$ has a slope of 2 and a y-intercept of $(0, 5)$.

PRACTICE PROBLEMS

For each of the following equations, what is the slope and y-intercept of the corresponding line?

1. $y = 3x + 2$

2. $y = -2x - 4$

3. $2y - 8x = 6$

4. $3y - 5x + 6 = 0$

ANSWERS AND EXPLANATIONS

1. In the slope-intercept form of an equation, $y = mx + b$, the numerical coefficient of the x-term, m, is the slope, and the constant at the end of the equation, b, is the y-coordinate of the y-intercept, $(0, b)$. Looking at the given equation, $y = 3x + 2$, we see that the slope $m = 3$, and the y-intercept $(0, b)$ is the point $(0, 2)$.

2. Looking at the given equation, $y = -2x - 4$, we see that the slope $m = -2$, and the y-intercept $(0, b)$ is the point $(0, -4)$.

3. In order to find the slope and y-intercept we must first solve for y so that we can put the equation in the slope-intercept form, $y = mx + b$.
   $2y - 8x = 6$
   $2y = 8x + 6$
   $y = 4x + 3$
   Therefore, the slope $m = 4$, and the y-intercept $(0, b)$ is the point $(0, 3)$.

4. In order to find the slope and y-intercept we must first solve for y so that we can put the equation in the slope-intercept form, $y = mx + b$.

$$3y - 5x + 6 = 0$$
$$3y = 5x - 6$$

$$y = \frac{5}{3}x - \frac{6}{2}$$

$$y = \frac{5}{3}x - 3$$

Therefore, the slope $m = \frac{5}{3}$, and the y-intercept $(0, b)$ is the point $(0, -3)$.

VOLUME

The **volume** of a three-dimensional solid figure is the amount of *space* contained within its surface. Volume is measured in units such as cubic inches, cubic feet, and cubic yards. As shown below, 1 cubic inch is defined to be the amount of space contained within a cube having an edge of 1 inch. The other cubic units are defined in a similar way.

Volume

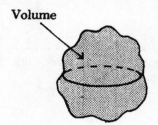

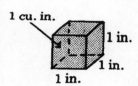

BASIC FORMULAS

The formulas for the volume of several common solid figures are given in the table below. Note that the first three formulas are derived from the more general volume formula, $V = Bh$, where B is the area of the base, and h is the height.

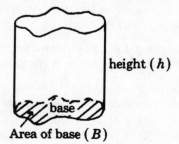

Volume = Area of base × height

$$V = Bh$$

Volume Formulas

The volume of a **rectangular solid** is equal to its length times its width times its height.

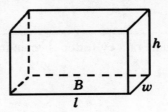

$$V = Bh$$
$$V = (lw)h$$
$$V = lwh$$

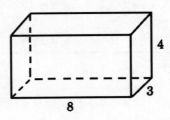

$$V = lwh$$
$$V = (8)(3)(4)$$
$$V = 96$$

The volume of a **cube** is equal to its edge cubed.

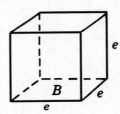

$$V = Bh$$
$$V = (e^2)e$$
$$V = e^3$$

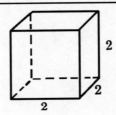

$$V = e^3$$
$$V = (2)^3$$
$$V = 8$$

The volume of a **cylinder** is equal to times the square of its radius times its height.

$$V = Bh$$
$$V = (\pi r^2)h$$
$$V = \pi r^2 h$$

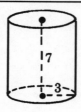

$$V = \pi r^2 h$$
$$V = \pi (3)^2 (7)$$
$$V = 63\pi$$

The volume of a **pyramid** is equal to $\frac{1}{3}$ the volume of a rectangular solid having the same base and the same height.

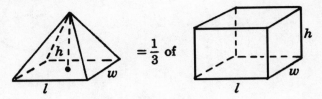

$$V = \frac{1}{3}lwh$$

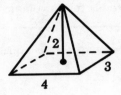

$$V = \frac{1}{3}lwh$$

$$V = \frac{1}{3}(4)(3)(2)$$

$$V = 8$$

The volume of a **cone** is equal to $\frac{1}{3}$ the volume of a cylinder having the same base and the same height.

$$V = \frac{1}{3}\pi r^2 h$$

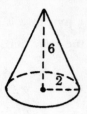

$$V = \frac{1}{3}\pi r^2 h$$

$$V = \frac{1}{3}\pi(2)^2(6)$$

$$V = 8\pi$$

Another common solid figure is the sphere. Like its two-dimensional counterpart, the circle, the formula for its volume contains the number π. Specifically we have:

The volume of a **sphere** is equal to $\frac{4}{3}$ times π times its radius cubed.

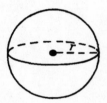

$$V = \frac{4}{3}\pi r^3$$

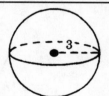

$$V = \frac{4}{3}\pi r^3$$

$$V = \frac{4}{3}\pi(3)^3$$

$$V = 36\pi$$

Example 1

What is the surface area of a cube whose volume is 64 cu. ft?

Procedure

1. Using the formula for the volume of a cube, set the volume equal to 64 and solve for the edge, e.

$$V = e^3$$
$$64 = e^3$$
$$4 = e$$

2. Draw a diagram of the cube and find the area of one of its square faces.

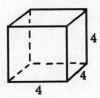

$$A_{sq.} = s^2$$
$$= (4)^2$$
$$= 16 \text{ sq. ft.}$$

3. To find the total surface area, multiply the result by 6. (There are 6 congruent faces.)

$$\text{Surface Area} = 6(16)$$
$$= 96 \text{ sq. ft.}$$

The surface area is 96 sq. ft.

Example 2

Cylinder A and cylinder B have the same height. If cylinder B has twice the radius of cylinder A what is the ratio $\dfrac{\text{volume of A}}{\text{volume of B}}$?

Procedure

1. Draw a diagram of the two cylinders, representing the height of both by h ("the same height"). Represent the radius of cylinder A by x and the radius of cylinder B by $2x$ ("B has twice the radius of A").

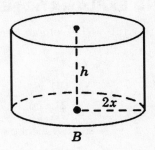

A   B

2. Find the volume of each cylinder.

$$V = \pi r^2 h$$

$$V_A = \pi(x)^2 h \qquad \bigg| \qquad V_B = \pi(2x)^2 h$$
$$= \pi x^2 h \qquad \qquad = 4\pi x^2 h$$

3. Form the required ratio and cancel common factors.

$$\frac{\text{volume of A}}{\text{volume of B}} = \frac{\cancel{\pi}\, x^{\cancel{2}}\, \cancel{h}}{4\cancel{\pi}\, x^{\cancel{2}}\, \cancel{h}}$$
$$= \frac{1}{4}$$

The ratio is $\frac{1}{4}$.

PRACTICE PROBLEMS

1. A cube, 6 inches on each edge, is $\frac{3}{4}$ full of water. How many cubic inches of water does it contain?

2. In order to make an open rectangular box from a rectangular piece of cardboard, 16 inches by 12 inches, four squares, each 2 inches on a side, are cut from the corners, and the remainder is folded along the dotted lines, as shown in the figure below. What is the volume of the resulting open box?

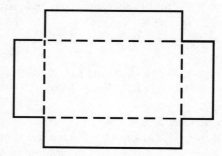

3. The volume of a cone having a height of 6 in. is 32π cu. in. What is the circumference of its circular base? Leave answer in terms of π.

4. The radius of sphere A is 3 times as large as the radius of sphere B. What is the value of the ratio $\dfrac{\text{Volume of A}}{\text{Volume of B}}$?

ANSWERS AND EXPLANATIONS

1. The volume of a cube is given by the formula

    $$V = e^3$$
    $$V = (6)^3$$
    $$V = 216 \text{ cu. in.}$$

    Since the cube is only $\frac{3}{4}$ full, the amount of water in the cube is $\frac{3}{4}(216) = 162$ cu. in.

2.

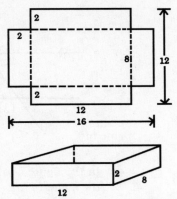

When the sides are folded up along the dotted lines, an open box is formed, with length 12, width 8, and height 2. Using the formula for the volume of a rectangular solid,

$$V = L \cdot W \cdot H$$
$$V = 12 \cdot 8 \cdot 2$$
$$V = 192 \text{ cu. in.}$$

3.

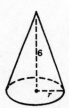

Using the formula for the volume of a cone,

$$V = \frac{1}{3}\pi r^2 h$$
$$32\pi = \frac{1}{3}\pi r^2 (6)$$
$$32\pi = 2\pi r^2$$
$$16 = r^2$$
$$4 = r$$

The diameter of the circular base is twice the radius, or 2(4). = 8. Thus, the circumference of the circular base is C = πd = 8π.

4.   The volume of sphere B is $\frac{4}{3}\pi r^3$. The volume of sphere A is $\frac{4}{3}\pi(3r)^3 = \frac{4}{3}\pi(27r^3)$. Thus,

$$\frac{\text{volume of A}}{\text{volume of B}} = \frac{\frac{4}{3}\pi(27r^3)}{\frac{4}{3}\pi r^3}$$

$$= \frac{27}{1}$$

351

PRACTICE TEST

1. How many degrees are between the hands of a clock at 3:30?

   A. 105°
   B. 90°
   C. 75°
   D. 37°
   E. 70°

2. How many degrees are in an angle that is 30° less than twice its supplement?

   A. 70°
   B. 110°
   C. 50°
   D. 165°
   E. 130°

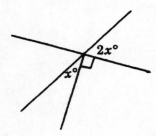

3. In the figure above, what is the value of x?

   A. 30
   B. 50
   C. 60
   D. 80
   E. 45

4. In the figure above, l_1 is parallel to l_2. What is the value of x?

   A. 110
   B. 50
   C. 20
   D. 30
   E. 40

5. The angles of a triangle are in the ratio of 2:5:8. How many degrees are in the largest angle?

   A. 83°
   B. 48°
   C. 20°
   D. 104°
   E. 96°

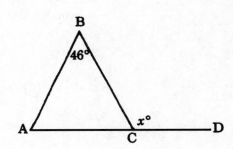

6. In the figure above, AB = BC. What is the value of x?

   A. 167
   B. 92
   C. 134
   D. 113
   E. 146

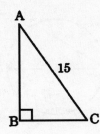

7. In the right triangle above, AB is twice BC. What is the length of BC?

    A. $10\sqrt{3}$

    B. $3\sqrt{5}$

    C.   10

    D. $5\sqrt{3}$

    E. $6\sqrt{5}$

8. Two cars leave the same location at 2:00 P.M. If one car travels north at the rate of 30 m.p.h. and the other travels east at the rate of 40 m.p.h., how many miles are the two cars apart at 4:00 P.M.?

    A.   50
    B.   500
    C.   100
    D.   120
    E.   140

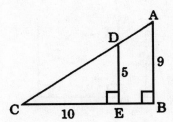

9. In the figure above, what is the length of EB?

    A.   8

    B. $1\frac{4}{5}$

    C.   18
    D.   5
    E.   2

10. If one side of a square is increased by 3, and an adjacent side is multiplied by 2, the resulting rectangle has a perimeter that is 3 times the perimeter of the original square. What is the perimeter of the original square?

    A.   12
    B.   1

    C. $6\frac{2}{3}$

    D.   3
    E.   4

11. If the length of a rectangle is increased by 10%, and the width is decreased by 20%, by what percent does the area decrease?

    A.   28%
    B.   2%
    C.   12%
    D.   21%
    E.   20%

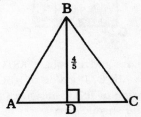

12. In triangle ABC above, height $BD = \frac{4}{5}$. If the area of ABC $= \frac{1}{3}$, what is the length of AC?

    A. $\frac{4}{15}$

    B. $\frac{5}{12}$

    C. $\frac{7}{15}$

    D. $\frac{5}{6}$

    E. $\frac{3}{5}$

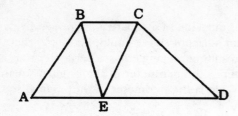

13. In trapezoid ABCD above, BC = 2 and AD = 8. If the area of ABCD is 30, what is the area of triangle BCE?

  A. 6
  B. 7
  C. 8
  D. 10
  E. 12

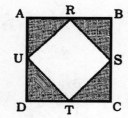

14. In the figure above, square RSTU is inscribed in square ABCD. If a side of ABCD measures x, and a side of RSTU measures y, what is the area of the shaded part?

  A. $\dfrac{xy}{2}$

  B. $x^2 - y^2$

  C. $\dfrac{x^2 y^2}{4}$

  D. $y^2 - x^2$
  E. $4x - 4y$

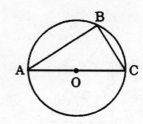

15. In the figure above, triangle ABC is inscribed in circle O. If the radius of the circle is 13, and BC = 10, what is the length of AB?

  A. 13
  B. 16
  C. 18
  D. 24
  E. 26

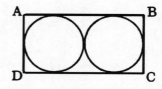

16. In the figure above, the two circles just fit inside rectangle ABCD. If the circumference of each circle is 5π, what is the perimeter of ABCD?

  A. 50
  B. 30
  C. 12π
  D. 10π
  E. 15

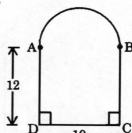

17. In the figure above, arc $\overset{\frown}{AB}$ is a semi-circle. What is the perimeter of figure ABCD?

  A. $34 + 5\pi$
  B. 44
  C. $120 + 25\pi$
  D. 44π
  E. $34 + 10\pi$.

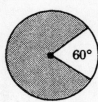

18. In the circle above, if the angle shown is a central angle, and the radius of the circle is 6, what is the area of the shaded part?

    A. 6π
    B. 10π
    C. 7π
    D. 30π
    E. 5π

19. In the figure above, square RSTU is inscribed in circle O. If a side of RSTU equals 8, what is the area of the shaded part?

    A. $4\pi - 64$
    B. $28\pi - 64$
    C. $8\pi - 32$
    D. $32\pi - 64$
    E. $32\pi - 32$

20. The vertices of a parallelogram are located at the points (0, 0), (1, 3), (5, 0), and (6, 3). What is the area of the parallelogram?

    A. 16
    B. $5\sqrt{10}$
    C. $10 + 2\sqrt{10}$
    D. $15\sqrt{10}$
    E. 15

21. What is the distance between the points located at (2, −3) and (8, 5)?

    A. 14
    B. 8
    C. $2\sqrt{10}$
    D. 10
    E. 12

22. What is the slope of the line passing through the points (6, 0) and (0, 6)?

    A. $\dfrac{1}{6}$
    B. -1
    C. 0
    D. 1
    E. 6

23. What is the y-intercept of the line whose equation is $3y - 6x = 12$

    A. (0, 0)
    B. (0, 1)
    C. (0, 2)
    D. (0, 3)
    E. (0, 4)

24. The volume of a cylinder is 45π. If its height is 5, what is the radius of its circular base?

    A. 6
    B. 6π
    C. 3
    D. 9π
    E. $3\sqrt{\pi}$

25. A circle has the same radius as a sphere whose volume is 36π cu. ft. What is the area of the circle, in sq. ft.?

    A. 9π
    B. 36
    C. 6π
    D. 36π
    E. 3π

ANSWERS AND EXPLANATIONS

1. C	6. D	10. E	14. B	18. D	22. B
2. B	7. B	11. C	15. D	19. D	23. E
3. A	8. C	12. D	16. B	20. E	24. C
4. B	9. A	13. A	17. A	21. D	25. A
5. E					

1. **The correct answer is (C).**

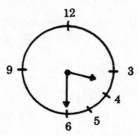

The number of degrees between each hour on a clock is $\frac{360°}{12} = 30°$.

The number of degrees between the hands of a clock at 3:30 is $2\frac{1}{2}$ hours $\times$ $30° = 75°$.

2. **The correct answer is (B).** Let x = the number of degrees in the angle, and $180 - x$ = the number of degrees in the supplement of the angle.

$$x = 2(180 - x) - 30$$
$$x = 360 - 2x - 30$$
$$x = 330 - 2x$$
$$3x = 330$$
$$x = 110°$$

3. **The correct answer is (A).**

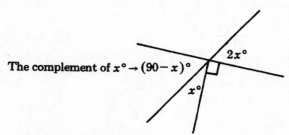

The complement of $x° \rightarrow (90 - x)°$

Since vertical angles are equal,

$$90 - x = 2x$$
$$90 = 3x$$
$$30 = x$$

4. The correct answer is (B).

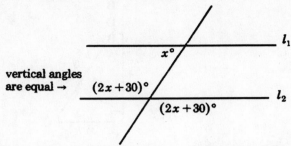

vertical angles
are equal →

Since interior angles on the same side of the transversal are supplementary,

$$x + 2x + 30 = 180$$
$$3x + 30 = 180$$
$$3x = 150$$
$$x = 50$$

5. The correct answer is (E). Let $2x$ = the number of degrees in the smallest angle of the triangle, $5x$ = the number of degrees in the middle sized angle of the triangle, and $8x$ = the number of degrees in the largest angle of the triangle.

Since the sum of the angles of a triangle is $180°$,

$$2x + 5x + 8x = 180$$
$$15x = 180$$
$$x = 12$$

Thus, the largest angle of the triangle is $8x = (8)(12) = 96°$.

6. The correct answer is (D).

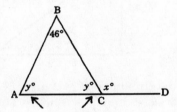

The base angles of an isosceles triangle are equal.
Since the sum of the angles of a triangle is $180°$,

$$46 + y + y = 180$$
$$46 + 2y = 180$$
$$2y = 134$$
$$y = 67$$

Since $\angle BCA$ and $\angle BCD$ are supplementary angles,

$$y + x = 180$$
$$67 + x = 180$$
$$x = 113$$

357

7. The correct answer is (B).

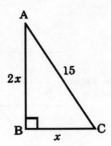

Using the Pythagorean theorem,

$$(AB)^2 + (BC)^2 = (AC)^2$$
$$(2x)^2 + x^2 = 15^2$$
$$4x^2 + x^2 = 225$$
$$5x^2 = 225$$
$$x^2 = 45$$
$$x = \sqrt{45}$$
$$x = \sqrt{9 \cdot 5}$$
$$x = 3\sqrt{5}$$

8. The correct answer is (C).

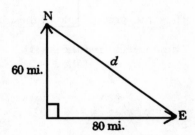

The car travelling north travels 30 m.p.h. $\times$ 2 hrs. = 60 mi.
The car travelling east travels 40 m.p.h. $\times$ 2 hrs. = 80 mi.
Using the Pythagorean theorem,

$$60^2 + 80^2 = d^2$$
$$3600 + 6400 = d^2$$
$$10000 = d^2$$
$$\sqrt{10000} = d$$
$$100 = d$$

9.   **The correct answer is (A).**

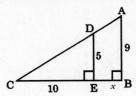

Since $\triangle ABC$ is similar to $\triangle DEC$,

$$\frac{AB}{DE} = \frac{BC}{EC}$$

Let $x = EB$

$$\frac{9}{5} = \frac{10 + x}{10} \quad \text{(cross-multiply)}$$

$$5(10 + x) = 9(10)$$

$$50 + 5x = 90$$

$$5x = 40$$

$$x = 8$$

10.   **The correct answer is (E).**

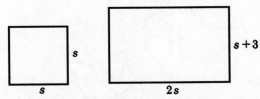

The perimeter of the original square $= 4s$
The perimeter of the rectangle $= 2(s + 3) + 2(2s) = 6s + 6$

$$6s + 6 = 3(4s)$$

$$6s + 6 = 12s$$

$$6 = 6s$$

$$1 = s$$

Thus, the perimeter of the original square $= 4s = (4)(1) = 4$.

11.   **The correct answer is (C).**

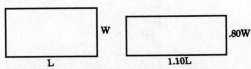

The length of the new rectangle is $(100\% + 10\%)L = 1.10L$
The width of the new rectangle is $(100\% - 20\%)W = .80W$
The area of the original rectangle is LW.
The area of the new rectangle is $(1.10L)(.80W) = .88LW$

Thus, the change in area $= .88LW - LW$

$$= -.12LW$$

This represents a decrease in area of 12%.

359

12. **The correct answer is (D).**

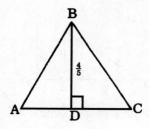

The area of triangle $ABC = \dfrac{1}{2}(AC)(BD)$

$$\dfrac{1}{3} = \dfrac{1}{2}(AC)\left(\dfrac{4}{5}\right)$$

$$\dfrac{1}{3} = \dfrac{4}{10}(AC)$$

$$\dfrac{10}{3} = 4(AC)$$

$$\dfrac{10}{12} = (AC)$$

$$\dfrac{5}{6} = (AC)$$

13. **The correct answer is (A).**

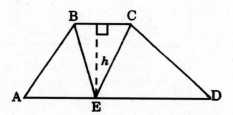

The area of trapezoid $ABCD = \left(\dfrac{BC + AD}{2}\right)h$

$$30 = \left(\dfrac{2+8}{2}\right)h$$

$$30 = 5h$$

$$6 = h$$

The area of triangle $BCE = \dfrac{1}{2}(BC)(h)$

$$= \dfrac{1}{2}(2)(6)$$

$$= 6$$

14.   **The correct answer is (B).**

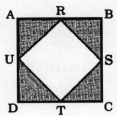

The area of square ABCD $= x^2$
The area of square RSTU $= y^2$
Thus, the area of the shaded part $= x^2 - y^2$.

15.   **The correct answer is (D).**

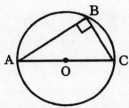

Since $\triangle$ABC is inscribed in a semi-circle, then angle B is a right angle. Since the radius of the circle is 13, then the diameter, AC = 26.
Using the Pythagorean theorem,

$$\left(AB\right)^2 + \left(BC\right)^2 = \left(AC\right)^2$$
$$\left(AB\right)^2 + \left(10\right)^2 = \left(26\right)^2$$
$$\left(AB\right)^2 + 100 = 676$$
$$\left(AB\right)^2 = 576$$
$$AB = \sqrt{576}$$
$$AB = 24$$

16.   **The correct answer is (B).**

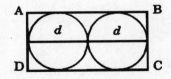

The circumference of each circle $= \pi d$
$$5\pi = \pi d$$
$$5 = d$$
Since the length of the rectangle = 2d = (2)(5) = 10, and the width = d = 5, then the perimeter = (2)(10) + (2)(5) = 30.

17. **The correct answer is (A).**

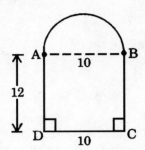

Arc $\overset{\frown}{AB}$ is a semi-circle having a diameter of 10. Thus, the length of

$\overset{\frown}{AB} = \dfrac{1}{2}\pi$ (diameter) $= \dfrac{1}{2}\pi(10) = 5\pi$.

The perimeter of figure ABCD

$= \overset{\frown}{AB} + BC + DC + AD$

$= 5\pi + 12 + 10 + 12$

$= 34 + 5\pi$

18. **The correct answer is (D).**

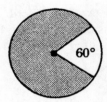

The area of the circle $= \pi(\text{radius})^2$

$\qquad\qquad\qquad\quad = \pi(6)^2$

$\qquad\qquad\qquad\quad = 36\pi$

The area of the unshaded part $= \dfrac{1}{6}$ of the circle.

$\left(\dfrac{60°}{360°} = \dfrac{1}{6} \text{ of the circle.}\right)$

Thus, the area of the shaded part $= \dfrac{5}{6}$ of the circle

$\qquad\qquad\qquad\qquad\qquad\qquad = \dfrac{5}{6}(36\pi)$

$\qquad\qquad\qquad\qquad\qquad\qquad = 30\pi$

19.   **The correct answer is (D).**

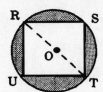

Using the Pythagorean theorem,

$$(RU)^2 + (UT)^2 = (RT)^2$$
$$(8)^2 + (8)^2 = (RT)^2$$
$$64 + 64 = (RT)^2$$
$$128 = (RT)^2$$
$$\sqrt{128} = RT$$
$$\sqrt{64 \cdot 2} = RT$$
$$8\sqrt{2} = RT$$

Since the diameter of circle O is $8\sqrt{2}$, , the radius is $4\sqrt{2}$.

$$\text{The area of circle O} = \pi(\text{radius})^2$$
$$= \pi\left(4\sqrt{2}\right)^2$$
$$= \pi(16 \cdot 2)$$
$$= 32\pi$$

$$\text{The area of square RSTU} = (\text{side})^2$$
$$= 8^2$$
$$= 64$$

Thus the area of the shaded part $= 32\pi - 64$.

20.   **The correct answer is (E).**

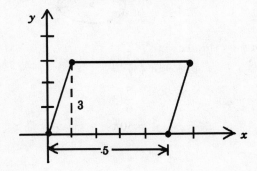

$$\text{The area of the parallelogram} = (\text{base})(\text{height})$$
$$= (5)(3)$$
$$= 15$$

21.   **The correct answer is (D).** Using the distance formula,

$$d = \sqrt{(x_2 - x_1)^2 + (y_2 - y_1)^2}$$
$$= \sqrt{(8-2)^2 + (5-(-3))^2}$$
$$= \sqrt{(6)^2 + (8)^2}$$
$$= \sqrt{36 + 64}$$
$$= \sqrt{100}$$
$$= 10$$

22.   **The correct answer is (B).**

$$m = \frac{y_2 - y_1}{x_2 - x_1}$$
$$= \frac{6-0}{0-6}$$
$$= \frac{6}{-6}$$
$$= -1$$

23.   **The correct answer is (E).** In order to find the y-intercept we must first solve for y so that we can put the equation in the slope-intercept form, $y = mx + b$, where m is the slope and $(0, b)$ is the y-intercept.
$3y - 6x = 12$
$3y = 6x + 12$
$y = 2x + 4$
Therefore, the y-intercept is the point $(0, 4)$.

24.   **The correct answer is (C).**

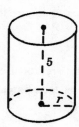

The volume of the cylinder $= \pi r^2 h$

$$45\pi = \pi r^2 (5)$$
$$9 = r^2$$
$$\sqrt{9} = r$$
$$3 = r$$

25. **The correct answer is (A).**

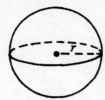 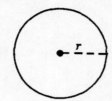

$$\text{The volume of the sphere } = \frac{4}{3}\pi r^3$$

$$36\pi = \frac{4}{3}\pi r^3$$

$$108\pi = 4\pi r^3$$

$$27 = r^3$$

$$3 = r$$

Thus, the area of the circle $= \pi r^2$

$$= \pi(3)^2$$

$$= 9\pi$$

Part III

PRACTICE TESTS AND
SPECIAL FORMAT QUESTIONS

MULTIPLE-CHOICE ANSWER SHEET

PRACTICE TEST I

1 Ⓐ Ⓑ Ⓒ Ⓓ Ⓔ	6 Ⓐ Ⓑ Ⓒ Ⓓ Ⓔ	11 Ⓐ Ⓑ Ⓒ Ⓓ Ⓔ	16 Ⓐ Ⓑ Ⓒ Ⓓ Ⓔ	21 Ⓐ Ⓑ Ⓒ Ⓓ Ⓔ	26 Ⓐ Ⓑ Ⓒ Ⓓ Ⓔ
2 Ⓐ Ⓑ Ⓒ Ⓓ Ⓔ	7 Ⓐ Ⓑ Ⓒ Ⓓ Ⓔ	12 Ⓐ Ⓑ Ⓒ Ⓓ Ⓔ	17 Ⓐ Ⓑ Ⓒ Ⓓ Ⓔ	22 Ⓐ Ⓑ Ⓒ Ⓓ Ⓔ	27 Ⓐ Ⓑ Ⓒ Ⓓ Ⓔ
3 Ⓐ Ⓑ Ⓒ Ⓓ Ⓔ	8 Ⓐ Ⓑ Ⓒ Ⓓ Ⓔ	13 Ⓐ Ⓑ Ⓒ Ⓓ Ⓔ	18 Ⓐ Ⓑ Ⓒ Ⓓ Ⓔ	23 Ⓐ Ⓑ Ⓒ Ⓓ Ⓔ	28 Ⓐ Ⓑ Ⓒ Ⓓ Ⓔ
4 Ⓐ Ⓑ Ⓒ Ⓓ Ⓔ	9 Ⓐ Ⓑ Ⓒ Ⓓ Ⓔ	14 Ⓐ Ⓑ Ⓒ Ⓓ Ⓔ	19 Ⓐ Ⓑ Ⓒ Ⓓ Ⓔ	24 Ⓐ Ⓑ Ⓒ Ⓓ Ⓔ	29 Ⓐ Ⓑ Ⓒ Ⓓ Ⓔ
5 Ⓐ Ⓑ Ⓒ Ⓓ Ⓔ	10 Ⓐ Ⓑ Ⓒ Ⓓ Ⓔ	15 Ⓐ Ⓑ Ⓒ Ⓓ Ⓔ	20 Ⓐ Ⓑ Ⓒ Ⓓ Ⓔ	25 Ⓐ Ⓑ Ⓒ Ⓓ Ⓔ	30 Ⓐ Ⓑ Ⓒ Ⓓ Ⓔ

PRACTICE TEST II

1 Ⓐ Ⓑ Ⓒ Ⓓ Ⓔ	6 Ⓐ Ⓑ Ⓒ Ⓓ Ⓔ	11 Ⓐ Ⓑ Ⓒ Ⓓ Ⓔ	16 Ⓐ Ⓑ Ⓒ Ⓓ Ⓔ	21 Ⓐ Ⓑ Ⓒ Ⓓ Ⓔ	26 Ⓐ Ⓑ Ⓒ Ⓓ Ⓔ
2 Ⓐ Ⓑ Ⓒ Ⓓ Ⓔ	7 Ⓐ Ⓑ Ⓒ Ⓓ Ⓔ	12 Ⓐ Ⓑ Ⓒ Ⓓ Ⓔ	17 Ⓐ Ⓑ Ⓒ Ⓓ Ⓔ	22 Ⓐ Ⓑ Ⓒ Ⓓ Ⓔ	27 Ⓐ Ⓑ Ⓒ Ⓓ Ⓔ
3 Ⓐ Ⓑ Ⓒ Ⓓ Ⓔ	8 Ⓐ Ⓑ Ⓒ Ⓓ Ⓔ	13 Ⓐ Ⓑ Ⓒ Ⓓ Ⓔ	18 Ⓐ Ⓑ Ⓒ Ⓓ Ⓔ	23 Ⓐ Ⓑ Ⓒ Ⓓ Ⓔ	28 Ⓐ Ⓑ Ⓒ Ⓓ Ⓔ
4 Ⓐ Ⓑ Ⓒ Ⓓ Ⓔ	9 Ⓐ Ⓑ Ⓒ Ⓓ Ⓔ	14 Ⓐ Ⓑ Ⓒ Ⓓ Ⓔ	19 Ⓐ Ⓑ Ⓒ Ⓓ Ⓔ	24 Ⓐ Ⓑ Ⓒ Ⓓ Ⓔ	29 Ⓐ Ⓑ Ⓒ Ⓓ Ⓔ
5 Ⓐ Ⓑ Ⓒ Ⓓ Ⓔ	10 Ⓐ Ⓑ Ⓒ Ⓓ Ⓔ	15 Ⓐ Ⓑ Ⓒ Ⓓ Ⓔ	20 Ⓐ Ⓑ Ⓒ Ⓓ Ⓔ	25 Ⓐ Ⓑ Ⓒ Ⓓ Ⓔ	30 Ⓐ Ⓑ Ⓒ Ⓓ Ⓔ

PRACTICE TEST III

1 Ⓐ Ⓑ Ⓒ Ⓓ Ⓔ	6 Ⓐ Ⓑ Ⓒ Ⓓ Ⓔ	11 Ⓐ Ⓑ Ⓒ Ⓓ Ⓔ	16 Ⓐ Ⓑ Ⓒ Ⓓ Ⓔ	21 Ⓐ Ⓑ Ⓒ Ⓓ Ⓔ	26 Ⓐ Ⓑ Ⓒ Ⓓ Ⓔ
2 Ⓐ Ⓑ Ⓒ Ⓓ Ⓔ	7 Ⓐ Ⓑ Ⓒ Ⓓ Ⓔ	12 Ⓐ Ⓑ Ⓒ Ⓓ Ⓔ	17 Ⓐ Ⓑ Ⓒ Ⓓ Ⓔ	22 Ⓐ Ⓑ Ⓒ Ⓓ Ⓔ	27 Ⓐ Ⓑ Ⓒ Ⓓ Ⓔ
3 Ⓐ Ⓑ Ⓒ Ⓓ Ⓔ	8 Ⓐ Ⓑ Ⓒ Ⓓ Ⓔ	13 Ⓐ Ⓑ Ⓒ Ⓓ Ⓔ	18 Ⓐ Ⓑ Ⓒ Ⓓ Ⓔ	23 Ⓐ Ⓑ Ⓒ Ⓓ Ⓔ	28 Ⓐ Ⓑ Ⓒ Ⓓ Ⓔ
4 Ⓐ Ⓑ Ⓒ Ⓓ Ⓔ	9 Ⓐ Ⓑ Ⓒ Ⓓ Ⓔ	14 Ⓐ Ⓑ Ⓒ Ⓓ Ⓔ	19 Ⓐ Ⓑ Ⓒ Ⓓ Ⓔ	24 Ⓐ Ⓑ Ⓒ Ⓓ Ⓔ	29 Ⓐ Ⓑ Ⓒ Ⓓ Ⓔ
5 Ⓐ Ⓑ Ⓒ Ⓓ Ⓔ	10 Ⓐ Ⓑ Ⓒ Ⓓ Ⓔ	15 Ⓐ Ⓑ Ⓒ Ⓓ Ⓔ	20 Ⓐ Ⓑ Ⓒ Ⓓ Ⓔ	25 Ⓐ Ⓑ Ⓒ Ⓓ Ⓔ	30 Ⓐ Ⓑ Ⓒ Ⓓ Ⓔ

PRACTICE TEST IV

1 Ⓐ Ⓑ Ⓒ Ⓓ Ⓔ	6 Ⓐ Ⓑ Ⓒ Ⓓ Ⓔ	11 Ⓐ Ⓑ Ⓒ Ⓓ Ⓔ	16 Ⓐ Ⓑ Ⓒ Ⓓ Ⓔ	21 Ⓐ Ⓑ Ⓒ Ⓓ Ⓔ	26 Ⓐ Ⓑ Ⓒ Ⓓ Ⓔ
2 Ⓐ Ⓑ Ⓒ Ⓓ Ⓔ	7 Ⓐ Ⓑ Ⓒ Ⓓ Ⓔ	12 Ⓐ Ⓑ Ⓒ Ⓓ Ⓔ	17 Ⓐ Ⓑ Ⓒ Ⓓ Ⓔ	22 Ⓐ Ⓑ Ⓒ Ⓓ Ⓔ	27 Ⓐ Ⓑ Ⓒ Ⓓ Ⓔ
3 Ⓐ Ⓑ Ⓒ Ⓓ Ⓔ	8 Ⓐ Ⓑ Ⓒ Ⓓ Ⓔ	13 Ⓐ Ⓑ Ⓒ Ⓓ Ⓔ	18 Ⓐ Ⓑ Ⓒ Ⓓ Ⓔ	23 Ⓐ Ⓑ Ⓒ Ⓓ Ⓔ	28 Ⓐ Ⓑ Ⓒ Ⓓ Ⓔ
4 Ⓐ Ⓑ Ⓒ Ⓓ Ⓔ	9 Ⓐ Ⓑ Ⓒ Ⓓ Ⓔ	14 Ⓐ Ⓑ Ⓒ Ⓓ Ⓔ	19 Ⓐ Ⓑ Ⓒ Ⓓ Ⓔ	24 Ⓐ Ⓑ Ⓒ Ⓓ Ⓔ	29 Ⓐ Ⓑ Ⓒ Ⓓ Ⓔ
5 Ⓐ Ⓑ Ⓒ Ⓓ Ⓔ	10 Ⓐ Ⓑ Ⓒ Ⓓ Ⓔ	15 Ⓐ Ⓑ Ⓒ Ⓓ Ⓔ	20 Ⓐ Ⓑ Ⓒ Ⓓ Ⓔ	25 Ⓐ Ⓑ Ⓒ Ⓓ Ⓔ	30 Ⓐ Ⓑ Ⓒ Ⓓ Ⓔ

PRACTICE TEST V

1 Ⓐ Ⓑ Ⓒ Ⓓ Ⓔ	6 Ⓐ Ⓑ Ⓒ Ⓓ Ⓔ	11 Ⓐ Ⓑ Ⓒ Ⓓ Ⓔ	16 Ⓐ Ⓑ Ⓒ Ⓓ Ⓔ	21 Ⓐ Ⓑ Ⓒ Ⓓ Ⓔ	26 Ⓐ Ⓑ Ⓒ Ⓓ Ⓔ
2 Ⓐ Ⓑ Ⓒ Ⓓ Ⓔ	7 Ⓐ Ⓑ Ⓒ Ⓓ Ⓔ	12 Ⓐ Ⓑ Ⓒ Ⓓ Ⓔ	17 Ⓐ Ⓑ Ⓒ Ⓓ Ⓔ	22 Ⓐ Ⓑ Ⓒ Ⓓ Ⓔ	27 Ⓐ Ⓑ Ⓒ Ⓓ Ⓔ
3 Ⓐ Ⓑ Ⓒ Ⓓ Ⓔ	8 Ⓐ Ⓑ Ⓒ Ⓓ Ⓔ	13 Ⓐ Ⓑ Ⓒ Ⓓ Ⓔ	18 Ⓐ Ⓑ Ⓒ Ⓓ Ⓔ	23 Ⓐ Ⓑ Ⓒ Ⓓ Ⓔ	28 Ⓐ Ⓑ Ⓒ Ⓓ Ⓔ
4 Ⓐ Ⓑ Ⓒ Ⓓ Ⓔ	9 Ⓐ Ⓑ Ⓒ Ⓓ Ⓔ	14 Ⓐ Ⓑ Ⓒ Ⓓ Ⓔ	19 Ⓐ Ⓑ Ⓒ Ⓓ Ⓔ	24 Ⓐ Ⓑ Ⓒ Ⓓ Ⓔ	29 Ⓐ Ⓑ Ⓒ Ⓓ Ⓔ
5 Ⓐ Ⓑ Ⓒ Ⓓ Ⓔ	10 Ⓐ Ⓑ Ⓒ Ⓓ Ⓔ	15 Ⓐ Ⓑ Ⓒ Ⓓ Ⓔ	20 Ⓐ Ⓑ Ⓒ Ⓓ Ⓔ	25 Ⓐ Ⓑ Ⓒ Ⓓ Ⓔ	30 Ⓐ Ⓑ Ⓒ Ⓓ Ⓔ

PRACTICE TEST VI

1 Ⓐ Ⓑ Ⓒ Ⓓ Ⓔ	6 Ⓐ Ⓑ Ⓒ Ⓓ Ⓔ	11 Ⓐ Ⓑ Ⓒ Ⓓ Ⓔ	16 Ⓐ Ⓑ Ⓒ Ⓓ Ⓔ	21 Ⓐ Ⓑ Ⓒ Ⓓ Ⓔ	26 Ⓐ Ⓑ Ⓒ Ⓓ Ⓔ
2 Ⓐ Ⓑ Ⓒ Ⓓ Ⓔ	7 Ⓐ Ⓑ Ⓒ Ⓓ Ⓔ	12 Ⓐ Ⓑ Ⓒ Ⓓ Ⓔ	17 Ⓐ Ⓑ Ⓒ Ⓓ Ⓔ	22 Ⓐ Ⓑ Ⓒ Ⓓ Ⓔ	27 Ⓐ Ⓑ Ⓒ Ⓓ Ⓔ
3 Ⓐ Ⓑ Ⓒ Ⓓ Ⓔ	8 Ⓐ Ⓑ Ⓒ Ⓓ Ⓔ	13 Ⓐ Ⓑ Ⓒ Ⓓ Ⓔ	18 Ⓐ Ⓑ Ⓒ Ⓓ Ⓔ	23 Ⓐ Ⓑ Ⓒ Ⓓ Ⓔ	28 Ⓐ Ⓑ Ⓒ Ⓓ Ⓔ
4 Ⓐ Ⓑ Ⓒ Ⓓ Ⓔ	9 Ⓐ Ⓑ Ⓒ Ⓓ Ⓔ	14 Ⓐ Ⓑ Ⓒ Ⓓ Ⓔ	19 Ⓐ Ⓑ Ⓒ Ⓓ Ⓔ	24 Ⓐ Ⓑ Ⓒ Ⓓ Ⓔ	29 Ⓐ Ⓑ Ⓒ Ⓓ Ⓔ
5 Ⓐ Ⓑ Ⓒ Ⓓ Ⓔ	10 Ⓐ Ⓑ Ⓒ Ⓓ Ⓔ	15 Ⓐ Ⓑ Ⓒ Ⓓ Ⓔ	20 Ⓐ Ⓑ Ⓒ Ⓓ Ⓔ	25 Ⓐ Ⓑ Ⓒ Ⓓ Ⓔ	30 Ⓐ Ⓑ Ⓒ Ⓓ Ⓔ

PRACTICE TEST VII

1 Ⓐ Ⓑ Ⓒ Ⓓ Ⓔ	6 Ⓐ Ⓑ Ⓒ Ⓓ Ⓔ	11 Ⓐ Ⓑ Ⓒ Ⓓ Ⓔ	16 Ⓐ Ⓑ Ⓒ Ⓓ Ⓔ	21 Ⓐ Ⓑ Ⓒ Ⓓ Ⓔ	26 Ⓐ Ⓑ Ⓒ Ⓓ Ⓔ
2 Ⓐ Ⓑ Ⓒ Ⓓ Ⓔ	7 Ⓐ Ⓑ Ⓒ Ⓓ Ⓔ	12 Ⓐ Ⓑ Ⓒ Ⓓ Ⓔ	17 Ⓐ Ⓑ Ⓒ Ⓓ Ⓔ	22 Ⓐ Ⓑ Ⓒ Ⓓ Ⓔ	27 Ⓐ Ⓑ Ⓒ Ⓓ Ⓔ
3 Ⓐ Ⓑ Ⓒ Ⓓ Ⓔ	8 Ⓐ Ⓑ Ⓒ Ⓓ Ⓔ	13 Ⓐ Ⓑ Ⓒ Ⓓ Ⓔ	18 Ⓐ Ⓑ Ⓒ Ⓓ Ⓔ	23 Ⓐ Ⓑ Ⓒ Ⓓ Ⓔ	28 Ⓐ Ⓑ Ⓒ Ⓓ Ⓔ
4 Ⓐ Ⓑ Ⓒ Ⓓ Ⓔ	9 Ⓐ Ⓑ Ⓒ Ⓓ Ⓔ	14 Ⓐ Ⓑ Ⓒ Ⓓ Ⓔ	19 Ⓐ Ⓑ Ⓒ Ⓓ Ⓔ	24 Ⓐ Ⓑ Ⓒ Ⓓ Ⓔ	29 Ⓐ Ⓑ Ⓒ Ⓓ Ⓔ
5 Ⓐ Ⓑ Ⓒ Ⓓ Ⓔ	10 Ⓐ Ⓑ Ⓒ Ⓓ Ⓔ	15 Ⓐ Ⓑ Ⓒ Ⓓ Ⓔ	20 Ⓐ Ⓑ Ⓒ Ⓓ Ⓔ	25 Ⓐ Ⓑ Ⓒ Ⓓ Ⓔ	30 Ⓐ Ⓑ Ⓒ Ⓓ Ⓔ

PRACTICE TEST VIII

1 Ⓐ Ⓑ Ⓒ Ⓓ Ⓔ	6 Ⓐ Ⓑ Ⓒ Ⓓ Ⓔ	11 Ⓐ Ⓑ Ⓒ Ⓓ Ⓔ	16 Ⓐ Ⓑ Ⓒ Ⓓ Ⓔ	21 Ⓐ Ⓑ Ⓒ Ⓓ Ⓔ	26 Ⓐ Ⓑ Ⓒ Ⓓ Ⓔ
2 Ⓐ Ⓑ Ⓒ Ⓓ Ⓔ	7 Ⓐ Ⓑ Ⓒ Ⓓ Ⓔ	12 Ⓐ Ⓑ Ⓒ Ⓓ Ⓔ	17 Ⓐ Ⓑ Ⓒ Ⓓ Ⓔ	22 Ⓐ Ⓑ Ⓒ Ⓓ Ⓔ	27 Ⓐ Ⓑ Ⓒ Ⓓ Ⓔ
3 Ⓐ Ⓑ Ⓒ Ⓓ Ⓔ	8 Ⓐ Ⓑ Ⓒ Ⓓ Ⓔ	13 Ⓐ Ⓑ Ⓒ Ⓓ Ⓔ	18 Ⓐ Ⓑ Ⓒ Ⓓ Ⓔ	23 Ⓐ Ⓑ Ⓒ Ⓓ Ⓔ	28 Ⓐ Ⓑ Ⓒ Ⓓ Ⓔ
4 Ⓐ Ⓑ Ⓒ Ⓓ Ⓔ	9 Ⓐ Ⓑ Ⓒ Ⓓ Ⓔ	14 Ⓐ Ⓑ Ⓒ Ⓓ Ⓔ	19 Ⓐ Ⓑ Ⓒ Ⓓ Ⓔ	24 Ⓐ Ⓑ Ⓒ Ⓓ Ⓔ	29 Ⓐ Ⓑ Ⓒ Ⓓ Ⓔ
5 Ⓐ Ⓑ Ⓒ Ⓓ Ⓔ	10 Ⓐ Ⓑ Ⓒ Ⓓ Ⓔ	15 Ⓐ Ⓑ Ⓒ Ⓓ Ⓔ	20 Ⓐ Ⓑ Ⓒ Ⓓ Ⓔ	25 Ⓐ Ⓑ Ⓒ Ⓓ Ⓔ	30 Ⓐ Ⓑ Ⓒ Ⓓ Ⓔ

Chapter 6
STANDARD MULTIPLE-CHOICE MATH QUESTIONS

Standard multiple-choice math questions are based on the mathematics assumed to have been learned in high school—arithmetic, algebra, and geometry. This type of question is usually found on both the GMAT and GRE exams.

TIPS FOR ANSWERING STANDARD MULTIPLE-CHOICE MATH QUESTIONS

1. Read each question carefully to determine what is given, what relationships and conditions must be satisfied, and what is the unknown.

2. Whenever necessary, draw a diagram depicting the given information. This is particularly useful when solving geometry problems.

3. Focus on the unknown and the other quantities involved in the problem. See if there is any element in the problem that reminds you of a similar problem you have solved before.

4. Look at the multiple-choice answers. They may provide you with some idea of how to proceed.

5. Write down any formulas you know involving the type of quantities involved in the problem. Decide whether any of them are applicable to the particular problem you are trying to solve.

6. Represent the unknown by a letter. Whenever possible, write an equation containing this letter by translating some given condition into symbolic form. Solve the resulting equation for the unknown.

7. Do not waste time doing unnecessary computations. Estimate as much as possible.

8. Be sure to express your answer in the same unit as the choices given.

9. Reduce all fractions to lowest terms, and simplify all square roots. In problems involving circles, see if the answers are left in terms of π or whether you are supposed to substitute some value like 3.14 or $\frac{22}{7}$.

10. Even though the answer you obtain does not match any of the given choices, it might still be correct. See if you can rewrite your answer in a different form. For example, the expression $ab + ac$ can also be written as $a(b + c)$.

Often, the questions in this section are based on data given in the form of tables and graphs. The most common types of graphs are bar graphs, line graphs, and circle graphs (pie graphs.) An example of each type is shown below.

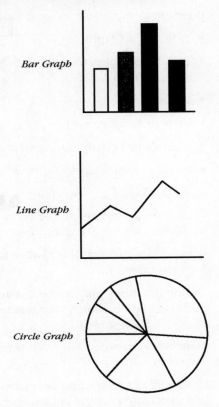

Bar Graph

Line Graph

Circle Graph

Bar graphs are used either to compare different quantities, or to compare the same quantity at different times. The value of a quantity is determined by the height of the bar.

Line graphs are used either to show how two different quantities change with respect to each other or how one quantity changes over time. In the latter case, if the line slopes up, the quantity is increasing; if the line slopes down, the quantity is decreasing; if the line is horizontal, the quantity is remaining the same.

Circle graphs are used to show how a whole quantity is divided up into different parts. The sectors in the circle are drawn proportional to the parts they represent. For example, a sector that represents $\frac{1}{4}$ of the whole quantity will have a central angle measuring $\frac{1}{4}$ of 360°, or 90°. The values given in the sectors are usually not actual values, but percents. Since the sectors represent all the parts of the whole, the sum of their percents must equal 100%. In addition to being given the percents represented by each of the sectors, the total value of the whole is usually stated somewhere near the circle.

TIPS FOR ANSWERING STANDARD MULTIPLE-CHOICE MATH QUESTIONS BASED ON GRAPHS

1. Briefly scan the graph, looking for important pieces of information such as:

   - Title of the graph

   - Quantities represented along the axes of a bar or line graph, or in the sectors of a circle graph

   - Dates

   - Units of measurement

   - Legends or keys indicating what certain shadings or other symbols represent

   - Range of values along the axes of a bar or line graph

   - Total value of a circle graph

   Do not try to understand the entire graph at once. Become familiar with it gradually as you answer the questions.

2. If more than one graph is involved, be very careful to look at the appropriate one for each question.

3. Do the questions that can be answered without computation first. For example, a question like "In which year was the quantity the largest?" can usually be answered by observation alone.

4. Look at the answers. They will tell you the extent to which you can approximate the result.

5. Be careful not to confuse decimals and percents. Remember, to change a decimal to a percent, move the decimal point two places to the right (D→P); to change a percent to a decimal, move the decimal point two places to the left (D←P). For example, .173 = 17.3% and 6.5% = .065.

6. Instead of performing computations with very large values, use the units along the axes and convert to actual values at the end. For example, if each unit represents $2,000,000, then $3\frac{1}{2}$ units + $4\frac{1}{2}$ units = 8 units, or $16,000,000.

7. If you are asked to find the ratio of the values represented by two sectors of a circle graph, simply find the ratio of their percents. You do not have to change the percents to actual values.

8. In questions that ask you to make inferences, only use the information given in the graph. Do not use any outside knowledge you might have about the quantities involved in the graph.

9. Whenever possible, visualize answers instead of computing them. For example, it might be possible to determine the average of two values simply by locating a point halfway between the two values.

PRACTICE TEST I

Directions: Solve each of the problems that follow, and then indicate the best answer in the appropriate space on the answer sheet.
Note: Figures that accompany problems in this test are intended to provide information useful in solving the problems. They are drawn as accurately as possible EXCEPT when it is stated in a specific problem that its figure is not drawn to scale. All figures lie in a plane unless otherwise stated. All numbers used are real numbers.

1. 68.4 is 34.2 percent of

    (A) 50
    (B) 68.4
    (C) 34.2
    (D) 200
    (E) 100

2. If a train travels M miles in H hours, how many hours will it take the train to travel the next N miles at the same rate?

    (A) $\dfrac{H}{MN}$

    (B) $\dfrac{HM}{N}$

    (C) $\dfrac{HN}{M}$

    (D) $\dfrac{M}{HN}$

    (E) $\dfrac{MN}{H}$

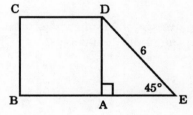

3. In the figure above, what is the area of square ABCD?

    (A) $3\sqrt{2}$
    (B) 18
    (C) 24
    (D) 36
    (E) 72

4. If the average of A and B is Q, and the average of C, D, and E is R, what is the average of A, B, C, D, and E in terms of Q and R?

    (A) $\dfrac{Q+R}{2}$

    (B) $\dfrac{2Q+R}{5}$

    (C) $\dfrac{Q+3R}{5}$

    (D) $\dfrac{6QR}{5}$

    (E) $\dfrac{2Q+3R}{5}$

373

5. A bottle of water is 80% full. After $\frac{3}{4}$ of the water is poured out, what percent of the bottle is empty?

(A) 10%
(B) 20%
(C) 25%
(D) 75%
(E) 80%

6. A certain copying machine can make 8 copies in 12 seconds. How many copies can this same machine make in 7 minutes?

(A) 630
(B) 672
(C) 336
(D) 224
(E) 280

7. The average of 20 numbers is what percent of the sum of the 20 numbers?

(A) 20%
(B) 5%
(C) 10%
(D) 50%
(E) 2%

8. If $\frac{x}{2} + \frac{x}{3} = 20$, then $\frac{x}{4} =$

(A) 24
(B) 12
(C) 5
(D) 6
(E) 25

9. The radius of a circle is the same length as the side of a square. What is the ratio of the circumference of the circle to the perimeter of the square?

(A) $\frac{\pi}{2}$

(B) $\frac{4}{\pi}$

(C) $\frac{\pi}{1}$

(D) $\frac{\pi}{4}$

(E) $\frac{2}{\pi}$

10. Which of the following is closest to $\frac{(.75)(.6667)}{(.8)(.8333)}$?

(A) $\frac{5}{7}$

(B) $\frac{2}{3}$

(C) $\frac{3}{4}$

(D) $\frac{27}{40}$

(E) 1

11. If the simple interest earned on $500 after 4 months is $25, what is the annual rate of interest?

(A) $33\frac{1}{3}\%$
(B) 25%
(C) 20%
(D) 5%
(E) 15%

12. A certain truck can travel M miles on G gallons of gasoline. How many gallons of gasoline are needed for 7 of these trucks if each one must travel 300 miles?

(A) $\frac{2100\ G}{M}$

(B) $\frac{2100\ M}{G}$

(C) $\frac{M}{2100\ G}$

(D) $\frac{G}{2100\ M}$

(E) $\frac{300\ M}{7G}$

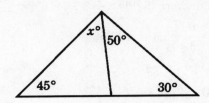

13. In the figure above, what is the value of x?

    (A) 55
    (B) 30
    (C) 40
    (D) 100
    (E) 65

14. If the ratio of x to y is $\frac{3}{4}$, and the ratio of y to z is $\frac{12}{13}$, what is the ratio of z to x?

    (A) $\dfrac{9}{13}$

    (B) $\dfrac{16}{13}$

    (C) $\dfrac{3}{13}$

    (D) $\dfrac{13}{9}$

    (E) $\dfrac{13}{16}$

15. A guitar, which is valued at $800 new, increases in value by 10% per year. What is its value at the end of 2 years?

    (A) $880
    (B) $900
    (C) $968
    (D) $1,000
    (E) $1,068

16. If $x^2 - y^2 = 100$ and $x - y = 4$, then $x + y =$

    (A) 96
    (B) 46
    (C) 25
    (D) 10
    (E) 14

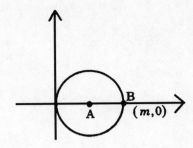

17. In the figure above, point A is the center of the circle, and point B is located at $(m, 0)$. If the area of the circle is 36π, what is the value of m?

    (A) 6
    (B) 36
    (C) 18
    (D) 12
    (E) 24

18. Mark earns $16,000 per year, which is $\frac{2}{3}$ of Ken's annual salary. If Ken's annual salary is $\frac{3}{5}$ of Rupert's annual salary, how much money does Rupert earn per year?

    (A) $26,000
    (B) $40,000
    (C) $6,400
    (D) $14,400
    (E) $48,000

19. If 30% of 40% of 50 equals $60x$, what is the value of x?

    (A) 100
    (B) 10
    (C) 1
    (D) .1
    (E) .01

20. Which of the following represents the largest value?

(A) $3 + 3(3)^4$

(B) 3^5

(C) $\dfrac{3^5}{3}$

(D) $3(3)^4$

(E) $3^2(3)^3 - 3$

21. A rectangle of area 60 is divided into exactly 5 nonoverlapping squares of equal area. What is the perimeter of the rectangle?

(A) $2\sqrt{3}$

(B) 120

(C) 144

(D) $24\sqrt{3}$

(E) $20\sqrt{3}$

22. On a final exam, the average grade of the class was 84. If 10% of the class averaged 90, and 30% of the class averaged 80, what was the average grade of the rest of the class?

(A) 83

(B) 84

(C) 85

(D) 86

(E) 87

23. A family budgets 30% of its monthly income for rent and 20% of what is left for food. What percent of the monthly income is budgeted for rent and food?

(A) 56%

(B) 54%

(C) 52%

(D) 50%

(E) 44%

24. In the formula $r = \sqrt{x^2 + y^2}$, if $r = \dfrac{10}{3}$ and $y = \dfrac{8}{3}$, what is the value of x?

(A) 4 or -4

(B) $\sqrt{6}$ or $-\sqrt{6}$

(C) 3 or -3

(D) 2 or -2

(E) $\sqrt{2}$ or $-\sqrt{2}$

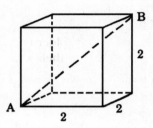

25. In the cube above, what is the length of diagonal AB?

(A) $2\sqrt{6}$

(B) $2\sqrt{2}$

(C) $2\sqrt{5}$

(D) 4

(E) $2\sqrt{3}$

26. Eddie earns $12 per hour for a normal 8-hour workday and $1\dfrac{1}{2}$ times this rate for hours worked overtime. If, on a certain day, Eddie earned $141, how long did he work?

(A) 9 hrs. 30 min.

(B) 10 hrs. 15 min.

(C) 10 hrs. 36 min.

(D) 11 hrs.

(E) 10 hrs. 30 min.

27. Lenny bought 4 dozen oranges at $6 per dozen, and sold all of them at a price of 75 cents per orange. What was the percent of profit on his cost?

(A) 50%

(B) $33\frac{1}{3}$%

(C) 150%

(D) $66\frac{2}{3}$%

(E) $133\frac{1}{3}$%

28. Tony is now 3 years older than Howard. If 5 years ago the sum of their ages was 59, how old is Tony now?

(A) 26

(B) 29

(C) 33

(D) 36

(E) 39

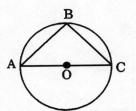

29. In the figure above, isosceles triangle ABC is inscribed in a semi-circle. What is the ratio of the area of circle O to the area of triangle ABC?

(A) $\dfrac{2}{\pi}$

(B) $\dfrac{\pi}{1}$

(C) $\dfrac{2\pi}{3}$

(D) $\dfrac{1}{\pi}$

(E) $\dfrac{\pi}{2}$

30. If a taxi driver charges C cents for the first quarter-mile, and $\dfrac{C}{4}$ cents for each additional quarter-mile, how much does it cost, in cents, for a trip of M miles?

(A) $C\left(M+\dfrac{1}{4}\right)$

(B) $\dfrac{C}{4}\left(M+\dfrac{4}{15}\right)$

(C) $C\left(M+\dfrac{3}{4}\right)$

(D) $C\left(M-\dfrac{1}{4}\right)$

(E) $C\left(M-\dfrac{3}{4}\right)$

ANSWERS AND EXPLANATIONS

1. **D**	6. **E**	11. **E**	16. **C**	21. **D**	26. **E**
2. **C**	7. **B**	12. **A**	17. **D**	22. **C**	27. **A**
3. **B**	8. **D**	13. **A**	18. **B**	23. **E**	28. **D**
4. **E**	9. **A**	14. **D**	19. **D**	24. **D**	29. **B**
5. **E**	10. **C**	15. **C**	20. **A**	25. **E**	30. **C**

1. **The correct answer is (D).**

$$\frac{\text{Part}}{\text{Whole}} = \frac{\text{Percent}}{100\%}$$

$$\frac{68.4}{x} = \frac{34.2}{100} \ (\text{cross-multiply})$$

$$34.2x = 6840$$

$$x = 200$$

2. **The correct answer is (C).** Let x = the number of hours it will take the train to travel the next N miles.

$$\frac{\text{miles} \rightarrow \text{M}}{\text{hours} \rightarrow \text{H}} = \frac{\text{N}}{x} \ (\text{cross-multiply})$$

$$\text{M}x = \text{HN}$$

$$x = \frac{\text{HN}}{\text{M}}$$

3. **The correct answer is (B).**

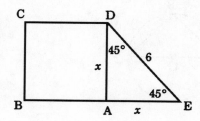

Since $\angle \text{ADE} = \angle \text{AED}$, side AE = side AD. Using the Pythagorean theorem,

$$(\text{AD})^2 + (\text{AE})^2 = (\text{DE})^2$$

$$x^2 + x^2 = 6^2$$

$$2x^2 = 36$$

$$x^2 = 18$$

The area of square ABCD $= (\text{AD})^2$

$$= x^2$$

$$= 18$$

4. **The correct answer is (E).**

$$\frac{\text{A} + \text{B}}{2} = \text{Q} \qquad \frac{\text{C} + \text{D} + \text{E}}{3} = \text{R}$$

$$\text{A} + \text{B} = 2\text{Q} \qquad \text{C} + \text{D} + \text{E} = 3\text{R}$$

Thus, the average of A, B, C, D, and E $= \dfrac{\text{A} + \text{B} + \text{C} + \text{D} + \text{E}}{5}$

$$= \frac{2\text{Q} + 3\text{R}}{5}$$

5. **The correct answer is (E).** After $\frac{3}{4}$ of the water is poured out, $\frac{1}{4}$ of 80% $= \frac{1}{4} \times 80\%$ $= 20\%$ of the bottle remains filled with water. Thus, the percent of the bottle that is now empty $= 100\% - 20\% = 80\%$.

6. **The correct answer is (E).** Let x = the number of copies the machine can make in 7 minutes. Since 7 minutes = 7(60 seconds) = 420 seconds,

$$\frac{copies \rightarrow}{seconds \rightarrow} \frac{8}{12} = \frac{x}{420} \ \left(\text{cross-multiply}\right)$$
$$12x = 3360$$
$$x = 280 \text{ copies}$$

7. **The correct answer is (B).** Let S = the sum of the 20 numbers. Thus, the average of the 20 numbers $= \frac{S}{20}$. Let x = the percent that the average of the 20 numbers is of the sum of the 20 numbers.

$$\frac{\text{Part}}{\text{Whole}} = \frac{\text{Percent}}{100\%}$$
$$\frac{\text{Average}}{\text{Sum}} = \frac{x}{100}$$

$$\frac{\frac{S}{20}}{S} = \frac{x}{100} \ \left(\text{cross-multiply}\right)$$
$$Sx = \frac{S}{20} \cdot 100$$
$$\cancel{S}x = 5\cancel{S}$$
$$x = 5\%$$

8. **The correct answer is (D).**
$$\frac{x}{2} + \frac{x}{3} = 20 \ \left(\text{multiply by 6}\right)$$
$$\overset{3}{\cancel{6}} \cdot \frac{x}{\cancel{2}} + \overset{2}{\cancel{6}} \cdot \frac{x}{\cancel{3}} = 6 \cdot 20$$
$$3x + 2x = 120$$
$$5x = 120$$
$$x = 24$$
$$\text{Thus, } \frac{x}{4} = \frac{24}{4} = 6.$$

379

9. **The correct answer is (A).** Let x = the radius of the circle and the side of the square.

$$\text{The circumference of the circle} = \pi(\text{diameter})$$
$$= \pi(2x)$$
$$= 2\pi x$$

$$\text{The perimeter of the square} = 4(\text{side})$$
$$= 4x$$

Thus, $\dfrac{\text{circumference}}{\text{perimeter}} = \dfrac{2\pi \cancel{x}}{4\cancel{x}}$

$$= \dfrac{\pi}{2}$$

10. **The correct answer is (C).**

$$\frac{(.75)(.6667)}{(.8)(.8333)} \approx \frac{\left(\dfrac{3}{4}\right)\left(\dfrac{2}{3}\right)}{\left(\dfrac{8}{10}\right)\left(\dfrac{5}{6}\right)}$$

$$\approx \frac{\dfrac{1}{2}}{\dfrac{2}{3}}$$

$$\approx \frac{1}{2} \div \frac{2}{3}$$

$$\approx \frac{1}{2} \times \frac{3}{2}$$

$$\approx \frac{3}{4}$$

11. **The correct answer is (E).** Since 4 months is $\dfrac{1}{3}$ of a year, the interest earned in a year is 3($25), or $75. Let x = the annual rate of interest.

$$\frac{\text{Part}}{\text{Whole}} = \frac{\text{Percent}}{100\%}$$

$$\frac{\$75}{\$500} = \frac{x}{100} \quad (\text{cross-multiply})$$

$$500x = 7500$$

$$x = 15\%$$

12. **The correct answer is (A).** Since 7 trucks must each travel 300 miles, the total distance travelled will be 2100 miles. Let x = the number of gallons of gasoline needed to travel 2100 miles.

$$\frac{\text{miles}}{\text{gallons}} \begin{array}{c} \to \\ \to \end{array} \frac{\text{M}}{\text{G}} = \frac{2100}{x} \ \left(\text{cross-multiply}\right)$$

$$\text{M}x = 2100 \ \text{G}$$

$$x = \frac{2100 \ \text{G}}{\text{M}}$$

13. **The correct answer is (A).**

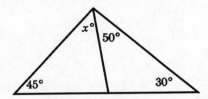

Since the sum of the angles in a triangle is 180°,

$$45 + 30 + \left(x + 50\right) = 180$$

$$x + 125 = 180$$

$$x = 55$$

14. **The correct answer is (D).**

$$\frac{x}{y} = \frac{3}{4} \text{ and } \frac{y}{z} = \frac{12}{13}$$

Thus, $\dfrac{x}{\cancel{y}} \cdot \dfrac{\cancel{y}}{z} = \dfrac{3}{4} \cdot \dfrac{12}{13}$

$$\frac{x}{z} = \frac{9}{13}$$

$$\text{or } \frac{z}{x} = \frac{13}{9}$$

15. **The correct answer is (C).** After one year, the value of the guitar is 110% of $800 = 1.10 \times \$800 = \$880$. After two years, the value of the guitar is 110% of $880 = 1.10 \times \$880 = \$968$.

16. **The correct answer is (C).**

$$x^2 - y^2 = 100$$

$$\left(x - y\right)\left(x + y\right) = 100$$

Since $x - y = 4$,

$$\left(4\right)\left(x + y\right) = 100$$

$$x + y = 25$$

17. **The correct answer is (D).**

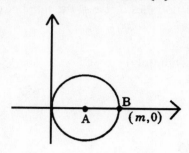

The area of the circle $= \pi(\text{radius})^2$

$$36\pi = \pi(\text{AB})^2$$
$$36 = (\text{AB})^2$$
$$\sqrt{36} = \text{AB}$$
$$6 = \text{AB}$$

Since AB = 6, the distance from the origin to point B$=2(6) = 12$. Thus, point B has coordinates (12, 0), or $m = 12$.

18. **The correct answer is (B).** Let K = Ken's annual salary, and R = Rupert's annual salary.

$$\$16,000 = \frac{2}{3}\text{K}$$
$$\$48,000 = 2\text{K}$$
$$\$24,000 = \text{K}$$
Thus, $\quad \$24,000 = \frac{3}{5}\text{R}$
$$\$120,000 = 3\text{R}$$
$$\$40,000 = \text{R}$$

19. **The correct answer is (D).** 30% of 40% of 50 equals $60x$

Thus, $.30 \times .40 \times 50 = 60x$
$$6 = 60x$$
$$.1 = x$$

20. **The correct answer is (A).**

$$3 + 3(3)^4 = 3 + 3^5 \leftarrow \text{largest}$$
$$3^5 = 3^5$$
$$\frac{3^5}{3} = 3^4$$
$$3(3)^4 = 3^5$$
$$3^2(3)^3 - 3 = 3^5 - 3$$

21. **The correct answer is (D).**

Let x = the side of each square

The area of the rectangle $= (\text{length})(\text{width})$

$$60 = (5x)(x)$$
$$60 = 5x^2$$
$$12 = x^2$$
$$\sqrt{12} = x$$
$$\sqrt{4 \cdot 3} = x$$
$$2\sqrt{3} = x$$

Thus, the perimeter of the rectangle $= 12x$

$$= 12(2\sqrt{3})$$
$$= 24\sqrt{3}$$

22. **The correct answer is (C).** Let x = the average grade of the rest of the class (the remaining 60%).

$$84 = \frac{10\%(90) + 30\%(80) + 60\%(x)}{100\%}$$
$$84 = \frac{.10(90) + .30(80) + .60(x)}{1.00}$$
$$84 = \frac{9 + 24 + .60x}{1}$$
$$84 = 33 + .60x$$
$$51 = .60x$$
$$85 = x$$

23. **The correct answer is (E).** 30% of the monthly income is budgeted for rent. Thus, the percent budgeted for food is 20% of the 70% left, or $.20 \times 70\% = 14\%$. The percent budgeted for rent and food $= 30\% + 14\% = 44\%$

24. **The correct answer is (D).**

$$r = \sqrt{x^2 + y^2}$$

$$\frac{10}{3} = \sqrt{x^2 + \left(\frac{8}{3}\right)^2}$$

$$\frac{10}{3} = \sqrt{x^2 + \frac{64}{9}} \quad \text{(square both sides)}$$

$$\left(\frac{10}{3}\right)^2 = \left(\sqrt{x^2 + \frac{64}{9}}\right)^2$$

$$\frac{100}{9} = x^2 + \frac{64}{9}$$

$$\frac{36}{9} = x^2$$

$$4 = x^2$$

$$+2 \text{ or } -2 = x$$

25. **The correct answer is (E).**

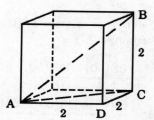

Using the Pythagorean theorem with right triangle ADC on the base of the cube,

$$(AD)^2 + (DC)^2 = (AC)^2$$

$$(2)^2 + (2)^2 = (AC)^2$$

$$4 + 4 = (AC)^2$$

$$8 = (AC)^2$$

$$\sqrt{8} = AC$$

Using the Pythagorean theorem with right triangle ACB,

$$(AC)^2 + (BC)^2 = (AB)^2$$

$$\left(\sqrt{8}\right)^2 + (2)^2 = (AB)^2$$

$$8 + 4 = (AB)^2$$

$$12 = (AB)^2$$

$$\sqrt{12} = AB$$

$$\sqrt{4 \cdot 3} = AB$$

$$2\sqrt{3} = AB$$

26. **The correct answer is (E).** The overtime rate of pay is If $1\frac{1}{2} \times \$12 = \$18$ hour.

Let x = the number of hours worked overtime.

$$\begin{array}{cc} \textit{Normal} & \textit{Overtime} \end{array}$$
$$\$141 = \$8(\$12) \;\; + \;\; x(\$18)$$
$$141 = 96 + 18x$$
$$45 = 18x$$
$$2\frac{1}{2}\,\text{hrs.} = x$$

Thus, the total time worked = 8 hrs. + $2\frac{1}{2}$ hrs. = 10 hrs. 30 min.

27. **The correct answer is (A).**

$$\begin{aligned} \text{Sales} &= 4 \text{ doz. oranges} \times \$.75 \text{ per orange} \\ &= 48 \text{ oranges} \times \$.75 \text{ per orange} \\ &= \$36 \end{aligned}$$
$$\begin{aligned} \text{Cost} &= 4 \text{ doz. oranges} \times \$6 \text{ per doz.} \\ &= \$24 \end{aligned}$$
$$\begin{aligned} \text{Thus, the Profit} &= \text{Sales} - \text{Cost} \\ &= \$36 - \$24 \\ &= \$12 \end{aligned}$$

$$\frac{\text{Profit}}{\text{Cost}} = \frac{\% \text{ of Profit}}{100\%}$$
$$\frac{\$12}{\$24} = \frac{x}{100} \;\; (\text{cross-multiply})$$
$$24x = 1200$$
$$x = 50\%$$

28. **The correct answer is (D).**

Let H = Howard's age now,

and H + 3 = Tony's age now.

Thus, H − 5 = Howard's age 5 years ago,

and H + 3 − 5 = H − 2 = Tony's age 5 years ago.

$$(H - 5) + (H - 2) = 59$$
$$2H - 7 = 59$$
$$2H = 66$$
$$H = 33$$

Thus, Tony is now H + 3 = 33 + 3 = 36.

29. **The correct answer is (B).** Since $\triangle$ ABC is inscribed in a semi-circle, angle B is a right angle. Using the Pythagorean theorem,

$$(AB)^2 + (BC)^2 = (AC)^2$$
$$x^2 + x^2 = (AC)^2$$
$$2x^2 = (AC)^2$$
$$\sqrt{2x^2} = AC$$
$$x\sqrt{2} = AC$$

Thus, the radius of the circle $= \dfrac{1}{2}(AC)$

$$= \dfrac{1}{2}\left(x\sqrt{2}\right)$$
$$= \dfrac{x\sqrt{2}}{2}$$

The area of circle O $= \pi(\text{radius})^2$

$$= \pi\left(\dfrac{x\sqrt{2}}{2}\right)^2$$
$$= \pi\left(\dfrac{x^2 \cdot 2}{4}\right)$$
$$= \dfrac{\pi x^2}{2}$$

The area of $\triangle$ABC $= \dfrac{1}{2}(AB)(BC)$

$$= \dfrac{1}{2}(x)(x)$$
$$= \dfrac{x^2}{2}$$

Thus, $\dfrac{\text{area of circle O}}{\text{area of } \triangle \text{ ABC}} = \dfrac{\dfrac{\pi x^2}{2}}{\dfrac{x^2}{2}}$

$$= \dfrac{\pi x^2}{2} \div \dfrac{x^2}{2}$$
$$= \dfrac{\pi x^2}{2} \cdot \dfrac{2}{x^2}$$
$$= \dfrac{\pi}{1}$$

30. **The correct answer is (C).** After the first quarter-mile, the number of miles remaining in the trip $= M - \dfrac{1}{4}$. This is equivalent to $4\left(M - \dfrac{1}{4}\right) = 4M - 1$ quarter-miles.

$$
\begin{aligned}
\text{Total Cost} \ = \ & \text{Cost of first quarter-mile + cost of} \\
& \text{remaining part} \\
= \ & C + \frac{C}{4}(4M - 1) \\
= \ & C + CM - \frac{C}{4} \\
= \ & C\left(1 + M - \frac{1}{4}\right) \\
= \ & C\left(M + \frac{3}{4}\right)
\end{aligned}
$$

PRACTICE TEST II

Directions: Solve each of the problems that follow, and then indicate the best answer in the appropriate space on the answer sheet.

Note: Figures that accompany problems in this test are intended to provide information useful in solving the problems. They are drawn as accurately as possible EXCEPT when it is stated in a specific problem that its figure is not drawn to scale. All figures lie in a plane unless otherwise stated. All numbers used are real numbers.

1. If 80% of R is 20% of S, then R is what percent of S?

   (A) 16%
   (B) 25%
   (C) 60%
   (D) 75%
   (E) 400%

2. Zachry travels 110 miles in 2 hours and 43 minutes. Which of the following is closest to his average rate of speed, in miles per hour?

   (A) 30
   (B) 35
   (C) 40
   (D) 45
   (E) 50

3. If $\frac{2}{3}$ of a number is 8, what is $\frac{5}{6}$ of the number?

   (A) 12
   (B) $4\frac{2}{7}$
   (C) 8
   (D) $13\frac{3}{7}$
   (E) 10

4. An item that normally sells for X dollars is marked down to Y dollars. What is the percent of markdown?

   (A) $\left(\dfrac{X-Y}{Y}\right)100$

   (B) $\left(\dfrac{Y-X}{Y}\right)100$

   (C) $(X-Y)100$

   (D) $\left(\dfrac{X-Y}{X}\right)100$

   (E) $\left(\dfrac{Y-X}{X}\right)100$

5. How many cubes, each having a surface area of 54 sq. in., will fit exactly inside a larger cube having a surface area of 216 sq. in.?

   (A) 8
   (B) 7
   (C) 6
   (D) 5
   (E) 4

6. In a promotional sale, Roxanne bought one item for its regular price and a second item for $1. If she paid $20 for both items, what fraction of the price of the first item is the price of the second item?

(A) $\dfrac{1}{20}$

(B) $\dfrac{1}{19}$

(C) $\dfrac{19}{20}$

(D) $\dfrac{1}{10}$

(E) $\dfrac{9}{10}$

7. After a $33\dfrac{1}{3}\%$ discount, a suit sells for $84. What is the price of the suit before the discount?

(A) $112
(B) $140
(C) $150
(D) $126
(E) $117

8. If $\dfrac{2x^3}{5} = \dfrac{25}{4}$, then $x^2 =$

(A) $\dfrac{5}{2}$

(B) $\dfrac{125}{12}$

(C) $\dfrac{125}{24}$

(D) $\dfrac{4}{25}$

(E) $\dfrac{25}{4}$

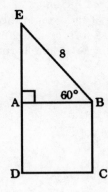

9. In the figure above, what is the area of square ABCD?

(A) 16
(B) 32
(C) 48
(D) $16\sqrt{3}$
(E) 8

10. $(0.5)(37.5)(0.04) =$

(A) $\dfrac{37}{50}$

(B) $\dfrac{5}{8}$

(C) $\dfrac{3}{4}$

(D) $\dfrac{3}{5}$

(E) $\dfrac{1}{2}$

11. Betty's 2004 salary is 12% higher than her 2003 salary. What is the ratio of her 2004 salary to her 2003 salary?

(A) $\dfrac{31}{28}$

(B) $\dfrac{19}{11}$

(C) $\dfrac{28}{25}$

(D) $\dfrac{27}{23}$

(E) $\dfrac{25}{22}$

12. In a race, three members of a relay team each run one lap. If they run at the rates of 10 ft./sec., 15 ft./sec., and 20 ft./sec, what fraction of the total time is run by the fastest runner?

(A) $\dfrac{3}{10}$

(B) $\dfrac{4}{15}$

(C) $\dfrac{4}{9}$

(D) $\dfrac{3}{13}$

(E) $\dfrac{2}{9}$

13. If the radius of a circle decreases by 10%, by what percent does its area decrease?

(A) 10%
(B) 11%
(C) 19%
(D) 20%
(E) 22%

14. Not including 1 and 24, what is the sum of the positive integer divisors of 24?

(A) 35
(B) 40
(C) 27
(D) 9
(E) 23

15. Laura invested a certain amount of money at $6\dfrac{1}{2}\%$ simple annual interest. At the end of 4 years, the amount was worth $7560. What was the original amount invested?

(A) $7100
(B) $6500
(C) $7000
(D) $6700
(E) $6000

16. If $A = \dfrac{Br}{3 + r}$, then $r =$

(A) $\dfrac{B}{3A}$

(B) $\dfrac{4A}{B}$

(C) $\dfrac{A - B}{3A}$

(D) $\dfrac{3A}{B - A}$

(E) $\dfrac{B - 3A}{A}$

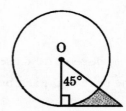

17. In the figure above, if the radius of circle 0 is 6, what is the area of the shaded part?

(A) $36 - \dfrac{3\pi}{2}$

(B) $18 - \dfrac{9\pi}{2}$

(C) $18 - \dfrac{3\pi}{2}$

(D) $18 - 3\pi$

(E) $36 - 9\pi$

18. A teacher changes his annual salary payment plan from 10 monthly checks to 12 monthly checks. If, after the change, he receives a gross monthly income of D dollars, what was the amount of his gross monthly income before the change?

(A) $\dfrac{5D}{6}$

(B) $\dfrac{7D}{6}$

(C) $\dfrac{6D}{5}$

(D) $\dfrac{5}{6D}$

(E) $\dfrac{6}{5D}$

19. Betsy invests a certain amount of money in stocks A, B, and C. If the amount she invests in A is three times the amount she invests in B and one-half the amount she invests in C, what percent of her money does she invest in A?

    (A) 25%
    (B) 30%
    (C) $33\frac{1}{3}$%
    (D) 40%
    (E) $66\frac{2}{3}$%

20. The area of a triangle is 30. If its base is 4 more than its height, what is the length of its height?

    (A) 10
    (B) 8
    (C) $\sqrt{15}$
    (D) 6
    (E) 4

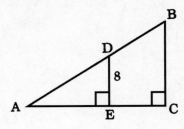

21. In the figure above, if AD = DB, what is the length of BC?

    (A) 32
    (B) 24
    (C) 12
    (D) 18
    (E) 16

22. The average height of three boys is 52 inches. If one boy grows 1 inch, the second boy grows 2 inches, and the third boy grows 3 inches, what is their new average height, in inches?

    (A) 54
    (B) 54.5
    (C) 55
    (D) 55.5
    (E) 56

23. In a recent survey, people were asked to state their preference for brand X, brand Y, or brand Z. If 15% said they preferred brand X, 2 out of 5 said they preferred brand Y, and 90 people said they preferred brand Z, how many people said they preferred brand X?

    (A) 200
    (B) 30
    (C) 50
    (D) 80
    (E) 60

24. If $(x + y)^2 = 17$, and $xy = 3$, then $x^2 + y^2 =$

   (A) 11
   (B) 14
   (C) 17
   (D) 20
   (E) 23

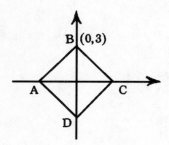

25. In the figure above, what is the area of square ABCD?

   (A) $8\sqrt{3}$
   (B) 9
   (C) 12
   (D) 18
   (E) $12\sqrt{2}$

26. A certain blend of coffee is made of coffee A, coffee B, and coffee C, in the ratio of 2:3:4 respectively. If 12 pounds of coffee B are used, what is the total weight of the blend, in pounds?

   (A) 30
   (B) 42
   (C) 66
   (D) 36
   (E) 38

27. On a bus carrying 30 passengers, 20% of the passengers are men. After 6 women get off the bus, what percent of the remaining passengers are men?

   (A) 23%
   (B) 30%
   (C) $33\frac{1}{3}\%$
   (D) 25%
   (E) 28%

28. If the sum of two numbers is 26, and their difference is 12, what is their product?

   (A) 228
   (B) 312
   (C) 100
   (D) 108
   (E) 133

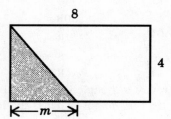

29. In the rectangle above, what is the ratio of the shaded area to the unshaded area?

   (A) $\dfrac{m}{16 - m}$

   (B) $\dfrac{2m}{16 - m}$

   (C) $\dfrac{16 - m}{m}$

   (D) $\dfrac{m}{16 + m}$

   (E) $\dfrac{m}{32 - m}$

30. If, working alone, Phil can complete a job in R hours, and Henny can complete the same job in S hours, how many hours would it take them to complete the job working together?

   (A) $R + S$

   (B) $\dfrac{1}{R + S}$

   (C) $\dfrac{RS}{R + S}$

   (D) $\dfrac{R + S}{RS}$

   (E) $\dfrac{RS}{R - S}$

ANSWERS AND EXPLANATIONS

1. **B**	6. **B**	11. **C**	16. **D**	21. **E**	26. **D**
2. **C**	7. **D**	12. **D**	17. **B**	22. **A**	27. **D**
3. **E**	8. **E**	13. **C**	18. **C**	23. **B**	28. **E**
4. **D**	9. **A**	14. **A**	19. **B**	24. **A**	29. **A**
5. **A**	10. **C**	15. **E**	20. **D**	25. **D**	30. **C**

1. **The correct answer is (B).** Since 80% of R is 20% of S,

$$.80R = .20S$$

$$\frac{R}{S} = \frac{.20}{.80}$$

$$\frac{R}{S} = \frac{1}{4}$$

Thus, $\frac{R}{S} = \frac{1}{4} \times 100\% = 25\%$

2. **The correct answer is (C).** 2 hours 43 minutes ≈ 2 hours 45 minutes

$$\approx 2\frac{3}{4} \text{ hours}$$

$$R = \frac{D}{T}$$

$$R \approx \frac{110 \text{ miles}}{2\frac{3}{4} \text{ hours}}$$

$$\approx \frac{110}{\frac{11}{4}}$$

$$\approx 110 \div \frac{11}{4}$$

$$\approx \frac{\overset{10}{\cancel{110}}}{1} \times \frac{4}{\cancel{11}}$$

$$\approx 40 \text{ miles per hour}$$

3. **The correct answer is (E).** Let x = the number.

$$\frac{2}{3}x = 8$$

$$2x = 24$$

$$x = 12$$

Thus, $\frac{5}{6}x = \frac{5}{6}(12) = 10$

393

4. **The correct answer is (D).** Let N = the percent of markdown.

$$\frac{\text{Amount of markdown}}{\text{Original value}} = \frac{\text{Percent of markdown}}{100\%}$$

$$\frac{X - Y}{X} = \frac{N}{100}$$

$$\left(\frac{X - Y}{X}\right)100 = N$$

5. **The correct answer is (A).**

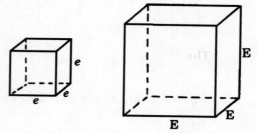

Each face of a cube has a surface area of $(\text{edge})^2$. Since there are 6 faces, the total surface area of a cube is $6 \cdot (\text{edge})^2$.

smaller cubes	*larger cubes*
$6e^2 = 54$	$6E^2 = 216$
$e^2 = 9$	$E^2 = 36$
$e = 3$	$E = 6$

The volume of each of the smaller cubes is $e^3 = (3)^3 = 27$, and the volume of the larger cube is $E^3 = (6)^3 = 216$.

Thus, the number of smaller cubes that fit inside the larger cube is $216 \div 27 = 8$.

6. **The correct answer is (B).** The price of the first item is $20 - 1 = 19$.

Thus, $\dfrac{\text{price of second item}}{\text{price of first item}} = \dfrac{1}{19}$

7.   **The correct answer is (D).** Let N = the original price of the suit.

Discount Price = $(100\% - \%$ of discount$) \times$ Original Price

$$\$84 = \left(100\% - 33\frac{1}{3}\%\right) \times N$$

$$84 = \left(66\frac{2}{3}\%\right) \times N$$

$$84 = \frac{2}{3}N$$

$$252 = 2N$$

$$\$126 = N$$

8.   **The correct answer is (E).**

$$\frac{2x^3}{5} = \frac{25}{4} \text{ (cross-multiply)}$$

$$8x^3 = 125$$

$$x^3 = \frac{125}{8}$$

$$x = \frac{5}{2}$$

Thus, $x^2 = \left(\frac{5}{2}\right)^2 = \frac{25}{4}$

9.   **The correct answer is (A).**

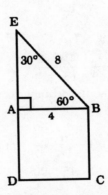

Since the sum of the angles of a triangle is 180°, angle E equals 30°. In a 30°−60°−90° right triangle, the side opposite the 30° angle is one-half the hypotenuse. Thus, AB = $\frac{1}{2}(8)$ = 4.

The area of square ABCD = $(AB)^2 = (4)^2 = 16$

10. **The correct answer is (C).** $(0.5)(37.5)(0.04)$

$$= \left(\frac{1}{2}\right)\left(37\frac{1}{2}\right)\left(\frac{4}{100}\right)$$

$$= \left(\frac{1}{\cancel{2}}\right)\left(\frac{\cancel{75}^{3}}{\cancel{2}}\right)\left(\frac{\cancel{4}^{1}}{\cancel{100}_{4}}\right)$$

$$= \frac{3}{4}$$

11. **The correct answer is (C).** $\dfrac{\text{Betty's 1981 salary}}{\text{Betty's 1980 salary}} = \dfrac{112\%}{100\%}$

$$= \frac{28}{25}$$

12. **The correct answer is (D).**

Let L = the length of one lap,

T$_1$ = the time of the first runner,

T$_2$ = the time of the second runner,

and T$_3$ = the time of the third runner.

$$\text{Time} = \frac{\text{Distance}}{\text{Rate}}$$

$$T_1 = \frac{L}{10} \qquad \bigg| \qquad T_2 = \frac{L}{15} \qquad \bigg| \qquad T_3 = \frac{L}{20}$$

$$T_{\text{total}} = T_1 + T_2 + T_3$$

$$= \frac{L}{10} + \frac{L}{15} + \frac{L}{20}$$

Since the third runner is the fastest,

$$\frac{T_3}{T_{\text{total}}} = \frac{\dfrac{L}{20}}{\dfrac{L}{10} + \dfrac{L}{15} + \dfrac{L}{20}} \quad \text{(multiply by 60)}$$

$$= \frac{\cancel{60}^{3} \cdot \dfrac{L}{\cancel{20}}}{\cancel{60}^{6} \cdot \dfrac{L}{\cancel{10}} + \cancel{60}^{4} \cdot \dfrac{L}{\cancel{15}} + \cancel{60}^{3} \cdot \dfrac{L}{\cancel{20}}}$$

$$= \frac{3L}{6L + 4L + 3L}$$

$$= \frac{3\cancel{L}}{13\cancel{L}}$$

$$= \frac{3}{13}$$

13.　**The correct answer is (C).** Let R = the radius of the original circle. Since the radius decreases by 10%, the new radius is (100% − 10%)R = (90%)R = .90R
The area of the original circle $= \pi R^2$
The area of the new circle $= \pi(.90R)^2 = .81\pi R^2$
The change in area $= .81\pi R^2 - \pi R^2 = -.19\pi R^2$
This represents a decrease of 19%.

14.　**The correct answer is (A).** Not including 1 and 24, the positive integer divisors of 24 are 2, 3, 4, 6, 8, and 12. Their sum is 2 + 3 + 4 + 6 + 8 + 12 = 35.

15.
The correct answer is (E). The interest rate for the 4 years $= 4\left(6\dfrac{1}{2}\%\right) = 26\%$.

Let A = the original amount invested.
The value of the investment after 4 years = (100% + 26%) × original amount invested

$$\$7560 = (126\%) \times A$$
$$\$7560 = 1.26A$$
$$\$6000 = A$$

16.　**The correct answer is (D).**

$$A = \frac{Br}{3+r}$$
$$\frac{A}{1} = \frac{Br}{3+r} \quad (\text{cross-multiply})$$
$$Br = A(3+r)$$
$$Br = 3A + Ar$$
$$Br - Ar = 3A$$
$$(B-A)r = 3A$$
$$r = \frac{3A}{B-A}$$

17.   **The correct answer is (B).**

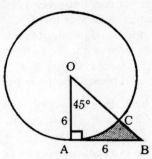

Angle B is also 45°, and thus △OAB is an isosceles triangle having AB = OA = 6.

$$\text{The area of } \triangle OAB = \frac{1}{2}(OA)(AB)$$

$$= \frac{1}{2}(6)(6)$$

$$= 18$$

$$\text{The area of sector } OAC = \frac{45°}{360°} \cdot \pi(6)^2$$

$$= \frac{1}{8} \cdot 36\pi$$

$$= \frac{9\pi}{2}$$

The area of the shaded part = the area of △OAB − the area of sector OAC

$$= 18 - \frac{9\pi}{2}$$

18.   **The correct answer is (C).** Let M = the gross monthly income before the change.
The gross annual income before the change was 10 · M.
The gross annual income after the change is 12 · D.
Since the gross annual income is the same,

$$10 \cdot M = 12 \cdot D$$

$$M = \frac{12D}{10}$$

$$M = \frac{6D}{5}$$

19.   **The correct answer is (B).** Let A = the amount invested in stock A,
B = the amount invested in stock B,
and C = the amount invested in stock C.

$$A = 3B \quad \text{or} \quad B = \frac{A}{3}$$

$$A = \frac{1}{2}C \quad \text{or} \quad C = 2A$$

Fraction invested in $A = \dfrac{A}{A + B + C}$

$$\left(\text{substitute } B = \frac{A}{3} \text{ and } C = 2A \right)$$

$$= \frac{A}{A + \dfrac{A}{3} + 2A} \quad \text{(multiply by 3)}$$

$$= \frac{3 \cdot A}{3 \cdot A + 3 \cdot \dfrac{A}{3} + 3 \cdot 2A}$$

$$= \frac{3A}{3A + A + 6A}$$

$$= \frac{3A}{10A}$$

$$= \frac{3}{10}$$

Thus, the percent invested in $A = \dfrac{3}{10} \times 100\% = 30\%$.

20.   **The correct answer is (D).** Let H = the height of the triangle, and H + 4 = the base of the triangle.

The area of the triangle $= \dfrac{1}{2}$ (base)(height)

$$30 = \frac{1}{2}(H + 4)(H)$$

$$60 = (H + 4)(H)$$

$$60 = H^2 + 4H$$

$$0 = H^2 + 4H - 60$$

$$0 = (H + 10)(H - 6)$$

$$
\begin{array}{c|c}
H + 10 = 0 & H - 6 = 0 \\
H = -10 & H = 6
\end{array}
$$

Since the height must be a positive number, H = 6.

21. **The correct answer is (E).**
Since $\triangle$ BCA is similar to $\triangle$ DEA,

$$\frac{BC}{DE} = \frac{BA}{DA}$$

$$\frac{BC}{8} = \frac{2x}{x}$$

$$BC = 16$$

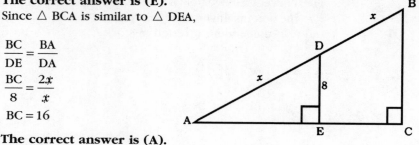

22. **The correct answer is (A).**

$$Average = \frac{Sum}{N}$$

$$52 \text{ inches} = \frac{Sum}{3}$$

$$156 \text{ inches} = Sum \text{ of the heights}$$

After the boys grow, the sum of their heights increases by $1 + 2 + 3 = 6$ inches. Thus, the new sum of their heights is $156 + 6 = 162$ inches.

$$The \text{ new average} = \frac{The \text{ new sum}}{3}$$

$$= \frac{162}{3}$$

$$= 54 \text{ inches}$$

23. **The correct answer is (B).** 15% preferred brand X.

$\frac{2}{5} = 40\%$ preferred brand Y.

Thus, $100\% - (15\% + 40\%) = 45\%$ preferred brand Z.

Let T = the total number of people surveyed. Since 90 people preferred brand Z,

$$\frac{Part}{Whole} = \frac{Percent}{100\%}$$

$$\frac{90}{T} = \frac{45}{100} \text{ (cross-multiply)}$$

$$45T = 9000$$

$$T = 200 \text{ people}$$

Thus, brand X was preferred by 15% of 200 $= .15 \times 200 = 30$

24. **The correct answer is (A).**

$$(x + y)^2 = 17$$

$$(x + y)(x + y) = 17$$

$$x^2 + 2xy + y^2 = 17$$

Since $xy = 3$,

$$x^2 + 2(3) + y^2 = 17$$

$$x^2 + 6 + y^2 = 17$$

$$x^2 + y^2 = 11$$

25.   **The correct answer is (D).**
       Since ABCD is a square, the coordinates
       of point C are (3,0).
       Using the Pythagorean theorem,

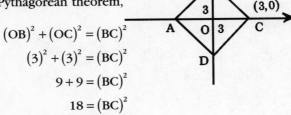

$$(OB)^2 + (OC)^2 = (BC)^2$$
$$(3)^2 + (3)^2 = (BC)^2$$
$$9 + 9 = (BC)^2$$
$$18 = (BC)^2$$

The area of square ABCD $= (BC)^2$
$$= 18$$

26.   **The correct answer is (D).** Let $2x =$ the number of pounds of coffee A,
       $3x =$ the number of pounds of coffee B,
       and $4x =$ the number of pounds of coffee C.
       Since 12 pounds of coffee B are used,

$$3x = 12$$
$$x = 4$$

Thus, the total weight $= 2x + 3x + 4x$
$$= 9x$$
$$= 9(4)$$
$$= 36 \text{ pounds}$$

27.   **The correct answer is (D).** The number of men on the bus is 20% of 30 = .20 ×
       30 = 6. After 6 women get off the bus, the total number of people on the bus is
       30 − 6 = 24.
       Let $x =$ the percent of men on the bus.

$$\frac{\text{Part}}{\text{Whole}} = \frac{\text{Percent}}{100\%}$$
$$\frac{6}{24} = \frac{x}{100} \text{ (cross-multiply)}$$
$$24x = 600$$
$$x = 25\%$$

28. **The correct answer is (E).** Let x = one of the numbers, and y = the other number.

$$x + y = 26$$
$$\underline{x - y = 12}$$
$$2x \quad = 38$$
$$x = 19$$

(substitute into $x + y = 26$)

$$x + y = 26$$
$$19 + y = 26$$
$$y = 7$$

Thus, the product of the numbers = $x \cdot y$
$$= 19 \cdot 7$$
$$= 133$$

29. **The correct answer is (A).**

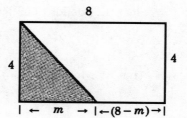

The area of the shaded triangle $= \dfrac{1}{2}(\text{base})(\text{height})$

$$= \dfrac{1}{2}(m)(4)$$

$$= 2m$$

The area of the unshaded trapezoid $= \left(\dfrac{\text{base}_1 + \text{base}_2}{2} \right)\text{height}$

$$= \left(\dfrac{(8-m)+8}{2} \right)4$$

$$= \left(\dfrac{16-m}{\cancel{2}} \right)\cancel{4}^{2}$$

$$= 32 - 2m$$

Thus, $\dfrac{\text{shaded area}}{\text{unshaded area}} = \dfrac{2m}{32 - 2m}$ (divide by 2)

$$= \dfrac{m}{16 - m}$$

30. **The correct answer is (C).** Let H = the number of hours it would take Henny and Phil to complete the job working together.

Phil   *Henny*

$$\frac{H}{R} + \frac{H}{S} = 1 \ (\text{multiply by RS})$$

$$RS \cdot \frac{H}{R} + RS \cdot \frac{H}{S} = RS \cdot 1$$

$$SH + RH = RS$$
$$(S + R)H = RS$$
$$H = \frac{RS}{S + R}$$

Chapter 7
DATA SUFFICIENCY QUESTIONS

A data sufficiency question is a special type of math question in which, instead of being asked to solve a problem, you are asked only to determine whether there is *sufficient information* to solve the problem. This type of question is usually found on the GMAT.

The format of each question is the same: a question, containing *incomplete* information, is followed by two statements, providing additional information. After analyzing the information in these statements, you must decide whether either or both of the statements provide *enough* additional information to answer the question. Based on your decision, you then choose one of the answers given in the directions shown below. These directions accompany all data sufficiency questions.

Each of the data sufficiency problems below consists of a question and two statements, labeled (1) and (2), in which certain data are given. You have to decide whether the data given in the statements are sufficient for answering the question. Using the data given in the statements plus your knowledge of mathematics and everyday facts (such as the number of days in July or the meaning of counterclockwise), you are to blacken space:

(A) if statement (1) ALONE is sufficient, but statement (2) alone is not sufficient to answer the question asked;

(B) if statement (2) ALONE is sufficient, but statement (1) alone is not sufficient to answer the question asked;

(C) if BOTH statements (1) and (2) TOGETHER are sufficient to answer the question asked, but NEITHER statement ALONE is sufficient.

(D) if EACH statement ALONE is sufficient to answer the question asked;

(E) if statements (1) and (2) TOGETHER are NOT sufficient to answer the question asked, and additional data specific to the problem are needed.

NOTE: A figure in a data sufficiency problem will conform to the information given in the question, but will not necessarily conform to the additional information given in statements (1) and (2).

To obtain a better understanding of the choices, A−E, let us look at five examples. Note that Example 1 has been designed so that choice A is the correct answer, Example 2 so that choice B is the correct answer, Example 3 so that choice C is the correct answer, and so on.

Example 1

In triangle ABC, what is the value of x?

    (1) $y + z = 140$

    (2) $z = 60$

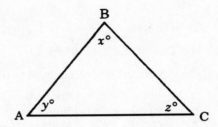

Analysis

    Statement (1)   Since $x + y + z = 180$, x must equal $180 - 140$, or 40. (Sufficient)

    Statement (2)   Without a value for y, we cannot determine x. (Insufficient)

Answer

A—Statement (1) alone is sufficient.

Example 2

Marybeth bought a piano on an installment plan. How much does she still owe?

    (1)   She made a downpayment of $300.

    (2)   She still owes 12 monthly payments of $100 each.

Analysis

    Statement (1)   Without knowing the full price of the piano, we cannot determine what she still owes. (Insufficient)

    Statement (2)   Since she still owes 12 payments of $100 each, she still owes $1200. (Sufficient)

Answer

B—Statement (2) alone is sufficient.

Example 3

What is the value of x?

    (1) $x + y = 6$

    (2) $x - y = 4$

Analysis

    Statement (1)   Without a specific value for y, we cannot determine a specific value for x. (Insufficient)

    Statement (2)   Same as above. (Insufficient)

Statements (1) and (2) together By adding the two equations together, we get $2x = 10$, or $x = 5$. (Sufficient)

Answer
C—Both statements together are sufficient.

Example 4
What is the radius of circle M?

    (1) The area of circle M is 9π.

    (2) The circumference of circle M is 6π.

Analysis

Statement (1)   Since the area of a circle equals πr^2, we can set $\pi r^2 = 9\pi$, and determine that $r^2 = 9$, or $r = 3$. (Sufficient)

Statement (2)   Since the circumference of a circle equals πd, we can set $\pi d = 6\pi$, and determine that $d = 6$, or $r = 3$. (Sufficient)

Answer
D—Each statement alone is sufficient.

Example 5
If A and B are points on the *x*-axis, what is the area of triangle ABC?

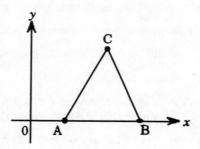

    (1) The coordinates of A are (2,0).

    (2) The coordinates of B are (5,0).

Analysis

Statement (1)   Without knowing the lengths of the base and height of the triangle, we cannot determine its area. (Insufficient)

Statement (2)   Same as above. (Insufficient)

Statements (1) and (2) together: Using the two statements together, we can determine that the length of base AB is 3. Without the coordinates of point C, however, we cannot determine the length of the height. (Insufficient)

Answer
E—Both statements alone, and together, are insufficient.

TIPS FOR ANSWERING DATA SUFFICIENCY QUESTIONS

1. Since the answers A−E are the same on every test, you can save valuable time during the test by memorizing their meanings in advance. In the summary below, S means that the statement (or combination of statements) is Sufficient, and I means that the statement (or combination of statements) is Insufficient.

Data Sufficiency Answers

Answer A	Answer B	Answer C	Answer D	Answer E
(1) S	(1) I	(1) I ⎫ S	(1) S	(1) I ⎫ I
(2) I	(2) S	(2) I ⎭	(2) S	(2) I ⎭

---

2. Remember that each of the additional statements must be considered *alone*, before both statements can be considered together. When considering statement (1) alone, you should avoid looking ahead at statement (2). When considering statement (2) alone, you must disregard the information just looked at in statement (1).

3. Sometimes one statement alone is sufficient, and both statements together are *also* sufficient. Although this may appear to be a conflict between either choice A or B and choice C, it is not. Choice C cannot be the answer since it includes the phrase, "... but NEITHER statement ALONE is sufficient."

4. If you are certain about a part of the additional information, but are unsure about another part, you can logically eliminate several answers, and thus greatly improve your chances of guessing correctly. For example, if you are certain that statement (1) is sufficient, but are unsure about statement (2), then the only possible answers are A or D. Similarly, if you are certain that statement (2) is sufficient, but are unsure about statement (1), then the only possible answers are B or D. Furthermore, if you are certain that each statement alone is insufficient, but are unsure about both statements together, then the only possible answers are C or E. These situations are depicted below.

Answer A or D
(1) S
(2) ??

Answer B or D
(1) ??
(2) S

Answer C or E
(1) I ⎫ ??
(2) I ⎭

Note that in each of these situations, the chances of guessing correctly have been improved from the usual 1 out of 5 to 1 out of 2.

THE "WHAT IS THE VALUE OF...?" TYPE OF QUESTION

Many of the data sufficiency questions on the GMAT ask for the *value* of a certain quantity. Remember that for this type of question a statement (or combination of statements) is sufficient *only* if it determines a *single numerical value*. Statements that determine two or more values, a range of values, or a maximum or minimum value are all insufficient.

Example 1

What is the value of x?

    (1) $2x = 6$

    (2) $3x < 12$

Analysis

Statement (1)   Since x can only be 3, statement (1) is sufficient.

Statement (2)   Since x can be any number less than 4, statement (2) is insufficient.

Answer

A—Statement (1) alone is sufficient.

Example 2

What is the value of x?

    (1) $x = 2y$

    (2) $x^2 = 9$

Analysis

Statement (1)   Since x varies with y, and therefore can be any number, statement (1) is insufficient.

Statement (2)   Since x can be *two* possible numbers, $+3$ or -3, statement (2) is insufficient.

Statements (1) and (2) together: Same as above. Therefore, statements (1) and (2) together are still insufficient.

Answer

E—Both statements together are insufficient, and additional data is needed.

Example 3

What is the value of x?

    (1) $x + y = 6$

    (2) $x - y = 4$

Analysis

Statement (1)   Without knowing the value of y, you cannot determine a single numerical value for x. Therefore, statement (1) is insufficient.

Statement (2)   Same as above. Therefore, statement (2) is insufficient.

Statements (1) and (2) together: When you add the two equations together, you get $2x = 10$, or $x = 5$. Since x can only be 5, statements (1) and (2) together are sufficient.

Answer

C—Neither statement alone is sufficient, but both statements together are sufficient.

THE "IS...?" TYPE OF QUESTION

The other type of data sufficiency question on the GMAT asks whether a certain quantity is some specific value or whether some geometric figure is a specific shape (for example, "Is $x = 0$?", or "Is $\triangle ABC$ a right triangle?") Remember that for this type of question you must interpret the question "Is . . .?" to mean *Does it have to be . . .?* rather than simply "Could it be . . .?"

A good way to approach this type of question is to first read the additional statement (or combination of statements) and then read the "Is...?" question. If your response to this question is "Yes, it has to be.", then the statement is sufficient. If your response is "No, it doesn't have to be.", then the statement is insufficient.

Example 1

Is $x = 0$?

    (1) The sum of x and 4 is 4.

    (2) The product of x and 0 is 0.

Analysis

Statement (1) First read the statement, "The sum of x and 4 is 4", or $x + 4 = 4$. Then read the question, "Is $x = 0$?" as "Does x have to equal 0?" Since the response to this question is "Yes, x has to equal 0", then statement (1) is sufficient.

Statement (2) First read the statement, "The product of x and 0 is 0.", or $x \cdot 0 = 0$. Then read the question, "Is $x = 0$?" as "Does x have to equal 0?" Since the response to this question is "No, x does not have to equal 0", then statement (2) is insufficient.

Answer

A—Statement (1) alone is sufficient.

Example 2

Is $\triangle ABC$ a right triangle?

    (1) The measure of $\angle A$ is 40°.

    (2) The measure of $\angle C$ is 50°.

Analysis

Statement (1) Since $\angle B$ and $\angle C$ can be any two angles whose sum is 140°, $\triangle ABC$ does not have to be a right triangle. Therefore, statement (1) is insufficient.

Statement (2) Since $\angle A$ and $\angle B$ can be any two angles whose sum is 130°, $\triangle ABC$ does not have to be a right triangle. Therefore, statement (2) is insufficient.

Statements (1) and (2) together: Since the sum of the measures of $\angle A$ and $\angle C$ is 90°, $\angle B$ measures $180° - 90° = 90°$, and, thus, $\triangle ABC$ must be a right triangle. Therefore, statements (1) and (2) together are sufficient.

Answer

C—Neither statement alone is sufficient, but both statements together are sufficient.

PRACTICE TEST III

Directions: Each problem that follows consists of a question and two statements, labeled (1) and (2), in which certain data are given. You have to decide whether the data given in the statements are sufficient for answering the question, and on the answer sheet blacken space:

(A) if statement (1) ALONE is sufficient, but statement (2) ALONE is not sufficient;

(B) if statement (2) ALONE is sufficient, but statement (1) ALONE is not sufficient;

(C) if BOTH statements TOGETHER are sufficient, but NEITHER statement ALONE is sufficient;

(D) if EACH statement ALONE is sufficient;

(E) if statements (1) and (2) TOGETHER are NOT sufficient.

1. What was the average grade in a class of 20 students?

    (1) The lowest grade was 60% and the highest grade was 96%.
    (2) The average grade of 10 students was 72%, and the average grade of the other 10 students was 88%.

2. How old is Dave now?

    (1) Twelve years ago he was two-thirds as old as he is now.
    (2) In ten years he will be twice as old as he was 13 years ago.

3. What is the perimeter of $\triangle RST$?

    (1) $RS = 5$
    (2) $\triangle RST$ is isosceles.

4. What was the percent of profit made on a house sold at $50,000?

    (1) The house cost $40,000.
    (2) The profit was $10,000.

5. A board 17 inches long is cut into 3 pieces. What is the length of the longest piece?

    (1) One piece is 9 inches long.
    (2) One piece is 5 inches long.

6. What is the value of $x^2 + y^2$?

    (1) $x + 2y = 11$
    (2) $2x + y = 10$

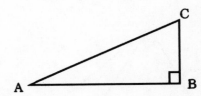

7. In the right triangle above, the ratio of the length of AB to the length of BC is 3 to 1. What is the perimeter of the triangle?

    (1) $BC = 6$
    (2) The area of the triangle is 54.

8. M is what percent of N?

    (1) $M + N = 14$
    (2) $4M = 3N$

9. How many children attended the matinee?

    (1) Two hundred people attended the matinee.
    (2) There were three times as many children as adults that attended the matinee.

10. What is the value of $\frac{x}{y}$?

    (1) $3x = 2y$
    (2) $x + y = 20$

11. In the figure above, is $x = y$?

    (1) $y = t$
    (2) $s = t$

12. At a party of 30 people, how many people had both brown hair and blue eyes?

    (1) 18 people had brown hair.
    (2) 10 people had blue eyes.

13. What is the value of $a^2 - b^2$?

    (1) $a + b = 0$
    (2) $a - b = 8$

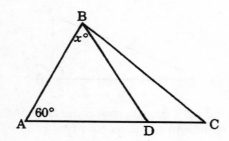

14. In the figure above, what is the value of x?

    (1) Angle BDC equals 110°.
    (2) Angle BCD equals 50°.

15. Dave, Steve, and Doug played a game of Scrabble. Who had the highest score?

    (1) Doug's score was higher than one of the scores and lower than the other score.
    (2) Doug's score was closer to Dave's score than it was to Steve's score.

16. What is the value of $2a + 3b$?

    (1) $a + b = 3$
    (2) $10a + 15b = 35$

17. Is a triangle with sides r, s, and t a right triangle?

    (1) $r^2 + s^2 = 9$
    (2) $t = 3$

18. Of its net monthly income, a family budgets 25% for rent and 20% for food. How much money is budgeted each month for food?

    (1) The family's net monthly income is $1,200.
    (2) The family budgets $300 each month for rent.

19. In an election for club president there are three candidates, A, B, and C. What fraction of the total vote does candidate A receive?

    (1) C receives $\frac{3}{4}$ as many votes as B.
    (2) B receives $\frac{2}{3}$ as many votes as A.

20. What is the value of x?

    (1) $x^2 = 9$
    (2) $x^4 = 81$

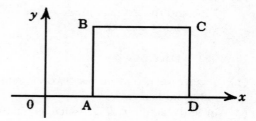

21. In the figure above, what is the area of rectangle ABCD?

    (1) The coordinates of point A are (2,0).
    (2) The coordinates of point C are (6,3).

22. Is x an odd integer?

    (1) $2x$ is an even integer.
    (2) $2x + 1$ is an odd integer.

23. Is $xy > 0$?

    (1) $x^4y^5 < 0$
    (2) $x^3y^2 < 0$

24. After a diet, Moira weighed 108 pounds. What percent of her former weight did she lose?

    (1) Before the diet, Moira weighed 120 pounds.
    (2) Moira lost 12 pounds during the diet.

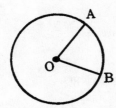

25. In the figure above, circle O has a radius of 3. What is the area of sector AOB?

    (1) Angle AOB equals 60°.
    (2) The area of circle O is 9π.

26. How long would it take pipe A and pipe B operating together to fill a swimming pool?

    (1) Operating alone, pipe A takes 3 hours to fill the swimming pool.
    (2) Operating alone, pipe B takes 6 hours to fill the swimming pool.

27. What is the smallest of 4 consecutive odd integers?

    (1) The sum of the integers is 32.
    (2) The average of the smallest integer and the largest integer is 8.

28. In an election for team captain, 3 players received votes. If 20 votes were cast and at least 11 votes were needed to win, did Steve win the election?

    (1) Neither of Steve's opponents received more than 4 votes.
    (2) Steve received at least 5 votes more than either of his opponents.

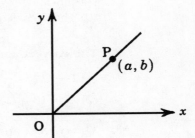

29. In the figure above, what is the length of OP?

    (1) $\dfrac{a}{b} = 1$
    (2) $a = b = 1$

30. M is an integer. Is M divisible by 6?

    (1) M is divisible by 3.
    (2) M is divisible by 12.

ANSWERS AND EXPLANATIONS

1. **B**	6. **C**	11. **B**	16. **B**	21. **C**	26. **C**
2. **D**	7. **D**	12. **E**	17. **C**	22. **E**	27. **D**
3. **E**	8. **B**	13. **A**	18. **D**	23. **C**	28. **A**
4. **D**	9. **C**	14. **A**	19. **C**	24. **D**	29. **B**
5. **A**	10. **A**	15. **E**	20. **E**	25. **A**	30. **B**

1. **The correct answer is (B).**
   (1) The average grade cannot be determined from the lowest and highest grade. (Insufficient)
   (2) The average grade $= \dfrac{10(72\%) + 10(88\%)}{20} = 80\%$. (Sufficient)

2. **The correct answer is (D).** Let D = Dave's age now.
   (1) $D - 12 = \dfrac{2}{3}$, which gives D = 36. (Sufficient)
   (2) $D + 10 = 2(D - 13)$, which gives D = 36. (Sufficient)

3. **The correct answer is (E).** (1) Without the lengths of the other two sides, the perimeter cannot be determined. (Insufficient)
   (2) Without the lengths of the sides, the perimeter cannot be determined. (Insufficient)
   (1) + (2) The length of at least one side is still unknown. (Insufficient)

4. **The correct answer is (D).** $\dfrac{\text{Profit}}{\text{Cost}} = \dfrac{\text{Percent of Profit}}{100\%}$
   (1) $\dfrac{\$50,000 - \$40,000}{\$40,000} = \dfrac{x}{100}$, which gives
   $x = 25\%$. (Sufficient)

   (2) $\dfrac{\$10,000}{\$50,000 - \$10,000} = \dfrac{x}{100}$, which gives
   $x = 25\%$. (Sufficient)

5. **The correct answer is (A).** (1) After cutting one piece of 9 inches, the other two pieces are cut from a piece 8 inches long, thus making each piece less than the first piece of 9 inches. (Sufficient)
   (2) After cutting one piece of 5 inches, the other two pieces are cut from a piece 12 inches long. This piece can be cut in a variety of different ways, thus making it impossible to determine the length of the longest piece. (Insufficient)

6. **The correct answer is (C).** (1) Without a specific value of x or y, the value of $x^2 + y^2$ cannot be determined. (Insufficient)
   (2) Same as above. (Insufficient)
   (1) + (2) The two equations can be solved simultaneously, giving $x = 3$ and $y = 4$, and thus $x^2 + y^2 = 3^2 + 4^2 = 25$. (Sufficient)

7.   **The correct answer is (D).**

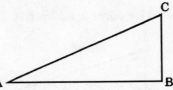

$$\frac{AB}{BC} = \frac{3}{1} \quad \text{or}$$

$$AB = 3BC$$

(1) If BC = 6, then AB = 3(6) = 18. Using the Pythagorean theorem, $6^2 + 18^2 = (AC)^2$, which gives $AC = 6\sqrt{10}$. Thus, the perimeter = $6 + 18 + 6\sqrt{10} = 24 + 6\sqrt{10}$. (Sufficient)

(2) The area of triangle ABC = $\frac{1}{2}$(AB)(BC). (Substitute AB = 3BC)

$$54 = \frac{1}{2}(3BC)(BC)$$

$$54 = \frac{3}{2}(BC)^2$$

$$36 = (BC)^2$$

$$6 = BC$$

Then, continuing as in (1), AB = 18, AC = $6\sqrt{10}$, and the perimeter = $24 + 6\sqrt{10}$. (Sufficient)

8.   **The correct answer is (B).** (1) M cannot be determined as a fractional part of N. (Insufficient)

(2) 4M = 3N gives $M = \frac{3}{4}N$, or M is 75% of N. (Sufficient)

9.   **The correct answer is (C).** (1) Without knowing the number of adults that attended, the number of children cannot be determined. (Insufficient)
(2) Without knowing the total number of people that attended, the number of children cannot be determined. (Insufficient)
(1) + (2) Let A = the number of adults that attended, and 3A = the number of children that attended.

$$A + 3A = 200$$

$$4A = 200$$

$$A = 50$$

Thus, the number of children that attended is 3A = 150. (Sufficient)

10. **The correct answer is (A).** (1) $3x = 2y$, which gives $\frac{x}{y} = \frac{2}{3}$. (Sufficient)

(2) A numerical value for $\frac{x}{y}$ cannot be determined from the equation $x + y = 20$. (Insufficient)

11. **The correct answer is (B).**

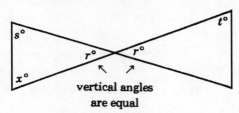

(1) Without knowing the relationship between s and t, the relationship between x and y cannot be determined. (Insufficient)

(2) In each triangle, the sum of the angles is 180°. Since $s = t$, and $r = r$, then the remaining angles must be equal. Thus, $x = y$. (Sufficient)

12. **The correct answer is (E).** (1) No information is given about the number of people with blue eyes. (Insufficient)

(2) No information is given about the number of people with brown hair. (Insufficient)

(1) + (2) No information is given about the number of people with neither brown hair nor blue eyes. (Insufficient)

13. **The correct answer is (A).** $a^2 - b^2 = (a + b)(a - b)$

(1) Since $a + b = 0$, $a^2 - b^2 = (0)(a - b) = 0$. (Sufficient)

(2) Since $a - b = 8$, $a^2 - b^2 = (a + b)(8)$. Without the value of $a + b$, the value of $a^2 - b^2$ cannot be determined. (Insufficient)

14. **The correct answer is (A).**

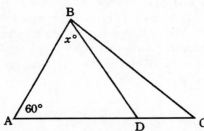

(1) If angle $BDC = 110°$, then angle $ADB = 70°$, and thus $x = 180 - (60 + 70) = 50$. (Sufficient)

(2) No other angle can be determined from this information. (Insufficient)

15. **The correct answer is (E).** (1) This statement only determines that Doug had the middle score. (Insufficient)

(2) This statement does not determine who had the highest score. (Insufficient)

(1) + (2) Same as above. (Insufficient)

16. **The correct answer is (B).** (1) Without a specific value of a or b, the value of $2a + 3b$ cannot be determined. (Insufficient)

(2) Dividing both sides of the equation $10a + 15b = 35$ by 5 gives $2a + 3b = 7$. (Sufficient)

17. **The correct answer is (C).** (1) Without knowing the value of t, the specific type of triangle cannot be determined. (Insufficient)

    (2) Without knowing the values of r and s, the specific type of triangle cannot be determined. (Insufficient)

    (1) + (2) Since $r^2 + s^2 = 9$, and $t^2 = 9$, then $r^2 + s^2 = t^2$. If the sides of a triangle satisfy the Pythagorean relationship, the triangle is a right triangle. (Sufficient)

18. **The correct answer is (D).** (1) 20% of $1,200 = .20 \times \$1,200 = \$240$ for food. (Sufficient)

    $$(2) \quad \frac{\text{Part}}{\text{Whole}} = \frac{\text{Percent}}{100\%}$$

    $$\frac{\$300}{\text{W}} = \frac{25}{100}$$

    $$25\text{W} = \$30,000$$

    $$\text{W} = \$1,200 \text{ net monthly income}$$

    Then, proceeding as in (1), 20% of $1,200 = \$240$ for food. (Sufficient)

19. **The correct answer is (C).** (1) No information is given relating the number of votes received by A to the number of votes received by either B or C. (Insufficient)

    (2) No information is given relating the number of votes received by C to the number of votes received by either A or B. (Insufficient)

    (1) + (2) Since $C = \frac{3}{4} B$ and $B = \frac{2}{3} A$, then

    $$C = \frac{3}{4}\left(\frac{2}{3}A\right) = \frac{1}{2}A$$

    Fraction of vote received by A

    $$= \frac{A}{A + B + C}$$

    $$\left(\text{substitute } B = \frac{2}{3}A \text{ and } C = \frac{1}{2}A\right)$$

    $$= \frac{A}{A + \frac{2}{3}A + \frac{1}{2}A} \text{ (multiply by 6)}$$

    $$= \frac{6A}{6A + 4A + 3A}$$

    $$= \frac{6\cancel{A}}{13\cancel{A}}$$

    $$= \frac{6}{13} \text{ (Sufficient)}$$

20. **The correct answer is (E).** (1) Since $x^2 = 9$, x can be either $+3$ or -3. (Insufficient)

    (2) Since $x^4 = 81$, x can be either $+3$ or -3. (Insufficient)

    (1) + (2) Same as above. (Insufficient)

21. **The correct answer is (C).**

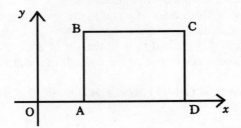

(1) Without knowing the length and width of the rectangle, the area cannot be determined. (Insufficient)

(2) Same as above. (Insufficient)

(1) + (2) Since the coordinates of A are (2, 0), and the coordinates of C are (6, 3), the length, AD, equals $6 - 2 = 4$, and the width, CD, equals $3 - 0 = 3$. Thus, the area of the rectangle equals (AD) (CD) $= (4)(3) = 12$. (Sufficient)

22. **The correct answer is (E).** (1) $2x$ is always an even integer, for *any* integer value of x. (Insufficient)

(2) $2x + 1$ is always an odd integer, for *any* integer value of x. (Insufficient)

(1) + (2) Same as above. (Insufficient)

23. **The correct answer is (C).** (1) This statement only determines that, since x^4 is always positive, y^5, and thus y, must be negative. (Insufficient)

(2) This statement only determines that, since y^2 is always positive, x^3, and thus x, must be negative. (Insufficient)

(1) + (2) Since y must be negative and x must be negative, the product xy must be positive, or $xy > 0$. (Sufficient)

24. **The correct answer is (D).** $\dfrac{\text{Amount of loss}}{\text{original weight}} = \dfrac{\text{Percent of loss}}{100\%}$

(1) $\dfrac{120 - 108}{120} = \dfrac{x}{100}$, which gives

$x = 10\%$. (Sufficient)

(2) $\dfrac{12}{108 + 12} = \dfrac{x}{100}$, which gives

$x = 10\%$. (Sufficient)

25. **The correct answer is (A).**

(1) Since angle AOB = 60°, then the area of sector AOB is $\dfrac{60°}{360°} = \dfrac{1}{6}$ of the area of the full circle. Thus,

$$
\begin{aligned}
\text{the area of sector AOB} &= \frac{1}{6} \cdot \pi \left(\text{radius}\right)^2 \\
&= \frac{1}{6}\pi(3)^2 \\
&= \frac{3}{2}\pi \ \text{(Sufficient)}
\end{aligned}
$$

(2) Without knowing the measure of angle AOB, the area of sector AOB cannot be determined. (Insufficient)

26. **The correct answer is (C).** (1) Without knowing the time it takes pipe B to fill the pool, the time it takes to fill the pool operating together cannot be determined. (Insufficient)
(2) Without knowing the time it takes pipe A to fill the pool, the time it takes to fill the pool operating together cannot be determined. (Insufficient)
(1) + (2) Let H = the number of hours it takes pipe A and pipe B operating together to fill the pool.

pipe A   pipe B

$$\frac{H}{3} + \frac{H}{6} = 1 \ \left(\text{multiply by 6}\right)$$

$$^2\cancel{6} \cdot \frac{H}{\cancel{3}} + {}^1\cancel{6} \cdot \frac{H}{\cancel{6}} = 6 \cdot 1$$

$$2H + H = 6$$

$$3H = 6$$

$$H = 2 \text{ hours (Sufficient)}$$

27. **The correct answer is (D).**

Let x = the first odd integer,

$x + 2$ = the second odd integer,

$x + 4$ = the third odd integer,

and $x + 6$ = the fourth odd integer.

(1) $x + x + 2 + x + 4 + x + 6 = 32$

$$4x + 12 = 32$$

$$4x = 20$$

$$x = 5 \ \text{(Sufficient)}$$

(2) $\dfrac{x + x + 6}{2} = 8$

$\dfrac{2x + 6}{2} = 8$

$2x + 6 = 16$

$2x = 10$

$x = 5 \ \text{(Sufficient)}$

28. **The correct answer is (A).** (1) Since neither of Steve's two opponents received more than 4 votes, Steve received at least 12 votes, and thus won the election. (Sufficient)

(2) Steve's two opponents could have received 5 votes and 4 votes, in which case Steve would have received 11 votes, and won the election. On the other hand, Steve's two opponents could have received 5 votes and 5 votes, in which case Steve would have received only 10 votes, and not won the election. (Insufficient)

29. **The correct answer is (B).**

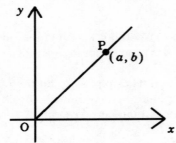

(1) Without knowing specific values of a and b, the length of OP cannot be determined. (Insufficient)

(2) Since $a = b = 1$, the coordinates of point P are (1, 1). Using the distance formula,

$d = \sqrt{\left(x_2 - x_1\right)^2 + \left(y_2 - y_1\right)^2}$

$d = \sqrt{\left(1 - 0\right)^2 + \left(1 - 0\right)^2}$

$d = \sqrt{1 + 1}$

$d = \sqrt{2} \ \text{(Sufficient)}$

30. **The correct answer is (B).** (1) 6 is divisible by 3 and is also divisible by 6. However, 9 is divisible by 3 but is not divisible by 6. (Insufficient)

(2) All numbers divisible by 12 have 6 as a factor, and are thus also divisible by 6. (Sufficient)

PRACTICE TEST IV

Directions: Each problem that follows consists of a question and two statements, labeled (1) and (2), in which certain data are given. You have to decide whether the data given in the statements are sufficient for answering the question, and on the answer sheet blacken space:

(A) if statement (1) ALONE is sufficient, but statement (2) ALONE is not sufficient;

(B) if statement (2) ALONE is sufficient, but statement (1) ALONE is not sufficient;

(C) if BOTH statements TOGETHER are sufficient, but NEITHER statement ALONE is sufficient;

(D) if EACH statement ALONE is sufficient;

(E) if statements (1) and (2) TOGETHER are NOT sufficient.

1. Two trains leave from the same station, at the same time, and travel in opposite directions. How far are they apart after 3 hours?

    (1) The average rate of one train is 10 m.p.h. faster than that of the other train.
    (2) The average rate of one train is 70 m.p.h., and the average rate of the other train is 80 m.p.h.

2. What is the volume of cube A?

    (1) The surface area of cube A is 54 sq. ft.
    (2) The length of an edge of cube A is 3 ft.

3. What was the list price of an item before a discount?

    (1) The sales price, after the discount, was $8.
    (2) The discount was $2, or 20% of the list price.

4. Ellen received a raise of 8% of her former salary. What was the amount of her raise?

    (1) Her new salary is $21,600.
    (2) Her former salary was $20,000.

5. How many faculty members are women?

    (1) There are 4 more men than women on the faculty.
    (2) The number of women on the faculty is 80% of the number of men on the faculty.

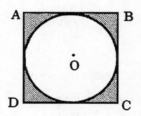

6. In the figure above, circle O is inscribed in square ABCD. What is the area of the shaded part?

    (1) The diameter of circle O is 8.
    (2) The length of the side of square ABCD is equal to twice the radius of circle O.

7. On January 1, 2001, the population of town A was 5,000 people. During what year did the population exceed 27,000 people?

    (1) On January 1, 2004, the population of town A was 40,000.
    (2) The population of town A doubled each year.

8. Is $\dfrac{x}{y}$ an integer?

    (1) $2x = 6y$

    (2) $x = \sqrt{18}$, $y = \sqrt{2}$

9. What is the value of $(x + y)^2$?

    (1) $x^2 + y^2 = 13$
    (2) $xy = 6$

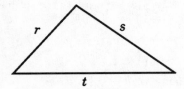

10. In the triangle above, is r greater than 3?

    (1) $r + s = 9$
    (2) $s = 4$, $t = 7$

11. What percent of those surveyed said they had tried both brand A and brand B?

    (1) 50% said they had tried brand A.
    (2) 40% said they had tried brand B.

12. What is the value of $\dfrac{1}{x} + \dfrac{1}{y}$?

    (1) $x + y = 5xy$
    (2) $x = 4y$

13. Does line L contain the point (2, 2)?

    (1) L contains the point (1, 1).
    (2) L contains the point (−1, −1).

14. What was the closing price of stock D on February 2?

    (1) On February 1, the closing price of stock D was $10 per share.
    (2) The closing price of stock D rose at a constant daily rate from February 1 to February 4, when it closed at $19 per share.

15. How many students in the class passed the final exam?

    (1) There are 15 women in the class.
    (2) 80% of the women in the class passed the final exam.

16. Is $x > 0$?

    (1) $xy > 0$
    (2) $x - y > 0$

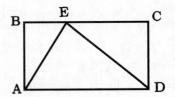

17. In the figure above, ABCD is a rectangle, and point E is anywhere on BC. What is the area of triangle AED?

    (1) $AD = 7$
    (2) The area of ABCD is 28.

18. Is x an even integer?

    (1) x is equal to 4 plus an integer.
    (2) x plus 4 is equal to an even integer.

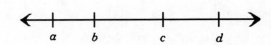

19. On the number line above, is $bd < 0$?

    (1) $c = 0$
    (2) $a = -3$

20. How many books did Roy buy?

    (1) The total cost of the books was $90.
    (2) The average cost of the books was $6 per book.

21. What is the distance from town A to town C?

    (1) The distance from town A to town B is 5 miles.
    (2) The distance from town B to town C is 12 miles.

22. Five friends decide to buy a van. If each person pays an equal amount, how much should each person pay?

  (1) The total cost of the van is $7500.
  (2) If one of the friends drops out before the purchase, the amount paid per person will increase by $375.

23. Is $a > b$?

  (1) $ax > bx$
  (2) $x^3 > 0$

24. Did it snow last night?

  (1) If it snowed last night, the meeting was cancelled.
  (2) The meeting was cancelled.

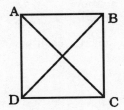

25. Is parallelogram ABCD above a square?

  (1) AC = BD
  (2) AC is perpendicular to BD.

26. Doris flipped a coin 60 times. How many flips were tails?

  (1) 30% of the flips were tails.
  (2) The number of tails was 3 less than half the number of heads.

27. If $x > 0$, is $x < 1$?

  (1) $x^2 < x$

  (2) $\sqrt{x} > x$

28. What is the ratio of the number of games won by the baseball team to the number of games lost?

  (1) The team won 60% of its games.
  (2) The team won 20 more games than it lost.

29. How many degrees are in each angle of regular polygon P?

  (1) P has 6 sides.
  (2) The length of each side of P is 5 inches.

30. Is x an integer?

  (1) $\dfrac{x}{8}$ is an integer.

  (2) $\dfrac{8}{x}$ is an integer.

ANSWERS AND EXPLANATIONS

1. **B**	6. **A**	11. **E**	16. **E**	21. **E**	26. **D**
2. **D**	7. **B**	12. **A**	17. **B**	22. **D**	27. **D**
3. **B**	8. **D**	13. **C**	18. **B**	23. **C**	28. **A**
4. **D**	9. **C**	14. **C**	19. **A**	24. **E**	29. **A**
5. **C**	10. **B**	15. **E**	20. **C**	25. **C**	30. **A**

1. **The correct answer is (B).** (1) Without knowing the specific rate of at least one of the trains, the distance apart cannot be determined. (Insufficient)

   (2) After 3 hours, one train has traveled 3(70) = 210 miles, and the other train has traveled 3(80) = 240 miles. Since they traveled in opposite directions, they are 210 + 240 = 450 miles apart. (Sufficient)

2. **The correct answer is (D).**

   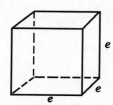

   (1) The surface of a cube consists of 6 congruent squares, each having an area of e^2. Thus,

   $$\text{Surface Area} = 6e^2$$
   $$54 = 6e^2$$
   $$9 = e^2$$
   $$3 = e$$

   Therefore, the volume of the cube is $e^3 = (3)^3 = 27$. (Sufficient)
   (2) The volume of the cube is $e^3 = (3)^3 = 27$. (Sufficient)

3. **The correct answer is (B).** (1) Without knowing the amount of discount, the list price cannot be determined. (Insufficient)

   (2) $$\frac{\text{Discount}}{\text{List Price}} = \frac{\%\ \text{of Discount}}{100\%}$$
   $$\frac{2}{L} = \frac{20}{100}$$
   $$20L = 200$$
   $$L = \$10 \text{ list price.} \quad \text{(Sufficient)}$$

4. **The correct answer is (D).** (1) New Salary = (100 + % of Raise) × Former Salary

   $$\$21,600 = \left(100\% + 8\%\right) \times F$$
   $$\$21,600 = 1.08F$$
   $$\$20,000 = \text{Former Salary}$$

   Thus, the raise was $21,600 − $20,000 = $1,600. (Sufficient)
   (2) The raise was 8% of $20,000 = .08 × $20,000 = $1,600. (Sufficient)

5. **The correct answer is (C).** (1) Without knowing either the number of men or the total number of faculty members, the number of women cannot be determined. (Insufficient)

    (2) Same as above. (Insufficient)

    (1) + (2)   Let W = the number of women,

    and W + 4 = the number of men.

    $$W = .80(W + 4)$$
    $$W = .80W + 3.2$$
    $$.2W = 3.2$$
    $$W = 16 \quad \text{(Sufficient)}$$

6. **The correct answer is (A).**

    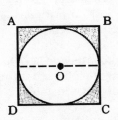

    (1) The side of the square has the same length as the diameter of the circle, 8. Thus,

Area of the square	*Area of the circle*
$= (\text{sides})^2$	$= \pi(\text{radius})^2$
$= (8)^2$	$= \pi(4)^2$
$= 64$	$= 16\pi$

    Therefore, the area of the shaded part = $64 - 16\pi$. (Sufficient)

    (2) Without knowing a specific length for the side of the square or the radius of the circle, the area of the shaded part cannot be determined. (Insufficient)

7. **The correct answer is (B).** (1) No information is given about the rate at which the population is growing. (Insufficient)

    (2) Since the population doubled each year, after one year the population was 10,000, after two years the population was 20,000, and after three years the population was 40,000. Thus, the population exceeded 27,000 between the second and third years, or during 2003. (Sufficient)

8. **The correct answer is (D).** (1) Since $2x = 6y, \dfrac{x}{y} = \dfrac{6}{2} = 3$, an integer. (Sufficient)

    (2) Since $x = \sqrt{18}$, and $y = \sqrt{2}, \dfrac{x}{y} = \dfrac{\sqrt{18}}{\sqrt{2}} = \sqrt{9} = 3$, an integer. (Sufficient)

9. **The correct answer is (C).** $(x + y)^2 = (x + y)(x + y) = x^2 + 2xy + y^2$

    (1) Without knowing the value of xy, the value of $(x + y)^2$ cannot be determined. (Insufficient)

    (2) Without knowing the value of $x^2 + y^2$, the value of $(x + y)^2$ cannot be determined. (Insufficient)

    (1) + (2) Since $x^2 + y^2 = 13$, and $xy = 6$, then $(x + y)^2 = 13 + 2(6) = 25$. (Sufficient)

10.   The correct answer is (B).

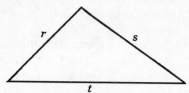

(1) Without knowing the value of s, the value of r cannot be determined. (Insufficient)

(2) The sum of any two sides of a triangle must be greater than the third side. Thus, in order for $r + s$ to be greater than t, $r + 4$ must be greater than 7, or r must be greater than 3. (Sufficient)

11.   The correct answer is (E). (1) No information is given about the percent that had tried brand B. (Insufficient)

(2) No information is given about the percent that had tried brand A. (Insufficient)

(1) + (2) No information is given about the percent that had tried neither brand A nor brand B. (Insufficient)

12.   The correct answer is (A). (1) The sum of two fractions can be determined by cross-multiplying the numerators and denominators and placing their sum over the product of the denominators. Thus,

$$\frac{1}{x} + \frac{1}{y} = \frac{1(y) + 1(x)}{(x)(y)} = \frac{x + y}{xy}$$

Since $x + y = 5xy$, $\dfrac{x + y}{xy} = 5$. (Sufficient)

(2) Without a specific value of x or y, the value of the given expression cannot be determined. (Insufficient)

13.   The correct answer is (C). (1) No information is given about the direction of the line. (Insufficient)

(2) Same as above. (Insufficient)

(1) + (2)

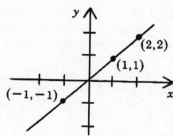

Since the line passes through both (1,1) and (−1, −1), it must also pass through (2,2). (Sufficient)

14.   The correct answer is (C). (1) No information is given about the daily rate of change in the price of the stock. (Insufficient)

(2) No information is given about the closing price of the stock on February 1. (Insufficient)

(1) + (2) The stock rose $9 in 3 days, or $3 per day. Since the stock closed at $10 on February 1, it closed at $13 on February 2. (Sufficient)

15. **The correct answer is (E).** (1) No information is given about the number of women or men that *passed* the final exam. (Insufficient)

    (2) No information is given about the number of men in the class that passed the final exam. (Insufficient)

    (1) + (2) Same as above. (Insufficient)

16. **The correct answer is (E).** (1) If $y > 0$, then $x > 0$. However, if $y < 0$, then $x < 0$. (Insufficient)

    (2) Since $x - y > 0$, then $x > y$. If $y > 0$, then $x > 0$. However, if $y < 0$, then x can be greater than 0 or less than 0. (Insufficient)

    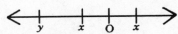

    (1) + (2) Same as above. (Insufficient)

17. **The correct answer is (B).**

    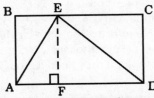

    (1) Without knowing the height of the triangle, the area cannot be determined. (Insufficient)

    (2) The height of the triangle, EF, is the same length as the width of the rectangle. Thus,

    $$\text{The area of triangle AED} = \frac{1}{2}(AD)(EF)$$

    $$= \frac{1}{2}(AD)(CD)$$

    $$= \frac{1}{2}(\text{the area of ABCD})$$

    $$= \frac{1}{2}(28)$$

    $$= 14 \text{ (Sufficient)}$$

18. **The correct answer is (B).** (1) $x = 4 +$ an integer. If the integer is even, then x is even. However, if the integer is odd, then x is odd. (Insufficient)

    (2) $x + 4 =$ an even integer, or $x =$ an even integer $- 4$, which is always even. (Sufficient)

19. **The correct answer is (A).**

    (1) Since $c = 0$, then $b < 0$ and $d > 0$, and thus their product, $bd < 0$. (Sufficient)

    (2) Without knowing the location of b and d with respect to 0, the sign of the product, bd, cannot be determined. (Insufficient)

20. **The correct answer is (C).** (1) No information is given about the cost per book. (Insufficient)

(2) No information is given about the total cost of the books. (Insufficient)

(1) + (2) The average cost per book

$$= \frac{\text{The total cost}}{\text{The number of books}}$$

$$\$6 = \frac{\$90}{N}$$

$$6N = 90$$

$$N = 15 \text{ books}$$

(Sufficient)

21. **The correct answer is (E).** (1) No information is given about the location of town C. (Insufficient)

(2) No information is given about the location of town A. (Insufficient)

(1) + (2) No information is given about the direction from one town to another. For example, if they lie in a straight line, as shown, the distance from A to C is 17 miles.

However, if they lie in some other configuration, as shown, the distance from A to C is less than 17 miles. (Insufficient)

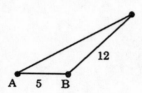

22. **The correct answer is (D).** (1) Each person should pay $\frac{\$7500}{5} = \$1500$. (Sufficient)

(2) Let T = the total cost of the van,

$$\frac{T}{5} = \text{the original cost per person,}$$

and $\frac{T}{4} = $ the cost per person after one person drops out.

$$\frac{T}{4} = \frac{T}{5} + 375 \,(\text{multiply by 20})$$

$$\overset{5}{\cancel{20}} \cdot \frac{T}{\cancel{4}} = \overset{4}{\cancel{20}} \cdot \frac{T}{\cancel{5}} + 20 \cdot 375$$

$$5T = 4T + 7500$$

$$T = \$7500$$

Thus, each person should pay $\frac{\$7500}{5} = \$1500$. (Sufficient)

23. **The correct answer is (C).** (1) If x is positive, $a > b$. However, if x is negative, $a < b$. (Insufficient)

(2) No information is given about a and b. (Insufficient)

(1) + (2) Since $x^3 > 0$, then x is positive. Thus, from (1), $a > b$. (Sufficient)

24. **The correct answer is (E).** (1) No information is given about whether it snowed last night. (Insufficient)

(2) Same as above. (Insufficient)

(1) + (2) Since the meeting could have been cancelled for many different reasons, whether it snowed last night cannot be determined. (Insufficient)

25. **The correct answer is (C).**

(1) Knowing that AC = BD only determines that ABCD is a rectangle. (Insufficient)

(2) Knowing that AC is perpendicular to BD only determines that ABCD is a rhombus. (Insufficient)

(1) + (2) A parallelogram that is both a rectangle and a rhombus must be a square. (Sufficient)

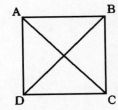

26. **The correct answer is (D).** (1) 30% of 60 = .30 × 60 = 18 tails. (Sufficient)

(2)

Let H = the number of heads,

and $\frac{1}{2}H - 3 =$ the number of tails.

$$H + \frac{1}{2}H - 3 = 60 \,(\text{multiply by 2})$$

$$2 \cdot H + \cancel{2} \cdot \frac{1}{\cancel{2}}H - 2 \cdot 3 = 2 \cdot 60$$

$$2H + H - 6 = 120$$

$$3H - 6 = 120$$

$$3H = 126$$

$$H = 42$$

Thus, the number of tails $= \frac{1}{2}H - 3 = \frac{1}{2}(42) - 3 = 18$. (Sufficient)

27. **The correct answer is (D).** (1) If $x > 0$ and $x^2 < x$, then $x < 1$. For example, $\left(\frac{1}{5}\right)^2 < \frac{1}{5}$. (Sufficient)

(2) If $x > 0$ and $\sqrt{x} > x$, then $x < 1$. For example, $\sqrt{\frac{1}{49}} > \sqrt{\frac{1}{49}}$. (Sufficient)

28. **The correct answer is (A).** (1) Since the team won 60% of its games, it lost 40% of its games. Thus,

$\frac{\text{games won}}{\text{games lost}} = \frac{60}{40} = \frac{3}{2}$. (Sufficient)

(2) Games won = games lost + 20. This equation cannot be transformed into a ratio of games won to games lost. (Insufficient)

29. **The correct answer is (A).** (1) The sum of the angles of any polygon = $(N - 2) \times 180°$, where N is the number of sides. Thus, the sum of the angles = $(6 - 2) \times 180°$
$$= 720°$$

Since P is a regular polygon, all its angles are equal. Thus, the number of degrees in each angle is $\dfrac{720°}{6} = 120°$. (Sufficient)

(2) Without knowing the number of sides of P, the measure of each angle cannot be determined. (Insufficient)

30. **The correct answer is (A).** (1) Since $\dfrac{x}{8}$ is an integer, x must be a multiple of 8. Thus, x is also an integer. (Sufficient)

(2) If $\dfrac{8}{x}$ is an integer, x does not necessarily have to be an integer. For example,

$$\frac{8}{2} = 4 \text{ and } \frac{8}{\frac{1}{3}} = 8 \div \frac{1}{3} = 8 \times \frac{3}{1} = 24. \text{ In both cases, the result is an integer.}$$

(Insufficient)

PRACTICE TEST V

Directions: Each problem that follows consists of a question and two statements, labeled (1) and (2), in which certain data are given. You have to decide whether the data given in the statements are sufficient for answering the question, and on the answer sheet blacken space:

(A) if statement (1) ALONE is sufficient, but statement (2) ALONE is not sufficient;

(B) if statement (2) ALONE is sufficient, but statement (1) ALONE is not sufficient;

(C) if BOTH statements TOGETHER are sufficient, but NEITHER statement ALONE is sufficient;

(D) if EACH statement ALONE is sufficient;

(E) if statements (1) and (2) TOGETHER are NOT sufficient.

1. What is the value of the integer x?

   (1) x is a multiple of 2.
   (2) $x + 8 = 10$

2. What was the average (arithmetic mean) of the scores on quiz Q for 40 students?

   (1) The lowest score on quiz Q was 30 and the highest score was 96.
   (2) The sum of the 40 students' scores on quiz Q was 3,040.

3. Is $\dfrac{x}{y} < 0$?

   (1) $x^2 = 9$
   (2) $y^3 = -8$

4. If a certain CD player and earphones were purchased separately, what was the cost of the CD player?

   (1) The total cost of the CD player and the earphones was $72.
   (2) The CD player cost 5 times as much as the earphones.

5. If $xy \neq 0$, then x is what fraction of y?

   (1) y is $\dfrac{4}{5}$ of x.
   (2) x is $\dfrac{4}{5}$ of 25.

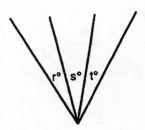

6. In the figure above, is r equal to s?

   (1) $r + s = 50$
   (2) $r = t$

7. How many defective light bulbs are there in a shipment of 5,000 light bulbs?

   (1) In a particular sample of 100 light bulbs selected from the shipment, 3 were defective.
   (2) In a particular sample of 10 light bulbs selected from the shipment, 2 were defective.

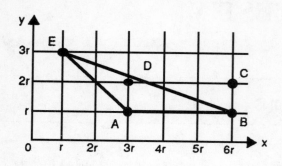

8. In the graph above, what is the area of triangular region AEB?

    (1) The area of ABCD is 48.
    (2) BC = 4.

9. Is $x = 0$?

    (1) $x + 2 > 0$
    (2) $x = -x$

10. What is the value of $2x + 8y$?

    (1) $x - 4y = 4$
    (2) $x + 4y = 10$

11. What is the value of a?

    (1) $a - b + 4 = 0$
    (2) $a = -a$

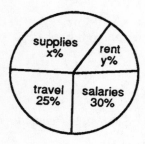

12. The graph above shows the distribution of expenses for Company M last year. What were Company M's total expenses last year?

    (1) Last year expenses for rent were exactly half the expenses for salaries.
    (2) Last year expenses for travel were $926 million.

13. Is $x^4 - y^4$ a positive number?

    (1) $x^2 - y^2$ is a positive number.
    (2) $x^2 + y^2$ is a positive number.

14. What is the value of x?

    (1) $3x + 6 = 2(x - 1) + 5x$
    (2) $3x + 6 > 2(x - 1)$

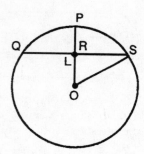

15. In the figure above, O is the center of the circle. If OP and QS are perpendicular and bisect each other, what is the length of OS?

    (1) The length of PR is $\sqrt{3}$.
    (2) The length of QS is 6.

16. What is the value of x?

    (1) $4^x = 16$
    (2) $x^4 = 16$

17. Is quadrilateral Q a square?

    (1) The sides of Q have the same length.
    (2) The diagonals of Q have the same length.

18. What is the value of $[rs - t(r - 3s)]$?

    (1) $r = 3s$
    (2) $t = 0$

19. What is Steve's annual salary and Maria's annual salary?

    (1) The combined total of the annual salaries of Steve and Maria is $80,000.
    (2) If Steve were to receive a 10 percent increase in annual salary and Maria an 8 percent increase, their combined annual salaries would be $87,000.

20. If b is an integer, is $\sqrt{b}$ an integer?

    (1) b is a multiple of 4.
    (2) b is a multiple of 9.

21. What is the value of xy?

    (1) $(x + y)^2 = 54$
    (2) $(x - y)^2 = 34$

22. How many hours were budgeted for a certain job?

    (1) The number of hours budgeted for the job plus the actual number of hours used for the job was 100.
    (2) The actual number of hours used for the job minus the number of hours budgeted for the job was 10.

23. By what percent was the price of a suit reduced?

    (1) The original price was $300.
    (2) The original price was $60 more than the reduced price.

24. Is $\triangle ABC$ isosceles?

    (1) Exactly two of the angles, $\angle A$ and $\angle C$, have the same measure.
    (2) $\angle B$ and $\angle C$ do not have the same measure.

25. What is the value of $5^a \cdot 5^b$?

    (1) $a = 2$
    (2) $a + b = 3$

26. What is the ratio of a to b?

    (1) The ratio of $2a$ to b is 8:1.
    (2) $b = 4$

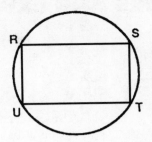

27. Rectangle RSTU is inscribed in a circle as shown above. What is the radius of the circle?

    (1) The length of the rectangle is 6 and the width of the rectangle is 8.
    (2) The length of arc RT is $\frac{1}{2}$ of the circumference of the circle.

28. If n is an integer, is $n(n + 2)(n + 4)(n + 6)$ odd?

    (1) n is an odd number.
    (2) $n + 1$ is an even number.

29. What is the value of $3\pi x^2 y$?

    (1) The ratio of x to y is 1 to 5.
    (2) The value of $y - 2x$ is 12.

30. What was Kathy's average driving speed in miles per hour during a 20-minute interval?

    (1) She drove 15 miles during this interval.
    (2) Her maximum speed was 55 miles per hour and her minimum speed was 35 miles per hour during this interval.

ANSWERS AND EXPLANATIONS

1. **B**	6. **E**	11. **B**	16. **A**	21. **C**	26. **A**
2. **B**	7. **E**	12. **B**	17. **C**	22. **C**	27. **A**
3. **E**	8. **D**	13. **A**	18. **E**	23. **C**	28. **D**
4. **C**	9. **B**	14. **A**	19. **C**	24. **A**	29. **C**
5. **A**	10. **B**	15. **D**	20. **E**	25. **B**	30. **A**

1. **The correct answer is (B).** (1) Without knowing the specific multiple, the value of x cannot be determined. (Insufficient)
   (2) $x + 8 = 10$, or $x = 2$. (Sufficient)

2. **The correct answer is (B).** (1) Knowing the lowest and highest score does not give the average. (Insufficient)
   (2) The average = Sum/Number. Thus, the average = 3040/40 = 76. (Sufficient)

3. **The correct answer is (E).** (1) x could be $+3$ or -3. (Insufficient)
   (2) Since $y^3 = -8$, $y = -2$. But no value of x is given. (Insufficient)
   (1) + (2) Since x could be either $+3$ or -3, the sign of $\dfrac{x}{y}$ cannot be determined. (Insufficient)

4. **The correct answer is (C).** Let x = the cost of the CD player and y = the cost of the earphones. (1) $x + y = 72$. Without the value of y, the value of x cannot be determined. (Insufficient)
   (2) $x = 5y$. Same as above. (Insufficient)
   (1) + (2) Substituting $x = 5y$ into $x + y = 72$, we get $5y + y = 72$, or $y = 12$, and thus $x + 12 = 72$, or $x = 60$. (Sufficient)

5. **The correct answer is (A).** (1) $y = \dfrac{4}{5}x$, or $x = \dfrac{5}{4}y$. (Sufficient).
   (2) Without a value for y, the fraction cannot be determined. (Insufficient)

6. **The correct answer is (E).**
   (1) No relationship is given between r and s. (Insufficient)
   (2) No information is given about s. (Insufficient)
   (1) + (2) Same as above. (Insufficient)

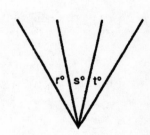

7. **The correct answer is (E).** (1) No information is given about the rate at which the bulbs are defective. (Insufficient)
   (2) Same as above (Insufficient)
   (1) + (2) Same as above. (Insufficient)

8. The correct answer is (D).

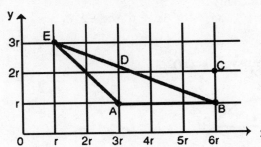

(1) The area of rectangle ABCD = length × width = $3r \times r = 3r^2 = 48$.

Therefore, $r^2 = 16$ and $r = 4$. The area of triangle AEB = $\frac{1}{2}$ × base × height = $\frac{1}{2}$ × $3r \times 2r = 3r^2 = 3(4)^2 = 48$. (Sufficient)

(2) $r = BC = 4$. Same as above. (Sufficient)

9. The correct answer is (B). (1) $x + 2 > 0$, or $x > -2$. But no specific value of x is given. (Insufficient)

(2) Since $x = -x$, $2x = 0$, or $x = 0$. (Sufficient)

10. The correct answer is (B). (1) No information is given about the specific values of x and y. (Insufficient)

(2) Multiplying both sides by 2, we get $2x + 8y = 20$. (Sufficient)

11. The correct answer is (B). (1) Without knowing b, the value of a cannot be determined. (Insufficient)

(2) Since $a = -a$, $2a = 0$, or $a = 0$. (Sufficient)

12. The correct answer is (B).

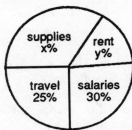

(1) Without knowing how much money was spent for salaries, the value of the total expenses cannot be determined. (Insufficient)

(2) Since travel was 25%, or $\frac{1}{4}$, of the total expenses, the total expenses were $4 \times \$926$ million, or $\$3.704$ billion. (Sufficient)

13. The correct answer is (A). (1) $x^4 - y^4 = (x^2 - y^2)(x^2 + y^2)$. If $x^2 - y^2$ is positive, and we know that not both x and y can be zero, we can deduce that $x^2 + y^2$ will always be positive. So $x^4 - y^4$ is the product of two positive factors, and must be positive.

14. **The correct answer is (A).** (1) Since $3x + 6 = 2(x - 1) + 5x$, $3x + 6 = 7x - 2$, or $x = 2$. (Sufficient)
(2) Since $3x + 6 > 2(x - 1)$, $3x + 6 > 2x - 2$, or $x > -8$. This does not specify a value for x. (Insufficient)

15. **The correct answer is (D).**

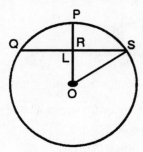

(1) OR = PR = $\sqrt{3}$.
Both OS and OP are radii. Thus OS = OP = $2\sqrt{3}$. (Sufficient)
(2) Since QS = 6, RS = 3.

Both OS and OP are radii. Thus OR = $\frac{1}{2}$OS. Using the Pythagorean theorem,

$$(RS)^2 + (OR)^2 = (OS)^2$$
$$(3)^2 + \left(\frac{1}{2}OS\right)^2 = (OS)^2$$
$$9 + \frac{(OS)^2}{4} = (OS)^2$$
$$36 + (OS)^2 = 4(OS)^2$$
$$36 = 3(OS)^2$$
$$OS = \sqrt{12} = 2\sqrt{3} \text{ (Sufficient)}$$

16. **The correct answer is (A).** (1) $4^x = 16$. Thus, $x = 2$. (Sufficient)
(2) If $x^4 = 16$, x could be $+2$ or -2. (Insufficient)

17. **The correct answer is (C).** (1) Q could be a square or a rhombus. (Insufficient)
(2) Q could be a square or a rectangle. (Insufficient)
(1) + (2) Q must be a square. (Sufficient)

18. **The correct answer is (E).** (1) If $r = 3s$, $[rs - t(r - 3s)] = rs = 3s^2$.
But we do not know the value of s. (Insufficient)
(2) If $t = 0$, $[rs - t(r - 3s)] = rs$.
But we do not know the value of r or s. (Insufficient)
(1) + (2) Same as above. (Insufficient)

19. **The correct answer is (C).** Let x = Steve's salary and y = Maria's salary.
     (1) $x + y = \$80,000$. Without knowing another relationship between x and y, we cannot determine the value of x or y. (Insufficient)
     (2) $x + .10x + y + .08y = \$87,000$, or $1.1x + 1.08y = \$87,000$. Same as above. (Insufficient)
     (1) + (2) Solving the two equations simultaneously, we get $x = \$30,000$ and $y = \$50,000$. (Sufficient)

20. **The correct answer is (E).** (1) If $b = 4$, $\sqrt{b} = 2$. But if $b = 8$, $\sqrt{b}$ is not an integer. (Insufficient)
     (2) If $b = 9$, $\sqrt{b} = 3$. But if $b = 18$, $\sqrt{b}$ is not an integer. (Insufficient)
     (1) + (2) If $b = 36$, $\sqrt{b} = 6$. But if $b = 72$, $\sqrt{b}$ is not an integer. (Insufficient).

21. **The correct answer is (C).** (1) Expanding $(x + y)^2 = 54$, we get $x^2 + 2xy + y^2 = 54$. Without specific values for x and y, we cannot determine the value of xy. (Insufficient)
     (2) Expanding $(x - y)^2 = 34$, we get $x - 2xy + y^2 = 34$. Same as above. (Insufficient)
     (1) + (2) Subtracting equation (2) from equation (1) we get

$$
\begin{aligned}
x^2 + 2xy + y^2 &= 54 \\
-\left(x^2 - 2xy + y^2\right) &= 34 \\
\hline
4xy &= 20
\end{aligned}
$$

Thus, $xy = 5$. (Sufficient)

22. **The correct answer is (C).** Let x = the number of hours budgeted for the job, and y = the actual number of hours used.
     (1) $x + y = 100$. Without a value for y, we cannot determine the value of x. (Insufficient)
     (2) $y - x = 10$. Same as above. (Insufficient)
     (1) + (2) Adding the two equations together, we get $2y = 110$, or $y = 55$. Thus, $x = 45$. (Sufficient)

23. **The correct answer is (C).** (1) Without knowing the amount of reduction, the percent of reduction cannot be determined. (Insufficient)
     (2) Without knowing the original price, the percent of reduction cannot be determined. (Insufficient)
     (1) + (2) The percent of reduction is $\dfrac{60}{300}$, or 20%. (Sufficient)

24. **The correct answer is (A).** (1) If two angles of a triangle are equal, then the sides opposite them are also equal. Therefore, the triangle is isosceles. (Sufficient)
     (2) No information is given about $\angle A$. (Insufficient)

25. **The correct answer is (B).** (1) No information is given about the value of b. (Insufficient)
     (2) Since the bases are the same, we get $5^a \cdot 5^b = 5^{a + b}$, or $5^3 = 125$. (Sufficient)

26. **The correct answer is (A).** (1) $\dfrac{2a}{b} = \dfrac{8}{1}$. Thus, $\dfrac{a}{b} = \dfrac{4}{1}$. (Sufficient)
     (2) No information is given about the value of a. (Insufficient)

27.   The correct answer is (A).

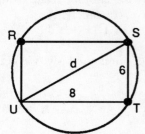

(1) Using the Pythagorean theorem we get $d^2 = 6^2 + 8^2$, or $d^2 = 100$, and $d = 10$. Thus, the radius is 5. (Sufficient)

(2) No information is given about the length of any side in the rectangle. (Insufficient)

28.   The correct answer is (D). (1) If n is an odd number, then each of the factors is odd, and so is their product. (Sufficient)

(2) If $n + 1$ is an even number, then n is an odd number. Same as above. (Sufficient)

29.   The correct answer is (C). (1) $\dfrac{x}{y} = \dfrac{1}{5}$, or $y = 5x$. No information is given about the numerical value of x or y. (Insufficient)

(2) $y - 2x = 12$. Same as above. (Insufficient)

(1) + (2) Substituting equation (1) into equation (2) we get $5x - 2x = 12$, or $x = 4$, and $y = 20$. Thus, the value of $3\pi x^2 y = 3\pi\,(4)2(20) = 960\pi$. (Sufficient)

30.   The correct answer is (A). (1) Her driving speed is

$$\frac{D}{T} = \frac{15\ \text{mi.}}{20\ \text{min.}} = \frac{15\ \text{mi.}}{1/3\ \text{hr.}} = 45\ \text{mph.} \quad \text{(Sufficient)}$$

(2) Knowing her maximum speed and minimum speed does not give the average speed. (Insufficient)

Chapter 8

QUANTITATIVE COMPARISON QUESTIONS

A quantitative comparison question is a special type of math question in which you are asked to compare the relative values of two quantities. This type of question is usually found on the GRE.

The format of each question is the same: two quantities, which are to be compared, are placed next to each other in columns labeled A and B; information concerning one or both of the quantities is centered above the two columns. After comparing the values of the two quantities, you must decide which, if either, is greater. Based on your decision, you then choose one of the answers given in the directions shown below. These directions accompany all quantitative comparison questions. Note that unlike other multiple-choice questions, quantitative comparison questions have only *four* possible choices.

Each question in this section consists of two quantities, one in Column A and one in Column B. You are to compare the two quantities and on the answer sheet blacken space:

(A) if the quantity in Column A is greater;

(B) if the quantity in Column B is greater;

(C) if the two quantities are equal;

(D) if the relationship cannot be determined from the information given.

Common Information: In a question, information concerning one or both of the quantities to be compared is centered above the two columns. A symbol that appears in both columns represents the same thing in Column A as it does in Column B.

Numbers: All numbers used are real numbers.

Figures: Positions of points, angles, regions, etc. can be assumed to be in the order shown.

Lines shown as straight can be assumed to be straight.

Figures are assumed to lie in the plane unless otherwise indicated.

Figures which accompany questions are intended to provide information useful in answering the questions. However, unless a note states that a figure is drawn to scale, you should solve these problems NOT by estimating sizes by sight or by measurement, but by using your knowledge of mathematics.

To obtain a better understanding of the choices, A−D, let us look at four examples. Note that Example 1 has been designed so that choice A is the correct answer, Example 2 so that choice B is the correct answer, and so on.

	Column A	**Column B**
Example 1	$\sqrt{10} + \sqrt{26}$	$\sqrt{10 + 26}$

Analysis

Column A: Since $\sqrt{10}$ is slightly greater than 3, and $\sqrt{26}$ is slightly greater than 5, their sum is slightly greater than 8.

Column B: $\sqrt{10 + 26} = \sqrt{36} = 6$. (Note that the sum of the square roots in Column A is not equal to, but greater than, the square root of the sum in Column B.)

Answer

A—Column A is greater than Column B.

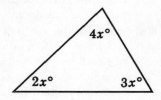

	Column A	**Column B**
Example 2	x	30

Analysis

Column A: Since the sum of the angles of a triangle is 180°, we can write $2x + 3x + 4x = 180$, which gives us $9x = 180$, or $x = 20$.

Column B: Given as 30.

Answer

B—Column B is greater than Column A.

	Column A	**Column B**
Example 3	The area of a circle with radius 1	The area of a square with side $\sqrt{\pi}$

Analysis

Column A: Since the area of a circle is πr^2, the area of the given circle is $\pi(1)^2$, or π.

Column B: Since the area of a square is $(\text{side})^2$, the area of the given square is $\left(\sqrt{\pi}\right)^2$, or π.

Answer

C—The two quantities are equal.

$$x^2 = y^2$$

Example 4	**Column A**	**Column B**
	x	y

Analysis

Without knowing the signs of x and y, we cannot determine which quantity is greater. For example, x can equal $+3$ and y can equal -3, in which case x is greater. On the other hand, x can equal -3 and y can equal $+3$, in which case y is greater.

Answer

D—The relationship *cannot* be determined.

TIPS FOR ANSWERING QUANTITATIVE COMPARISON QUESTIONS

1. Since the answers A–D are the same on every test, you can save valuable time during the test by memorizing their meanings in advance. In the summary below, v(A) means the *value of the quantity in Column A*, and v(B) means *the value of the quantity in Column B*.

Quantitative Comparison Answers			
Answer A	**Answer B**	**Answer C**	**Answer D**
$v(A) > v(B)$	$v(B) > v(A)$	$v(A) = v(B)$	$v(A)??v(B)$

2. Make sure you understand that the answer to a quantitative comparison question is (A) only if the quantity in Column A is *always* (not just sometimes) greater than that in Column B. Similarly, an answer of (B) means that the quantity in Column B is *always* greater, and an answer of (C) means that the quantities are *always* equal.

3. At first glance, many of the quantitative comparison questions on the GRE appear easy because they are based on topics that you have already studied (arithmetic, algebra, and geometry), and seem not to require much work to determine a solution. On the contrary, a lot of these questions are actually quite tricky. Answers that initially appear to be correct will often be incorrect. Doing well on quantitative comparison questions involves not only knowing the math topics but also knowing a variety of alternate problem-solving approaches.

TIPS FOR ANSWERING PURELY NUMERICAL QUESTIONS

In many of the quantitative comparison questions on the GRE, the quantities in both columns will be purely numerical (no variables, just numbers). These are illustrated in the problems that follow.

1. The Answer to a Purely Numerical Question is Never (D)

Since the relative sizes of two purely numerical quantities can always be determined, the answer to such a question is never (D).

The following strategies will be useful in solving purely numerical questions:

2. Perform the Computations

Whenever the given computations can be easily performed, simply do them and then compare the results.

Example 1	**Column A**	**Column B**
	$\dfrac{5}{6} + 1$	$\dfrac{10}{3} - 1$

Analysis

Column A: $\dfrac{5}{6} + 1 = 1\dfrac{5}{6}$

Column B: $\dfrac{10}{3} - 1 = \dfrac{10}{3} - \dfrac{3}{3} = \dfrac{7}{3} = 2\dfrac{1}{3}$

Answer

B—Column B is greater than Column A.

3. Reduce or Factor

Operations that appear to be too time-consuming can often be simplified by first reducing fractions or by factoring the given expressions. In general, if you find yourself doing a lengthy computation, you may have missed a shortcut.

Example 2	**Column A**	**Column B**
	$\dfrac{3 \cdot 3 \cdot 3 \cdot 3}{6 \cdot 6 \cdot 6 \cdot 6}$	$\left(\dfrac{1}{2}\right)^4$

Analysis

Column A: $\dfrac{3 \cdot 3 \cdot 3 \cdot 3}{6 \cdot 6 \cdot 6 \cdot 6} = \dfrac{1 \cdot 1 \cdot 1 \cdot 1}{2 \cdot 2 \cdot 2 \cdot 2} = \dfrac{1}{16}$

Column B: $\left(\dfrac{1}{2}\right)^4 = \dfrac{1^4}{2^4} = \dfrac{1}{16}$

Answer

C—Column A is equal to column B.

Example 3	**Column A**	**Column B**
	$(403)^2 - (402)^2$	$2(402)$

Analysis

Column A: $(403)^2 - (402)^2$ can be simplified using the formula $x^2 - y^2 = (x + y)(x - y)$

$$(403)^2 - (402)^2 = (403 + 402)(403 - 402)$$
$$= (805)(1) = 805$$

Column B: $2(402) = 804$

Answer

A—Column A is greater than Column B.

Example 4	**Column A**	**Column B**
	$8^{24} - 8^{23}$	$8^{23}(7)$

Analysis

Column A: $8^{24} - 8^{23} = 8^{23}(8 - 1)$

Column B: Given as $8^{23}(7)$

Answer

C—Column A is equal to Column B.

4. Compare Terms and Factors

Only do as much work as is necessary to determine which quantity is larger. Sums and products can often be compared term-by-term or factor-by-factor.

Example 5	**Column A**	**Column B**
	$\dfrac{2}{3} + \dfrac{3}{4} + \dfrac{5}{6}$	$\dfrac{2}{4} + \dfrac{3}{5} + \dfrac{5}{7}$

Analysis

Simply note that each one of the three terms in Column A is larger than the corresponding term in Column B. That is.

$$\frac{2}{3} > \frac{2}{4}, \frac{3}{4} > \frac{3}{5}, \text{ and } \frac{5}{6} > \frac{5}{7}$$

Answer

A—Column A is greater than Column B.

Example 6	**Column A**	**Column B**
	The number of seconds in a day	The number of minutes in 50 days

Analysis

Column A: The number of seconds in a day is $60 \cdot 60 \cdot 24$

Column B: The number of minutes in 50 days is $60 \cdot 24 \cdot 50$

Note that the expressions in Column A and Column B have two factors in common, 60 and 24. Since the third factor in Column A is 60, and the third factor in Column B is 50, Column A is greater than Column B.

Answer

A—Column A is greater than Column B.

5. Estimate

Whenever possible, estimate the sizes of the quantities.

Example 1	Column A	Column B
	$\dfrac{334}{999}$	$\dfrac{110}{333}$

Analysis

Note that the quantity in Column A is slightly greater than $\dfrac{1}{3}$ while the quantity in Column B is slightly less than $\dfrac{1}{3}$.

Answer

A—Column A is greater than Column B.

Example 2	Column A	Column B
	$\sqrt{10} + \sqrt{17}$	$\sqrt{27}$

Analysis

Column A: $\sqrt{10}$ is slightly larger than 3, and $\sqrt{17}$ is slightly larger than 4. Thus, $\sqrt{10} + \sqrt{17}$ is slightly larger than 7.
Column B: $\sqrt{27}$ is slightly larger than 5.

Answer

A—Column A is greater than Column B.

6. Treat as an Algebraic Inequality

Each quantitative comparison question can be treated as an algebraic inequality. Thus, any operation that can be performed on both sides of an inequality can also be performed on both columns of a quantitative comparison question: (1) you can add the same number to or subtract the same number from both columns; (2) you can multiply or divide both columns by the same *positive* number; (3) you can square both columns (if the entries are positive).

These principles can be used to transform the operations of subtraction and division to the relatively easier operations of addition and multiplication, respectively.

Example 1	Column A	Column B
	$4.1 + \dfrac{1}{3}$	$5.1 - \dfrac{2}{3}$

Analysis

To eliminate the subtraction in Column B, add $\dfrac{2}{3}$ to both columns.

	Column A	Column B
	$4.1 + \dfrac{1}{3} + \dfrac{2}{3}$	$5.1 - \dfrac{2}{3} + \dfrac{2}{3}$
	$4.1 + 1$	5.1
	5.1	5.1

Answer

C—Column A is equal to Column B.

Example 2	**Column A**	**Column B**
Analysis	$\dfrac{1}{5}$	$\dfrac{1}{5}-\dfrac{1}{6}+\dfrac{1}{7}-\dfrac{1}{8}+\dfrac{1}{9}$

Begin by "canceling" the term $\dfrac{1}{5}$ from both columns.

	0	$-\dfrac{1}{6}+\dfrac{1}{7}-\dfrac{1}{8}+\dfrac{1}{9}$

Then, to eliminate the subtraction in Column B, add $\dfrac{1}{6}$ and $\dfrac{1}{8}$ to both columns.

	$\dfrac{1}{6}+\dfrac{1}{8}$	$\dfrac{1}{7}+\dfrac{1}{9}$

Now simply note that each of the two terms in Column A is larger than the corresponding two terms in Column B.

Answer
A—Column A is greater than Column B.

Example 3	**Column A**	**Column B**
Analysis	$\dfrac{4}{\sqrt{2}}$	$\sqrt{2}$

To eliminate the division in Column A, multiply both columns by $\sqrt{2}$.

	4	$\sqrt{2}\cdot\sqrt{2}$

Since $\sqrt{2}\cdot\sqrt{2}=2$, Column A is greater than Column B.

Answer
A—Column A is greater than Column B.

Example 4	**Column A**	**Column B**
	$\sqrt{89,900}$	300

Analysis
To eliminate the square root in Column A, square both columns. Column A then becomes 89,900, while Column B becomes 90,000

Answer
B—Column B is greater than Column A.

7. Use Properties of Proper Fractions
Remember that when you raise a proper fraction (a fraction less than 1) to a power, the result is *smaller* than the original fraction. Also, when you take the square root of a proper fraction, the result is *larger* than the original fraction (but still, of course, less than 1).

Example 1	**Column A**	**Column B**
	$(0.63)^2$	$\sqrt{0.63}$

Analysis

Simply note that when 0.63 is *squared*, the result is a number smaller than 0.63, but that when the square root of 0.63 is taken, the result is larger than 0.63.

Answer

B—Column B is larger than Column A.

Example 2	**Column A**	**Column B**
	$(1 - 0.8)^4$	$(0.2)^6$

Analysis

Since $(1 - 0.8)^4$ is equal to $(0.2)^4$, we are actually comparing $(0.2)^4$ to $(0.2)^6$. Then, recall that the higher the power to which a proper fraction is raised, the smaller the result.

Answer

A—Column A is greater than Column B.

TIPS FOR ANSWERING QUESTIONS INVOLVING VARIABLES

The other quantitative comparison questions on the GRE involve expressions containing both *numbers* and *variables*. Since the relative size of the two quantities depends on the particular values of the variables, additional strategies can be used. These are illustrated in the problems below.

1. Use Strategies for Purely Numerical Questions

Many of the principles that have already been discussed for purely numerical questions will also apply to questions involving variables. In particular, make use of the concept of treating the two columns as if they were the two sides of an inequality.

Example 1	**Column A**	**Column B**
	$x < 0$	
	$x - 3$	$3 - x$

Analysis

To eliminate the subtraction, add both 3 and x to both columns.

$$2x \qquad\qquad 6$$

Since x is negative, $2x$ is also negative and thus less than 6.

Answer

B—Column B is greater than Column A.

Example 2	**Column A**	**Column B**

$$x \neq 0$$

$$\dfrac{x^2 + 4x}{2} \qquad\qquad 2x$$

Analysis

To eliminate the division in Column A, multiply both columns by 2.

$$x^2 + 4x \qquad\qquad 4x$$

Now, subtract $4x$ from both columns.

$$x^2 \qquad\qquad 0$$

Since $x \neq 0$, x^2 is positive and thus greater than 0.

Answer

A—Column A is greater than Column B.

Example 3	**Column A**	**Column B**

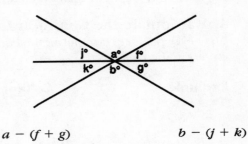

$$a - (f + g) \qquad\qquad b - (j + k)$$

Analysis

To eliminate the subtractions, add both $(f + g)$ and $(j + k)$ to both columns.

$$a + (j + k) \qquad\qquad b + (f + g)$$

Since each column represents three angles that form a straight angle, the sum in each column is 180.

Answer

C—Column A is equal to Column B.

2. Solve the Equations in the Common Information

Whenever possible, solve the equations in the common information to determine the numerical values of the variables in the columns.

Example	**Column A**	**Column B**

$$k + n = 13$$
$$n + 3 = 8$$

$$k \qquad\qquad n$$

Analysis

Solving the equation $n + 3 = 8$, we find $n = 5$. Substituting $n = 5$ into the equation $k + n = 13$, we get $k + 5 = 13$, or $k = 8$.

Answer

A—Column A is greater than Column B.

3. Perform the Algebraic Operations

If algebraic operations are involved in an expression, it is often helpful to begin by performing these operations.

Example	**Column A**	**Column B**

$$y>0$$

$$(2 + x)(3 + y) \qquad\qquad 6 + 3x + xy$$

Analysis

Multiply the expressions in Column A.

$$6 + 3x + 2y + xy \qquad\qquad 6 + 3x + xy$$

Column A is the same as Column B with the addition of the term $2y$. Since y is positive, so is $2y$.

Answer

A—Column A is greater than Column B.

4. Manipulate the Common Information

Whenever possible, manipulate the common information into a form similar to one of the entries in the columns.

Example	**Column A**	**Column B**

$$3x - y = 10$$

$$\frac{6x-2y}{3} \qquad\qquad \frac{19}{3}$$

Analysis

Notice that in Column A, $6x - 2y$ in the numerator of the fraction is $2(3x - y)$. Since $3x - y$ is given as 10, $2(3x - y) = 2(10) = 20$. Thus, Column A is equal to $\frac{20}{3}$.

Answer

A—Column A is greater than Column B.

5. Substitute Numbers for the Variables

One of the most useful techniques for solving questions involving variables is to choose sample numerical values for the variables. A single substitution will always eliminate two of the four answer choices. For example, suppose that for a particular numerical value the expression in Column A is larger than the expression in Column B. Then, the answer to the question must either be (A) (Column A is *always* larger) or (D) (Column A is *sometimes* larger and *sometimes* not larger).

To determine which of the two remaining possible answer choices is correct, choose a few other values. Be sure to try numbers of different types (negative numbers, fractions, 0, etc.). If, for any of these values, Column A is not larger than Column B, then the answer must be (D). If, on the other hand, Column A is larger for each value you try, then you can reasonably assume that (A) is the correct answer.

Example	**Column A**	**Column B**

x is an integer
$$x > 0$$

x^2		2^x

Analysis

Try some sample values for x. For example, if $x = 1$, $x^2 = 1^2 = 1$ and $2^x = 2^1 = 2$. In this case, Column B is larger than Column A. If, on the other hand, $x = 3$, $x^2 = 3^2 = 9$ and $2^x = 2^3 = 8$. In this case, Column A is larger than Column B. Therefore, the relative size of the two columns depends on the value of x.

Answer

D—The relationship cannot be determined.

6. Use Properties of Proper Fractions and Negative Numbers

Remember that powers of, roots of, and divisions by numbers between 0 and 1 (proper fractions) behave the opposite of those greater than 1. Also, negative numbers raised to even powers behave differently than do negative numbers raised to odd powers.

Thus, when solving a quantitative comparison question involving variables, carefully note which types of numbers are involved, that is, whether the numbers are greater than 1, between 0 and 1, or negative. These variations are illustrated below:

Example 1	**Column A**	**Column B**

$$x > 1$$

x^2		x^3

Analysis

When a number greater than 1 is squared, it becomes larger. When the same number is cubed, it becomes even larger.

Answer

B—Column B is greater than Column A.

Example 2	**Column A**	**Column B**

$$0 < x < 1$$

x^2		x^3

Analysis

When proper fractions (numbers between 0 and 1) are raised to powers, they behave the opposite of numbers greater than 1. That is, squaring a proper fraction results in a smaller number. When the same proper fraction is cubed, it becomes even smaller.

Answer

A—Column A is greater than Column B.

Example 3 | **Column A** | **Column B**

$$x < 0$$

x^2 | x^3

Analysis

When a negative number is squared, the result is always positive. When a negative number is cubed, the result is always negative.

Answer

A—Column A is greater than Column B.

Example 4 | **Column A** | **Column B**

x^2 | x^3

Analysis

Since no information is given about x, x could be a negative number, zero, a proper fraction, one, or a number greater than one. Therefore, it is impossible to determine the relative sizes of x^2 and x^3.

Answer

D—The relationship cannot be determined.

Example 5 | **Column A** | **Column B**

$$x > 1$$

x | $\sqrt{x}$

Analysis

When the square root of a number greater than 1 is taken, the result is smaller than the original number.

Answer

A—Column A is greater than Column B.

Example 6 | **Column A** | **Column B**

$$0 < x < 1$$

x | $\sqrt{x}$

Analysis

When the square root of a proper fraction is taken, the result is larger than the original number.

Answer

B—Column B is greater than Column A.

Example 7	**Column A**	**Column B**
	x	$\sqrt{x}$

Analysis

Since no information is given about the value of x, it is impossible to determine the relationship between x and $\sqrt{x}$.

Answer

D—The relationship cannot be determined.

Example 8	**Column A**		**Column B**
		$x > 1$	
	$\dfrac{8}{x}$		$8x$

Analysis

When a positive whole number is divided by a number larger than 1, the result is smaller than the original number. When a positive number is multiplied by a number larger than 1, the result is larger than the original number.

Answer

B—Column B is greater than Column A.

Example 9	**Column A**		**Column B**
		$0 < x < 1$	
	$\dfrac{8}{x}$		$8x$

Analysis

When a positive whole number is divided by a proper fraction, the result is larger than the original number (e.g., $8 \div \dfrac{1}{2} = 8 \times 2 = 16$). When a positive whole number is multiplied by a proper fraction, the result is smaller than the original number.

Answer

A—Column A is greater than Column B.

Example 10	**Column A**	**Column B**
	$\dfrac{8}{x}$	$8x$

Analysis

Since no information is given about the value of x, it is impossible to determine the relative value of $\dfrac{8}{x}$ and $8x$.

Answer

D—The relationship cannot be determined.

Example 11   **Column A**   **Column B**

$$\frac{x}{y} = \frac{7}{9}$$

$$x > 0, \ y > 0$$

x y

Analysis

First, remember that $\frac{x}{y} = \frac{7}{9}$ does not mean that $x = 7$ and $y = 9$, but that the ratio of x to y is 7 to 9. For example, x could be 14 and y could be 18. In any case, since x and y are both positive, x must be less than y.

Answer

B—Column B is greater than Column A.

Example 12   **Column A**   **Column B**

$$\frac{x}{y} = \frac{7}{9}$$

x y

Analysis

If x and y are both positive, then x is less than y. However, if x and y are both negative, then y is less than x. For example, if $x = -7$ and $y = -9$, y is less than x.

Answer

D—The relationship cannot be determined.

Example 13   **Column A**   **Column B**

$$x^3 = y^3$$

x y

Analysis

Since both x and y are raised to the same odd power, they must have both the same numerical value and the same sign. That is, they must be the same number.

Answer

C—Column A is equal to Column B.

Example 14   **Column A**   **Column B**

$$x^2 = y^2$$

x y

Analysis

Since both x and y are raised to the same even power, they must have the same numerical value, but not necessarily the same sign. For example, x could be $+3$ and y could be -3, in which case $x^2 = y^2$, but x is greater than y. Of course, just the opposite could be the case. That is, x could be -3 and y could be $+3$.

Answer

D—The relationship cannot be determined.

PRACTICE TEST VI

Directions: Each problem that follows consists of a question and two statements, labeled (1) and (2), in which certain data are given. You have to decide whether the data given in the statements are sufficient for answering the question, and on the answer sheet blacken space:

(A) if the quantity in Column A is greater;

(B) if the quantity in Column B is greater;

(C) if the two quantities are equal;

(D) if the relationship cannot be determined from the information given

	Column A	Column B
1.	$\dfrac{5}{9}$	$\dfrac{7}{13}$
2.	$\sqrt{28} - \sqrt{18}$	$\sqrt{10}$

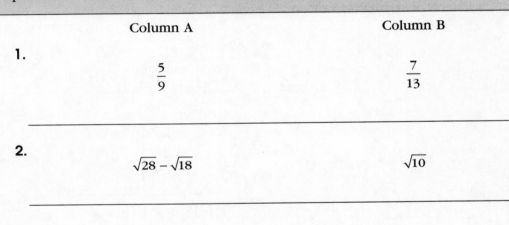

3.	BC	4
4.	60% of 80	80% of 60

$$x > 0$$

5.	x^2	x^3

Column A	Column B

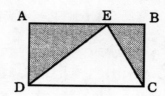

ABCD is a rectangle

6.   The area of $\triangle$DEC   The area of the shaded part

---

7.   .5% $\dfrac{1}{2}$

$$x > y > 0$$

8. $\dfrac{1}{x}$ $\dfrac{1}{y}$

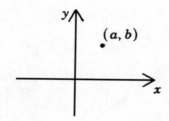

9. a b

---

10.   The percent of increase from \$40 to \$50   The percent of decrease from \$50 to \$40

$$x = 2$$
$$y = -3$$

11. $x^3 - 3y$ $x - 5y$

<table>
<tr><td>Column A</td><td>Column B</td></tr>
</table>

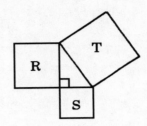

Figures R, S, and T are squares

12. Area of R + Area of S   Area of T

---

13. The number of   The number of
         different   different prime divisors
         prime divisors of 50   of 64

$$0 < a < 1$$

14. a a^2

---

15. The volume of a   The volume of a
         cylinder   cylinder
         with radius 1   with radius 2

---

16.   8.34692   8.354

$$\frac{x}{y} = \frac{7}{8}$$

17. x y

Column A   Column B

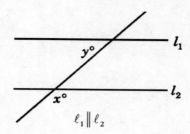

$\ell_1 \parallel \ell_2$

18. $x + y$ 170

___

19. $(8)(574)(6)$ $(4)(574)(12)$

___

$$x > y$$

20. $(x - y)^5$ $(y - x)^5$

___

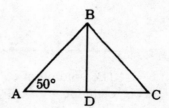

21.   AD   DC

___

22.   66.6% $\dfrac{2}{3}$

___

$$y \neq 1$$
$$x = \frac{y}{y - 1}$$

23. y $\dfrac{x}{x - 1}$

___

	Column A	Column B

24. The area of a circle with diameter 10 | The area of a square with side 9

25. The amount of profit on a house sold at $35,000 | The amount of profit on a house sold at $40,000

26. $(x - y)^2$ | $(y - x)^2$

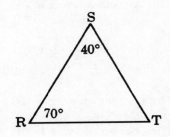

27. RS | ST

28. 74 | 90% of 110% of 74

$$x^4 = 16$$

29. x | 2

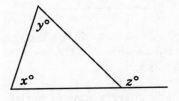

30. $x + y$ | z

ANSWERS AND EXPLANATIONS

1. **A**	6. **C**	11. **C**	16. **B**	21. **D**	26. **C**
2. **B**	7. **B**	12. **C**	17. **D**	22. **B**	27. **C**
3. **B**	8. **B**	13. **A**	18. **A**	23. **C**	28. **A**
4. **C**	9. **D**	14. **A**	19. **C**	24. **B**	29. **D**
5. **D**	10. **A**	15. **D**	20. **A**	25. **D**	30. **C**

In each of the explanations that follow,

$v(A) > v(B)$	means the value of the quantity in Column A is greater than the value of the quantity in Column B.
$v(B) > v(A)$	means the value of the quantity in Column B is greater than the value of the quantity in Column A.
$v(A) = v(B)$	means the values of the two quantities are equal.
$v(A) \ ?? \ v(B)$	means the relationship cannot be determined.

1. **The correct answer is (A).**

Since $65 > 63$, $\dfrac{5}{9} > \dfrac{7}{13}$, and thus $v(A) > v(B)$.

2. **The correct answer is (B).** $\sqrt{28} - \sqrt{18} \approx 5 - 4 \approx 1$. Since $\sqrt{10} \approx 3$, $v(B) > v(A)$.

3. **The correct answer is (B).** In a $30° - 60° - 90°$ right triangle, the side opposite the $30°$ angle is one-half the hypotenuse. Thus, $BC = \dfrac{1}{2}(6) = 3$, and $v(B) > v(A)$.

4. **The correct answer is (C).** 60% of 80 = $.60 \times 80 = 48$, and 80% of 60 = $.80 \times 60 = 48$. Thus, $v(A) = v(B)$.

5. **The correct answer is (D).** If $x > 1$, then $x^3 > x^2$. However, if $x < 1$, then $x^3 < x^2$. Thus, $v(A) ?? v(B)$.

6. **The correct answer is (C).**

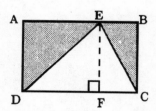

Since shaded triangle DAE equals unshaded triangle DFE, and shaded triangle CBE equals unshaded triangle CFE, the shaded area equals the unshaded area. Thus, $v(A) = v(B)$.

7. **The correct answer is (B).**

$$.5\% = \frac{.5}{100} = \frac{5.}{1000} = \frac{1}{200}$$

Thus, $v(B) > v(A)$.

8. **The correct answer is (B).**

Since $x > y$, $\dfrac{1}{y} > \dfrac{1}{x}$, and thus $\upsilon(B) > \upsilon(A)$.

9. **The correct answer is (D).** Since the point is in the first quadrant, both a and b are positive. However, without knowing the exact position of the point, it is impossible to determine the relative size of a and b. Thus, $\upsilon(A)??\upsilon(B)$.

10. **The correct answer is (A).** The percent of increase from \$40 to \$50

$$= \frac{10}{40} \times 100\% = 25\%$$

The percent of decrease from \$50 to \$40

$$= \frac{10}{50} \times 100\% = 20\%$$

Thus, $\upsilon(A) > \upsilon(B)$.

11. **The correct answer is (C).** $x^3 - 3y = (2)^3 - 3(-3) = 8 + 9 = 17$, and $x - 5y = (2) - 5(-3) = 2 + 15 = 17$. Thus, $\upsilon(A) = \upsilon(B)$.

12. **The correct answer is (C).**

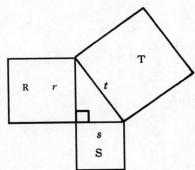

The area of square R + the area of square S = $r^2 + s^2$.
The area of square T = t^2. Since, by the Pythagorean theorem,
$r^2 + s^2 = t^2$, $\upsilon(A) = \upsilon(B)$.

13. **The correct answer is (A).** The distinct prime divisors of 50 are 2 and 5. 64 has only one distinct prime divisor 2. Thus $\upsilon(A) > \upsilon(B)$.

14. When $0 < a < 1$, $a^2 < a$. For example,
$\left(\dfrac{1}{3}\right)^2 < \dfrac{1}{3}$. Thus, $\upsilon(A) > \upsilon(B)$.

15. **The correct answer is (D).** The volume of a cylinder = $\pi(\text{radius})^2(\text{height})$. Without knowing the heights, $\upsilon(A)??\upsilon(B)$.

16. **The correct answer is (B).** Since 8.35400>8.34692, $v(B)>v(A)$.

17. **The correct answer is (D).** If x and y are positive, $x<y$. However, if x and y are negative, $x>y$. Thus, $v(A)??v(B)$.

18. **The correct answer is (A).**

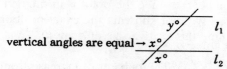

vertical angles are equal → $x°$

Since the interior angles on the same side of the transversal are supplementary, $x + y = 180$. Thus, $v(A)>v(B)$.

19. **The correct answer is (C).** $(8)(574)(6) = (4)(2)(574)(6) = (4)(574)(2)(6) = (4)(574)(12)$. Thus, $v(A) = v(B)$.

20. **The correct answer is (A).** Since $x>y$, $(x - y)^5$ is positive, and $(y - x)^5$ is negative. Thus, $v(A)>v(B)$.

21. **The correct answer is (D).** Without knowing either the exact position of point D, or the measure of angle BDA, $v(A)??v(B)$.

22. **The correct answer is (B).** Since $\dfrac{2}{3} = 66.666\cdots\%$, $v(B)>v(A)$.

23. **The correct answer is (C).**

$$\frac{x}{1} = \frac{y}{y-1} \ \left(\text{cross-multiply}\right)$$
$$xy - x = y$$
$$xy = y + x$$
$$xy - y = x$$
$$y(x - 1) = x$$
$$y = \frac{x}{x - 1}$$

Thus, $v(A) = v(B)$.

24. **The correct answer is (B).** The area of a circle $= \pi(\text{radius})^2$. Thus, the area of a circle with diameter $10 = \pi(5)^2 = 25\pi$. Since $\pi \approx 3.14$, the area of the circle ≈ 75. The area of a square $= (\text{side})^2$. Thus, the area of a square with side $9 = (9)^2 = 81$. Therefore, $v(B)>v(A)$.

25. **The correct answer is (D).** Without knowing the cost of each house, $v(A)??v(B)$.

26. **The correct answer is (C).** $(x - y)^2 = (x - y)(x - y) = x^2 - 2xy + y^2$, and
$$(y - x)^2 = (y - x)(y - x) = y^2 - 2xy + x^2.$$
Thus, $v(A) = v(B)$.

27. **The correct answer is (C).**

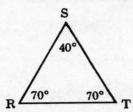

Since the sum of the angles of a triangle is 180°, angle T = 180° − (70° + 40°) = 70°. Thus, △ RST is isosceles, having RS = ST, and $v(A) = v(B)$.

28. **The correct answer is (A).** 90% of 110% of 74 = .90 × 1.10 × 74 = .99 × 74. Thus, $v(A) > v(B)$.

29. **The correct answer is (D).** Since $x = 2$ or -2, $v(A)??v(B)$.

30. **The correct answer is (C).**

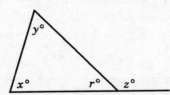

Since $r + z = 180$, $z = 180 − r$. Since the sum of the angles of a triangle is 180°, $x + y + r = 180$, or $x + y = 180 − r$. Thus, $x + y = z$, and $v(A) = v(B)$.

PRACTICE TEST VII

Directions: Each problem that follows consists of a question and two statements, labeled (1) and (2), in which certain data are given. You have to decide whether the data given in the statements are sufficient for answering the question, and on the answer sheet blacken space:

(A) if the quantity in Column A is greater;

(B) if the quantity in Column B is greater;

(C) if the two quantities are equal;

(D) if the relationship cannot be determined from the information given

	Column A	Column B
1.	3476	$6 + 7 \cdot 10 + 4 \cdot 10^2 + 3 \cdot 10^3$
2.	$\sqrt{10} + \sqrt{17}$	$\sqrt{27}$

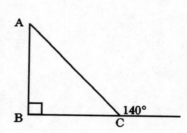

3.	AB	BC
4.	The largest prime divisor of 100	The largest prime divisor of 56

$$6 < x < 8$$
$$7 < y < 9$$

5.	x	y

<table>
<tr><th>Column A</th><th>Column B</th></tr>
</table>

Column A   Column B

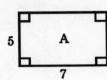   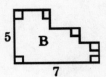

6.   Perimeter of A   Perimeter of B

---

7. $\dfrac{5}{9} - \dfrac{1}{2}$ $\dfrac{4}{7}$

$$y \neq 0$$
$$y \neq -1$$

8. $\dfrac{x}{y}$ $\dfrac{x+1}{y+1}$

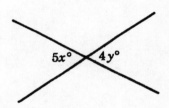

9. x y

---

10.   The number of   The number of
           seconds   minutes
           in a day   in 50 days

$$xy > 0$$

11. $x^2 + y^2$ $(x + y)^2$

	Column A	Column B

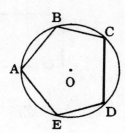

12. Perimeter of pentagon ABCDE | Circumference of circle O

13. $86 - .14$ | $14 - .86$

14. $(734)^2 - 1$ | $(735)(733)$

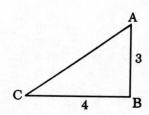

15. AC | 5

16. $\frac{1}{4}\%$ | .25

$$xy = 0$$

17. x | y

18. The number of degrees in each angle of a regular polygon | $60°$

	Column A	Column B

19. $\dfrac{2}{3} \times \dfrac{5}{7} \times \dfrac{4}{9}$ $\dfrac{4}{7} \times \dfrac{2}{9} \times \dfrac{5}{3}$

$$0 < a < 1$$

20. $\sqrt{a}$ a

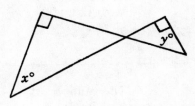

21. x y

---

22. The amount of simple interest earned on $500 over 2 years The amount of simple interest earned on $1000 over 1 year

---

$$x \neq 0$$

23. $-x^2$ $(-x)^2$

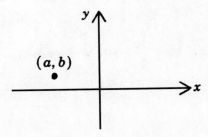

24. a b

	Column A	Column B

25. .5 $\dfrac{1}{.2}$

26. The average of 2x, 4x, and 9 | The average of x, 2x, 5x, and 12

27. The circumference of a circle with radius 2 | The perimeter of a square with side 3

28. The number of tens in 65 | The number of hundreds in 590

29. $(a^4b^3)^6$ | $(a^{12}b^9)^2$

$\ell_1 \parallel \ell_2$

30. The area of △ABC | The area of △ADC

ANSWERS AND EXPLANATIONS

1. C	6. C	11. B	16. B	21. C	26. C
2. A	7. B	12. B	17. D	22. D	27. A
3. B	8. D	13. A	18. D	23. B	28. A
4. B	9. B	14. C	19. C	24. B	29. C
5. D	10. A	15. D	20. A	25. B	30. C

In each of the explanations that follow,

$v(A) > v(B)$	means the value of the quantity in Column A is greater than the value of the quantity in Column B.
$v(B) > v(A)$	means the value of the quantity in Column B is greater than the value of the quantity in Column A.
$v(A) = v(B)$	means the values of the two quantities are equal.
$v(A) ?? v(B)$	means the relationship cannot be determined.

1. **The correct answer is (C).** $6 + 7 \cdot 10 + 4 \cdot 10^2 + 3 \cdot 103 = 6 + 70 + 400 + 3000 = 3476$. Thus, $v(A) = v(B)$.

2. **The correct answer is (A).** $\sqrt{10} + \sqrt{17} \approx 3 + 4 \approx 7$. Since $\sqrt{27} \approx 5$, $v(A) > v(B)$.

3. **The correct answer is (B).**

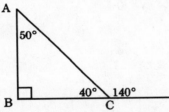

   Angle ACB is the supplement of 140°and thus measures 40°. Angle BAC is the complement of 40° and thus measures 50° Since side BC is opposite an angle of 50° and side AB is opposite a smaller angle BC>AB, and thus, $v(B) > v(A)$.

4. **The correct answer is (B).** The largest prime divisor of 100 is 5, and the largest prime divisor of 56 is 7. Thus, $v(B) > v(A)$.

5. **The correct answer is (D).** x could be 7.9 and y could be 7.1, in which case x would be greater than y. However, x could be 6.1 and y could be 8.9, in which case y would be greater than x. Thus, $v(A) ?? v(B)$.

6. **The correct answer is (C).**

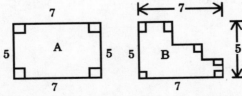

   In figure B, the sum of the three horizontal line segments is 7, and the sum of the three vertical line segments is 5. Thus, the two perimeters are the same, and $v(A) = v(B)$.

7. **The correct answer is (B).** $\frac{5}{9} - \frac{1}{2} = \frac{1}{18}$ which is less than $\frac{4}{7}$. Thus, $v(B) > v(A)$.

8. **The correct answer is (D).**

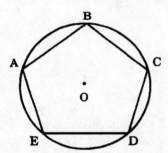

   If $x > y$, then $x > xy + y$. However, if $x < y$, then $xy + x < xy + y$. Thus, $v(A)??v(B)$.

9. **The correct answer is (B).** Since vertical angles are equal,

   $5x = 4y$, or $x = \frac{4}{5}y$

   Thus, $y > x$, and $v(B) > v(A)$.

10. **The correct answer is (A).** The number of seconds in a day = (60 sec./min.) · (60 min./hr.) · (24 hr./day) The number of minutes in 50 days = (60 min./hr.) · (24 hr./day) · (50 days) Comparing factors, $v(A) > v(B)$.

11. **The correct answer is (B).** $(x + y)^2 = (x + y)(x + y) = x^2 + 2xy + y^2$. Since $xy > 0$, $x^2 + 2xy + y^2 > x^2 + y^2$, and thus $v(B) > v(A)$.

12. **The correct answer is (B).**

   Since each arc on the circle is longer than the corresponding side of the pentagon, $v(B) > v(A)$.

13. **The correct answer is (A).** $86 - .14 = 85.86$, and $14 - .86 = 13.14$. Thus, $v(A) > v(B)$.

14. **The correct answer is (C).** Since $a^2 - b^2 = (a + b)(a - b)$, $(734)^2 - 1 = (734 + 1)(734 - 1) = (735)(733)$. Thus, $v(A) = v(B)$.

15. **The correct answer is (D).** Without knowing the number of degrees in angle B, the length of AC cannot be determined. Thus, $v(A)??v(B)$.

16. **The correct answer is (B).**

$$\frac{1}{4}\% = \frac{\frac{1}{4}}{100} = \frac{1}{4} \div 100 = \frac{1}{4} \times \frac{1}{100} = \frac{1}{400}$$

$$.25 = \frac{25}{100} = \frac{1}{4}$$

Thus $v(B) > v(A)$.

17. **The correct answer is (D).** If $x = 0$, then y can be anything. Similarly, if $y = 0$, then x can be anything. Thus, $v(A)??v(B)$.

18. **The correct answer is (D).** If the regular polygon is a triangle, then each angle measures $60°$. However, if the regular polygon is a quadrilateral, then each angle measures $90°$. Thus, $v(A)??v(B)$.

19. **The correct answer is (C).** Since all the numerators are the same, and all the denominators are the same, the two products are equal. Thus, $v(A) = v(B)$.

20. **The correct answer is (A).** When $0 < a < 1$, $\sqrt{a} > a$. For example, $\sqrt{\frac{1}{9}} > \frac{1}{9}$. Thus, $v(A) > v(B)$.

21. **The correct answer is (C).**

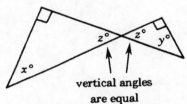

vertical angles
are equal

In each triangle the sum of the angles is $180°$. Since both triangles contain a right angle and an angle of $z°$, the remaining angles must be equal. Thus, $x = y$, and $v(A) = v(B)$.

22. **The correct answer is (D).** Without knowing the interest rates, $v(A)?? v(B)$.

23. **The correct answer is (B).** Since $-x^2 = -(x^2)$, which is always negative, and $(-x)^2 = +x^2$, which is always positive, $v(B) > v(A)$.

24. **The correct answer is (B).** Since the point is in the second quadrant, a is negative and b is positive. Thus, $v(B) > v(A)$.

25. **The correct answer is (B).** $\frac{1}{.2} = \frac{1}{\frac{2}{10}} = 1 \div \frac{2}{10} = 1 \times \frac{10}{2} = 5$. Thus $v(B) > v(A)$.

26. **The correct answer is (C).** The average of $2x$, $4x$, and 9

$$= \frac{2x + 4x + 9}{3} = \frac{6x + 9}{3} = 2x + 3$$

The average of x, $2x$, $5x$, and 12

$$= \frac{x + 2x + 5x + 12}{4} = \frac{8x + 12}{4} = 2x + 3$$

Thus, $v(A) = v(B)$.

27. **The correct answer is (A).** The circumference of a circle $= \pi(\text{diameter})$. Thus, the circumference of a circle with radius $2 = \pi\,(4) = 4\pi$. Since $\pi \approx 3.14$, the circumference $\approx 4(3.14) \approx 12.56$. The perimeter of a square $= 4(\text{side})$. Thus, the perimeter of a square with side $3 = 4(3) = 12$. Therefore, $v(A) > v(B)$.

28. **The correct answer is (A).** The number of tens in 65 is 6, and the number of hundreds in 590 is 5. Thus, $v(A) > v(B)$.

29. **The correct answer is (C).** $(a^4b^3)^6 = a^{4 \cdot 6}b^{3 \cdot 6} = a^{24}b^{18}$
$(a^{12}b^9)^2 = a^{12 \cdot 2}b^{9 \cdot 2} = a^{24}b^{18}$
Thus $v(A) = v(B)$.

30. **The correct answer is (C).**

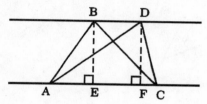

The area of triangle $= \frac{1}{2}(\text{base})(\text{height})$. Since both triangles have the same base, AC, and the same heights, BE $=$ DF, they have the same area. Thus, $v(A) = v(B)$.

PRACTICE TEST VIII

SUGGESTED TIME—**30** MINUTES • **30** QUESTIONS

Directions: Each problem that follows consists of a question and two statements, labeled (1) and (2), in which certain data are given. You have to decide whether the data given in the statements are sufficient for answering the question, and on the answer sheet blacken space:

(A) if the quantity in Column A is greater;

(B) if the quantity in Column B is greater;

(C) if the two quantities are equal;

(D) if the relationship cannot be determined from the information given

	Column A	Column B
1.	2^5	5^2

$$x + 7 = 9$$
$$y - 7 = 4$$

	Column A	Column B
2.	$x + y$	13

$$x > 0$$

	Column A	Column B
3.	$\dfrac{x}{15}$	$\dfrac{15}{x}$

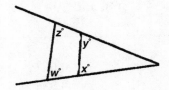

	Column A	Column B
4.	$x + y$	$w + z$
5.	$\left(\dfrac{1}{6} \times \dfrac{13}{14}\right) + \left(\dfrac{1}{6} \times \dfrac{3}{14}\right)$	$\dfrac{1}{6}$

Column A	Column B

The discount price of a radio is 85 percent of its original cost, and the discount price of an amplifier is 80 percent of its original cost.

6.   The discount price of the radio.   The discount price of the amplifier.

$$x(x + 3) + 2 = 3x + 2$$

7. x 0

---

8. $a^4 + b$ $a^4 - b$

---

x, y and z are positive integers

9. $x(z + y)$ $xz + y$

$x < 0$, $y > 0$, and $z > 0$

10. $(3x)(3y)(3z)$ $3[(x)(y)(z)]$

$$x = 3$$

11. $5x^2$ 225

---

12.   The average (arithmetic mean) of 57, 68, and 79   The average (arithmetic mean) of 56, 68, and 79

---

13. $\dfrac{0.667}{0.833}$ $\dfrac{\frac{2}{3}}{\frac{5}{6}}$

$r < -1$ and $s > 1$

14. r^2 s^2

Column A	Column B

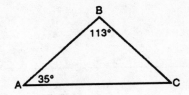

15. The length of *AB* — The length of *BC*

---

16. $\left(3\sqrt{5}+2\right)\left(3\sqrt{5}-2\right)$ — 42

When Janet drives from her home to the nearest lake, it takes 5 hours at an average speed of 40 mph. When Janet drives from her home to the beach house, it takes 4.5 hours at an average speed of 46 mph.

17. Janet's driving distance from her home to the lake. — Janet's driving distance from her home to the beach.

$AQ > 0$

$BQ < 0$

18. *A* — *B*

$x + y = 3$

$y + z = 5$

19. $x + 3 + 2y + z$ — 11

Two machines took a total of 35 hours to complete a job. One of the machines spent 25% fewer hours on the job than the other.

20. The difference between the number of hours spent by each machine. — 4

	Column A	Column B

$$x^5 = -32$$

21.　　　　　x　　　　　　　　　　　　　-1

22.　　　　　$\dfrac{x}{0.25}$　　　　　　　　　　$4x$

$$x = 3y + 1$$

23.　　　　　$2x$　　　　　　　　　　　$6y + 1$

24.　　$2^3 \cdot 3 \cdot 7^9 \cdot 9^{10}$　　　　　　$3^3 \cdot 7^9 \cdot 9^{10}$

$$r > 0, s > 0$$

25.　$\left(\dfrac{r+s}{2}\right)^2 - \left(\dfrac{r-s}{2}\right)^2$　　　　　0

$$n > 0$$

26.　　　$\dfrac{7^n}{7^{n+1}}$　　　　　　　　$\dfrac{7^{n+1}}{7^{n+2}}$

$$b^2 = a^2 - 1$$
$$a \neq 0$$

27.　　　　b^4　　　　　　　　　　$a^4 + 1$

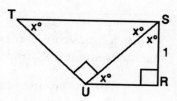

28.　　The perimeter of *RSTU*　　　　　　6

Column A	Column B

In a certain school, 50 students are enrolled in English, 60 students are enrolled in math, and 45 students are enrolled in both.

29. The ratio of the number of students enrolled in both English and math to the number of students enrolled in English.

8

For all numbers r and s, where

$$s \neq 0, r * s = \frac{10r}{s}$$

30. $(0.01) * (0.01)$

10

ANSWERS AND EXPLANATIONS

1. **A**	6. **D**	11. **B**	16. **B**	21. **B**	26. **C**
2. **C**	7. **C**	12. **A**	17. **B**	22. **C**	27. **B**
3. **D**	8. **D**	13. **A**	18. **D**	23. **A**	28. **B**
4. **C**	9. **D**	14. **D**	19. **C**	24. **B**	29. **A**
5. **A**	10. **B**	15. **B**	20. **A**	25. **A**	30. **C**

In each of the explanations that follow,

$v(A) > v(B)$	means the value of the quantity in Column A is greater than the value of the quantity in Column B.
$v(B) > v(A)$	means the value of the quantity in Column B is greater than the value of the quantity in Column A.
$v(A) = v(B)$	means the values of the two quantities are equal.
$v(A) ?? v(B)$	means the relationship cannot be determined.

1. **The correct answer is (A).** $2^5 = 32$ and $5^2 = 25$. Thus, $v(A) > v(B)$.

2. **The correct answer is (C).** Adding the two equations together, we get $x + y = 13$. Thus, $v(A) = v(B)$.

3. **The correct answer is (D).** If $x < 15$, then $\dfrac{x}{15} < \dfrac{15}{x}$. If $x > 15$, then $\dfrac{x}{15} > \dfrac{15}{x}$. Thus, $v(A) ?? v(B)$.

4. **The correct answer is (C).**

    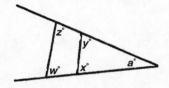

    $x + y + a = 180$, and $w + z + a = 180$. Thus, $x + y + a = w + z + a$, or $x + y = w + z$, and $v(A) = v(B)$.

5. **The correct answer is (A).**

    $$\left(\frac{1}{6} \times \frac{13}{14}\right) + \left(\frac{1}{6} \times \frac{3}{14}\right) =$$

    $$\frac{1}{6}\left(\frac{13}{14} + \frac{3}{14}\right) = \frac{1}{6}\left(\frac{16}{14}\right).$$

    Since $\dfrac{16}{14} > 1$, $v(A) > v(B)$.

6. **The correct answer is (D).** Without knowing the original cost of the radio or of the amplifier, we cannot compare the discount prices. Thus, $v(A) ?? v(B)$.

7. **The correct answer is (C).** $x(x + 3) + 2 = 3x + 2$. Therefore, $x^2 + 3x + 2 = 3x + 2$, or $x^2 = 0$, and $x = 0$. Thus, $v(A) = v(B)$.

8. **The correct answer is (D).** After eliminating the term a^4 in both expressions, we have b and $-b$. If $b > 0$, then $b > -b$. But if $b < 0$, then $b < -b$. Thus, $v(A) ?? v(B)$.

9. **The correct answer is (D).** $x(z + y) = xz + xy$. If $x = 1$, $xz + xy = xz + y$. But if $x > 1$, $xz + xy > xz + y$. Thus, $v(A)??v(B)$.

10. **The correct answer is (B).** $(3x)(3y)(3z) = 27xyz$.
    $3[(x)(y)(z)] = 3xyz$. This becomes $27x$ vs. $3x$. Since $x < 0$, $3x > 27x$. Thus, $v(B) > v(A)$.

11. **The correct answer is (B).** Since $x = 3$, $5x^2 = 5(3)^2 = 45$. Thus, $v(B) > v(A)$.

12. **The correct answer is (A).** Since $57 > 56$, and the other two numbers are the same, $v(A) > v(B)$

13. **The correct answer is (A).** 0.667 is slightly larger than $\frac{2}{3}$. 0.833 is slightly smaller than $\frac{5}{6}$. Thus, $v(A) > v(B)$.

14. **The correct answer is (D).** Since $r < -1$, $r^2 > 1$. Since $s > 1$, $s^2 > 1$. We do not have any information with which to determine actual values. Thus, $v(A)??v(B)$.

15. **The correct answer is (B).**

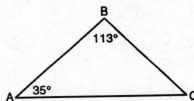

$\angle C = 180° - (113° + 35°) = 32°$. Since AB is opposite the 32° angle and BC is opposite the 35° angle, $v(B) > v(A)$.

16. **The correct answer is (B).**

$$\left(3\sqrt{5} + 2\right)\left(3\sqrt{5} - 2\right) = (9)(5) + 6\sqrt{5} - 6\sqrt{5} - 4 = 45 - 4 = 41$$

Thus, $v(B) > v(A)$.

17. **The correct answer is (B).** The distance Janet drives to the lake is 40 mph $\times$ 5 hrs. = 200 miles. The distance she drives to the beach house is 46 mph $\times$ 4.5 hrs. = 207 miles. Thus, $v(B) > v(A)$.

18. **The correct answer is (D).** If $Q > 0$, $A > 0$ and $B < 0$, then $A > B$. If $Q < 0$, $A < 0$ and $B > 0$, then $B > A$. Thus, $v(A)??v(B)$.

19. **The correct answer is (C).** Adding the two equations, we get $x + 2y + z = 8$. Thus, $x + 3 + 2y + z = 3 + 8 = 11$. Therefore, $v(A) = v(B)$.

20. **The correct answer is (A).** Let x = the number of hours taken by one machine and $.75x$ = the number of hours taken by the other machine. Thus, $x + .75x = 35$, or $x = 20$. Therefore, the difference between the number of hours is $20 - 15 = 5$, and $v(A) > v(B)$.

21. **The correct answer is (B).** Since $x^5 = -32$, $x = -2$. Thus, $v(B) > v(A)$.

22. **The correct answer is (C).** $\dfrac{x}{0.25} = \dfrac{x}{\frac{1}{4}} = 4x$. Thus, $v(A) = v(B)$.

23. **The correct answer is (A).** Since $x = 3y + 1$, $2x = 2(3y + 1) = 6y + 2$. Thus, $v(A) > v(B)$.

24. **The correct answer is (B).** After eliminating the common factors of 7^9 and 9^{10}, we have $2^3 \cdot 3$ and 3^3. Since $2^3 \cdot 3 = 24$, and $3^3 = 27$, $v(B) > v(A)$.

25. **The correct answer is (A).**

$$\left(\frac{r+s}{2}\right)^2 - \left(\frac{r-s}{2}\right)^2 =$$

$$\frac{r^2 + 2rs + s^2}{4} - \frac{r^2 - 2rs + s^2}{4} = \frac{4rs}{4} = rs$$

Since $r > 0$ and $s > 0$, $rs > 0$, and $v(A) > v(B)$.

26. **The correct answer is (C).** Multiplying the numerator and denominator of $\dfrac{7^n}{7^{n+1}}$ by 7, we get $\dfrac{7^{n+1}}{7^{n+2}}$. Thus, $v(A) = v(B)$.

27. **The correct answer is (B).** Since $b^2 = a^2 - 1$, $b^4 = (a^2 - 1)^2 = a^4 - 2a^2 + 1$. Also, since $a \neq 0$, $2a^2$ is positive. Thus, $v(B) > v(A)$.

28. **The correct answer is (B).**

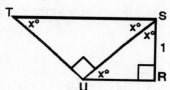

In each triangle, $x = 45$. Thus $RU = RS = 1$. Also,

$SU = UT = \sqrt{2}$, and $ST = \sqrt{2} \cdot \sqrt{2} = 2$. Therefore, the perimeter of $RSTU = 1 + 1 + \sqrt{2} + 2 = 4 + \sqrt{2} \approx 5.14$ and $v(B) > v(A)$.

29. **The correct answer is (A).** The ratio of the number of students in both English and math to the number of students enrolled in English is $45:5 = 9:1 = 9$. Thus, $v(A) > v(B)$.

30. **The correct answer is (C).** $(0.01) * (0.01) = \dfrac{10(0.01)}{(0.01)} = 10$. Thus, $v(A) = v(B)$.

Part IV

APPENDIX

SUMMARY OF DEFINITIONS, PROCEDURES, AND FORMULAS

ARITHMETIC

WHOLE NUMBERS

Prime Numbers: 2, 3, 5, 7, 11, 13, 17,...
Composite Numbers: 4, 6, 8, 9, 10, 12, 14, 15,...

FRACTIONS

$$\text{Fraction} = \frac{\text{part}}{\text{whole}} = \frac{\text{dividend}}{\text{divisor}} = \frac{\text{quantity A}}{\text{quantity B}}$$

Comparing Two Fractions:

If $a \times d > b \times c$, then $\dfrac{a}{b} > \dfrac{c}{d}$

If $a \times d = b \times c$, then $\dfrac{a}{b} = \dfrac{c}{d}$

If $a \times d < b \times c$, then $\dfrac{a}{b} < \dfrac{c}{d}$

PERCENTS

$$\text{Fraction} \xrightleftharpoons[\text{Divide by 100}]{\text{Multiply by 100}} \text{Percent}$$

$$\text{Decimal} \xrightleftharpoons[\substack{\text{Move Point 2 Places} \\ \text{to the Left}}]{\substack{\text{Move Point 2 Places} \\ \text{to the Right}}} \text{Percent}$$

Percent Product

$$\text{Percent} \times \text{Whole} = \text{Part}$$

Percent Proportion

$$\frac{\text{Part}}{\text{Whole}} = \frac{\text{Percent}}{100\%}$$

ALGEBRA

EVALUATING NUMERICAL EXPRESSIONS

The Order of Operations

(1) Perform all operations within parentheses, under square root symbols, and above and below fractions bars.

(2) Evaluate all powers and square roots.

(3) Perform all multiplications and divisions, from left to right.

(4) Perform all additions and subtractions, from left to right.

SIGNED NUMBERS

To Add Two Signed Numbers: If the numbers have the *same sign*, add their absolute values and keep the common sign. If the numbers have *different signs*, subtract the smaller absolute value from the larger and keep the sign of the larger.

To Subtract Two Signed Numbers: Change subtraction to addition, and change the sign of the number being subtracted to its opposite sign.

To Multiply or Divide Two Signed Numbers: Multiply or divide their absolute values. If the numbers have the *same sign*, make the result *positive*. If the numbers have *different signs*, make the result *negative*.

Powers of Signed Numbers

$$(+)^{\text{even}} = (+) \qquad (-)^{\text{even}} = (+)$$
$$(+)^{\text{odd}} = (+) \qquad (-)^{\text{odd}} = (-)$$

EXPONENTS

$$x^m = \underbrace{x \cdot x \cdots x}_{m \text{ factors}}$$

$$x^m \cdot x^n = x^{m+n}$$

$$\frac{x^m}{x^n} = \begin{cases} x^{m-n} & , \text{ for } m > n \\ 1 & , \text{ for } m = n \\ \dfrac{1}{x^{n-m}} & , \text{ for } m < n \end{cases}$$

$$x^0 = 1$$

$$x^{-m} = \frac{1}{x^m}$$

$$\left(x^m\right)^n = x^{m \cdot n}$$

THE DISTRIBUTIVE LAW

$$A(B+C) = AB + AC$$

$$\frac{B+C}{A} = \frac{B}{A} + \frac{C}{A}$$

SOLVING LINEAR EQUATIONS AND INEQUALITIES

If A = B, *then*:

$$A + c = B + c$$

$$A - c = B - c$$

$$c \cdot A = c \cdot B$$

$$\frac{A}{c} = \frac{B}{c} (c \neq 0)$$

If A > B, *then*:

$$A + c > B + c$$

$$A - c > B - c$$

$$c \cdot A > c \cdot B \quad \text{when } c \text{ is positive}$$

$$c \cdot A < c \cdot B \quad \text{when } c \text{ is negative}$$

$$\frac{A}{c} > \frac{B}{c} \quad \text{when } c \text{ is positive}$$

$$\frac{A}{c} < \frac{B}{c} \quad \text{when } c \text{ is negative}$$

THE FOIL METHOD OF MULTIPLYING BINOMIALS

$$(A+B)(C+D) = AC + AD + BC + BD$$

First   Outer   Inner   Last

FACTORING POLYNOMIALS

Common Monomial Factor: $AB + AC = A(B + C)$
Trinomial: $ax^2 + bx + c = (mx + n)(rx + s)$
The Difference of Two Squares: $A^2 - B^2 = (A + B)(A - B)$

OPERATIONS WITH SQUARE ROOTS

$$\sqrt{a} \cdot \sqrt{b} = \sqrt{a \cdot b}$$

$$\frac{\sqrt{a}}{\sqrt{b}} = \sqrt{\frac{a}{b}}$$

$$\sqrt{x^m} = x^{\frac{1}{2}m} \ (m \text{ is even})$$

OPERATIONS WITH FRACTIONS

Addition and Subtraction of Like Fractions:

$$\frac{a}{c} + \frac{b}{c} = \frac{a+b}{c} \qquad \frac{a}{c} - \frac{b}{c} = \frac{a-b}{c}$$

Addition and Subtraction of Unlike Fractions:

$$\frac{a}{b} + \frac{c}{d} = \frac{ad + bc}{bd} \qquad \frac{a}{b} - \frac{c}{d} = \frac{ad - bc}{bd}$$

Multiplication and Division:

$$\frac{a}{b} \cdot \frac{c}{d} = \frac{a \cdot c}{b \cdot d} \qquad \frac{a}{b} \div \frac{c}{d} = \frac{a}{b} \cdot \frac{d}{c} = \frac{a \cdot d}{b \cdot c}$$

WORD PROBLEMS

FRACTION WORD PROBLEMS

$$\text{Fraction} \times \text{Whole} = \text{Part} \qquad \text{Fraction} = \frac{\text{Part}}{\text{Whole}}$$

PROPORTION WORD PROBLEMS

If $\dfrac{A}{B} = \dfrac{C}{D}$, then $A \cdot D = B \cdot C$

PERCENT WORD PROBLEMS

$$\text{Percent} \times \text{Whole} = \text{Part} \qquad \frac{\text{Part}}{\text{Whole}} = \frac{\text{Percent}}{100\%}$$

Percent of Change (Increase or Decrease):
% of Change $\times$ Original Value = Amount of Change
or

$$\frac{\text{Amount of Change}}{\text{Original Value}} = \frac{\text{\% of Change}}{100\%}$$

New Value After a Percent of Increase:
New Value = Original Value + Amount of Increase
or
New Value = (100% + % of Increase) $\times$ Original Value

New Value After a Percent of Decrease:
New Value = Original Value − Amount of Decrease
or
New Value = (100% − % of Decrease) $\times$ Original Value

Profit and Discount:
Profit = Sales − Cost
Selling Price = (100% + % of Profit) $\times$ Cost
Selling Price = (100% − % of Discount) $\times$ List Price

CONSECUTIVE INTEGER PROBLEMS

Integers: ..., −3, −2, −1, 0, + 1, +2, +3,...
Consecutive Integers: N, N + 1, N + 2,...
Consecutive Even Integers: N, N + 2, N + 4,...
Consecutive Odd Integers: N, N + 2, N + 4,...

AGE PROBLEMS

Age N years in the future = Present Age + N
Age N years in the past = Present Age − N

AVERAGE PROBLEMS

The average (mean) of the numbers $a_1, a_2,..., a_N$ is

$$\text{Average (mean)} = \frac{a_1 + a_2 + ... a_N}{N}$$

The median is the middle number in the set after the numbers are arranged in increasing order. If there are an even number of numbers in the set, then the median is the simple average (the mean) of the two middle numbers.

The mode is the number that occurs most frequently.

RANGE PROBLEMS

The range of a set of numbers measures the amount of spread between the numbers, and is determined by subtracting the smallest number in the set from the largest.

Range = Largest Number − Smallest Number

WEIGHTED AVERAGE

The combined (weighted) average of a group of N_1 numbers, having an average of A_1, and another group of N_2 numbers having an average of A_2 is

$$\text{Combined Average} = \frac{N_1 \cdot A_1 + N_2 \cdot A_2}{N_1 + N_2}$$

MIXTURE PROBLEMS

If N_1 units of an item having a unit value of U_1 are mixed with N_2 units of an item having a unit value of U_2, then

The Value of the Mixture = $N_1 \cdot U_1 + N_2 \cdot U_2$

MOTION PROBLEMS

Distance = Rate × Time

$$D = RT \qquad T = \frac{D}{R} \qquad R = \frac{D}{T}$$

WORK PROBLEMS—INDIVIDUALS

$$\text{The Fractional Part of the Job Completed} = \frac{\text{Actual Time Worked}}{\text{Total Time Required}}$$

If one individual can complete a job in H_1 hours alone, and another individual can complete the same job in H_2 hours alone, then the amount of hours it would take them to complete the job working together, T, is given by the equation

$$\frac{T}{H_1} + \frac{T}{H_2} = 1$$

WORK PROBLEMS—GROUPS

If a group of size N_1 completes a job in H_1 hours, and another group of size N_2 completes the same job in H_2 hours, then

$$N_1 \cdot H_1 = N_2 \cdot H_2$$

SET PROBLEMS

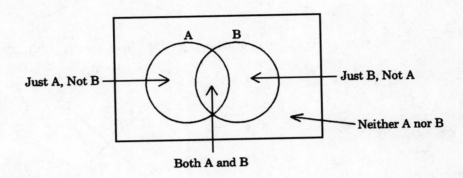

Just A, Not B

Just B, Not A

Neither A nor B

Both A and B

PROBABILITY PROBLEMS

The probability that an event occurs is defined to be the ratio of the number of outcomes in which the event occurs to the total number of possible outcomes.

$$P(E) = \frac{\text{Number of outcomes in which E occurs}}{\text{Total number of possible outcomes}}$$

The probability that an event does NOT occur is equal to 1—the probability that it does occur.

$$P(\text{Not } E) = 1 - P(E)$$

GEOMETRY

LINES AND ANGLES

If the sum of two angles, is 90°, the angles are complementary.

$$a° + b° = 90°$$

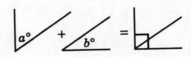

If the sum of two angles is 180°, the angles are supplementary.

$$a° + b° = 180°$$

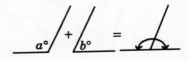

When two lines intersect, the opposite angles, called vertical angles, are equal.

$$a° = c°, b° = d°$$

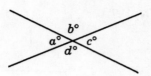

If two lines intersect at right angles, the lines are perpendicular.

$$AB \perp CD$$

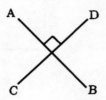

When parallel lines are crossed by a transversal, the corresponding angles are equal.

$$a° = b°$$

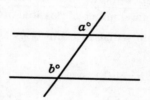

When parallel lines are crossed by a transversal, the alternate interior angles are equal.

$$a° = b°$$

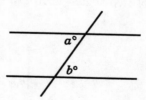

When parallel lines are crossed by a transversal, the interior angles on the same side of the transversal are supplementary.

$$a° + b° = 180°$$

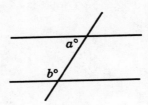

The sum of the angles of a polygon having N sides is

$$\text{Sum} = (N - 2) \times 180°$$

TRIANGLES

The sum of the angles of a triangle is 180°.

$$a° + b° + c° = 180°$$

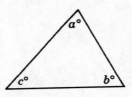

The base angles of an isosceles triangle are equal. The altitude from the vertex angle to the base bisects both the vertex angle and the base.

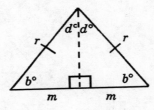

Each angle of an equilateral triangle measures 60°.

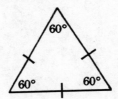

In a right triangle, the sum of the squares of the two legs is equal to the square of the hypotenuse.

$$r^2 + s^2 + = h^2$$

Common Pythagorean Triples: 3−4−5, 5−12−13, 8−15−17

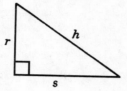

In a 30°−60°−90° right triangle, the side opposite the 30° angle is exactly one-half the hypotenuse.

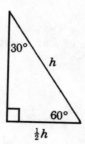

The corresponding sides and altitudes of similar triangles are in proportion.

$$\frac{AB}{RS} = \frac{BC}{ST} = \frac{AC}{RT} = \frac{BD}{SU}$$

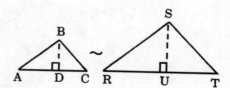

All triangles inscribed in a semi-circle are right triangles having the diameter as their hypotenuse.

PERIMETER AND AREA FORMULAS

Rectangle: $P = 2L + 2W$

$A = LW$

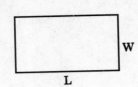

Square: $P = 4s$

$A = s^2$

Parallelogram: $P = 2a + 2b$

$A = bh$

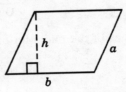

Trapezoid: $P = r + s + b_1 + b_2$

$A = \left(\dfrac{b_1 + b_2}{2}\right)h$

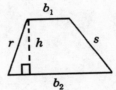

Triangle: $P = a + b + c$

$A = \dfrac{1}{2}bh$

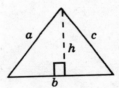

Circle: $C = \pi d$

$A = \pi r^2$

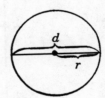

COORDINATE GEOMETRY

The distance between two points is

$$D = \sqrt{(x_2 - x_1)^2 + (y_2 - y_1)^2}$$

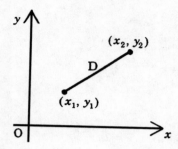

The coordinates of the midpoint of the line segment joining two points is

$$(x_m, y_m) = \left(\frac{x_1 + x_2}{2}, \frac{y_1 + y_2}{2} \right)$$

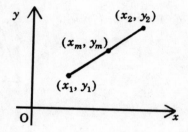

SLOPE OF A LINE

The slope of a line is $\quad m = \dfrac{y_2 - y_1}{x_2 - x_1}$

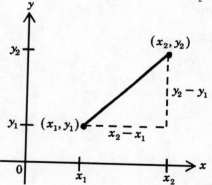

SLOPE-INTERCEPT EQUATION OF A LINE

The slope-intercept equation of a line is $y = mx + b$

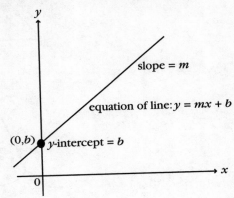

slope = m

equation of line: $y = mx + b$

$(0,b)$ y-intercept = b

VOLUME FORMULAS

Rectangular Solid: $V = lwh$

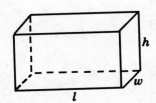

Cube: $V = e^3$

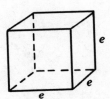

Cylinder:
$$V = \pi r^2 h$$

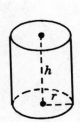

Pyramid:

$$V = \frac{1}{3}lwh$$

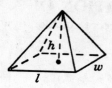

Cone:

$$V = \frac{1}{3}\pi r^2 h$$

Sphere:

$$V = \frac{4}{3}\pi r^3$$

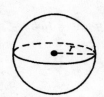